Presidential Doctrines

Presidential Doctrines

U.S. National Security from George Washington to Barack Obama

Joseph M. Siracusa and Aiden Warren

ROWMAN & LITTLEFIELD
Lanham • Boulder • New York • London

Published by Rowman & Littlefield
A wholly owned subsidiary of The Rowman & Littlefield Publishing Group, Inc.
4501 Forbes Boulevard, Suite 200, Lanham, Maryland 20706
www.rowman.com

Unit A, Whitacre Mews, 26-34 Stannary Street, London SE11 4AB

British Library Cataloguing in Publication Information Available

Library of Congress Cataloging-in-Publication Data

Names: Siracusa, Joseph M., author. | Warren, Aiden, author.
Title: Presidential doctrines : U.S. national security from George Washington to Barack Obama /
    Joseph M. Siracusa and Aiden Warren.
Description: Lanham, Maryland : Rowman & Littlefield Education, 2016. | Includes bibliographical
    references and index.
Identifiers: LCCN 2016012244 (print) | LCCN 2016022560 (ebook) | ISBN 9781442267473 (cloth :
    alk. paper) | ISBN 9781442267480 (pbk. : alk. paper) | ISBN 9781442267497 (electronic)
Subjects: LCSH: United States--Foreign relations--Philosophy--History. | National security--United
    States--Philosophy--History. | National security--United States--History. | Strategic culture--
    United States--History. | Military doctrine--United States--History.
Classification: LCC JZ1480 .S5 2016 (print) | LCC JZ1480 (ebook) | DDC 355/.033573--dc23

Printed in the United States of America

For our fathers
John Paul Siracusa
Michael John Warren

Contents

Acknowledgments

We would both like to thank our respective families in supporting us in this endeavor. Thank you so much for your love, patience, support, and encouraging words.

We also would like to thank Adam Bartley, our valued research assistant, for his fine work on this project.

Professor Joseph Siracusa and Dr. Aiden Warren
Royal Melbourne Institute of Technology University, Melbourne

Acronyms

ABMT or ABM Treaty – Anti-Ballistic Missile Treaty
ASIL – American Society on International Law
AUMF – authorization for the use of military force
CBW – chemical and biological weapons
CIA – Central Intelligence Agency
CTBT – Comprehensive Nuclear-Test-Ban Treaty
DMZ – demilitarized zone
DOD – Department of Defense
DOS – Department of State
DOT – Department of Treasury
DPRK – Democratic People's Republic of Korea
EDC – European Defense Community
EU – European Union
FOA – Foreign Operations Administration
GLCM – ground-launched cruise missiles
GOP – Grand Old Party (the U.S. Republican Party)
IAEA – International Atomic Energy Agency
ICBMs – intercontinental ballistic missiles
IMF – International Monetary Fund
INF Treaty – Intermediate Nuclear Force Treaty
INR – Department of State's Bureau of Intelligence and Research
IRBM – intermediate-range ballistic missile
ISIS – Islamic State of Iraq and Syria
LTBT – Limited Test Ban Treaty
MENWFZ – Middle East nuclear-weapon-free zone
MIRV – Multiple Independently Targeted Re-entry Vehicle
NAS – National Academy of Sciences

NATO – North Atlantic Treaty Organization
NIE – National Intelligence Estimate
NLF – National Liberation Front
NPR – Nuclear Posture Review
NPT – Nuclear Non-proliferation Treaty
NSC – National Security Council
NSC 68 – National Security Council Report 68
NSCWMD – National Strategy to Combat Weapons of Mass Destruction
NSPD – National Security Presidential Directive
NSS – National Security Strategy
PRC – People's Republic of China
ROK – Republic of Korea
SAC – Strategic Air Command
SALT – Strategic Arms Limitation Talks
SDI – Strategic Defense Initiative
SFRC – Senate Foreign Relations Committee
SHAPE – Supreme Headquarters, Allied Powers in Europe
SLBM – submarine-launched ballistic missile
SORT (also the Moscow Treaty) – Strategic Offensive Reductions Treaty
SSBN – strategic submarine ballistic nuclear
START – Strategic Arms Reduction Treaty
U.N. – United Nations
U.S. – United States
U.S.S.R. – Union of Soviet Socialist Republics
WEU – Western European Union
WMD – weapons of mass destruction

Introduction

American foreign policy has long been caught between conflicting desires to influence world affairs yet at the same time avoid becoming entangled in the burdensome conflicts and damaging rivalries of other states. With the term "doctrine" seemingly (re)attaining charged prominence in the early 21st century and, more recently, in regard to the many contested debates surrounding Obama's very own "set of guidelines," this book will argue that the doctrinal thrust in articulating the United States' foreign policy direction has long embodied the desire to maintain a "balance of influence" in meeting U.S. interests. This has necessitated attaining an equilibrium between domestic and international considerations, involvement and detachment from global security issues, unilateralism and multilateralism, interventionism and expansionism, and exceptionalism and hegemony. While some of these factors have been extensively discussed by historians, political scientists, and varying international relations commentators, much of the discourse on presidential doctrines has often been confined to research on singular doctrines.[1] As such, in proving a comprehensive and more holistic approach across multiple presidencies, this book will assess what we deem to be the most significant doctrines and doctrinal themes in defining, and in some cases redefining, U.S. foreign policy and national security over the course of the last 200-plus years. Thus, paying heed to Mark Lagon's words, "[in] fully understanding U.S. foreign policy," the book will "explore where U.S. declaratory doctrines come from,"[2] and ultimately explain considerations for both the present and future.

While the definitional debates surrounding presidential doctrines are wide and varied, there are many commonalities that commentators agree on. In the broadest sense, presidential foreign policy doctrines, like much of presidential rhetoric, have a defensive and explanatory component that serve to defend actions already underway or to persuade others to support new plans. Presidents articulate their foreign policy ideas in response to immediate political concerns, and "their broader doctrinal significance becomes apparent years later."[3] In simpler terms, presidential doctrines "serve as axiomatic guide to policy" and encompass "simple, concise, and lucid statements of purpose or strategy."[4] While not overly detailed in their explanation, Overholt and Chou argue that a rhetorical thematic message and defining strategic "thread" have been the common features in most, if not all, doctrines extending back to Washington, albeit delivered in varying fashion over the course of 44 presidents. For example, in specifically outlining the course of action in relation to Greece and Turkey and his broader position in containing communism, President Truman at the joint session of Congress on March 12, 1947, called for the "the United States to support free peoples who are resisting attempted subjugation by armed minorities and outside pressures." Similarly, in his own controversial doctrine, George W. Bush concisely argued that "[t]o forestall or prevent such hostile acts by our adversaries, the United States will, if necessary, act pre-emptively in exercising its right of self-defense." In justifying the invasion of Afghanistan and Iraq in 2001 and 2003, respectively, Bush clearly posited—and formalized—his doctrinal penchant for prevention.

Notwithstanding the strategic thread embodied in most doctrines, not all are as straightforward in their execution, or, according to Jeffrey Kimball, as true to the notion of a doctrine as a guide for policy. He states that rather than acting as a sense of "grand strategy or a master set of principles and guidelines controlling policy decisions," Nixon's doctrine, for instance—also referred to as "Vietnamization" or the "Guam doctrine"—struggled to accurately articulate and meet its core ideals.[5] The "measures for which it [the doctrine] stood were secondary to others he [Nixon] had in mind for dealing with the Vietnam War, Asia, and the world," underscored by the level of escalation in bombing of the Ho Chi Minh trail and the campaigns into Cambodia by U.S. military forces.[6] This occurred despite that the doctrine, in essence, advocated the gradual extraction of U.S. forces and commitment from the Vietnam conflict. Comparatively, however, Jeffrey Michaels argues that there is a difference between a statement "intended purely for a public or foreign audience" and one that is rather of executive intent for the bureaucracy to follow—thereby indicating that the Nixon Doctrine viewed in this light can be considered a legitimate doctrine.[7] If it is for public consumption, Michaels argues, "simplistic and sometimes moralizing terminology will be used."[8] Yet, as he also claims, a doctrine implied for public consumption will almost certainly have implications for the bureaucracy, though what constitutes these implications is to be determined and applied *by* the bureaucracy.[9]

Presidential doctrines have had a tendency to adapt to new eras and circumstances in addressing the defining security threat of the day and conveying the United States' broader national-interest objectives. In some instances, a doctrine may function as an imperative policy to follow, or, as stated, be purely for public and foreign consumption. In other cases they embody broader guiding sentiments that endorse the "exceptionalist mission." Indeed, from its inception in 1823, the Monroe Doctrine, named after President James Monroe, has been well noted for its enduring quality in combining such notions of exceptionalism and manifest destiny with what was viewed as a necessary policy prescription for the time. According to Mark Gilderhus, the doctrine's strength lies in its language of "idealism and high principle . . . purported to advance the cause of humankind . . . by upholding values such as freedom, democracy, and peace," principles highly cherished by an American population determined over the course of history to unleash their entrepreneurial and expansionist spirit unchecked—and, in their own minds, justified in doing so. [10] For Dexter Perkins, whose writings touched on the fundamental reading of the intentions of Monroe and his secretary of state, John Quincy Adams, the extended development of the doctrine came about more simply because of its two fundamental tenets of dealing with "(1) the problem of possible European territorial aggrandizements or conquests [in America]; and (2) the problem of the possible translation to this hemisphere of forms of government alien to American ideals." [11] The implication for Perkins, writing in 1942, was that these two problems faced by the United States in 1823 would be longstanding problems in American history, whether it be the Europeans or other powers in the future, such as the Japanese or Chinese. [12]

By the time of Theodore Roosevelt's corollary to the Monroe Doctrine in 1904, the unequivocal rise in international status of America, coinciding with the slow demise of European monarchies, had legitimized new interventionist and expansionist policies and somewhat offered protection to the exceptionalist values and virtues, however flawed they may have been. As stated by Jay Sexton, author of *The Monroe Doctrine: Empire and Nation in Nineteenth Century America*, the national dogma that became the Monroe Doctrine emerged from the belief that a so-called American century was in full swing and that an American exceptionalism, as espoused by the revered founding fathers, Monroe and Roosevelt, had triumphed over the Old World and was here to stay. [13] That the doctrine was able to be easily adapted into future presidential doctrines—from anti-colonialist to interventionist and at times expansionist—and continually updated and reinforced, cultivated an American mindset where exceptionalism was perceived as an intrinsic part of the American trajectory. [14]

In slightly different, but simpler, terms, Roosevelt's "linkage" turned the Monroe Doctrine into a mechanism for policing America's backyard in the long term, while standing as an "ideal illustration of the United States' righteous, paternalistic attitude towards Latin America." [15] This attitude, and indeed the Cold War attitude of many policy makers that would inevitably emerge after 1945, deeply impacted the subsequent administrations and subsequent doctrines of the Presidents Kennedy, Johnson, Carter, and Reagan.[16] According to Middlebrook and Rico, Washington's hegemonic claim over all of Latin America "included a corresponding paternalistic desire to monopolize or jealously control any relationship between its wards and third countries," the basis of which can be found in "the United States overwhelming power vis-à-vis both Latin America and the rest of the world."[17] Subsequently, for T. D. Allman writing in *Unmanifest Destiny*, the virtue of the Monroe Doctrine eventually became a stunning ideological and political metamorphosis—where Americans went "from the benefactors of the hemisphere to the benefactors of the universe."[18] Of course, given the Middle Eastern focus of the Eisenhower Doctrine, the international focus of the Wilson and Truman Doctrines, and the globalization of the Carter Doctrine,[19] Allman's words were not entirely unjustified.

The attachment of similar doctrines to the Kennedy, Johnson, and Reagan administrations offered indistinguishable paternalistic features, but, as attested to by others, such as Michaels, Middlebrook, and Rico, contained a heightened sense of ideological and material insecurity associated with the Cold War.[20] The Cuban missile crisis added to President John F. Kennedy's, and later administrations', anxiety of what Communist regimes, from small beginnings, could lead to. The short and tragic end to Kennedy's presidency, and presidential doctrine, would be carried forth in the Johnson Doctrine, with the United States' military blocking of communist insurrections in Latin America.[21] "[S]teadfast U.S. opposition to communism in the Western Hemisphere" asserts Stephen Rabe, "represented a continuation . . . in postwar U.S. foreign policy" and "should be seen as part of the historic desire of the United States to preserve its hegemony in the Western Hemisphere."[22] Reagan's unintentional addition to the doctrinal archive, according to Chester Pach, "called for both challenging communism and extending freedom" internationally, but in a far more forceful way.[23] In other words, Reagan's doctrine asserted a more militaristic intervention of his predecessors' doctrines, nominally a reinvigoration of Truman's struggle against Soviet (international) expansion, and an extension of the moral values of the Monroe Doctrine.

Presidential doctrines do not mark, necessarily, a departure in U.S. foreign policy, but in most cases adaptations of it. For instance, as the Roosevelt corollary is an adaptation to the Monroe Doctrine, the Eisenhower and Carter Doctrines are similar corollaries to the Truman Doctrine. In line with the Truman Doctrine, Eisenhower authorized in a special message to Congress the commitment of American forces "to secure and protect the territorial integrity and political independence of such nations, requesting such aid against overt armed aggression from any nation controlled by international communism." Yet, according to Jeffrey H. Michaels, what the doctrine became in the essence of clear and simple language and practical foreign policy was misplaced in Eisenhower's Middle East policy. In *Dysfunctional Doctrines? Eisenhower, Carter and U.S. Military Intervention in the Middle East*, he argues that in Eisenhower's case, policy did not often meet rhetoric, nor was the doctrine ever invoked.[24] The reason for this, Michaels suggests, is that the administration needed the rhetorical significance of a doctrine to counter the criticisms of Eisenhower's Middle East policy. The doctrine provided the administration with public support, offering the pretext that nationalist uprisings in Jordan and Syria at the time were, rather, communist insurrections.[25] The ambiguous language used in the doctrine, Michaels asserts, is best captured by then-Senator J. William Fulbright's declaration that what the administration was essentially asking for was "a blank amount of power, for a blank length of time, under blank conditions with respect to blank nations in a blank area. . . . Who will fill in these blanks?"[26]

Nevertheless, as various administrations evidently attest, and this book highlights, similar parallels of "blankness," and indeed a propensity for shifting delineations of time and place in the fine lines of policy description, are inherent within many of the doctrines of the 20th and 21st centuries. At the State of the Union address on January 3, 1980, President Jimmy Carter announced that the United States' position was, in fact, absolutely clear: "An attempt by any outside force to gain control of the Persian Gulf region will be regarded as an assault on the *vital interests* of the United States of America, and such an assault will be repelled by any means necessary, including military force."[27] While the doctrine was meant to serve as a warning to the Soviet Union, which was at the time involved in the invasion of Afghanistan, its evolution centered on the term "vital interest." According to Michael T. Klare, the Carter Doctrine went on to justify action "in the Caspian Sea region, Latin America, and the west coast of Africa," slowly but surely converting the U.S. military into "a global oil protection service."[28] Vital interests became synonymous with oil, while the Persian Gulf moved up in the equation as a "beholder" of such assets, as attested to by the Bush Administration's 2003 invasion of Iraq.[29] Subsequently, the Carter Doctrine was the only Cold War doctrine to survive the fall of the Berlin Wall.

Walter LaFeber's analysis of the Bush Doctrine similarly places the term "doctrine" in the contrasts of domestic consumption and practical, pragmatic, policy. He argues, however, that while Bush did indeed invoke the doctrine to combat terrorist organizations anathema to the American way of life, the Bush Doctrine, like all presidential doctrines, was nevertheless aimed at preempting domestic debate.[30] The doctrine, LaFeber laments, was more about domestic interests and security, a provision obtained only through unilateralism, distinctive of but even less prescribed than Carter's "vital interests," and less about the realist doctrine, or power politics, of the Cold

War years.[31] Contrastingly, prominent international relations scholar Robert Jervis argues that the concept of realism *was* at play and was a highly significant plank in Bush's doctrinal drive. While the Cold War has ended and the U.S. is no longer a status quo power, he argues, a "combination of power, fear, and perceived opportunity leads it [the U.S.] to seek to reshape world politics."[32] Hence, not unlike Woodrow Wilson's idealism of self-determination and free democratic governments worldwide, Bush was similarly "preventing" the forces of evil (in this case Saddam Hussein) from creating fear, instability, and therefore the future breeding grounds for terrorist attacks against the United States by exporting democratic and freedom-supporting values.[33] That American policies were, as a by-product, amiable to the safeguarding of Iraq's oil industry, and hence U.S. oil contracts, was not a fundamental reason for war.[34]

Just as the Bush Doctrine is a politically contested concept, the Obama Doctrine is similarly mixed with ideology, politics, and paradoxes. As with presidential doctrines of the past, hindsight offers a sturdier basis from which to analyze the subject and direction of a presidential doctrine. Thus, the Obama Doctrine has proven a far more debated subject. To this effect, the line is drawn between those who argue for the existence of an Obama Doctrine and those who argue to the contrary. Fareed Zakaria is a proponent of the latter argument. President Obama's foreign policy, he argues, is not at all dissimilar from many past presidents, and is based on a fundamental sober logic of cost-benefit analysis.[35] For this reason, Obama is seen as realist minded, multilaterally friendly, militarily conservative, domestically focused, and a proponent of exceptionalism; an otherwise divisive composition of characteristics somewhat uncommon in the makeup of presidential doctrines.

This divisiveness is indeed representative of the various arguments that Obama's doctrine is inherently, according to Daniel Drezner, one of multilateral retrenchment and counterpunching.[36] For Kristin M. Lord and Marc Lynch of the Center for a New American Century, the pillar of Obama's foreign policy is engagement and diplomacy, from the "extended hand" to Iran, to working with nations in the United Nations Security Council.[37] Yet, as stated by Rahm Emanuel, former White House chief of staff, if one were to put Obama in a category it would be more about the realpolitik than idealism.[38] Indeed, despite the importance of personal relationships, he continues, "You've got to be cold-blooded about the self-interests of your nation."[39] Emblematic of this taxonomical classification is the modernization and revitalization of nuclear weapons, despite a first-term campaign of advocating for a "nuclear-free world." Of course, this does have a direct correlation with the deterioration of relations with Russia, heightened competition with China, and as discussed in the last chapter of this book, the penchant to use military force but readjust when necessary.[40] In comparative terms, Stepak and Whitlark's assessment of Obama's foreign-policy framework concludes that there is indeed a distinctive Obama Doctrine. Unlike previous doctrines composed of isolationist, interventionist, and even expansionist tendencies, they argue that the Obama version is centrist in course and driven by the confines of a liberal (international) institutionalist framework.[41] Decidedly, they confirm, Obama's doctrine is influenced predominantly by the still volatile conditions of the American economy, a strategic turn towards China and the Asian Pacific, and the continued dominance, but international downplay, of military power. It is these components that have at varying intervals signified a departure from previous U.S. presidential doctrines,[42] and a far cry from the simple, lucid, and concise statements of policy as according to Overhalt and Chou.

There is no simple answer to the question of what makes a presidential doctrine. While there are guidelines as to what qualities a doctrine may adopt in the sense of purposeful, clear language and standards of measurement, historical and empirical analysis also tells us that doctrines are useful as devices for domestic and foreign consumption. Indeed, as this book will illustrate, presidential doctrines have ranged from isolationist to interventionist, expansionist, and, as mentioned above, feasibly centrist in terms of orientation. While many are adaptations of previous frameworks, many also offer new and at times innovative approaches and challenges ideologically, politically, and materially. Fundamentally, at the level of doctrinal DNA, an exceptionalist mentality in the principles and values of democracy and freedom, as espoused by the founding fathers, pervades the mindset of many American presidents and policymakers and therefore much of the discussion pertaining to U.S. foreign policy.

In considering the above viewpoints, the book evaluates the key presidential doctrines in explaining the current dilemmas facing the U.S. as a continuation of "perennial foreign policy challenges," rather than necessarily being a fundamental departure from the issues the nation has faced previously. In linking these varied presidential arteries to the defining doctrines of the 21st century—the Bush Doctrine and the Obama Doctrine—the book will navigate and assess the key presidential doctrines encompassing both individual and defining transitional themes, including: Washington's Farewell Address (chapter 1), the Monroe Doctrine (chapter 2), liberation (chapter 3), containment and interventionism (chapter 4; chapter 5; chapter 6), prevention for the 21st century (chapter 7), and the "pragmatic realist" doctrine of the Obama administration (chapter 8). Positing new insights and linkages between the current context and past administrations, this analytical review of key presidential doctrines will reveal that while each was formulated and adopted by U.S. leaders in reaction to immediate foreign-policy concerns, each has been remarkably consistent in the way it has been inclined to contemplate the world in general and the international framework that would adhere to the

United States' national-interest objectives. Notwithstanding the many contested debates and marked variations, to a great extent presidential doctrines have crafted responses and directions conducive to an international order that would best advance American interests: a composition encompassing democratic states (in the confidence that democracies do not go to war with one another), open free markets (on the basis that they elevate living standards, engender collaboration, and create prosperity), self-determining states (on the supposition that empires were not only adversative to freedom but more likely to reject American influence),[43] and a secure global environment in which U.S goals can be pursued (ideally) unimpeded.

NOTES

1. Jeffrey H. Michaels, "Dysfunctional Doctrines? Eisenhower, Carter and U.S. Military Intervention in the Middle East," *Political Science Quarterly* 126, no. 3, 2011, p. 465. One of the few attempts to write holistically about doctrines is Cecil V. Crabb Jr.'s writing in *The Doctrines of American Foreign Policy: Their Meaning, Role, and Future.* Also see Richard Dean Burns, Joseph M. Siracusa, and Jason Flanagan, *American Foreign Relations since Independence,* Santa Barbara, CA: Praeger, 2013.

2. Mark P. Lagon, *The Reagan Doctrine: Sources of American Conduct in the Cold War's Last Chapter,* Westport, CT: Praeger, 1994, p. 1.

3. Julia Azari, "Defending the Nation, Defending Themselves: The Politics of Presidential Doctrines," *Washington Monthly,* May 30, 2014; available at: www.washingtonmonthly.com.

4. William H. Overholt and Marylin Chou, "Foreign Policy Doctrines," *Policy Studies Journal* 3, no. 2, 1974, p. 185.

5. Jeffrey Kimball, "The Nixon Doctrine: A Saga of Misunderstanding," *Presidential Studies Quarterly* 36, no. 1, 2006, p. 60.

6. *Ibid.,* p. 60.

7. Jeffrey H. Michaels, "Dysfunctional Doctrines? Eisenhower, Carter and U.S. Military Intervention in the Middle East," *Political Science Quarterly* 126, no. 3, 2011, pp. 465–492.

8. *Ibid.,* p. 466.

9. *Ibid.*

10. Mark T. Gilderhus, "The Monroe Doctrine: Meanings and Implications," *Presidential Studies Quarterly* 36, no. 1, 2006, p. 5.

11. Dexter Perkins, "Bringing the Monroe Doctrine Up to Date," *Foreign Affairs* 20, no. 2, 1942, p. 261.

12. *Ibid.*

13. Jay Sexton, *The Monroe Doctrine: Empire and Nation in Nineteenth Century America,* New York: Hill and Wang, 2011, p. 244.

14. *Ibid.*

15. Serge Ricard, "The Roosevelt Corollary," *Presidential Studies Quarterly* 36, no. 1, 2006, p. 24.

16. See Michael D. Gambone, *Capturing the Revolution: The United States, Central America, and Nicaragua, 1961–1972,* Greenwood Publishing Group, 2001.

17. Kevin J. Middlebrook and Carlos Rico, eds., *The United States and Latin America in the 1980s,* Pennsylvania: University of Pittsburgh Press, 1986, p. 355.

18. T. D. Allman, *Unmanifest Destiny,* Michigan: Dial Press, 1984, p. 102.

19. Michael T. Klare, "Oil, Iraq, and American Foreign Policy: The Continuing Salience of the Carter Doctrine," *International Journal* 62, 2006, p. 31.

20. Jeffrey H. Michaels, "Dysfunctional Doctrines? Eisenhower, Carter and US Military Intervention in the Middle East," in Middlebrook and Rico, eds. *The United States and Latin America in the 1980s.*

21. Stephen G. Rabe, "The Johnson Doctrine," *Presidential Studies Quarterly* 36, no. 1, 2006, p. 48.

22. *Ibid.*, pp. 54 and 57.

23. Chester Pach, "The Reagan Doctrine: Principle, Pragmatism, and Policy," *Presidential Studies Quarterly* 36, no. 1, 2006, p. 88.

24. Michaels, "Dysfunctional Doctrines?" p. 474.

25. *Ibid.*

26. Fulbright cited in *Ibid.*, p. 473.

27. Jimmy Carter, "The State of the Union Address Delivered Before a Joint Session of the Congress," January 23, 1980.

28. Michael Klare, "The Carter Doctrine Goes Global," *Progressive Magazine*, December 2004, p. 18.

29. *Ibid.*

30. Walter LaFeber, "The Bush Doctrine," *Diplomatic History* 26, no. 4, 2002, pp. 543–558.

31. *Ibid.*

32. Robert Jervis, "Understanding the Bush Doctrine," *Political Science Quarterly* 118, no. 3, 2003, p. 383.

33. *Ibid.*

34. *Ibid.*

35. Fareed Zakaria, "Stop Searching for an Obama Doctrine," *Washington Post*, 6, 2011.

36. Daniel W. Drezner, "Does Obama Have a Grand Strategy? Why We Need Doctrines in Uncertain Times," *Foreign Affairs* 90, 2011, p. 57.

37. Kristin M. Lord and Marc Lynch, "America's Extended Hand: Assessing the Obama Administration's Global Engagement Strategy," *Center for a New American Security*, 2010.

38. Cited in Peter Baker, "Obama Puts His Own Mark on Foreign Policy Issues," *New York Times*, 13, 2010.

39. *Ibid.*

40. William J. Broad and David E. Sanger, "US Ramping Up Major Renewal in Nuclear Arms," *New York Times,* 2014.

41. Amir Stepak and Rachel Whitlark, "The Battle over America's Foreign Policy Doctrine," *Survival* 54, no. 5, 2012, p. 66.

42. *Ibid.*

43. Michael Cox and Doug Stokes, *U.S. Foreign Policy*, Oxford: Oxford University Press, 2008, p. 5.

Chapter One

Non-Entangling Alliances

The most decisive strand of what can be deemed the first presidential doctrine was to limit the new state from being "entangled in European affairs." As warfare swept through Europe in the wake of the French Revolution, President Washington declared America a neutral but not isolationist state, resisted the efforts of Citizen Edmond Genêt to involve America in those conflicts, and negotiated the highly successful Pinckney's Treaty with Spain and the nearly disastrous Jay's Treaty with Britain. The 1787 Constitution written in Philadelphia provided the foundation on which Washington could undertake such actions. Encompassed in its passages, the new government declared that it could control commerce, raise revenue, and create and maintain armies and navies, while separate executive and judicial departments provided the machinery necessary for enforcement. As this chapter will argue, creating such mechanisms ensured that outside states or foreign governments could no longer scorn the promises or pay little heed to the threats of the United States. However, it was Washington's resolve on American detachment from the wars of the French Revolution that was perhaps his greatest accomplishment as president.

Pushed in one direction by the partisans of France, pulled in another by the proponents of Britain, Washington believed that during the crucial period of its inception as a new nation, the United States must be allowed to grow in its own way, to continue to prosper, to consolidate, and thus move to perpetuate national unification. He unwaveringly held to the belief that the diplomatic desideratum of his day was for Americans to abjure partiality for one power or the other and to follow an unswervingly neutral policy. To do otherwise would be to put the security of the state at risk, where foreign entanglements would lead to United States participation in foreign wars and ultimately to the loss of its independence.[1] For J. A. Carroll, in no other "instance during his tenure as chief executive did Washington demonstrate his role in government so abundantly, or his greatness in statecraft so dramatically. In the year 1793 he forged the neutral rule in its fundamental form, and through the next four years his every policy was built on it."[2] The adoption of the Constitution would help inaugurate this new era in American diplomacy, while the doctrine of avoiding entangling affairs with "outside states" would be a significant driver of U.S. foreign policy for well over the next hundred years.

PRECEDING THE "DE-ENTANGLEMENT"

The origins of American independence can best be understood in the context of the long struggle between England and France for both domination of North America and supremacy in Europe. The conclusion in 1763 of the Seven Years' War—or the French and Indian War as it is also known—left Britain victorious and at the pinnacle of its power. At the same time, however, the roots of the American Revolution may be traced to this victory and the Treaty of Paris in the said year.[3] The treaty marked the beginning of increasingly divergent attitudes and acrimonious policies in London and the colonies. For Britain, victory required reorganizing the vast North American territories acquired from France and Spain. Aimed at preventing frontier warfare with the natives, the Proclamation of 1763 closed the trans-Appalachian area to colonial settlement. To defend and police the new territories, the British maintained an unprecedented standing army in mainland America. Additionally, to meet the costs of this commitment and relieve the massive financial burden left by the war, London sought to impose new taxes and enforce imperial trade laws that had long been ignored by the colonists, ending the period of so-called salutary neglect.

These measures sought not only to bring peace and stability to North America, but also to require the colonies to share the cost of imperial defense and administration. The colonists, however, had played a vital role in the victory over the French and their native allies, a victory that encouraged the colonies to think of themselves as self-governing entities.[4] The removal of the French and Spanish threat to North America reinforced the notion that the colonists no longer required British protection. As such, a chasm developed where in simple terms the colonists refused to have their duties prescribed for them by Parliament and king, while Parliament and king rejected independent colonial self-government. Britain, consequently, found itself involved in a war not only with its colonies, but eventually most of Europe. The war, though not wholly disastrous to British arms, deprived Britain of the most valuable of its colonial possessions. The initial aim of armed revolt in 1775 was not independence, but rather, recognition of what the colonials held to be their rights as British subjects that they had enjoyed prior to 1763. The colonies only turned to independence when the British government adopted repressive measures. No one set forth the arguments for independence so persuasively as Thomas Paine, a recent immigrant from England. He arrived in America in late 1774, and less than two years later, in January 1776, he published *Common Sense*. This widely read pamphlet was the single most effective articulation of the case for independence.

An Entangling Franco-American Alliance

In asserting the benefits of independence, Paine argued that it was America's connection to Britain that drew it into "European wars and quarrels" and set it "at variance with nations, whom would otherwise seek our friendship, and against whom, we have neither anger nor complaint." He continued, "As Europe is our market for trade, we ought to form no partial connection with any part of it. It is the true interest of America to steer clear of European contentions." Such commerce, he explained, would also bring security, so far as it would "secure us the peace and friendship of all Europe; because it is in the interest of all Europe to have America a free port."[5] While such ideas would form the foundation of a basic American foreign policy principle and doctrinal drive, they were neither original nor unique to the American setting. These ideas can be traced back to earlier political debates between the English Whigs and Tories who were divided over whether England should actively participate in maintaining a continental balance of power or take advantage of its insular position and avoid European conflicts in the pursuit of trade.[6] In 1744, one pamphleteer posited a general rule that anticipated the founding fathers' views of foreign policy: "A Prince or State ought to avoid all Treaties, except such as tend towards promoting Commerce or Manufactures. . . . All other Alliances may be look'd upon as so many incumbrances."[7] Such views were tempered by realistic concerns, as an "entangling alliance" with France proved essential to securing independence.

Markedly inferior to Britain in numbers, wealth, industry, and military and naval power, the colonies' only hope for military success depended on aid by a major European power. Months before deciding on independence, Congress had set up a secret committee to make contact with friends in Paris. The committee's agent in Paris, Silas Deane, having come to Paris in July 1776 seeking supplies and credit, discovered secret arrangements for aid had been instituted before his arrival. He found the French government's motivation in assisting the rebelling colonies was to weaken England. The celebrated French playwright and amateur diplomat Caron de Beaumarchais and French foreign minister Comte de Vergennes had persuaded King Louis XVI that aid to the colonies was in France's interest.[8] Its material aid to the colonies, managed by Beaumarchais, consisted of gunpowder and other essential supplies from French arsenals. Spain, persuaded by France, also provided aid. All in all, measured in the dollars of that day, France contributed to the American cause nearly $2 million in subsidies and more than $6,350,000 in loans; Spain, approximately $400,000 and $250,000 in subsidies and loans, respectively. [9]

With the Declaration of Independence, Congress sent to France the most widely admired and persuasive American of his day, Benjamin Franklin. A celebrity in France, Franklin was regarded as the embodiment of the Enlightenment. His mission was to secure French recognition of the colonies' independence, which could be accomplished by a treaty between France and the new United States. In Paris he joined Deane and Arthur Lee, who had come from London, to form an American commission. Enemy agents, however, severely compromised the commission's work, the most important of them being Deane's secretary, Dr. Edward Bancroft, secretly in the pay of the British. [10] In addition to such debasing agents, Franklin frequently leaked information for political reasons, while Deane used inside information in pursuit of speculative schemes. Nevertheless, Franklin was still able to submit a draft of a proposed treaty of amity and commerce, which embodied the liberal commercial principles that Congress hoped to see adopted not only by France but by the entire trading world. The Plan of Treaties of 1776, primarily authored by John Adams, was the first major state paper dealing with American foreign policy and would have influence beyond the exigencies of the Revolution. [11] Writing in June 1776, Adams made his feelings regarding the French treaty clear: "I am not for soliciting any political connection, or military assistance, or indeed naval, from France. I wish for nothing but commerce, a mere marine treaty with them." [12] In this way Adams had begun to frame Washington's, and later his own adopted, doctrine of non-entangling alliances.

While supportive of the United States, Vergennes was initially unwilling to risk war with England by granting formal recognition to the Americans. The surrender of General Burgoyne's British army at Saratoga in October 1777 proved the colonists' determination to field a viable military force that, combined with the readiness of the French navy, encouraged a French commitment. [13] At Paris on February 6, 1778, two agreements—a Treaty of Amity and Commerce and a Treaty of Alliance—were signed, the latter to take effect if Britain went to war with France. Still, Vergennes's major concern was that Britain might seek reconciliation with its former colonies. Burgoyne's surrender led Parliament in March to pass legislation repealing all bills enacted since 1763, which had led to colonial resentment. In April, London dispatched a commission to America, empowered to offer to Congress virtually everything it had desired, independence alone excepted, if Americans would lay down their arms and resume their allegiance to the British Crown. The right to control their own taxation, to elect their governors and other officials formerly appointed, to be represented in Parliament if they so desired, to continue Congress as an American legislature, release from quitrents, assurance that their colonial characters would not be altered without their consent, full pardon for all who had engaged in rebellion—these concessions illustrate the extent to which Britain was prepared to go to save its empire. Despite offering "dominion status" to America,[14] however, the proposition was too late. With France's recognition, the prospect of an alliance, and the promise of substantial aid, independence seemed assured. Congress ratified the treaties with France without even hesitating to parley with London's commission.

The Treaty of Amity and Commerce placed each nation on a most-favored-nation basis with reference to the liberal principles of the Plan of 1776, principles that would protect the interest of either signatory should it be neutral when the other was at war. The Treaty of Alliance—to go into effect should France become embroiled in the war against Britain—had as its object "to maintain effectually the liberty, Sovereignty, and independence absolute and unlimited" of the United States. Neither party was to make a separate peace with Britain nor lay down its arms until American independence was won. Both parties mutually guaranteed "from the present time and forever against all other powers" the American possessions that they then held and with which they might emerge from the war. France, in addition, would guarantee the liberty, sovereignty, and independence of the United States.[15] As pointed to throughout this chapter, the Franco-American pact constituted the only entangling alliance in which the United States would participate until the North Atlantic Treaty in 1949,[16] and proved indispensable to the winning of independence. After the British declared war on France for recognizing U.S. independence, a French army was sent to America, and French fleets operated off the American coast. The importance of French aid was illustrated in the final chapter of the Revolution when, at Yorktown, a British army was trapped between a French fleet and an allied army, of which two-thirds were French.

The Spanish Impact

Spain, though bound to France by a dynastic alliance—the "Family Compact"—and though giving secret aid to the United States, refused to enter the war for over a year. The Spanish court hoped to recover Gibraltar (lost in 1713) and Florida (lost in 1763) as a reward for mediating between Britain and France. When London declined mediation, Spain signed a pact with France—the Convention of Aranjuez in April 1779—and declared war against Britain on June 21, 1779.[17] John Jay spent many bitter months in Madrid asking for recognition. Spain declined, however, to join the Franco-American alliance or, as a colonial power, to formally endorse rebellion by any colonies. Even an offer to waive the American claim of right to navigate the Mississippi River could not persuade the Spanish government to recognize the young republic. The Convention of Aranjuez pledged that France and Spain would not make peace until Spain had recovered Gibraltar. Since the United States had promised not to make peace without France, it could not, if all treaty engagements were observed, make peace until Gibraltar was restored to Spain. As Samuel Flagg Bemis put it, America found itself "chained by European diplomacy to the Rock of Gibraltar."[18] Spanish and American interests clashed over the United States' desire for the Mississippi River as its western boundary and the right of navigation on it to the Gulf of Mexico. Anxious to monopolize the navigation and commerce of both river and gulf, Spain was unwilling to concede either American use of the river or a foothold on its eastern bank. If the Spanish had their way, the United States' western boundary would be fixed at the summit of the Appalachians. Spain's bargaining position was strengthened by the daring of Bernardo de Galvez, the young governor of Louisiana and one of the war's most successful generals, who routed the British from West Florida.[19] He established Spain's claim to a cession of Florida at the end of the war and took full control of the lower Mississippi.

The young United States only necessarily involved itself in the international rivalries of Europe as their politics threatened to terminate hostilities with American independence not yet achieved. Spain, reluctant to enter the war in the first place, soon grew tired of it. Thus, Madrid received a British mission in 1780 anxious to discuss peace terms. For America, the Spanish ministers proposed a long truce between Britain and its colonies without specific recognition of independence and with a division of territory on the basis of the areas each party then occupied.[20] This would have left the British in control of Maine, the northern frontier, New York City, Long Island, and the principal seaports south of Virginia. While Vergennes disapproved of the Anglo-Spanish conversations, which violated the Convention of Aranjuez, he listened to a proposal for mediation from Catherine II of Russia and Austrian Emperor Joseph II, which would have had much the same effect in America.

John Adams, then American peace commissioner and minister at The Hague, rejected the proposal out of hand when Vergennes laid it before him. No truce, he said, until all British troops were withdrawn from the United States; no negotiation with England without guarantees that American sovereignty and independence would be respected. Back home, however, Congress was more easily persuaded than Adams. Under pressure (and in some instances via monetary persuasion) from the French minister to the United States, Congress on June 15, 1781, directed its commissioners in Europe to accept the mediation of Russia and Austria and to place themselves in the hands of the French ministers, "to undertake nothing in the negotiations for peace or truce without their knowledge and concurrence," and to be governed "by their advice and opinion."[21]

Emboldening Borders and Security

It was clear that defining borders and true points of sovereignty was considered a necessary plank on the "de-entangling" doctrine's development. The American Congress named five peace commissioners, three of whom actually handled the negotiations. Franklin was in Paris when the talks began. John Jay, who had been in Madrid, arrived in June 1782. John Adams, who had secured recognition and a loan from the Netherlands, reached Paris in October. Franklin and Jay handled most of the discussions, with Adams providing valuable aid toward the latter stages.

The American commissioners had three primary objectives: (1) recognition of independence, now assured; (2) the widest boundaries obtainable; and (3) retention of the inshore fishing privileges on the coasts of British North America that the colonials had previously enjoyed. London was prepared to recognize American independence and respond generously to the other American demands. In return, it hoped to secure from the United States: (1) payment of the pre-Revolutionary debts of American planters and others to British creditors, and (2) compensation for the Loyalists (Americans who had sided with Britain) for the lands and other property that had been seized by the states. Of these objectives, the most controversial American demands concerned boundaries, for their claims involved adjustments with Britain and Spain. Congress claimed the entire area between the Appalachian Mountains and the Mississippi River based chiefly on the sea-to-sea clauses in certain colonial charters. The British government in the years since 1763 acted as though the western lands belonged to the Crown. South of the Ohio River, American settlements in central Kentucky and eastern and central Tennessee gave the United States a solid basis for claiming those areas, but farther south the Spanish held the east bank of the Mississippi as far north as Natchez. They still hoped to deny the Americans access to the Mississippi and to draw the boundary near to the Appalachian watershed. In this endeavor they had French support.

In the summer of 1779, on August 14, Congress's first step toward peace negotiations was naming John Adams as commissioner to France. Adams was tasked with setting the proposed boundaries that included the area claimed by the states from the mountains to the Mississippi. The commission added that although it was "of the utmost importance to the peace and Commerce of the United States that Canada and Nova Scotia should be ceded" and that equal rights in the fisheries should be guaranteed, a desire to terminate the war led Congress to refrain from making these concerns an ultimatum.[22] Military necessity and pressure from the French minister prompted

Congress to issue new instructions on June 15, 1781, that insisted only on independence and the preservation of the treaties with France as indispensable conditions. With regard to boundaries, the commissioners were to regard the earlier instructions as indicating "the desires and expectations of Congress," but were not to adhere to them if they presented an obstacle to peace.[23]

The Peace Negotiations

The Spanish and French presented several obstacles to the doctrine's non-entanglement drive for separation. John Jay arrived in Paris suspicious of both countries after his futile mission in Madrid. The Spanish ambassador in Paris and a spokesman for Vergennes indicated that the Spanish, with French support, were bent on excluding the United States from the Mississippi Valley. Vergennes agreed that the American and French negotiations with the British should proceed separately, but with the understanding that neither settlement should become effective without the other. Franklin and Jay proceeded to negotiate their own preliminary terms with the British, neglecting, with considerable justification, to make those "most candid and confidential communications" to the French ministers.[24] In their negotiations with Britain, they simply disregarded Spanish claims in the western country north of the 31st parallel, assuming (as did London) that that country still belonged to Britain.

Franklin had already informally sketched out to Britain's special representative, Richard Oswald, what, as an American, he considered the "necessary" and the "advisable" terms of a lasting settlement. Among "necessary" terms he included, after independence and withdrawal of troops, "a confinement of the boundaries of Canada" to what they had been before the Quebec Act (that is, the St. Lawrence-Nipissing line), "if not to a still more contracted state," and the retention of fishing privileges. Among "advisable" terms that might be expected to contribute to a permanent reconciliation, he mentioned indemnification by Britain of those persons who had been ruined through the devastations of war, admission of American ships and trade to British and Irish ports on the same terms as those of Britain, and "giving up every part of Canada."[25] A delay now ensued, because when Oswald received his formal commission as an agent of the British government on August 8, it failed to authorize him to recognize the independence of the United States as preliminary to negotiation. It did, however, authorize him to make recognition of independence the first article of the proposed treaty. Franklin and Jay were at first inclined to insist on formal recognition of independence as a condition precedent to negotiation; but, becoming alarmed lest France use any further delay to their disadvantage, they agreed to accept recognition as stipulated in Oswald's commission.[26]

On September 1, Oswald received instructions to accept terms based on Franklin's proposed "necessary" terms, ceding to the United States the western country as far north as Canada, while accepting the rejection of payments for pre-war debts or the restitution of property confiscated from the Loyalists. A draft treaty on these terms was initialed by the commissioners on October 5 and referred to London. At the same time, news arrived that a major assault on Gibraltar had failed. With this victory, the Earl of Shelburne took a firmer tone, not only insisting that something be done for British creditors and Loyalists, but attempting to hold on to the "old" Northwest territory. The Americans, reinforced by Adams, insisted on retention of the Northwest, but they agreed to inclusion in the treaty of articles in the interest of the Loyalists and the British creditors. They accepted the St. Croix River instead of the St. John, as originally proposed, as the northeastern boundary. In the west, they accepted a line through the middle of the St. Lawrence and the Great Lakes and thence via the Lake of the Woods to the Mississippi. The preliminary treaty was signed at Paris on November 30, 1782, not to become effective until France also made peace with England. The treaty was less favorable to the United States than the draft initialed on October 5. It contained provisions for Loyalists and for British creditors, and the northern boundary as such followed the river and lake line instead of Lake Nipissing, costing the United States the most valuable part of the modern province of Ontario.

Still, it was remarkable that the United States got as much as it did, especially title to all territory east of the Mississippi between the Great Lakes and the 31st parallel. For the explanation of this, one must look to the enlightened policy of the Earl of Shelburne. Desirous of a peace of reconciliation, he saw a means of achieving it at small cost to the empire. The regulation of the fur trade in that area was proving alarmingly expensive to the royal treasury, and experience had indicated that the region was of little value without control of the mouth of the Mississippi, now firmly in the hands of Spain. The principal provisions of the preliminary treaty signed on November 30, 1782, established the boundaries of the United States, several of which would be disputed for several years, but included the territory west to the Mississippi River. Britain acknowledged the independence and sovereignty of the 13 states individually; promised to withdraw all its armies, garrisons, and fleets from their soil and waters "with all convenient speed"; and conceded to American fishermen the liberty to ply their trade much as before in the territorial waters of British North America. The United States, on its part, made certain promises in the interest of Loyalists and British creditors. The parties agreed that creditors on either side should "meet with no lawful impediment" in the recovery of the full value of bona fide debts previously contracted. The United States agreed that there should be no further prosecutions or confiscations of property against any persons for the part they had taken in the war and promised that it would "earnestly recom-mend" to the legislatures of the states that, with certain exceptions, rights and properties of Loyalists be restored.[27] The definitive treaty was signed on September 3, 1783, at the same time that Britain made peace with its other enemies. Britain ceded the Floridas, with limits undefined, to Spain, which did not endorse U.S. navigation of the Mississippi or the United States' southern boundary. With both Spain and Britain, the United States still faced many difficulties before the stipulations of the treaty could be converted into reality.

THE CHALLENGES OF INDEPENDENCE

Despite attaining the Washington Doctrine's goal of de-entangling the Unit-ed States from problematic alliances, this effort would remain an ongoing work in progress, and paradoxically required recognition from the very states from which the U.S. was trying to keep a reasonable distance. When hostil-ities officially ended in 1783, France, Britain, the Netherlands, and Sweden had recognized the United States. Inexperienced American diplomats had previously wandered over to Europe in vain to secure recognition from Rus-sia, Prussia, Austria, Spain, and the Grand Duke of Tuscany. In these courts they had been coldly received, for few monarchs cared to countenance rebel-lion and the institution of republican government. That said, several other recognitions followed independence: in 1784, Spain sent Don Diego de Gar-doqui as its first minister to the United States; Prussia signed a treaty in 1785 and Morocco in 1786. By 1787, the United States had commercial treaties with France (1778), the Netherlands (1782), and Sweden (1783), but would have to wait until 1794 and 1795 to secure ones with Britain and Spain, respectively. The British government thought so little of the importance of the United States that, though it received John Adams as minister in 1785, it did not send a full-fledged minister to Philadelphia until 1791.

The United States' temporary "underprivileged" status stemmed from it being a product of revolution, an experiment in democracy, small in popula-tion, and poor in fluid resources. But also the Articles of Confederation—which constituted a government without dependable revenue, without an army or navy, and without power to coerce the governments of the 13 indi-vidual states—lacked the respect of foreign powers. Such a government was unable to fulfill its treaty obligations, was not able to make commitments with assurance that they would be observed or threats with expectation that they would be carried out, and was incapable of securing equality of com-mercial treatment abroad. Additionally, it was incapable of enforcing its sovereignty over areas assigned to it or of putting an end, by either diploma-cy or force, to foreign occupation of its soil. Not until after it was replaced by the more effective government provided for by the Constitution of 1787 were these pressing issues resolved.

The Economic Drawbacks of Independence

The lack of a commercial treaty with Britain was particularly damaging to the nation's economy. The original 13 states had, as British colonies, been protected by the Royal Navy, and had developed a flourishing merchant marine and an extensive and profitable commerce. Colonial shipyards turned out ships more cheaply than the British. Ships built and owned in the colonies enjoyed the privileges of empire trade with American tobacco, rice, indigo, wheat, flour, meat, fish, rum, furs, and lumber, finding markets in England, on the continent of Europe, in Africa, and in the West Indies. There they exchanged these products for manufactured goods, sugar and molasses, coffee, rum, and slaves. During the Revolution, American ships and their cargoes were excluded from British Empire ports and were at the risk of capture by British cruisers or privateers. Many American ship owners took to privateering and harried British commerce, but peace in 1783 put an end to such employment. It compelled the United States, in the exercise of its newly won independence, to seek markets for its produce, cargoes and foreign ports for its merchantmen, and protection for ships and cargoes against the piracies of North African freebooters.

Trade with the various portions of the British Empire might have continued as before the war had the British been willing. The American peace commissioners of 1782 were instructed to secure, if possible, for citizens of the United States, "a direct commerce to all parts of the British dominions and possessions" in return for the admission of British subjects to trade with all parts of the United States.[28] The British government at that time declined. Its Parliament was in no mood to be generous to its former colonies; least of all to encourage a rival in the American merchant marine. American ships carrying American products were admitted to ports in the British Isles on fairly liberal terms, but their ships, like other foreign ships, were excluded from trading with the British colonies. New England merchants particularly missed what had once been a profitable trade with the British West Indies; only gradually, and at considerable risk, did they succeed in reopening this trade through clandestine and illegal channels. To varying degrees, and with some exceptions, other colonial powers adhered to the same mercantilist policy of reserving trade with their colonies to their own ships.

The Conundrum of the West

Despite the Washington Doctrine's contribution to securing spacious boundaries, American sovereignty within such boundaries was largely a legal fiction. Settlement beyond the mountains took the form of a narrow wedge, with its base stretching from Pittsburgh to the Watauga settlements in eastern Tennessee and its apex at Nashville on the Cumberland River. Within it lay the villages in the Kentucky bluegrass region and at the Falls of the Ohio (Louisville). To these should be added the old French villages on the Wabash and in the Illinois country. All told, there were perhaps 25,000 settlers between the crest of the mountains and the Mississippi. Beyond these limits, to the north, west, and south, were some 500 nations of natives; and the explorer or trader who ventured into these domains would also find garrisons of British or Spanish troops on land within the United States' treaty boundaries. The British army still occupied every strategic point on the Great Lakes, while Spanish soldiers held the Mississippi at Natchez and (a little later) at the sites of the future Vicksburg and Memphis. Moreover, both the British and Spanish had an alliance or understanding with the natives for the purpose of preventing the United States from taking possession of its legal territory.

Additionally, there was no assurance that the frontier settlers would be firm in their allegiance to the state governments in the East or to the weak Congress that represented their Union. The frontier found its natural outlets through the Ohio, Mississippi, and St. Lawrence Rivers, and the nations that controlled those watercourses exerted a powerful influence on the settlements on their waters. Frontier leaders were not above bartering their allegiance in return for special favors from the local British and Spanish agents. Before the United States could enforce its sovereign rights, it had to accomplish three difficult, interrelated tasks: it must gain the allegiance of the frontiersmen, bring the native tribes under its authority, and secure from England and Spain, respectively, the execution of the terms of the Treaty of Paris. Only through ousting the British and Spanish from their footholds on its soil could the United States hope to control the natives, and only by dealing effectively with the natives and Europeans could it win the "men of the western waters."[29] None of these problems proved capable of attaining a solution during the period of the Articles of Confederation. The British held seven fortified posts on U.S. soil, strung out from the foot of Lake Champlain to the junction of Lakes Huron and Michigan. They excused this violation of the peace treaty by asserting that the United States had not fulfilled its obligations. In reality, the decision to hold such posts had been taken before the treaty was formally proclaimed, for retention would maintain a valuable trade in furs and enabled the British government to meet its obligations to allied native tribes. British authorities encouraged these tribes, living south of the Canadian border, to resist American attempts to settle their lands. The British also hoped the dissatisfied American frontier communities in Vermont and Kentucky might detach themselves from the Confederation.

The treaty of 1783 had fixed the United States' southern boundary from the Chattahoochee to the Mississippi at the 31st parallel, had made the middle of the Mississippi the western boundary, and had declared: "The navigation of the river Mississippi, from its source to the ocean, shall forever remain free and open to the subjects of Great Britain, and the citizens of the United States." In the contemporaneous settlement with Spain, Britain had ceded East and West Florida without defining their boundaries. Louisiana, embracing the region west of the Mississippi and New Orleans east of that river, had been ceded by France to Spain in 1762. After 1783, therefore, a weak and nervous Spain was hemmed in by the United States on both the west and the south.

In simple terms, Spain refused to consider itself bound by terms of the Anglo-American treaty, either as to the southern boundary of the United States or as to the free navigation of the Mississippi. As a result of the successful campaign in 1779–1781, Spain claimed a large area in the Southwest by right of conquest and denied the right of Britain to cede it to the United States. Holding both banks of the Mississippi from its mouth to far above New Orleans, Spain likewise denied the right of Britain to guarantee to citizens of the United States its free navigation. Spanish policy after 1783 included the assertion of title to a region as far north as the Tennessee and Ohio Rivers, the denial to the Americans the use of the lower Mississippi except as a privilege granted by Spain, and the cultivation of the powerful native nations of the Southwest as a barrier against the Americans. Additionally, Spain also periodically schemed with those leaders in the American frontier communities who appeared ready to barter their allegiance for privileges or bounties conferred by the Spanish crown. Diego de Gardoqui, the first Spanish minister to the United States, was empowered to make liberal boundary concessions and to offer substantial trading privileges in return for the consent of the United States to waive its claim to the navigation of the Mississippi. John Jay, serving as secretary for foreign affairs under the direction of Congress, thought the trade offer advantageous and the navigation of the Mississippi of little immediate importance. He asked Congress for authority to consent to closure of the river for a period of 25 or 30 years. The vote on his proposal revealed sectional disparities as Virginia, the Carolinas, and Georgia, all with land claims extending to the Mississippi, voted against it. The seven states to the north (Delaware having no delegate in Congress) supported Jay. The majority of seven to five was sufficient to alter Jay's instructions, but any treaty that he might make would require the vote of nine states for ratification. Jay and Gardoqui continued their futile conversations. The following year (1787), however, Spanish authorities opened the river for Americans from the Kentucky settlements. One of these, Revolutionary War veteran James Wilkinson, paid for the privilege by taking a secret oath of allegiance to the Spanish Crown and advising the Spanish on the best means of winning over other Kentuckians. The establishment of satisfactory relations with Spain, as well as with Britain, would have to await the formation of a more efficient American government.

The Constitution and a New Era of Diplomacy

Written in Philadelphia in 1787, and effective two years later, the Constitution established a form of government that could control commerce and raise revenue, as well as create and maintain armies and navies. Treaties, both those already made and those to be made in the future, were declared to be "the supreme law of the land,"[30] overriding state enactments and even state constitutions, while separate executive and judicial departments provided the machinery necessary for enforcement. In this light, foreign governments would no longer scorn the promises or scoff at the threats of the United States.

While the adoption of the Constitution inaugurated a new era in American diplomacy, Washington had to contend with some tensions within his government. To borrow Doris Kearns Goodwin's phrase, his administration had the first and perhaps most bitter "team of rivals" in American history.[31] The appointment of Thomas Jefferson as secretary of state and Alexander Hamilton as secretary of the treasury led to a rivalry that not only divided the administration, but contributed to the formation of the nation's first political parties. The Hamilton-Jefferson divide was apparent from the first foreign policy challenge faced by the administration. In 1789, an Anglo-Spanish dispute erupted over possession of Nootka Sound in the remote Pacific Northwest. The territory was claimed by Spain, and when the British attempted to establish a post there, the Spanish drove them out and captured their ships. With both countries preparing for war, Washington was concerned the British might desire to move troops through American territory to strike at Spanish possessions in Louisiana and Florida. Since denying permission raised the specter of conflict with England, while granting such permission raised the possibility of war with Spain, he asked his advisers how the United States should respond. Jefferson essentially recommended giving no answer at all to such a request, believing that evading the question would not only guarantee American neutrality but allow time for the United States to extract some advantage from Anglo-Spanish tensions. Hamilton, on the other hand, recommended that permission be granted. Fortunately for Washington, he never had to make a decision on this matter. Spain, having lost its French ally to revolution, quickly capitulated. The unfolding French Revolution, and the war it triggered in 1792, contributed to Hamilton and Jefferson's increasingly divergent views, which would shape the American response to the unfolding international conflict.[32]

THE FIGHT FOR SEPARATION AND AUTONOMY

The French Revolution soon provoked a widespread conflict that would come to challenge the non-entanglement doctrine. The War of the First Coalition began in April 1792 when France declared war on Austria. In January the following year the French executed Louis XVI, and in February they declared war on Britain. The English phase of the war in 1793 launched a naval conflict that reached the shores of the United States. American popular sympathy initially favored France, a recent ally and now the exemplar of republicanism and democracy. In 1793, however, conservative Federalists recoiled at the terror in France, denying any resemblance between America's cause and that of their French counterparts.[33] Jeffersonian Republicans, in contrast, formed "Jacobin Clubs," patterned after those in France, addressing one another as "citizen" and "citizeness" after the current French fashion. Popular sentiment apart, the United States had treaty obligations, where under certain circumstances they were required to protect French possessions in America and to allow French naval vessels and privateers privileges denied to Britain. Support for France was also heightened by British interference with American trade at sea and consistent opposition to American interests on the frontier.

American officials were aware of the perils of the situation and were determined to remain neutral; on this point Jefferson and Hamilton agreed. Anticipating the arrival of the French Republic's first minister, Edmond Genêt, Washington submitted a list of 13 questions to his cabinet, consisting of Jefferson, Hamilton, Secretary of War Henry Knox, and Attorney General Edmund Randolph. The list encompassed three fundamental considerations: First, should the president issue a proclamation of neutrality? Second, were the treaties made with Louis XVI still binding on the United States, now that the monarchy had been overthrown? And finally, the question of whether Genêt should be received as the minister of the French Republic. The answers to these questions returned by Hamilton and Jefferson—Knox siding with Hamilton and Randolph with Jefferson—shaped the American concept of neutral rights and duties, and the rules of recognition. To the first question—issuing a proclamation of neutrality—Jefferson answered "no," Hamilton "yes." Jefferson argued that the question of neutrality (like that of war) was one for Congress to determine, and that American neutrality should be used as a bargaining chip, not freely given. Hamilton argued that America's neutrality was not a negotiable commodity and that delaying its announcement risked America being dragged into the war.[34]

To the second question—on the binding of treaties—Hamilton answered "no," since the government with which they were made had been overthrown. Even if the treaties were still in force, Hamilton added, the alliance was expressly a "defensive" one, and France, having declared war against

England, was the aggressor. Jefferson dissented, arguing that treaties were made by Louis XVI's government, acting as the agent of the French people, and that a change of agents did not invalidate the agreements. (Jefferson's position since has been universally accepted.) If Jefferson would not repudiate the French treaties, neither did he believe they committed the United States to join France in the war. France, he said, had not yet asked the United States to fulfill its guarantee under the alliance. Should it do so, the United States could excuse itself on the grounds that France had failed to aid in ending British occupation of the northwest posts. If Jefferson headed the pro-French faction, he was as anxious as pro-British Hamilton to preserve American neutrality. To the third question—should Genêt be received—both Hamilton and Jefferson answered "yes"; but where Jefferson would receive him unconditionally, Hamilton would give him notice that the United States did not consider itself bound by the treaties of 1778. On April 22, 1793, Washington issued a proclamation of neutrality, avoiding the word "neutrality," declaring the United States would "pursue a conduct friendly and impartial toward the belligerent Powers." He called on American citizens to avoid contrary acts and warned of the consequences of committing hostile acts against any belligerent. Offenders must expect prosecution for any violation of "the law of nations" committed "within the cognizance of the courts of the United States."[35]

Citizen Genêt arrived in the United States expecting, if not an outright military alliance, at least America's active assistance in his nation's war with Britain and Spain. If he did not demand activation of the alliance, he did engage in unwarranted activities that would have compromised U.S. neutrality. Genêt had landed in Charleston and only after a slow four-week journey arrived in Philadelphia. En route he used public meetings and banquets to mobilize support for the French cause, attempted to organize illegal military expeditions to seize the Spanish possessions of Florida and Louisiana, and commissioned privateers to cruise under the French flag and to prey on British commerce. When Washington sought to curtail Genêt's efforts, the Frenchman appealed to the American people over the president's head.[36] Genêt's actions, which even Jefferson could not condone, led to a request for his recall, and the French readily agreed. France's ready acceptance was due to a desire to maintain good terms with the United States and to the new Jacobin authorities' suspicions of Genêt.[37] Fearing the guillotine at home, Genêt remained in the United States as a private citizen. His actions, however, were largely responsible for Congress's enactment of a landmark neutrality law on June 5, 1794.

Rising Tensions

Tensions generated by maritime grievances soon put the country at odds with Britain. Rejecting the Plan of 1776, the British, following the accepted law of nations, ignored the dictum "free ships make free goods," condemning French property found on American ships to British prize courts. The British also seized cargoes of American wheat, corn, and flour en route to France—not for confiscation but for preemptive purchase, presumably to the injury of the shipper. Voiding the stipulation of 1776 that neutral ships were free to trade between enemy ports, the British insisted that trade illegal in peace was illegal in war. Thus France, which in peacetime limited trade between itself and its colonies to French ships, could not in wartime open that trade to neutral shipping. Neutral ships admitted to such trade, the British declared, would be subject to confiscation. But the British went further, seizing not only American ships trading between France and its colonies, but also those trading between the colonies and the United States—a trade that France permitted in peacetime—seizing some 250 ships in the West Indies.[38] The British also stopped American merchant vessels on the high seas and impressed members of their crews, presumed to be British subjects, for service in the Royal Navy.

Tensions were further exacerbated by events on the frontier. British troops still garrisoned in northwest posts despite the treaty of 1783, as well as British agents, continued to encourage the natives to resist American land claims. Viewing the native treaties of 1784 and later years as valid, Congress had provided for the government of the Northwest Territory in the Ordinance of 1787 and had sold large tracts of land north of the Ohio River to prospective settlers and speculators. By the spring of 1789, the settlement of the northwest had begun, but it had become apparent that the natives would not honor the land treaties. Two expeditions against the natives in 1789 and 1791 resulted, respectively, in an inconclusive campaign and a disastrous defeat. Washington appointed "Mad" Anthony Wayne to command a third expedition. When Wayne moved into the native country in the fall of 1793, the United States and Britain were already engaged in a heated dispute over the rights of neutrals. Congress had enacted a temporary embargo on American shipping, while other measures of retaliation were also introduced. Consequently, Lord Dorchester, Canadian governor general, assumed that war was inevitable and feared that Wayne, if successful against the natives, would attack Detroit. Hence, he ordered the fortification of a strategic point at the Maumee River many miles within U.S. territory. In February 1794, Dorchester told a delegation of western natives that the United States did not desire peace, that it had violated the 1783 treaty, and that he expected war within a year. At that time, he said, the natives could draw a new treaty line.[39] Such was the ominous atmosphere when Wayne, by August 18, 1794, had advanced just short of the British fort on the Maumee. In a mass of fallen timber, he scattered assembled natives, reinforced by Canadian volunteers, with a disciplined charge. The natives fell back under the guns of the British fort, but fortunately Wayne and the British commander avoided a dangerous clash that could have started a war. Having soundly defeated the Indians, Wayne set about laying waste to their villages and fields as a way of bringing them to terms.

Jay's Attempt to Quell Tensions

With Washington's doctrine under threat from the very outside influences it had intended to avoid, John Jay was sent to London in April 1794 in a final attempt to reach an agreement with England over the several matters discussed above. A staunch Federalist and experienced diplomat, Jay shared a desire for continued peace with Britain but understood the necessity to secure fulfillment of the treaty of 1783, including the surrender of the northwest posts. He was instructed to urge the British to accept the principles of 1776 and to seek compensation for seizures of American ships and cargoes in violation of those principles. Hamilton, in shaping Jay's instructions, had given preserving peace with Britain the highest priority, so as to maintain the flow of revenue from commerce that sustained the nation's credit.[40] However, in negotiating in this spirit, there was perhaps little that Jay could hope to achieve. In the subsequent treaty signed on November 19, 1794, the United States agreed that enemy goods might be taken from neutral ships, that naval stores could be considered contraband, and that provisions bound for an enemy might be taken from neutral ships if paid for. The rule of 1756 remained intact; moreover, the United States was left without clarification of the definition of a legal blockade. Under the initial 1778 treaty, French ships-of-war or privateers with enemy prizes were admitted freely to American ports, but British ships with enemy prizes were excluded. While the Jay treaty extended the same privilege to British ships-of-war and privateers and excluded its (French) enemies, the apparent contradiction of the Franco-American treaty was partly nullified by a clause declaring that nothing in the treaty should "operate contrary to former and existing public treaties with other sovereigns or States."[41]

The West fared rather better, for the treaty contained a British promise that the posts would be evacuated no later than June 1, 1796. The subjects or citizens of either country should be privileged "freely to pass and repass by land or inland navigation, into the respective territories and countries of the two parties." For the liberation of U.S. soil from British troops, Jay deserves no great credit since London had earlier decided to give up the posts. He attempted unsuccessfully to secure demilitarization of the lakes and an agreement that neither party would employ native allies in war against the other or supply the natives with arms. Nonetheless, Jay resisted London's attempt to secure a slice of territory reaching down the Mississippi River to navigable water near modern Minneapolis. Additionally, he did settle other controversial matters pertaining to the adjudication and payment, on the one side, of pre-Revolutionary debts owed by Americans to British subjects and of British claims for damages resulting from Genêt's irregular activities and, on the other, of claims of illegal seizures by British cruisers of American ships and cargoes. The commercial clauses of Jay's Treaty placed the United States on a most-favored-nation basis with reference to trade with the British Isles, opened the East Indian trade to Americans on fairly liberal terms, and also opened the important West Indian trade.

The treaty spurred controversy in Congress and a widespread and passionate public debate that heightened the emergence of a full-fledged party system.[42] In the House of Representatives, the Republican Frederick Muhlenberg cast a key vote to approve funding for the treaty. Feelings were so intense that Muhlenberg's vote destroyed his political career and led his own brother-in-law, a fellow Republican, to stab him in the streets of Philadelphia. Washington, however, skillfully managed the ratification process, giving the Federalists time to mobilize public sentiment behind the treaty.[43] Unsatisfactory in some respects, the Jay treaty not only kept the peace at a critical time, but brought about the fulfillment of the 1783 peace treaty and London's acceptance of the United States as an equal and sovereign state. Freeing the northern frontier from British garrisons led to a settlement with the natives. Defeated by General Wayne at Fallen Timbers and deprived of British support, the tribes came to terms. At Fort Greenville on August 3, 1795, they ceded the future state of Ohio to the United States, except the northwest corner and a strip running along the shore of Lake Erie to the Cuyahoga River. Of course, with these two treaties, control of the Northwest was passed to the United States for the first time and thereby secured an important pillar in the Washington Doctrine's prescription of de-entangled relations with Europe.

The Treaty with Spain

The other important element in Washington's doctrinal drive pertained to Spain. After Jay's agreement, Thomas Pinckney signed a treaty with Madrid that accomplished for the Southwest even greater things than Jay's Treaty had achieved for the Northwest. Pinckney's treaty—the Treaty of San Lorenzo—was in many regards a by-product of the Jay treaty. If Spain made peace with France and found itself at war with Britain, the Spanish feared an Anglo-American alliance would render Spanish colonies vulnerable, a fear heightened when Madrid learned of Jay's mission to England. Friendly relations with the United States, even at the cost of concessions, seemed the only safe policy for Spain. A hint that the Spanish might accept American claims as to the boundary line and the navigation of the Mississippi prompted President Washington, in November 1794, to appoint Thomas Pinckney minister to Spain. As Pinckney reached Madrid in late June 1795, circumstances were ripe for a successful negotiation. When a peace treaty between Spain and France was signed in July, the news of Jay's treaty with Britain also reached Madrid. Spanish authorities decided to accept the United States' principal demands without insisting on a treaty of alliance, yet negotiations proceeded until October 27, 1795.[44]

Spain conceded America's long-standing claims to the 31st parallel of latitude from the Mississippi to the Chattahoochee as the southern boundary of the United States and to the free navigation of the Mississippi. American citizens also could enjoy for three years the privilege of landing and storing their goods in New Orleans. This "right of deposit" was important for the westerners, who brought their cargoes down the river in flatboats and needed storage while awaiting suitable oceangoing vessels. The Spanish, however, displayed what has been referred to by some as characteristic procrastination in carrying out the terms of the treaty. They did not evacuate frontier posts north of the 31st parallel until 1798, but by the end of that year all Spanish garrisons had been withdrawn and westerners were freely navigating the great river and utilizing the storage facilities of New Orleans. In the Southwest as in the Northwest, the United States had at length achieved the treaty boundaries of 1783.

AN "ALMOST" WAR WITH FRANCE

While failing to promote neutral rights, Jay's Treaty ushered in a decade of generally cordial relations with Britain.[45] However, the French were not happy with this development to say the least. When Washington ratified Jay's Treaty, it was seen in Paris as contrary to the spirit and the letter of the engagements with France. A South Carolina Federalist, Charles C. Pinckney, was appointed minister to France in 1796. France, ruled now by the Directory, was elated as military successes reduced its smaller neighbors to the status of satellites and tributaries. Angered by Jay's Treaty, and perhaps even in a heavy-handed way, they sought to deal harshly with the United States. They refused to receive Pinckney; interfered in the election of 1796, hoping to put Jefferson and the Republicans in office; and by June 1797 seized more than 300 American ships. French actions were aimed at damaging American commerce without provoking formal hostilities. As the French diplomat Louis-Andre Pichon said, "An open war would reunite the parties [in America]. A little clandestine war, like England made on America for three years, would produce a constructive effect."[46]

Nonetheless, French interference in American politics actually inspired much of Washington's Farewell Address, published in September 1796.[47] In his address, Washington cautioned his fellow countrymen against "inveterate antipathies against particular nations and passionate attachments for others," and encouraged them to be "constantly awake" against the "insidious wiles of foreign influence." The address's authors, Washington and Hamilton, obviously had the initially vital but later problematic French alliance in mind when Washington declared: "It is our true policy to steer clear of permanent alliances with any portion of the foreign world" and to rely only on "temporary alliances for extraordinary emergencies." While the new republic would vigorously pursue commercial engagement with the world, its new doctrinal thrust was the permanent avoidance of political and military entanglements.[48]

John Adams, elected despite French machinations, named a commission consisting of Federalist John Marshall of Virginia, Republican Elbridge Gerry of Massachusetts, and the rejected Charles Pinckney to negotiate outstanding differences with France and seek compensation for the seized ships and cargoes. Upon arrival in Paris, the commissioners were approached by three French agents—designated X, Y, and Z in the printed dispatches—as spokesmen for the French foreign minister, Charles Maurice de Talleyrand-Périgord. Talleyrand may have been "an unscrupulous, pleasure-loving aristocrat of elegant taste and loose morals,"[49] but he was also an extremely talented diplomat. The three French agents demanded a loan to France, a substantial bribe for the Directors, and an apology for some unfriendly remarks by President Adams.[50] The commissioner's rejection of the proposal was less due to moral indignation than to the fact that agreement was beyond their instructions. Of course, publication of their correspondence set off an almost hysterical reaction in the United States. Talleyrand was burned in effigy, and the phrase "Millions for defense, but not one cent for tribute" became a popular slogan.[51] Congress authorized the president to raise a "provisional army" of 10,000 men in addition to the regular army and called George Washington back from retirement for its command. More significantly, they created a Navy Department, initiated construction of warships, and authorized U.S. naval vessels and armed merchantmen to challenge armed French vessels in the western Atlantic and Caribbean. This small navy—some 15 vessels in 1798—focused on the Caribbean and cooperated closely with the British navy.[52] Although the army was not used, Congress declared the treaties of 1778 with France abrogated. This became known as the "quasi-war" with France of 1798 to 1800.

Neither President Adams, Talleyrand, nor General Napoleon Bonaparte, who, in November 1799, became the head of the French government, desired a full-scale war. Bonaparte and Talleyrand, now intent on securing Louisiana, clearly desired peace with both the United States and Britain. Adams declared that he would never send another minister to France without assurance that he would be "received, respected, and honored as the representative of a great, free, powerful, and independent nation."[53] Talleyrand agreed and Adams named a new commission of three men, William Vans Murray, Oliver Ellsworth, and William R. Davie, to undertake negotiations with France. The American negotiators, received in Paris with proper respect, found that Talleyrand had ordered an end to the seizure of American ships and was arranging for the release of captured American sailors. Murray and his colleagues asked indemnity for French depredations on American commerce and bilateral abrogation of the treaties of 1778—already unilaterally abrogated by an act of Congress. No agreement proving possible on the claims for indemnity, the negotiators signed on September 30, 1800, a treaty that terminated the treaties of 1778 and left the question of indemnities undetermined, both to be the subject of further negotiation "at a convenient time." As amended by the Senate and further qualified by Bonaparte before ratification, the treaty nullified the earlier treaties and cancelled the claims for indemnity.[54]

The chief importance of the treaty of 1800 with France was that it released the United States from all obligations that compromised its neutral position in relation to the European belligerents. The restatement of the principles of 1776 was little more than a gesture, for Napoleon Bonaparte's promises were kept only as long as they suited his convenience and, in any event, a statement of neutral rights had little importance without the concurrence of Britain. The treaty of 1800, followed by the election of Thomas Jefferson to the presidency later that year, marked the end of the Federalist era in American diplomacy.

THE LOUISIANA PURCHASE

For the main part, the Washington Doctrine's attempt to keep foreign influence at a manageable distance seemed almost complete. But while the Jay and Pinckney treaties of 1794 and 1795 validated the boundary provisions of the peace treaty of 1783, these boundaries would not hold the young republic. It was "impossible not to look forward to distant times," Jefferson wrote in 1801, "when our rapid multiplication will . . . cover the whole Northern, if not Southern continent with people speaking the same language, governed in similar forms, and by similar laws."[55] American settlers threatened to dominate Upper Louisiana and the eastern bank of the Mississippi in West Florida. In New Orleans, where the right of deposit proved a boon to the growing settlements upriver, American sailing ships far outnumbered their counterparts. Eastward from New Orleans along the Gulf Coast lay West and East

Florida, sparsely inhabited but positioned at the mouths of rivers that would become important as Georgia and Mississippi filled with people.

Thomas Jefferson, who became president in March 1801, was content to let New Orleans and the Floridas remain in the hands of Spain, as its rule there ceased to menace the United States. "With respect to Spain our dispositions are sincerely amicable and even affectionate," he wrote in July 1801. "We consider her possession of the adjacent country as most favorable to our interests and should see, with extreme pain any other nation substituted for them."[56] Five months later, he received evidence that by a secret treaty of October 1, 1800, Spain had retroceded Louisiana to the French Republic, headed by Napoleon Bonaparte. Originally a French colony, Louisiana had been ceded by France to Spain in 1762, but Madrid found Louisiana unprofitable and impossible to defend against intrusions from the United States and Canada. Spain returned Louisiana and provided six ships-of-war for the French navy, and, in return, Napoleon promised the nephew of the king of Spain an Italian kingdom. He also promised never to transfer Louisiana to a third party.[57]

Napoleon valued Louisiana as part of a balanced colonial empire, the heart of which would be the sugar island of Santo Domingo. But at the time of acquiring Louisiana, French authority in Santo Domingo had been substantially reduced by a violent slave revolt, and control of the island had fallen to a charismatic ex-slave, Toussaint L'Ouverture. Nominally acknowledging allegiance to France, Toussaint was making himself an independent sovereign. The overthrow of Toussaint, the re-establishment of French authority in Santo Domingo, and the restoration of slavery were necessary steps in the building of the colonial empire of which Louisiana was to be a part. As such, in November 1801, Napoleon sent an army of 20,000 men to restore rule in Santo Domingo. This expedition, which witnessed the virtual annihilation of the army, was to be followed by another to take possession of Louisiana. Due to foul weather and the collapse of the Peace of Amiens, the Louisiana expedition never sailed. The rebels' victory in Santo Domingo, encouraged by Jefferson, ended Napoleon's grand plans for France's empire in the Western Hemisphere.[58] In response to news of the defeat, Napoleon exploded: "Damn sugar, damn coffee, damn colonies!"[59]

Jefferson had been alarmed by the prospect of a vigorous and powerful France replacing Spain in New Orleans. Writing to the U.S. minister in Paris, Robert R. Livingston, Jefferson noted that New Orleans, "through which the produce of three eighths of our territory must pass to market," was the one single spot on the globe "the possessor of which is our natural and habitual enemy." He argued that French possession of New Orleans would seal "the union of two countries who in conjunction can maintain exclusive possession of the ocean. From that moment we must marry ourselves to the British fleet and nation."[60] Friends in Paris advised the president that Napoleon might be more easily swayed by money than by the threat of an Anglo-American alliance. Accordingly on May 1, 1802, Livingston was instructed to ascertain if France would sell New Orleans. However, in November, Jefferson learned that Spain had transferred Louisiana to France. At almost the same time came information that the Spanish intendant at New Orleans had on October 16 withdrawn the right of deposit. The change of policy resulted from the smuggling activities of certain Americans who had abused their privileges at New Orleans. Nonetheless, the Spanish action was an undeniable violation of American treaty rights and, most alarming, seemed a foretaste of possible French policies.

Westerners were willing to leave the solution of the Mississippi question to Jefferson's diplomacy, but eastern Federalists were more assertive. Their political strategy was to force Jefferson to choose between war with France or surrender of western interests; ultimately, however, their strategy failed. Pierre Samuel DuPont de Nemours advised Jefferson that New Orleans and the Floridas might be purchased for $6 million. In response, Jefferson nominated James Monroe in January 1803 to be minister extraordinary to France and Spain to assist in securing American interests. Monroe was popular in the West, and his appointment was promptly confirmed. Should the French be willing to sell New Orleans and the Floridas, the American diplomats were authorized to offer as much as $10 million to obtain them. Should France refuse to cede any territory, they were to secure and improve the right of deposit guaranteed by the Spanish treaty of 1795. If France refused even the right of deposit, they were to refer the matter to Washington, for, in addition to the $10 million carrot, there was also the familiar stick—the prospect of America's "marriage" to the British fleet. Louis Andre Pichon, the French *chargé d'affaires* in Washington, informed Talleyrand that Monroe had "carte blanche and he is to go immediately to London if he is badly received at Paris."[61]

"The Greatest Land Deal Ever"

Before Monroe arrived in Paris, Napoleon had decided to offer the United States not only New Orleans but all of Louisiana. On April 11, 1803, he instructed his finance minister to open negotiations with Livingston. The new proposal, however, came through Talleyrand, who that same day inquired whether the United States would care to buy all of Louisiana. Napoleon had the price at 50 million livres; the thrifty minister asked 100 million. The commissioners' instructions authorized them to purchase only New Orleans and the Floridas, but there never was any serious doubt of accepting the offer. Since the price considerably exceeded instructions, the Americans haggled to lower it, finally agreeing on 80 million livres ($15 million). Three-fourths was to be paid to France, the remainder to Americans holding damage claims against the French government. Virtual agreement was reached on April 29, the treaty signed May 2, and the accompanying documents antedated as of April 30, 1803. France ceded to the United States "the colony or province of Louisiana, with the same extent that it now has in the hands of Spain, and that it had when France possessed it; and such as it should be after the treaties subsequently entered into between Spain and other states." Other articles of the treaty promised the incorporation of the inhabitants of Louisiana in the Union of the United States, with all the rights of citizens, while permitting French and Spanish ships to use the ports of Louisiana for 12 years on the same terms as American ships. [62] Jefferson and his ministers had achieved an impressive diplomatic success, though the decision to sell the territory was Napoleon's alone.

But of what did Louisiana consist? To requests from the American commissioners for a more specific definition of limits, Talleyrand replied: "I can give you no direction. You have made a noble bargain for yourselves, and I suppose you will make the most of it." [63] Jefferson and James Madison, his secretary of state, claimed that all of West Florida, west of the Perdido, was part of Louisiana; henceforth, that became the official American position. Spain insisted that Louisiana was bounded on the east by the Mississippi and the Iberville; this was also the French interpretation. Weak though the U.S. claim was, the disputed strip of Gulf Coast was of such potential value that Jefferson made repeated efforts to secure it via methods that are considered to be the least creditable chapters in American diplomacy. Jefferson tried first to bluff Spain into yielding possession of the territory; when Spain refused, he tried diplomatic persuasion. Finally, he offered Napoleon a large cash consideration if he would coerce Spain into humoring the United States. Napoleon was not above such a deal, but with his brother Joseph on the throne of Spain in 1808, he became a defender of Spanish interests. [64]

It remained for Jefferson's successor, James Madison (1809–1817), to make good the American claim to the disputed portion of West Florida. In the autumn of 1810, when revolts had begun in other Spanish colonies, the settlers along the Mississippi at the western extremity of West Florida seized the Spanish fort at Baton Rouge, proclaimed their independence, and invited the United States to annex them. President Madison acted promptly. In a proclamation of October 27, he stated anew the American claim to Florida, west of the Perdido, as a part of Louisiana and directed Governor W. C. C. Claiborne of Louisiana Territory to take possession of it without employing force against Spanish troops. The United States took formal possession of Baton Rouge on December 10, 1810, and American authority was extended eastward to the Perdido with the exception of the bay and town of Mobile. A Spanish garrison at Mobile was the sole obstacle to the acquisition by the United States of Louisiana. The removal of that garrison, in 1813, was to be an incident of a conflict with England over frontier rivalries and neutral rights. Nonetheless, that last piece of sovereign acquisition from the European powerhouses was attained and with it, a defining moment in U.S. foreign relations.

CONCLUSION

As the Washington Doctrine was bred from the turmoil of the years leading up to the American Revolution, so too would its significance continue to bear in the years following Washington's retirement. Though the Constitution ushered in a new supreme government and with it international recognition, standing, and loans, circumstances required the young republic maintain significant political and commercial ties with European powers. Despite independence, however, the precariousness of the American states in arms, finances, and foreign policy following the conclusion of war in 1783 would remain a thorn in the side of the government well into the terms encompassing the first three presidents. Reflected in the difficulties Washington would encounter in his first years as president, European interests along the northern, western, and southern borders of the American states illustrated the still-considerable European influence an American foreign policy would need to overcome. Significantly, nowhere was this more important than within the conflicting dialogues of Jefferson and Hamilton in the Departments of State and Treasury. In this way, as the British, Spanish, and French divided up the bordering American lands, so too did they divide Washington's cabinet.

Conspiring in the further division of Washington's two most valued advisors, and engendering Washington's toughest foreign policy decision, the outbreak of the French Revolution proved almost a fait accompli. Washington's desire was to continue the policy laid out in Adams's plan of treaties, avoiding war while continuing commerce with both sides under neutrality. To this end, despite Jefferson's objections, arguing in terms of the Franco-American treaty of alliance, Washington proved reluctant to enter the war, citing the fact that France's declaration was contrary to the alliance. Consequently, Washington's decision for neutrality ended the last alliance in which America would involve itself for more than a century, cementing his legacy of avoiding entangling alliances.

As the main progenitor of avoiding alliances with foreign nations, George Washington implored his successors in his farewell address to beware of the same "vicissitudes" of European politics he had to face and to detach America from the "frequent controversies" of European interests. That Adams's anti-Europeanism, as revealed in stations overseas, further engendered Washington's legacy as a core interest of American foreign policy was not necessarily due to Washington's warning. Rather, Adams took on a more hawkish stance, particularly in regards to the X, Y, Z scandal and the following quasi-war with France. More importantly, Jefferson's Republican pro-French party had grown distant from its French connection, threatened under the Napoleon dictatorship. Under Jefferson's two-term presidency, as a result, more progress was made in untangling the affairs of European interests on America's borders, purchasing Louisiana from the French. By the end of Jefferson's presidency the American nation had obtained for itself not just a clear government identity and sovereign consolidation, but had emboldened the Washington Doctrine as a core thread in American foreign-policy orientation.

NOTES

1. "George Washington: Second Term," President Profiles, 2015, available at: http://www.presidentprofiles.com/Washington-Johnson/George-Washington-Second-term.html.

2. *Ibid.* Also see Richard Dean Burns, Joseph M. Siracusa, and Jason Flanagan, *American Foreign Relations since Independence,* Santa Barbara, CA: Praeger, 2013.

3. Colin G. Galloway, *The Scratch of a Pen: 1763 and the Transformation of America,* New York: Oxford University Press, 2006.

4. Fred Anderson, *Crucible of War: The Seven Years' War and the Fate of Empire in British North America, 1754–1766,* New York: Alfred A. Knopf, 2000.

5. Thomas Paine, *Common Sense,* London: Penguin Classics, 1982, p. 86.

6. See Felix Gilbert, *To the Farewell Address: Ideas of Early American Foreign Policy,* Princeton, NJ: Princeton University Press, 1970; James H. Hutson, "Intellectual Foundations of Early American Diplomacy," *Diplomatic History* 1, 1972, pp. 1–19; David M. Fitzsimons, "Tom Paine's New World Order: Idealistic Internationalism in the Ideology of Early American Foreign Relations, *Diplomatic History* 19, 1995, pp. 569–82.

7. Gilbert, *To the Farewell Address,* p. 28.

8. Orville T. Murphy, "The View from Versailles: Charles Gravier Comte de Vergennes's Perceptions of the American Revolution," in Ronald Hoffman and Peter J. Albert, eds., *Diplomacy and Revolution: The Franco-American Alliance of 1778,* Charlottesville: University Press of Virginia, 1981, pp. 107–49.

9. See S. F. Bemis, *The Diplomacy of the American Revolution,* New York: Appleton-Century-Crofts, 1965, pp. 93.

10. Jonathan R. Dull, "Franklin the Diplomat: the French Mission," *Transactions of the American Philosophical Society* 72, 1982, p. 33.

11. Gregg L. Lint, "John Adams on the Drafting of the Treaty Plan of 1776," *Diplomatic History* 2, 1978, pp. 313–20.

12. John Adams, *The Works of John Adams, Second President of the United States: With a Life of the Author, Notes and Illustrations, by His Grandson Charles Francis Adams,* Boston: Little, Brown, 1856, 10 vols.; vol. 9, chapter "To John Winthrop," available at: http://oll.libertyfund.org/title/2107/161330/2838396 on 2010–07–01.

13. Jonathan R. Dull, *The French Navy and American Independence: A Study of Arms and Diplomacy, 1774–1787* Princeton, NJ: Princeton University Press, 1975; Chris Tudda, "'A Messiah That Will Never Come': A New Look at Saratoga, Independence, and Revolutionary War Diplomacy," *Diplomatic History* 32, 2008, pp. 779–810.

14. The Royal Instructions to the Peace Commission of 1778 are conveniently printed in S. E. Morison, ed., *Sources and Documents Illustrating the American Revolution, 1764–1788,* Oxford: Clarendon Press, 1923, pp. 186–203.

15. Copies of the treaties are available through the Avalon Project. The Treaty of Amity and Commerce, available at: http://avalon.law.yale.edu/18th_century/fr1788–1.asp and the Treaty of Alliance at: http://avalon.law.yale.edu/18th_century/fr1788–2.asp.

16. See Lawrence S. Kaplan, "The Treaties of Paris and Washington, 1778 and 1949: Reflections on Entangling Alliances," in Ronald Hoffman and Peter J. Albert, eds., *Diplomacy and Revolution: The Franco-American Alliance of 1778*, Charlottesville: University Press of Virginia, 1981, pp. 107–49.

17. Jonathan R. Dull, *A Diplomatic History of the American Revolution*, New Haven: Yale University Press, 1985, p. 109.

18. Bemis, *Diplomacy of the American Revolution*, p. 34.

19. Dull, *Diplomatic History of the American Revolution*, pp. 110–11.

20. Gregg L. Lint, "Preparing for Peace: The Objectives of the United States, France, and Spain in the War of the American Revolution," in Ronald Hoffman and Peter J. Albert, eds., *Peace and the Peacemakers: The Treaty of 1783*, Charlottesville: University Press of Virginia, 1986, pp. 30–51.

21. "Instructions to John Adams, Benjamin Franklin, John Jay, Henry Laurens, and Thomas Jefferson, signed by Saml. Huntington and witnessed by Chas Thompson, Signed 15 June 1781, III. Instructions to the Joint Commission to Negotiate a Peace Treaty," *Papers of John Adams Volume II*, Digital Editions, available at: www.masshist.org/publications/apde2/view?&id=PJA11dg1.

22. Timothy Pitkin, *A Political and Civil History of the United States of America from the Year 1763 to the Close of the Administration of President Washington, in March, 1797*, Carlisle, MA: Applewood Books, 2009, p. 84.

23. *Ibid.*, p. 109.

24. "Instructions to John Adams, Benjamin Franklin, John Jay, Henry Laurens, and Thomas Jefferson," 1781.

25. Benjamin Franklin, *The Works of Benjamin Franklin: With Notes and a Life of the Author by J. Sparks*, 1840, pp. 354–355.

26. James H. Hutson, "The American Negotiators: The Diplomacy of Jealousy," in Hoffman and Albert, eds., *Peace and the Peacemakers*, pp. 52–69.

27. "Treaty of Paris," September 30, 1783, Library of Congress Digital Reference Section Primary Documents in American History, available at: www.loc.gov/rr/program/bib/ourdocs/paris.html.

28. To Benjamin Franklin from Robert R. Livingston, January 2, 1783, National Archives, available at: http://founders.archives.gov/documents/Franklin/01-38-02-0405#BNFN-01-38-02-0405-fn-0005-ptr.

29. See Theodore Roosevelt, *The Winning of the West, Volume Four: Louisiana and the Northwest 1791–1807,* Echo Library, 2007, p. 214.

30. The Constitution of the United States of America, available at: www.archives.gov/exhibits/charters/constitution_transcript.html. The fullest account of the issue of foreign policy and the drafting of the Constitution is found in Norman A. Graebner, Richard Dean Burns, and Joseph M. Siracusa, *Foreign Affairs and the Founding Fathers: From Confederation to Constitution, 1776–1787*, Santa Barbara, CA: Praeger, 2011.

31. Doris Kearns Goodwin, *Team of Rivals: The Political Genius of Abraham Lincoln*, Camberwell, VIC: Penguin, 2009.

32. Alexander DeConde, *Entangling Alliance: Politics & Diplomacy under George Washington*, Durham, NC: Duke University Press, 1958, pp. 68–73; Albert Hall Bowman, *The Struggle for Neutrality: Franco-American Diplomacy during the Federalist Era*, Knoxville: University of Tennessee Press, 1974, pp. 34–36.

33. Charles D. Hazen, *Contemporary American Opinion of the French Revolution*, Baltimore: Johns Hopkins Press, 1897.

34. Stanley Elkins and Eric McKitrick, *The Age of Federalism*, New York: Oxford University Press, 1993, pp. 336–41.

35. George Washington, "Proclamation 4: Neutrality of the United States in the War Involving Austria, Prussia, Sardinia, Great Britain, and the United Netherlands Against France," April 22, 1793, The American Presidency Project, available at: http://www.presidency.ucsb.edu/ws/?pid=65475.

36. Harry Ammon, *The Genet Mission*, New York: W. W. Norton, 1973.

37. Eugene R. Sheridan, "The Recall of Edmond Charles Genet: A Study in Transatlantic Politics and Diplomacy" *Diplomatic History* 18:4, 1994, pp. 463–88.

38. Elkins and McKitrick, *The Age of Federalism*, pp. 388–91.

39. E. A. Cruikshank, ed., *The Correspondence of Lieut. Governor John Graves Simcoe, with Allied Documents Relating to His Administration of the Government of Upper Canada*, Toronto: Ontario Historical Society, 1923–1931, vol. 2, pp. 149–50.

40. Samuel Flagg Bemis, *Jay's Treaty, A Study in Commerce and Diplomacy*, New Haven: Yale University Press, 1962, p. 298.

41. Jay's Treaty, Article 25, Library of Congress, available at: http://www.loc.gov/rr/program/bib/ourdocs/jay.html

42. Joseph Charles, "The Jay Treaty: The Origins of the American Party System," *William and Mary Quarterly* 12:4, 1955, pp. 581–630.

43. Todd Estes, "Shaping the Politics of Public Opinion: Federalists and the Jay Treaty Debate," *Journal of the Early Republic* 20, 2000, pp. 393–422; Todd Estes, *The Jay Treaty Debate, Public Opinion, and the Evolution of Early American Political Culture*, Amherst: University of Massachusetts Press, 2006.

44. Samuel Flagg Bemis, *Pinckney's Treaty: America's Advantage from Europe's Distress, 1783–1800*, New Haven: Yale University Press, 1960.

45. Bradford Perkins, *The First Rapprochement: England and the United States, 1795–1805*, Philadelphia: University of Philadelphia Press, 1955.

46. Quoted in Bowman, *The Struggle for Neutrality*, p. 277.

47. Samuel Flagg Bemis, "Washington's Farewell Address: A Foreign Policy of Independence," *American Historical Review* 39, 1934, pp. 250–68.

48. A copy of Washington's Farewell Address can be found in Thomas G. Paterson and Dennis Merrill, *Major Problems in American Foreign Relations, Volume I: To 1920*, Lexington, MA: D. C. Heath, 1995, pp. 75–78.

49. Alexander DeConde, *The Quasi-War: The Politics and Diplomacy of the Undeclared War with France 1797–1801*, New York: Charles Scribner's Sons, 1966, p. 41.

50. William Stinchcombe, *The XYZ Affair*, Westport, CT: Greenwood Press, 1980.

51. Thomas A. Ray, "'Not One Cent for Tribute': The Public Addresses and American Popular Reaction to the XYZ Affair, 1798–1799," *Journal of the Early Republic* 3, 1983, p. 389.

52. Perkins, *The First Rapprochement*, pp. 96–98.

53. Quoted in DeConde, *The Quasi-War*, p. 95.

54. See Richard C. Rohrs, "The Federalist Party and the Convention of 1800," *Diplomatic History* 12:3, 1988, pp. 237–60.

55. Thomas Jefferson to James Monroe, Washington, November 24, 1801, in Barbara B. Oberg, ed., *The Papers of Thomas Jefferson*, vol. 35, Princeton, NJ: Princeton University Press, 2008, p. 719.

56. Thomas Jefferson to William C. C. Claiborne, Washington, July 13, 1801, *The Papers of Thomas Jefferson*, vol. 34, 560.

57. Alexander DeConde, *This Affair of Louisiana*, New York: Charles Scribner's Sons, 1976, pp. 91–105.

58. Tim Matthewson, "Jefferson and Haiti," *Journal of Southern History* 61:2, 1995, p. 209.

59. Quoted in Robert W. Tucker and David C. Hendrickson, *Empire of Liberty: The Statecraft of Thomas Jefferson*, Oxford: Oxford University Press, 1990, p. 131.

60. To the United States Minister in France (Robert E. Livingston), Washington, April 18, 1802, in Albert Ellery Bergh, ed., *The Writings of Thomas Jefferson*, vol. 10, Washington: Thomas Jefferson Memorial Association, 1907, pp. 311–16.

61. Quoted in Albert H. Bowman, "Pichon, the United States and Louisiana," *Diplomatic History* 1:3, 1977, p. 266.

62. For the Louisiana Purchase Treaty, April 30, 1803, see the Avalon Project of the Lillian Goldman Law Library of Yale Law School, available at: http://avalon.law.yale.edu/19th_century/louis1.asp.

63. Quoted in DeConde, *This Affair of Louisiana*, p. 174.

64. Tucker and Hendrickson, *Empire of Liberty*, pp. 137–44.

Chapter Two

Securing the Region

This chapter will focus on the doctrine that, for all intents and purposes, marked the determination of the United States to become and remain a significant player on the international stage. The Monroe Doctrine in simple terms stated that future efforts by European states to colonize land or interfere with states in North or South America would be viewed as acts of aggression, requiring U.S. intervention. The doctrine stands apart from others in that very few American leaders have questioned its legitimacy, while some have even gone further in invoking it.[1] In the famous fight over American participation in the League of Nations, for example, opponents of the league condemned such participation as contrary to the principles of the Monroe Doctrine. Woodrow Wilson and fellow proponents, on the other hand, praised the league as representing a kind of worldwide adoption of the doctrine.[2] The Monroe Doctrine owes its long-time popularity to the fact that it was the first official pronouncement of a deep-seated American belief—that the Atlantic and Pacific Oceans divide the world such that nations in the New World should be able to insulate themselves from the quarrels, the interferences, and the colonizing ambitions of Old World powers. On the one hand, this belief married American neutrality and abstention from European tensions, while on the other, exclusion from the Americas of the political interference and the colonizing activity of Europe. Of course, the former idea became a cardinal principle of American foreign policy in the late 18th century,[3] while the latter—and subject of this chapter—set forth in President Monroe's message to Congress of December 2, 1823, emboldened the strands of Washington's doctrine, but by no means can be considered a spontaneous or necessarily new invention.

The second part of the chapter concerns the role of western expansion and what would come to be defined as manifest destiny and notions of American exceptionalism. Despite having secured the southeast and central parts of the United States, not to mention having seemingly warned European powers to stay away from its regional domains, Washington's detachment notions would soon be challenged in the future states of Oregon, Washington, Texas and California. Within three short years, between 1845 and 1848, the United States expanded its size by two-thirds, pushing the nation's boundaries westward to the Pacific and southward to the Rio Grande. Territorial expansion provided land for new settlers, exacerbated politics over the issue of slavery, and improved American security against external threats. In addition, it intensified internal perils and moved the nation farther and farther down the road toward sectionalism and, ultimately, civil war. Despite the apparent domestic nature of these developments, they would come with powerful implication for the threads of government concerning foreign relations. Here, the doctrinal thrust of securing the region by the late 1840s was mired by the controversial expansionism of the Polk and Tyler administrations claimed by the similarly controversial notion of manifest destiny. This would obviously have a significant impact on U.S. foreign policy as notions of destiny quickly became embedded with notions of rightful and hard-earned exceptionalism— a thread that has pervaded strategic thought ever since.[4]

THE MONROE DOCTRINE

As indicated in the previous chapter, President Washington's concern in becoming overly entwined with European affairs has been well documented. Nowhere was this more pronounced than in his 1796 Farewell Address: "Europe has a set of primary interests, which to us have none or a very remote relation."[5] Similarly, Thomas Jefferson, writing in 1813 of the independence movement in Spain's American colonies, observed:

> But in whatever government they end, they will be American governments, no longer to be involved in the never-ceasing broils of Europe. The European nations constitute a separate division of the globe: their localities make them a part of a distinct system; they have a set of interests of their own in which it is our business never to engage ourselves. America has a hemisphere to itself. It must have its separate system of interests: which must not be subordinated to those of Europe.[6]

President Monroe's ideas were similarly engendered by the influence of both Washington and Jefferson's earlier prejudices towards the European powers, to the extent that he would often incorporate his predecessors' sentiments into his own rhetoric as specific situations arose. After describing recent negotiations with Russia concerning its claims to territory on the Pacific coast of North America, the president said:

In the discussions to which this interest has given rise . . . the occasion has been judged proper for asserting, as a principle in which the rights and interests of the United States are involved, that the American continents, by the free and independent condition which they have assumed and maintain, are henceforth not to be considered as subjects for future colonization by any European powers.

This statement embodies what is generally called the "non-colonization" principle. Later in the message, after alluding to the recent suppression of liberal movements in Spain and Italy, Monroe stated what has since been called the "non-interference" principle:

Of events in that quarter of the globe, with which we have so much intercourse and from which we derive our origin, we have always been anxious and interested spectators. . . . In the wars of the European powers in matters relating to themselves we have never taken any part, nor does it comport with our policy so to do. It is only when our rights are invaded or seriously menaced that we resent injuries or make preparation for our defense. . . . *We owe it, therefore, to candor and to the amicable relations existing between the United States and those powers to declare that we should consider any attempt on their part to extend their system to any portion of this hemisphere as dangerous to our peace and safety.* With the existing colonies or dependencies of any European power we have not interfered and shall not interfere.

He went on to warn European states the U.S. supported colonies that had declared their independence and that "we could not view any interposition for the purpose of oppressing them, or controlling in any other manner their destiny." In this regard, the United States would remain neutral in hostilities between Spain and its rebellious colonies, "provided no change shall occur which, in the judgment of the competent authorities of this Government, shall make a corresponding change on the part of the United States indispensable to their security."[7]

The Non-colonization Rationale

The non-colonization principle was the brainchild of John Quincy Adams, Monroe's secretary of state. Adams distrusted European colonial establishments in the strategic neighborhood of the United States. He disliked the commercial exclusiveness with which colonizing powers surrounded their dependencies, distrusted monarchical neighbors, and desired, according to one authority, to "keep North America open as a preserve for the republic of the United States to expand over at leisure." Thus, non-colonization was "a principle of territorial containment."[8] As indicated above, the timing for declaring the non-colonization principle stemmed from Russian claims on North America's Pacific coast. Russian traders had visited the northwest coast since 1727, but not until 1799 was the Russian American Company chartered, with exclusive trading rights and jurisdiction along the coast as far south as 55° north latitude. The company planted settlements north of that line and, in 1812, established Fort Ross at Bodega Bay a few miles north of San Francisco Bay. The American government was more alarmed by an imperial ukase of September 1821, in which Russia extended its exclusive claims down the coast to 51° and forbade all non-Russian ships to come within 100 miles of the American coast north of that latitude.[8][9] In discussions with Baron Tuyll, the Russian minister in Washington, Adams stated the idea that he had been considering for several years. The United States, he told Tuyll in July 1823, would not only "contest the right of Russia to any territorial establishment on this continent," but would "assume distinctly the principle that the American continents are no longer subjects for any new European colonial establishments."[10] A few days later he included the idea in instructions sent to U.S. ministers Richard Rush in London and Henry Middleton in St. Petersburg. Adams provided Monroe with similar language as his statement to Tuyll, and it became an integral part of the Monroe Doctrine.

The declaration of the non-colonization principle was likely aimed less at Russia than Britain, whose rivalry in territorial expansion concerned Adams the most.[11] An active candidate for the presidency in 1824, Adams may have been prodding the British for political purposes. Political enemies were charging him with having betrayed American, and particularly western, interests to Britain and Spain in the treaties of 1818 and 1819. As such, a forthright statement forbidding further European colonization in "the American continents" would perhaps silence such criticism. Notwithstanding this motive, however, the truth of the matter is that neither Adams nor the United States had any right to veto further colonial enterprises in unoccupied and unexplored territories. Two years earlier, he had told the British minister that Britain had no right to the northwest coast, and his cabinet colleagues restrained him from telling Tuyll that Russia had no right to any territory in North America. Yet in the treaty of 1818, he had essentially acknowledged British equality with American rights in the Oregon country; he was willing in 1824 and later to divide that region with the British at the 49th parallel. In 1824 he would accept the Russian claim to exclusive sovereignty north of 54°40'. Thus, Adams did not feel bound by the non-colonization principle, and no European government ever recognized it. "There is room to doubt its wisdom as a diplomatic move," noted Dexter Perkins, "and a harsh critic might even go so far as to describe it as a barren gesture."[12] That said, the principle of non-colonization did garner traction.

Non-interference

The second fundamental principle of the doctrine—U.S. opposition to European interference with the independent nations of the New World—has a more complicated origin. At the time, it was America's answer to a British proposal for a joint Anglo-American declaration of non-interference. The circumstances that produced the British proposal resulted from two different series of events, one in Europe and another in America. After the overthrow of Napoleon in 1815, Europe was guided for years by an alliance of Russia, Prussia, Austria, and Britain. At Vienna in 1815, the four jointly agreed to prevent France from again promoting "revolutionary principles" and to consider measures that might prove "most salutary for the repose and prosperity of Nations and for the maintenance of the Peace of Europe."[13] Members of the Quadruple Alliance found the liberal spirit, suppressed by the Vienna settlement, revived in revolutions involving the kingdoms of Naples, Piedmont, and Spain that compelled their sovereigns to accept constitutions limiting their prerogatives. In 1820 and 1821, the Quadruple Alliance, under the leadership of Prince Metternich, Austrian foreign minister and chancellor, commissioned Austria to send troops into Italy to suppress the uprisings there. In 1822, the alliance sent French armies into Spain to overturn the 1820 liberal constitution and restore Ferdinand VII as an absolute monarch. During these actions however, the composition of the Quadruple Alliance underwent change. If France's restored Bourbon sovereign, Louis XVIII, had employed its armies to enforce the alliance's aims, the conservative British government had objected repeatedly to the armed interventions in Italy and Spain. Having restored Ferdinand to power in Spain, continental statesmen also talked of restoring his authority in Spain's former American colonies. England again objected and sought U.S. cooperation.[14]

Napoleon's attempt in 1808 to put a French king on the Spanish throne had absolved Spain's colonies of their allegiance to the newly restored Spanish monarch, and as such they had been working toward independence since 1810. As Ferdinand's restoration failed to tempt them back to Spanish rule, by 1822 all the mainland colonies from Mexico to Argentina and Chile had effectively overthrown Spain's dominance. The elimination of Spain's trade monopoly with new states had been economically beneficial to Britain and, to a lesser extent, the United States. Neither wished to see Spanish rule restored, and both frowned on the rumor of intervention. Additionally, Britain feared that because of Spain's weakness, France might appropriate some of the colonies for itself, while the Americans felt a natural sympathy for colonial populations who had won their independence. Thus they resented any attempt to restore the despotic rule of Spain.

RECOGNIZING SPAIN'S COLONIES

The United States would go on to recognize the independence of Colombia, Mexico, the United Provinces of Rio de la Plata (Argentina), and Chile, and other recognitions followed in due course. However, recognition had come only after a period of watchful waiting. At first, emissaries of the new governments were cordially, though unofficially, received in Washington, while "agents for seamen and commerce" were sent to the new countries to protect American interests. When the European war ended and Spain sought to recover control of its American colonies, Washington adopted a position of neutrality, allowing colonial vessels to frequent U.S. ports so as to procure arms and other supplies. Henry Clay, speaker of the House of Representatives, championed immediate recognition of the new governments. "Let us become real and true Americans, and place ourselves at the head of the American System," he urged, and criticized Monroe and Adams for their timidity and subservience in postponing recognition.[15] The president and secretary of state had good reason for hesitation, for the recognition of rebellious subjects had often been a prelude to war. After all, France had recognized America's independence only when it was deemed ready to go to war with England. Similarly, the British government, after seizing an unauthorized draft treaty with the United States, used it as an excuse for attacking the Netherlands. Madrid, following the British precedent, might regard recognition as an act of war, and the United States had no desire to be dragged into a war with Spain, and possibly the Quadruple Alliance, on behalf of the breakaway colonies.

Under what conditions, then, could recognition be granted to a state that had established itself by revolution without giving just offense to the parent state? As international law had as yet no clear answer to that question, officials in Washington had to devise their own formula. Jefferson had argued the thesis in 1792, during the French Revolution, that "it accords with our principles to acknowledge any government to be rightful which is formed by the will of the nation substantially declared."[16] On another occasion he declared: "The only thing essential is the will of the nation."[17] But how was "the will of the nation" to be ascertained? Henry Clay, in 1818, offered a more practical test for recognition: "We have constantly proceeded on the principle that the government de facto is that which we could alone notice. . . . But as soon as stability and order were maintained, no matter by whom, we always had considered and ought to consider the actual as the true government."[18] If Clay came close to stating what would become the standard American doctrine of recognition, Adams added important qualifications. The government of a state or a colony in rebellion might properly be recognized, he said, "when independence is established as a matter of fact so as to leave the chance of the opposite party to recover their dominion utterly desperate."[19] He also insisted on certain standards of behavior by the new authorities: they must carry out their responsibilities and duties as members of the international community. Complaining of the lawless acts by privateers carrying letters of marque from the unrecognized Latin American governments, Adams wrote that they "cannot claim the rights & prerogatives of independent States, without conforming to the duties by which independent States are bound."[20]

Brought on by the Latin American wars of independence, these discussions posited the principles of U.S. recognition policy. That is, a government that has come to power by revolution (whether in an old or a new state) may properly be recognized when it: (1) is effectively exercising the powers of government; (2) shows promise of stability; and (3) shows willingness and ability to carry out its international obligations. The problem for Monroe and Adams was to ascertain, first, whether these requirements were met by the new Latin American governments and, second, whether Spain and its European allies would take an act of recognition as an excuse for hostile action against the United States. In 1817, when Clay began his campaign for recognition, victory for the revolutionists was still uncertain, and the quality of the new governments was open to doubt. Commissioners sent by President Monroe to Buenos Aires and elsewhere in South America disagreed as to whether the current status of various governments justified recognition. When Adams asked Britain, France, and Russia whether they would join the United States in recognizing the new governments, their responses were negative. In Washington, officials thought it best to postpone action until the new governments could provide better evidence of permanence and stability.

By 1822, victories over Spanish forces in South America had made it obvious that Spain, unaided, could never restore its rule. The emancipated colonies were making encouraging progress toward orderly government, and it seemed unlikely that recognition would lead to war. Monroe and Adams thought it appropriate to recognize the new governments to the south without approval of the European powers. A special message of March 8, 1822, conveyed that opinion to Congress, which authorized and funded diplomatic missions to such of the American nations as the president might deem appropriate. Accordingly, by the end of January 1823 the United States had entered into formal diplomatic relations with Colombia (including also Ecuador and Venezuela), Mexico, Chile, and the United Provinces of Rio de la Plata.

A Warning to European Allies

Meanwhile, in August 1823, reports reached George Canning, the British foreign secretary, that when France had completed its intervention in Spain, the alliance would likely include discussions on how to deal with the question of rebellious Spanish America. In the preceding March, Canning had already warned France that Britain would oppose any attempt to appropriate any of the Spanish colonies. He now suggested to Richard Rush, the American minister in London, that the British and American governments signify—either by signing a convention or by an exchange of notes—their disapproval of any attempt by the European powers to restore the rule of Spain to its lost colonies. Additionally, he argued, Britain subscribed to the following principles, which he believed to be also accepted by the United States:

1. We conceive the recovery of the Colonies by Spain to be hopeless.
2. We conceive the question of the recognition of them, as Independent States, to be one of time and circumstances.
3. We are, however, by no means disposed to throw any impediment in the way of an arrangement between them and the mother country by amicable negotiations.
4. We aim not at the possession of any portion of them ourselves.
5. We could not see any portion of them transferred to any other power, with indifference.

If any European power, Canning added, contemplated the forcible subjugation of the former colonies on behalf of Spain or the acquisition of any of them for itself, a joint declaration by Britain and the United States of the principles indicated "would be at once the most effectual and the least offensive mode of intimating our joint disapprobation of such projects."[21] Since Britain, with its unchallenged control of the seas, would have been able to prevent any attempt by the continental powers to restore Spanish rule in America, why should Canning have sought the cooperation of the United States? Scholars have suggested several reasons for Canning's proposal. The United States' acceptance of the fourth principle would be viewed in London as a disclaimer of any American intent to acquire Cuba. It also has been estimated that Canning hoped, through courting American cooperation, to secure a continuance of a tariff-free American market for British textiles and ironware, a hope that was rebuffed in protectionist proposals contained in Monroe's famous message.[22]

Rush had no instructions that would have empowered him to join with Canning in any such proposal. Nevertheless, he found it quite attractive. If he could have secured from Canning an immediate recognition of the independence of the Spanish American states, he was prepared to state on behalf of the United States that it would "not remain inactive under an attack upon the independence of those states by the Holy [Quadruple] Alliance,"[23] leaving it for Washington to disavow his action if it saw fit. Canning, backed by the prime minister, Lord Liverpool, but opposed by other cabinet members and the king, was not ready to risk recognition.[24] Nor was Rush willing to accept a mere promise of future recognition; therefore, he could only report the discussions to Washington and await instructions. Adams was at home in Quincy, Massachusetts, when Rush's account of his discussions with Canning reached Washington. Monroe sought the advice of two living ex-presidents, Jefferson and Madison. Should the United States join with Britain in the proposed declaration? Both elder statesmen answered affirmatively. Madison even proposed that the "avowed disapprobation" be extended to cover the French intervention in Spain and that the two governments issue also a declaration on behalf of the Greeks, then engaged in their war for independence against Turkey.

When Monroe's cabinet discussed Canning's proposal in November, however, Adams now opposed joint action with Britain. "It would be more candid, as well as more dignified," he argued, "to avow our principles explicitly to Russia and France, than to come in as a cock-boat in the wake of the British man-of-war."[25] Adams prevailed and Rush was instructed to decline Canning's proposal for a joint declaration, though at the same time assuring the foreign secretary that the United States accepted all of his stated principles except the second, which left the question of recognition to "time and circumstances." On this point, Adams said, "We considered that the people of these emancipated Colonies, were, of right independent of all other nations, and that it was our duty so to acknowledge them." He added, on behalf of the United States, that "we could not see with indifference, any attempt by one or more powers of Europe to restore those new states to the crown of Spain, or to deprive them, in any manner, whatever of the freedom and independence which they have acquired."[26] The note did not close the door to the possibility of a joint declaration,[27] should an emergency make it expedient, but the decision on such a declaration was reserved to the Washington authorities. They would, said Adams, "according to the principles of our Government, and in the forms prescribed by our Constitution, cheerfully join in any act by which we may contribute to support the cause of human freedom, and the Independence of the South American Nations."[28]

Of course, as history clearly highlights, it was President Monroe who proposed that the American position be announced to the whole world through a presidential message instead of being buried in diplomatic correspondence. The notes for his annual message, which he read to his cabinet, not only included a vigorous statement of the non-interference principle, but also expressed disapproval of the French intervention in Spain and sympathy with the Greek revolt. To these latter expressions Adams objected. "The ground I wish to take," he said, "is that of earnest remonstrance against the interference of European powers by force in South America, but to disclaim all interference on our part in Europe; to make an American cause, and adhere inflexibly to that."[29] The president yielded. The message, while branding European intervention in the New World as "dangerous to our peace and safety" and as "the manifestation of an unfriendly disposition toward the United States," likewise repudiated the United States of taking any part "in the wars of the European powers in matters relating to themselves."[30] This last phrase left the door open for American participation in the wars of Europe, should such wars seriously menace American rights or American security. When this passage was written, the Treaty of Ghent was less than eight years old. Monroe, who had been secretary of state and, for a short time, secretary of war during the War of 1812, had not forgotten that European powers engaged in conflicts that were not always concerned solely with "matters relating to themselves."

Response to the Doctrine

To James Monroe and the members of his cabinet, who concurred in the content and phraseology of his message to Congress of December 2, 1823, the threat of European intervention in America was real; to all, that is, except Adams, who remained unpersuaded. The British warnings had been reinforced by a communication from the Russian foreign office, exulting over the successes of the Quadruple Alliance in Europe and declaring it to be the Tsar's policy to guarantee "the tranquility of all the states of which the civilized world is composed." This expression, the Russian minister informed Adams, related to "the supremacy of Spain over the revolted colonies."[31] The warning against intervention was therefore appropriate. While the notion of a young and emerging state challenging four major powers of continental Europe appeared audacious, Monroe was not pretending and knew he had some degree of support from the British navy. And despite there being no agreement with Britain—nor even an "understanding"—Canning had revealed enough to Rush to assure Monroe that London also would oppose armed intervention in the Americas.

What neither Monroe nor Adams knew was that Canning had already served an ultimatum on France and received a satisfactory response. Discouraged by Rush's insistence on conditions that he was unwilling to meet, Canning had approached the Prince de Polignac, the French ambassador in London, and in a series of discussions during October had received assurances that France had no intention or desire to appropriate any of the Spanish possessions in America, nor "any design of acting against the Colonies by force of arms."[32] With the substance of these assurances embodied in a memorandum, Canning had lost interest in obtaining cooperation from the United States. He no longer needed it to secure British objectives, but he dropped the matter with an abruptness that shook American confidence in his good faith. After the secret Canning-Polignac conversations, there was no danger that the Quadruple Alliance powers would intervene by force in Latin America, if, indeed, any such danger had ever existed. None of the four governments involved—French, Russian, Austrian, and Prussian—had any real plan for the use-of-force against Spain's former colonies, and Prince Metternich, most influential of the Quadruple Alliance statesmen, was realistic enough to know that the restoration of Spain's rule in the New World was impossible.[33] Under these circumstances, it was unlikely that the alliance could have agreed on a military intervention in America.

A practically nonexistent danger had been completely dissipated by Canning's warning to Polignac nearly two months before Monroe's message went to Congress. Consequently, his message had little or no practical effect on the course of events in Europe. From the courts of the continental powers, the message elicited considerable unofficial abuse, being described as "blustering," "monstrous," "arrogant," "haughty," and "peremptory." That said, the United States was still considered by many to be a small power, and its attitude on international questions was of minor significance. Simply put, continental powers regarded the declaration as being impertinent but unimportant. George Canning, whose proposals had led to the inclusion of the non-interference principle in Monroe's message, was understandably annoyed at Monroe's independent pronouncement. Monroe, he felt, had stolen a march on him and was courting the favor of the Latin American republics as the principal protector of their independence. To establish British priority in that role, Canning published the Polignac memorandum of October 1823, which showed that the British government had anticipated the United States in warning the continental key states against intervention. After Britain had extended recognition to the new governments in December 1824, Canning boasted, "I called the New World into existence to redress the balance of the Old."[34] Through such claims, and in more direct ways, he sought to undermine the prestige of the United States with the Latin American governments and to establish England as their first and most powerful friend.

The other basic theme of Monroe's message—the non-colonization principle—contributed further to Canning's pique at the United States. With vast portions of North America still "unoccupied," Britain could not assent to the right of the United States to veto all further colonizing enterprises in that area. For this reason, Canning refused to join the United States in tripartite negotiations with Russia over claims on the northwest coast and took an unyielding stand toward the United States on the Oregon boundary question. In due course, Britain and the United States would come to see mutual advances in the Monroe Doctrine, but the initial effect of Monroe's message on Anglo-American relations was doubtless more irritating than soothing. As for Russia, against whose expanded territorial claims the non-colonization principle had been ostensibly directed, it readily consented—in separate treaties with the United States (1824) and Great Britain (1825)—to limit its territorial claims in North America to the area north of latitude 54°40' (the border of modern-day Alaska).

Monroe's message was received with some enthusiasm by the American press, while in Congress it earned both praise and criticism. Despite attaining a resolution of endorsement, introduced by Henry Clay in the House of Representatives, it never came to a vote. Therefore, the principles of the message remained a clear and simple pronouncement of the president of the United States, without legal standing at home or in the international community. In the Latin American capitals, supposedly the beneficiaries of the message, liberal and republican elements applauded the president's declaration, but as they would soon discover, the United States was unwilling to back up its words with action. Five of the new governments, Argentina, Brazil, Chile, Colombia, and Mexico, applied to authorities in Washington for either treaties of alliance or promises of assistance against possible European intervention. All received negative replies. Of special interest was John Quincy Adams's August 6, 1824, reply to the Colombian minister in Washington, since it plainly indicated that without the support of Britain, the United States could not undertake to defend the Americas against the Quadruple Alliance. Thus, Latin American liberals learned what their conservative and monarchist rivals had known from the beginning: that the British navy was the chief protector of their newly won independence.

WESTWARD CHALLENGES AND MANIFEST DESTINY

On the domestic front, the steady influx of settlers moving toward the most western boundaries initiated new discussion on expansionist polices. Touring America in the early 1830s, Alex de Tocqueville would go on to write of the inevitable and ineluctable expansionism of the white race toward the west as the natural progression of the American heritage. He noted that the "gradual and continuous progress of the European race toward the Rocky mountains, has the solemnity of a providential event; it is like the deluge of men rising unabatedly, and daily driven onward by the hand of god."[35] Three years after the first publication of de Tocqueville's *Democracy in America*, journalist John L. O'Sullivan wrote of the "divine destiny" of the American peoples and the bearing of the necessity for "better deeds" in America's destiny. Recognizing the expanding march of settlers to the west, O'Sullivan went on to ask, "Who will . . . set the limits to our onward march?"[36] By the 1840s, although not quite fulfilling Jefferson's grand vision, the decade of dramatic territorial expansion was indeed under way.[37] The doctrinal thrust of "securing the region" by the later 1840s was mired by the controversial expansionism of the Polk and Tyler administrations, claimed by the similarly controversial notion of manifest destiny.

The Oregon Question

The Oregon territory was, by the treaty of 1818, open to the use and occupation of both British subjects and American citizens. For many years, the British, who were on the ground, with organization and experience, exploited the country. The Hudson's Bay Company tightened its monopoly of the Oregon fur trade until there were few areas west of the Rockies in which traders from the United States dared compete with the great corporation. With the fur trade effectually closed to Americans, Oregon seemed to have little else to offer. Nevertheless, a few men in Congress, notably Senator Thomas Hart Benton of Missouri, viewed it as a route to the commerce of the Orient. In diplomatic negotiations during the 1820s, the United States, while claiming the entire area, offered to accept the 49th parallel as the boundary, while the British insisted on the Columbia River, from its mouth to its intersection with the 49th parallel, as the dividing line. With neither government willing to back down, and with the 10-year period of joint occupation due to terminate in 1828, the negotiators agreed to extend that arrangement indefinitely.

Not until the early 1840s did American migration to Oregon reach significant proportions. A census in 1845 showed 2,109 persons in Oregon, and the migration of that year brought nearly 3,000 more, posing the need for some regular form of government and for settlers to secure titles to the land they occupied. Following several petitions to Congress that asked for Washington to assume control of the area, the settlers, in July 1843, established the Oregon Provisional Government. In amending their organic act two years later, they stated that its provisions applied only "until such time as the United States of America extend their jurisdiction over us." The next move was up to the Congress and the diplomats.[38] While Oregon was never formally considered, informal discussions during the Webster-Ashburton negotiations of 1842 revealed Great Britain was still unwilling to concede the territory between the Columbia River and the 49th parallel. President John Tyler suggested, unsuccessfully, that if Great Britain induced Mexico to recognize Texas's independence and cede Upper California to the United States, he would accept the Columbia River as a northern boundary. U.S. naval officers discouraged surrendering the region north of the Columbia, however, because of the formidable bar at the mouth of the Columbia and excellent harbors on Puget Sound.

Rumors of an offer to surrender northern Oregon in exchange for California created uproar in the western states that climaxed in July 1843, when some 120 delegates from six states met in Cincinnati. Claiming that ceding the whole of Oregon from 42° to 54°40' north latitude was "unquestionable," the delegates asserted it to be "the imperative duty of the General Government forthwith to extend the laws of the United States over said territory."[39]

On the eve of a presidential campaign in which the annexation of Texas was certain to be a major issue, the Democratic Party decided it was expedient to link the two expansionist issues—Texas and Oregon—so that western votes for Texas might be obtained in return for southern votes for Oregon. After nominating James K. Polk, an advocate of possessing Oregon, the Democratic National Convention declared:

> *Resolved*, That our title to the whole of the territory of Oregon is clear and unquestionable; that no portion of the same ought to be ceded to England or any other power; and that the re-occupation of Oregon and the re-annexation of Texas at the earliest practicable period are great American measures, which this convention recommends to the cordial support of the Democracy of the Union. [40]

The syllable "re-" prefixed to "occupation" and "annexation" suggested that the nation was merely about to resume possession of what had once been American.

Assertive Negotiations

Texas figured more significantly in the campaign than Oregon; the phrase "Fifty-four forty or fight" actually was coined after the campaign. [41] Since there was no serious Whig opposition to the Democratic pronouncement on Oregon, President Polk could interpret his electoral victory as a popular verdict favoring a vigorous Oregon policy. In his inaugural address, Polk asserted that the American title to all of Oregon was "clear and unquestionable." [42] Yet, since his predecessors had offered to settle for the 49th parallel, he instructed Secretary of State James Buchanan to repeat the offer. When the British minister rejected the proposal without even referring it to London, Polk withdrew it, intimating that the United States would assert its claim to the whole of Oregon. On December 2, 1845, Polk informed Congress that he was persuaded "that the British pretensions of title could not be maintained to any portion of the Oregon territory upon any principle of public law recognized by nations." His offer of compromise, on being refused, had been withdrawn, "and our title to the whole Oregon territory asserted, and, as is believed, maintained by irrefragable facts and arguments." He asked Congress to authorize the required one year's notice of termination of joint occupation, to extend the laws and jurisdiction of the United States over American citizens in Oregon, to likewise extend to Oregon the laws regulating trade with the Indians, and to provide for a line of fortified posts from the Missouri to the Rockies and the establishment of an overland mail route to the Columbia. As stated:

At the end of the year's notice [said Polk], . . . we shall have reached a period when the national rights in Oregon must either be abandoned or firmly maintained. That they cannot be abandoned without a sacrifice of both national honor and interest, is too clear to admit of doubt. Oregon is a part of the North American continent, to which, it is confidently affirmed, the title of the United States is the best now in existence. . . . The British proposition of compromise . . . can never for a moment, be entertained by the United States without an abandonment of their just and clear territorial rights, their own self-respect, and the national honor. [43]

Polk appeared to have closed the door to compromise, and this was heightened when Buchanan declined two British offers of arbitration. To one congressman, who feared Polk's bold stand might lead to war with Britain, the president replied: "The only way to treat John Bull was to look him straight in the eye; . . . if Congress faltered or hesitated in their course, John Bull would immediately become arrogant and more grasping in his demands."[44]

In reality, Polk was much less firm. He indicated a willingness to submit to the Senate any reasonable proposal that London might make. Lord Aberdeen, British foreign secretary, was informed that although the president "would accept nothing less than the whole territory unless the Senate should otherwise determine," he might submit to the Senate a British proposal for a division at the 49th parallel. The foreign secretary, meanwhile, had expressed his opinion that Polk was no longer interested in compromise, and thus it was his duty to withdraw his opposition to "the adoption of measures, founded upon the contingency of war with the United States, and to offer no obstacle in [the] future to preparations which might be deemed necessary, not only for the defence and protection of the Canadas, but for offensive operations." Such measures would include "the immediate equipment of thirty sail of the line, besides steamers and other vessels of war."[45] Polk, perhaps, had carried his game of bluff too far. Though publicly preserving a bold front, he permitted Buchanan to make a further bid for a compromise settlement. The president, he said, had always been ready "to receive and to treat with the utmost respect" any compromise proposal from the British government. The U.S. minister in London thought that he could secure an offer of settlement at the 49th parallel with one of several alternative modifications. Such an offer, Buchanan assured him, would be sent to the Senate where it was thought it would comfortably win approval.[46]

In essence, Polk had abandoned the claim to 54°40' and secretly reverted to the repeatedly proposed 49th parallel boundary. The Oregon debate in both houses was notable for two things: the popularization of the phrase "manifest destiny" and a dispute between spokesmen of the Northwest and those of the South over the proposed compromise on the boundary question. The phrase "manifest destiny" had apparently been coined by John L. O'Sullivan and was first used in an editorial on the Texas question printed in

the *Democratic Review* of July and August 1845. It appeared again in the
New York *Morning News*—also by O'Sullivan—on December 27, 1845, in
an editorial setting forth "the true title" to Oregon. This "title" was not to be
found in rights of discovery, exploration, settlement, and contiguity—strong
though the American case was on these grounds—but rather in

> the right to our manifest destiny to overspread and to possess the whole of the
> continent which Providence has given us for the development of the great
> experiment of liberty and federated self-government entrusted to us. . . . The
> God of nature and of nations has marked it for our own; and with His blessing
> we will firmly maintain the incontestable rights He has given, and fearlessly
> perform the high duties he has imposed.

Within a few days the phrase "manifest destiny" was quoted in Congress by
both the opponents and advocates of terminating joint occupation.[47]

Of course, the sectional controversy arose from the fact that southern
leaders like John C. Calhoun, having secured Texas, now favored compromise with Britain on Oregon. Northwestern expansionists took literally the
slogan "Fifty-four forty or fight," though professing to believe that England
would not fight if the United States stood firm. The South was charged with
"Punic faith" in deserting the West after realizing its own objectives. Southern Democratic senators joined with Whigs to pave the way for compromise,
while Whig senators shared the alarm of business and commercial groups at
the possibility of a costly war with England. An anonymous pamphlet declared that "monied men, for the most part, think very unfavorably of belligerent measures for the acquisition of Oregon" and claimed that such men
would not invest money in government bonds "issued for the purpose of
asserting a claim to worse than useless territory on the coast of the Pacific."[48]
Under such influences, the curt resolution was finally passed by both houses
on April 23, 1846, authorizing the president to give the year's notice. It also
expressed a hope for "a speedy and amicable adjustment" of "the respective
claims of the United States and Great Britain."[49]

The Resolution

Buchanan forwarded the formal notice to the British government, but reiterated the president's willingness to consider any suitable British proposal.
Lord Aberdeen, personally, had long been ready to accept the 49th parallel as
a boundary. He attached little value to the disputed territory—and to the
whole of Oregon for that matter—but he resented Polk's declaration that the
American title to Oregon was "clear and unquestionable."[50] Aberdeen's
problem, in abandoning the British claim to the Columbia boundary, was
mainly to reconcile British opinion. He needed to convince the British public
that no vital British interests were being surrendered and guard the cabinet's

slender majority in Parliament. Because of the decline of the fur trade and friction between the company's establishment at Fort Vancouver and the American settlers south of the river, the company had moved to Vancouver Island, thus abandoning the river. Now Lord Aberdeen could argue that the Columbia River boundary was not worth contending for.[51]

Aberdeen's offer—in the form of a treaty—proposed to draw the boundary line along the 49th parallel from the Rocky Mountains to the channel separating Vancouver Island from the mainland, and thence through the channel around the south end of the island, leaving the entire island to the British. Polk objected to a provision that navigation of the Columbia from the boundary line to its mouth should be "free and open to the Hudson's Bay Company, and to all British subjects trading with the same." Concluding an agreement, however, had no time for a delay. War with Mexico had begun, making a settlement with England imperative. Polk therefore sent the treaty to the Senate as it stood and it advised acceptance of the British proposal without change. The treaty was signed on June 15 and on June 18 the Senate gave its advice and consent for ratification by a vote of 41 to 14. The treaty was proclaimed on August 5, 1846. Thus the doctrinal bearings of Monroe and Adams' proclamation of 1823 came to assert themselves in Polk's legitimacy to the Oregon region, ending the controversial saga to the satisfaction of nearly everyone.[52]

Annexation of Texas

The extent to which manifest destiny was to cut across the domestic threshold and into the foreign domain is no more evident than in the United States' "exceptionally based" treatment of Mexico. The said state's resentment over the annexation of Texas proved an insuperable obstacle to any notions of the United States attaining an amicable negotiation over claims and boundary. While President James K. Polk's desire to gain California probably made him less forbearing toward Mexico than he might have been otherwise, the Texan question remained a point of consternation. In simple terms, the war with Mexico consequently stemmed from four broad issues that interacted with one another in an adverse manner: (1) Mexico's resentment over the American annexation of Texas; (2) a dispute over what constituted the southwestern boundary of Texas; (3) the failure of Mexico to pay certain damage claims to citizens of the United States; and (4) President Polk's anxiety to acquire California for the United States.[53]

When the Tyler administration first contemplated the annexation of Texas, Mexico served notice that it would regard such action on the part of the United States as a *casus belli*. Repeated warnings had been delivered in the summer of 1843 and the spring of 1844. In March 1845, when Congress passed the joint resolution of annexation and President Tyler signed it, the

Mexican government terminated relations with the United States and all formal diplomatic interaction ceased. Mexico, however, fresh from one revolution and with another on the horizon, was in no condition to go to war with the United States. The dispute over annexation was further embittered by a controversy over just what Texas territory had been annexed. The United States adopted the Texan claim that its boundary was the Rio Grande River, while Mexico insisted that historically Texas had never extended west or south of the River Nueces. Texas's claim to the Rio Grande boundary rested on an early act of the Texas Congress and the fact that Santa Anna's armies had retired beyond the Rio Grande. Thereafter the area between the rivers had not been effectively occupied or controlled by either party. Texas had done little or nothing through de facto occupation to counter Mexico's historic claim. The joint resolution of annexation had merely provided that the boundaries of Texas should be subject to the adjustment. American diplomats sought to revive the claim that the Rio Grande had been the ancient boundary of Louisiana, but the United States had given up that claim by the treaty of 1819.

President Polk was determined to uphold the claim to the Rio Grande boundary. He was willing to recognize merit in Mexico's position to the extent of canceling several millions of dollars of damage claims against Mexico if it would accept the Rio Grande boundary. Polk was not willing, in the meantime, to forgo occupation of the disputed territory. In July 1845, as soon as the Texas legislature agreed to annexation, he ordered Brigadier General Zachary Taylor, with some 3,900 U.S. troops, to Texas for defense against an anticipated Mexican invasion. Taylor was instructed to take up a position south of the Nueces and as near the Rio Grande "as prudence will dictate," but not to disturb any posts occupied by Mexican troops or Mexican settlements not under Texan jurisdiction.[54] While asserting title to the disputed territory, the intent of these instructions was to avoid initiating any clash with Mexican forces. Exercising the discretion allowed Taylor, in August, to station his army at Corpus Christi at the mouth of the Nueces at a prudent distance from the Rio Grande, where he remained until March 1846.

A third dispute with Mexico pertained to its failure to settle claims of American citizens—in the amount of several million dollars—that had originated from unpaid supplies purchased by the Mexican government, and in damages to U.S. persons and property suffered during revolutionary disorders. An 1839 treaty established a mixed claims commission that considered claims of over $8 million and granted awards of slightly over $2 million. Additional claims of over $3 million had been submitted too late for adjudication. Mexico agreed to pay the $2 million in 20 installments over five years, but paid only 3 installments, together with arrears to April 30, 1843, before suspending payments. Since the Mexican treasury was chronically empty, there was little hope that cash payments would be resumed. Following the precedents set by the Louisiana and Florida transactions, Polk proposed a boundary settlement in lieu of money. If Mexico would recognize the annexation of Texas with the Rio Grande boundary, the U.S. would release Mexico from all monetary claims of American citizens, which would be paid by the U.S. Treasury. However, in this regard Polk wanted to carry the settlement further. If Mexico would yield additional territory, coveted by Polk, the president was prepared to fill the empty Mexican treasury with American dollars.

The California Strategy

Soon after taking office, Polk remarked that two of the "great measures" of his administration would be "the settlement of the Oregon boundary question" and "the acquisition of California."[55] He successfully settled the Oregon question; however, the acquisition of California would not be accomplished without bloodshed. Spanish and later Mexican control of California—its first Spanish settlers having arrived during the American Revolution—never extended farther north than San Francisco Bay or farther inland than the coastal area. Aside from the presidios and Franciscan missions, Spanish activities consisted principally of sheep and cattle ranching. As late as 1846, the entire population of Spanish descent did not exceed 7,000 persons. The first American visitors to California came by sea, and in the 1820s, fur traders were beginning to make their way overland. Reports of official explorations by Lieutenant Charles Wilkes and John C. Frémont, published in 1845, contributed to a growing interest in California. Thomas O. Larkin, first U.S. consul in Monterey, estimated that by 1846 there were some 900 Americans in California. The American contingent was rapidly growing and with it the prediction that the Americans would soon be "sufficiently numerous to play the Texas game."[56] The danger of a "Texas game" in California was apparent to authorities in Mexico City, but local officials disregarded orders to halt American immigration or expel Americans, having neither the will nor the power to enforce them. Mexico's hold on California grew steadily weaker, arousing suspicions in Washington that London might consider opposing the American acquisition.

Despite the embellished nature of these rumors, Polk was still not clear on the exact nature of British policy in California. As such, he pressed for two possible methods of acquiring California: by purchase, which the president was determined to try; and, if Mexico refused to negotiate, that Californians might be induced to join the United States. Polk's reliance here was on bona fide Spanish Californians. He understood the shaky hold of Mexico City on California and the impatience many native Californians had with the ineptitude and inefficiency of Mexican rule. These individuals might be persuaded to sever their ties with Mexico and join the United States, with the idea of eventual statehood. Larkin became a confidential agent on October 17, 1845, with specific duties. He was directed to win the friendship of the Californians and to assure them that if California should declare its independence, "we shall render her all the kind offices in our power as a sister republic." The United States, they were to be told, did not desire to extend its boundaries "unless by the free and spontaneous wish of all the independent people of adjoining territories." As further stated: "Whilst the President will make no effort and use no influence to induce California to become one of the free and independent States of this Union, yet if the people should desire to unite their destiny with ours, they would be received as brethren, whenever this can be done without affording Mexico just cause of complaint."[57] These instructions, which could easily be interpreted as an invitation to the Californians to revolt from Mexico and join the United States, reached Larkin on April 17, 1846.

Earlier Polk used his annual message on December 2, 1845, to remind Europe generally, and Britain specifically, of Monroe's non-colonization principle, becoming the first president to refer to the Monroe Doctrine as a statement of official American policy.[58] Polk stipulated another principle, often referred to as the "Polk corollary," stating:

> We must ever maintain the principle that the people of this continent alone have the right to decide their own destiny. Should any portion of them, constituting an independent state, propose to unite themselves with our Confederacy, this will be a question for them and us to determine without any foreign interposition.[59]

This declaration rebuked the British government for its efforts to prevent the annexation of Texas. Additionally, it also reproved the French premier, who had declared that there ought to be a "balance of power" in the Americas and a counterweight to the United States. Encompassed in this same message in most emphatic fashion, Polk also asserted America's claim to all of Oregon.

THE WAR OPTION

Meanwhile, Polk attempted a restoration of diplomatic relations with Mexico not only to purchase California but also to effect a peaceful settlement of all disputed questions. Peña y Peña, the Mexican foreign minister, wrote on October 15, 1845, that President Herrera was "disposed to receive the commissioner [*comisionado*] of the United States, who may come to this capital with full powers from his government to settle the present dispute in a peaceable, reasonable, and honorable manner."[60] In response, Polk dispatched John Slidell to Mexico bearing a commission as envoy extraordinary and U.S. minister plenipotentiary. Polk and his cabinet had previously agreed to propose a boundary line following the Rio Grande from its mouth to El Paso in latitude 32° north or thereabouts, and thence directly westward to the Pacific, thus gaining New Mexico and Upper California as well as the Rio Grande boundary. The president believed such a line might be obtained for $15 or $20 million, but he was willing to pay as much as $40 million.[61]

When Slidell arrived in Mexico City, President Herrera faced imminent overthrow and dared not antagonize public opinion by an appearance of concessions to the United States. Peña y Peña complained that Washington had sent an envoy extraordinary and minister plenipotentiary, which implied an attempt for full restoration of diplomatic relations. In that capacity, he said, Slidell could not be received. On January 2, 1846, General Paredes assumed presidential authority and was also in no position to be conciliatory. "Be assured," Slidell wrote in response as he prepared to leave, "that nothing is to be done with these people, until they shall have been chastised."[62] Polk's attitude toward Mexico combined simultaneous gestures with the "sword" and the "olive branch." Willing to settle with Mexico, he was determined to have as a minimum the Rio Grande boundary as compensation for the American claims. He was hopeful that Slidell's mission would result in such a settlement, but if Mexico declined, the "sword" was ready. Thus, on January 13, 1846, on learning of Herrera's refusal to negotiate, he ordered General Taylor to take up a position on the Rio Grande.

A month later, Polk was visited by one Colonel A. J. Atocha, a friend of Santa Anna then in exile at Havana, who assured Polk that should Santa Anna again gain power he would gladly negotiate the territorial settlement Polk desired. To reconcile Mexican public opinion to a cession of territory, the United States would have to take stronger measures and perhaps deliver an ultimatum supported by warships. Polk, favorably impressed by Atocha's suggestions, now proposed to his cabinet that Congress be requested to authorize the president, first, to present Mexico with an ultimatum and, second, if Mexico rejected his terms, "to take redress into our own hands by aggressive measures."[63] However, with the Oregon controversy approaching a crisis, Polk accepted the advice of Secretary of State James Buchanan not to precipitate war with Mexico until he was sure of peace with England. Later, on May 9, Polk proposed to send to Congress a message recommending a declaration of war against Mexico. George Bancroft, secretary of the navy, "dissented but said if any act of hostility should be committed by the Mexican forces he was then in favour of immediate war."[64] On that very evening came tidings that such an "act of hostility" had taken place.

Coming to Arms

General Zachary Taylor moved his army early in March from Corpus Christi to the Rio Grande. Reaching the river without meeting resistance, he proceeded to occupy and fortify the east bank at the present site of Brownsville, Texas, opposite the Mexican town of Matamoros. Taylor's advance brought Mexican General Ampudia to Matamoros, warning Taylor on April 12, on pain of hostilities, to withdraw his army beyond the Nueces. In reply, Taylor cited his orders from the secretary of war as authority for his advance. Furthermore, in retaliation for the Mexican refusal to permit him to use the river as a supply line, he instituted a blockade at its mouth, thereby denying its use to the Mexicans at Matamoros. While Taylor characterized it as "a simply defensive precaution," it was in reality an act of war.

Learning of Taylor's blockade, President Paredes, on April 23, proclaimed the existence of a "defensive war" against the United States. On the following day and unaware as yet of Paredes's proclamation, a Mexican force crossed the river above Taylor's position, and on the 25th, Mexican cavalry attacked a company of American dragoons, killing or wounding 16 and capturing the remainder. When this news reached President Polk on May 9, 1846, he responded with a "war message" to Congress that summarized Mexican offenses against the United States, including a specific emphasis on its "breach of faith" in refusing to receive Slidell. Finally, Polk also added a paragraph gauged towards the burgeoning patriotism of his young state:

> The cup of forbearance had been exhausted even before the recent information from the frontier of the Del Norte. But now, after reiterated menaces, Mexico has passed the boundary of the United States, has invaded our territory and shed American blood upon American soil. She has proclaimed that hostilities have commenced, and that the two nations are now at war. [65]

The shedding of American blood on "American soil" supplied the necessary emotional element to give Polk the war he wanted. [66] Within two days, Congress, by a vote of 173 to 14 in the House and 42 to 2 in the Senate, declared that a state of war existed "by the act of the Republic of Mexico," authorizing the president to call out 50,000 volunteers, and the appropriation of $10 million for military and naval expenditures. [67] Thanks to Polk's diary, it is clear that he and his advisers, with a single dissenting vote, had chosen war before they knew of the attack.

The Pursuit of Territory and Amity

Immediately, steps toward the attainment of peace were taken with the expectation that it would be a short and easy war. In Havana, Santa Anna expressed a desire to return to Mexico and "govern in the interest of the masses, instead of parties, and classes." [68] In expectation of this return to power, Secretary of State Buchanan on July 27 proposed negotiations to the Mexican foreign minister for "a peace just and honorable for both parties." When Santa Anna returned to Mexico, he assumed command of the "Liberating Army," and now proposed postponing consideration of a peace offer until a new Mexican congress met in December. Buchanan replied that no choice remained for the United States "but to prosecute the war with vigor," until Mexico exhibited a desire for peace.[69] Before hopes of an early peace faded, Polk's cabinet had discussed the war's objectives. While the acquisition of territory was not the aim, the United States, Polk noted, should take California for indemnification. He would "meet war with either England or France or all the Powers of Christendom" rather than disclaiming any intention of dismembering Mexico or acquiring New Mexico or California.[70] Weeks later, a general agreement was reached that as a minimum the United States must secure the Rio Grande line, New Mexico, and Upper California. General Taylor, already on the Rio Grande, would advance "toward the heart of the enemy's country" to bring Santa Anna to terms, while another expedition, setting out from Fort Leavenworth, Kansas, would proceed to Santa Fe and occupy both New Mexico and California.

Taylor's army captured Monterey in September, and before the close of 1846 the capitals of three Mexican states, Nueve Leon, Coahuila, and Tamaulipas, were in American hands. After taking Santa Fe, Brigadier General Stephen W. Kearny's forces headed for California. The United States gained California, but not through a peaceful agreement with the Spanish Californians. As directed, Larkin began conversations with some of the leading Californians, but his efforts to win their loyalty were interrupted by the strange behavior of Captain John C. Frémont. As a young army officer, and already a noted explorer, he had set out in the spring of 1845 for California, where he spent the winter. The Mexican commandant at Monterey ordered the Americans to leave the province, whereupon Frémont led his men up the Sacramento Valley and north into Oregon, where, in May 1846, he was overtaken by Lieutenant Gillespie, bringing instructions to Larkin and letters to Frémont. What the letters contained, or what verbal messages Gillespie may have brought, are debated. What is not debated is when Frémont returned to California and to the vicinity of San Francisco Bay, he assisted a group of American frontiersmen in an unprovoked rebellion against the Mexican authorities—the so-called "Bear Flag revolt"—bringing him into direct conflict with the very Spanish Californians whom Polk had wished to conciliate.[71]

Frémont learned unofficially of the war early in July and cooperated with Commodore John D. Sloat, and later Captain Robert F. Stockton, to occupy all of California; however, his erratic behavior had no doubt impacted the chances of gaining the Californians' goodwill. Before the end of July, the U.S. flag was flying over all the settlements north of Monterey when Stockton and Frémont took their commands by sea to southern California. In August they took possession of San Diego, San Pedro, and Los Angeles without armed resistance. With the first official news of the declaration of war, Stockton proclaimed the United States' annexation of California. At every point, American arms had occupied all the territory that the administration desired to wrest from Mexico. When the time came to terminate the war with a treaty by which Mexico would confirm the annexations, Santa Anna showed no inclination to discuss peace terms. In response, Polk finally resolved to dispatch an expedition to seize Vera Cruz and then advance against Mexico City. The expedition's commander was Major General Winfield Scott, a capable officer and a Whig. His army of some 10,000 men was put ashore south of Vera Cruz early in March 1847, and on March 29 received the city's surrender. General Santa Anna's Mexican forces were defeated by Scott at Puebla, Mexico's second city, and surrendered without opposition on May 15. The road to Mexico City lay open, but at Puebla, Scott had to await replacements for his one-year volunteers.

While Scott and his army rested at Puebla, a new attempt was made to bring Santa Anna to terms, but he still refused to negotiate. But with American victories at Buena Vista and Vera Cruz, Washington saw new opportunities for negotiation. Polk decided to send Nicholas P. Trist, formerly consul in Havana, and directed him to insist on the Rio Grande boundary and the cession of New Mexico and Upper California. In compensation, the United States would assume the claims against Mexico and pay, in addition, as much as $20 million. Moreover, he was authorized to pay an additional $5 million for Lower California and a similar sum for the right of transit across the Isthmus of Tehuantepec. Trist arrived at Vera Cruz on May 6, when almost at once he and Scott engaged in an epistolary duel that did neither credit. Fortunately, the antagonists reconciled and the two worked in friendship and harmony.[72] With reinforcements in place but no diplomatic progress, General Scott advanced on the Mexican capital and after several victories, occupied Mexico City, whereby Santa Anna resigned the presidency. A new government, headed provisionally by Peña y Peña, was set up at Querétaro.

Exasperated by Mexico's refusal to accept what he considered generous terms of peace, Polk and his cabinet talked of exacting from the defeated enemy much more than initially contemplated. Two members of the cabinet, Buchanan and Secretary of the Treasury Robert J. Walker, considered conquering and absorbing all of Mexico, and wished the president to intimate as much in his annual message. Buchanan suggested a statement that "we must fulfill that destiny which Providence may have in store for both countries." Polk chose to say that we should "take the measure of our indemnity into our own hands."[73] Walker and Buchanan, however, were expressing the thoughts of a vocal group of politicians and journalists. These "Continental Democrats" urged the annexation of Mexico. The long-prevalent view of this movement, like that of the war itself, ascribed the annexationist sentiment to the southern appetite for more slave territory and states. In reality, there was nothing peculiarly "southern" about either the promotion of the war or the talk of larger annexations of Mexican territory. Southern Whigs almost unanimously, as well as Calhoun and many southern Democrats, condemned the war and deplored acquisitions of new territory. The passage several times of the Wilmot Proviso by the House of Representatives, prohibiting slavery or involuntary servitude in any territory to be acquired from Mexico, had warned southerners that any attempt to extend slavery into new territory would be met with determined northern opposition.

The "all-Mexico" movement was neither pro-slavery nor anti-slavery. Its greatest vocal support was in New York and in the western states, from Ohio to Texas. Its adherents were Democrats, and the arguments used on its behalf were those of manifest destiny. The *Democratic Review*, original propagator of that phrase, declared in October 1847: "This occupation of territory by the people, is the great movement of the age, and until every acre of the North American continent is occupied by citizens of the United States, the foundations of the future empire will not have been laid."[74] The New York *Herald* and *Sun* expressed similar ideas, and the same sentiments were common in Congress. President Polk had not aligned himself with this faction, but his December message stated that if Mexico rejected peace offers, we "must continue to occupy her country with our troops, taking the full measure of indemnity into our own hands."[75] Then, quite unexpectedly, a messenger arrived in Washington bearing a peace treaty that Trist, ignoring his recall as commissioner, had negotiated with the provisional government of Mexico.

Trist's Treaty

Not until November 16 had Trist received Buchanan's letter recalling him to Washington for allegedly disregarding his instructions. Trist, meanwhile, had contacted the newly formed Mexican government at Querétaro and had been informed that the government was anxious for peace. He notified the Mexican government of his recall and asked for peace proposals to take to Washington. The Mexican authorities (and General Scott) urged Trist to remain for negotiations, and on December 3, he informed the Mexican commissioners that he would proceed to negotiate if assured that Mexico would accept the United States' minimum territorial demands. Trist's unprecedented act of insubordination was to his credit. He knew that the party in power, the *Moderado* or Moderate Party, was the only group in Mexico with which there was any hope of making a treaty to Polk's satisfaction. Given the "all-Mexico" movement in the United States and suspecting that Polk favored it, Trist saw that the choice lay between a peace made at once with the Moderates on the basis of his original instructions and a protracted military occupation of Mexico, complicated by guerrilla warfare, possibly ending in annexation of the whole country. The latter course he believed would be a major calamity for the United States.

Since the negotiations moved slowly, it was not until February 2, 1848, that the treaty was signed at Guadalupe Hidalgo, a suburb of Mexico City. The treaty embodied the minimum territorial demands and the minimum monetary compensation proposed in Trist's instructions of April 15, 1847. The United States secured the Rio Grande boundary and retained New Mexico and Upper California, both of which were already occupied. The United States would release Mexico from existing claims and pay to Mexico $15 million.

The arrival of the treaty placed Polk in a serious dilemma. He was indignant at Trist, not only for disregarding his recall but also because his recent communications had been critical of the president. Yet Trist's treaty conformed to his official instructions and to Polk's publicly professed war aims. If he rejected it and chose to carry on the war, the president knew he would meet with intensified opposition in Congress. Thus, with a cautious statement of approval, Polk sent it to the Senate. The treaty was opposed in the Senate by an alliance of those who wanted less territory than it secured and those who wanted more. The former were Whigs, the latter, expansionist Democrats. Daniel Webster declared that New Mexico and California together were "not worth a dollar."[76] But the two groups of malcontents faltered in the final vote, and the treaty was approved on March 10, 1848, by a majority of 38 to 14. On May 19, 1848, the Mexican Congress approved the amended treaty, and on the 30th, ratifications were exchanged. The war was over, and by July 30 the last American soldiers had embarked from Vera Cruz for home.

CONCLUSION

The transformation of American territory with the annexation of Texas and California and the treaty for Oregon cemented what had been an increasing struggle for the securitization of the American identity. While Polk was willing to entice the American republic and obtain California and Texas by peaceful means, as Jefferson had previously done with Louisiana, he was also willing to take by force the initiative for which many proclaimed was America's fundamental—and even exceptional—right. The claim, that "securing the region" not just from the Europeans for the Americans, but also from the Americas for the Americans, was a contested subject during its time. Nevertheless, the long history of interposition by European powers in American affairs proved incentive enough to parlay the anti-expansionist divide in government and conform to the deep-seated belief that a United States from the Pacific to the Atlantic was worth the trouble.

Despite being still considerably weak in foreign-policy terms compared to its European rivals, Washington found itself in a position to draw from a stronger policy than otherwise previously available. Capitalizing on the diminishing strength of European powers and with the overthrow of Spanish rule in the South American colonies, the Monroe Doctrine was an attempt to further disaggregate European rule from what Washington considered an "American sphere" of influence, a principal of Washington's original foreign-policy aims. The recognition of the new nations of South America following their victories over the Spanish, however, pronounced the true length to how far Washington's foreign policy would extend beyond its own borders, hitherto still in question. The United States understood that to exert its influence in the region as the Europeans had previously done it first needed to secure these boundaries. Manifest destiny provided the "exceptional" and philosophical authority for such expansionist claims while the Monroe Doctrine provided the policy framework, both of which would extend deep into the twentieth century and beyond.

NOTES

1. Mark T. Gilderhaus, "The Monroe Doctrine: Meanings and Implications," *Presidential Studies Quarterly* 36:1, 2006, pp. 5–16.

2. An Address to the Senate, January 22, 1917, in Arthur S. Link, ed., *The Papers of Woodrow Wilson,* vol. 40, Princeton, NJ: Princeton University Press, 1966–1994, p. 536.

3. T. R. Schellenberg, "Jeffersonian Origins of the Monroe Doctrine," *The Hispanic American Historical Review* 14:1, February 1934, pp. 1–31.

4. Also see Richard Dean Burns, Joseph M. Siracusa, and Jason Flanagan, *American Foreign Relations since Independence,* Santa Barbara, CA: Praeger, 2013.

5. Washington's Farewell Address can be found in Thomas G. Paterson and Dennis Merrill, *Major Problems in American Foreign Relations,* vol. 1, 1920, Lexington, MA: D. C. Heath, 1995, pp. 75–78.

6. A Letter to Alexander von Humboldt, December 6, 1813, in Helmut de Terra, "Alexander von Humboldt's Correspondence with Jefferson, Madison, and Gallatin," *Proceedings of the American Philosophical Society* 103:6, 1959, p. 793.

7. The Monroe Doctrine: Extracts from President Monroe's Seventh Annual Message to Congress, December 2, 1823, in Henry Steele Commager, ed., *Documents of American History,* New York: Appleton-Century-Crofts, 1958, vol. 1, p. 236.

8. Frederick Merk, *Albert Gallatin and the Oregon Problem, A Study in Anglo-American Diplomacy,* Cambridge, MA: Harvard University Press, 1950, p. 28.

9. The ukase actually forbade all non-Russian ships to come within 100 *Italian* miles of the American coast north of that latitude. Italian miles were slightly shorter than the standard American mile. See Irby C. Nicoles Jr., "The Russian Ukase and the Monroe Doctrine: A Re-Evaluation," *Pacific Historical Review* 36 (1967): pp. 13–26; Irby C. Nicoles Jr. and Richard A. Ward, "Anglo-American Relations and the Russian Ukase: A Reassessment," *Pacific Historical Review* 41, 1972, pp. 444–59.

10. *Memoirs of John Quincy Adams, Comprising Portions of His Diary from 1795–1848,* edited by Charles Francis Adams, vol. 6, Philadelphia: J. B. Lippincott, 1875, p. 163.

11. See Nikolai N. Bolkhovitinov, "Russia and the Declaration of the Noncolonization Principle: New Archival Evidence," *Oregon Historical Quarterly* 72, 1971, pp. 101–26.

12. Dexter Perkins, *A History of the Monroe Doctrine,* Boston: Little, Brown, 1963, p. 32.

13. See Ernest Llewellyn Woodward, *War and Peace in Europe 1815–1870*, London: Psychology Press, 1963, p. 3.

14. The Quadruple Alliance is often confused with the Holy Alliance. The Holy Alliance treaty, which was originated by Czar Alexander I of Russia, was a benign declaration to the effect that the signatory sovereigns would be guided by Christian principles in their relations with one another and with their subjects. It was signed by all the sovereigns of Europe except the pope, the sultan of Turkey, and the British prince regent. The United States was invited to adhere but sent a polite declination. Since the czar, the emperor of Austria, and the king of Prussia were also members of the Quadruple Alliance, it is not surprising that contemporary writers and later historians have confused the two alliances.

15. Speech in Congress, May 10, 1820, *Annals of Congress*, 16th Congress, 1st Session, p. 27.

16. Thomas Jefferson to Gouverneur Morris, Philadelphia, November 7, 1792, in John Catanzariti, ed., *The Papers of Thomas Jefferson*, vol. 24, Princeton, NJ: Princeton University Press, 1990, p. 593.

17. Thomas Jefferson to Thomas Pinckney, Philadelphia, December 30, 1792, in Catanzariti, *The Papers of Thomas Jefferson*, vol. 24, p. 803.

18. Speech in the House of Representatives, March 24, 1818, reproduced in *Niles' Weekly Register*, April 18, 1818, p. 127.

19. Adams to Monroe, August 24, 1818, in Worthington Ford, ed., *Writings of John Quincy Adams*, vol. 6, New York: Macmillan, 1916, p. 442.

20. John Quincy Adams, Secretary of State, to Baptis Irvine, Special Agent of the United States to Venezuela, Washington, January 31, 1818, in William R. Manning, ed., *Diplomatic Correspondence of the United States Concerning the Independence of the Latin American Nations*, vol. 1, New York: Oxford University Press, 1925, p. 55.

21. Letter from George Canning to Richard Rush, August 20, 1823, reproduced in Harold Temperley, *The Foreign Policy of Canning, 1822–1827: England, the Neo-Holy Alliance, and the New World*, London: Frank Cass, 1966, pp. 110–13.

22. George Dangerfield, *The Era of Good Feelings*, New York: Harcourt, Brace & World, 1952, pp. 291–292, 319.

23. Richard Rush, United States Minister to Great Britain, to John Quincy Adams, Secretary of State of the United States, London, August 18, 1823, in William R. Manning, ed., *Diplomatic Correspondence of the United States Concerning the Independence of the Latin American Nations*, vol. 3, New York: Oxford University Press, 1925, p. 1,484.

24. Bradford Perkins, *Castlereagh and Adams: England and America, 1812–1823*, Berkeley: University of California Press, 1964, pp. 321–23.

25. John Quincy Adams's Account of the Cabinet Meeting of November 7, 1823, in *Memoirs of John Quincy Adams, Comprising Portions of His Diary from 1795–1848*, ed. by Charles Francis Adams, vol. 6, Philadelphia: J. B. Lippincott, 1875, p. 179.

26. Adams's first draft of the answer to Canning, prepared November 17, and the amendments made by Monroe, November 20, reproduced in Worthington Chauncey Ford, "John Quincy Adams and the Monroe Doctrine," *American Historical Review* 8:1, 1902, pp. 33–38.

27. This point is well developed in G. W. McGee, "The Monroe Doctrine—A Stopgap Measure," *Mississippi Valley Historical Review* 38, 1951, pp. 223–50.

28. *Memoirs of John Quincy Adams, Comprising Portions of His Diary from 1795–1848*, edited by Charles Francis Adams, vol. 6, Philadelphia: J. B. Lippincott, 1875, 197–98.

29. *Ibid.*

30. Expressed in President Monroe's seventh annual message to Congress, December 2, 1823. See The Avalon Project, available at: http://avalon.law.yale.edu/19th_century/monroe.asp.

31. Walter Alison Phillips, *The Confederation of Europe: A Study of the European Alliance, 1813–1823*, New Jersey: The Lawbook Exchange, Ltd., 2005, p. 272.

32. The Polignac Conference and Memorandum (October 3–9, 1823) in Temperley, *Foreign Policy of Canning, 1822–1827*, pp. 114–18.

33. Dexter Perkins, *The Monroe Doctrine, 1823–1826*, Cambridge, MA: Harvard University Press, 1927, chap. 4.

34. George Canning's Address on the King's Message Respecting Portugal, December 12, 1826, in Temperley, *The Foreign Policy of Canning, 1822–1827*, pp. 379–81.

35. Alexis de Tocqueville, *Democracy in America*, Vol. 10, Washington, DC: Regnery Publishing, 2003, p. 430.

36. John L. O'Sullivan, "The Great Nation of Futurity," *The United States Democratic Review* 0006, No. 13, pp. 426–430.

37. Thomas Jefferson to James Monroe, Washington, November 24, 1801, in Barbara B. Oberg, ed., *The Papers of Thomas Jefferson*, vol. 35, Princeton, NJ: Princeton University Press, 2008, p. 719.

38. Robert J. Loewenberg, "Creating a Provisional Government in Oregon: A Revision," *Pacific Northwest Quarterly* 68:1, 1977, pp. 13–24.

39. M. C. Jacobs, *Winning Oregon: A Study of an Expansionist Movement*, Caldwell, ID: Caxton Printers, 1938, pp. 24–39, 169–76.

40. Democratic Party Platform of 1844, May 27, 1844, in John T. Woolley and Gerhard Peters, The American Presidency Project, Santa Barbara, CA, available at: http://www.presidency.ucsb.edu/ws/?pid=29573.

41. Edwin A. Miles, "'Fifty-four Forty or Fight'—An American Political Legend," *Mississippi Valley Historical Review* 44, 1957, pp. 291–309; Hans Sperber, "'Fifty-Four Forty or Fight': Facts and Fictions," *American Speech* 32, 1957, pp. 5–11.

42. Inaugural Address, March 4, 1845, in John J. Farrell, ed., *James K. Polk, 1795–1849: Chronology, Documents, Bibliographical Aids*, Dobbs Ferry, NY: Oceana, 1970, pp. 25–34.

43. *Ibid.*, pp. 35–48.

44. Diary entry, January 4, 1846, in Milo Milton Quaife, ed., *The Diary of James K. Polk During His Presidency, 1845 to 1849*, vol. 1, Chicago: A. C. McClurg, 1910, p. 155.

45. Quoted in Stuart Anderson, "British Threats and the Settlement of the Oregon Boundary Dispute," *Pacific Northwest Quarterly* 66:4, 1975, p. 159.

46. John Bassett Moore, ed., *The Works of James Buchanan: Comprising His Speeches, State Papers, and Private Correspondence*, vol. 6, 1844–1846, Philadelphia: J. B. Lippincott, 1909, pp. 377–87.

47. J. W. Pratt, "The Origin of 'Manifest Destiny,'" *American Historical Review* 32, 1927, pp. 795–98; "John L. O'Sullivan and Manifest Destiny," *New York History* 45, 1933, pp. 213–34.

48. *Oregon: The Cost and the Consequences*, by "a Disciple of the Washington School," Philadelphia: J. C. Clark's Bookstore, 1846.

49. See President James J. Buchanan's Second Annual Message to Congress on the State of the Union, December 6, 1858, The American Presidency Project, available at: http://www.presidency.ucsb.edu/ws/?pid=29499.

50. George Lockhart Rives, *The United States and Mexico, 1821–1848: A History of the Relations between the Two Countries from the Independence of Mexico to the Close of the War with the United States*, vol. 2, New York: Charles Scribner's Sons, 1918, p. 20.

51. Frederick Merk, *The Oregon Question: Essays in Anglo-American Diplomacy and Politics*, Cambridge, MA: Harvard University Press, 1967, Chapter 8.

52. The Oregon Treaty, June 15, 1846, in Henry Steele Commager, ed., *Documents of American History*, New York: Appleton-Century-Crofts, 1958, vol. 1, p. 311.

53. N. A. Graebner, *Empire on the Pacific: A Study in American Continental Expansion*, New York: Ronald Press Company, 1955; emphasizes commercial interest in Pacific harbors.

54. William L. Marcy to Taylor, July 30, 1845, in Rives, *The United States and Mexico*, p. 137.

55. James Schouler, *History of the United States of America under the Constitution*, rev. ed., 7 vols., New York: Dodd, Mead, 1894–1913, 4, p. 498. Bancroft to Schouler February 1887: Schouler says the conversation between Polk and Bancroft is "still preserved." This may mean that Bancroft had preserved a contemporary memorandum of the conversation.

56. Quoted in Robert Glass Cleland, "The Early Sentiment for the Annexation of California: An Account of the Growth of American Interest in California from 1835 to 1846," *Southwestern Historical Quarterly*, 18:1, 1914, p. 144.

57. Moore, *The Works of James Buchanan*, vol. 6, pp. 275–78.

58. Polk seemed to restrict the non-colonization principle to the Northern Hemisphere; see Dexter Perkins, *The Monroe Doctrine, 1826–1867*, Baltimore: Johns Hopkins Press, 1933, chapter 2.

59. First Annual Message, December 2, 1845, in Farrell, *James K. Polk, 1795–1849*, pp. 35–48.

60. Mr. Peña y Peña to Mr. Black, Mexico, October 15, 1845, reproduced in *Niles' National Register*, May 30, 1846, pp. 204–5.

61. Under the minimum proposal, the line would follow the Rio Grande from mouth to source, thus depriving Mexico of the eastern portion of New Mexico, including Santa Fe and Taos, and thence run due north to the 42nd parallel.

62. Slidell to Buchanan, March 15, 1846, in Jesse S. Reeves, *American Diplomacy under Tyler and Polk*, Baltimore: Johns Hopkins, 1907, p. 284.

63. Diary entry of February 17, 1846, in Quaife, *The Diary of James K. Polk*, vol. 1, p. 234.

64. Diary entry of May 9, 1846, in Quaife, *The Diary of James K. Polk*, p. 385.

65. Message to Congress on War with Mexico, May 11, 1846, in Farrell, *James K. Polk, 1795–1849*, pp. 49–52.

66. See N. A. Graebner, "The Mexican War: A Study in Causation," *Pacific Historical Review* 49, 1980, pp. 405–26.

67. An excellent analysis of the debate on the war resolutions in Charles Sellers, *James K. Polk, Jacksonian, 1795–1843*, 2 vols., Norwalk, CT: Easton Press, 1987, pp. 416–21.

68. Mackenzie's report on his conversations with Santa Anna, dated June 7, 1846, in Reeves, *American Diplomacy under Tyler and Polk*, pp. 299–307.

69. Buchanan to the Mexican Minister of Foreign Affairs, July 27, 1846, in Moore, *The Works of James Buchanan*, vol. 7, p. 40; September 26, 1846, *ibid.*, p. 88.

70. Diary entry of May 13, 1846, in Quaife, *The Diary of James K. Polk*, vol. 1, p. 398.

71. Andrew Rolle, "Exploring an Explorer: Psychohistory and John Charles Frémont," *Pacific Historical Review* 51, 1982, pp. 145–163; Richard R. Stenberg, "Polk and Fremont, 1845–1846," *Pacific Historical Review* 7, 1938, pp. 211–27; George Tays, "Fremont Had No Secret Instructions," *Pacific Historical Review* 9, 1940, pp. 157–72.

72. The best defense of Trist is still L. M. Sears, "Nicholas P. Trist, a Diplomat with Ideals," *Mississippi Valley Historical Review* 11, 1924, pp. 85–98.

73. See Edward G. Bourne, "The United States and Mexico, 1847–1848," *The American Historical Review* 5, no. 3, 1900, p. 495.

74. For excellent analysis see Frederick Merk, *Manifest Destiny and Mission in American History: A Reinterpretation*, New York: Alfred A. Knopf, 1963, chaps. 5–8; *The United States Democratic Review* 21:112, October 1847, p. 291.

75. Third Annual Message, December 7, 1847, in Farrell, *James K. Polk, 1795–1849*, pp. 63–72.

76. *The Works of Daniel Webster*, Boston: Little, Brown, vol. 5, 1881, p. 294.

Chapter Three

The Seeds of Democracy Promotion

Having secured the "domain" from the Atlantic to the Pacific, the new post-1865 expansion would not only see the continued movement of settlers across the land, but of traders and financiers across the oceans. While Americans had once viewed these oceans as great walls that could mitigate foreign invasion, they now viewed them as gateways through which they could ship ever-larger amounts of their farm and industrial goods to foreign markets. Americans continued to follow the advice of Washington and Jefferson not to form any overseas political alliances, and the resulting freedom of action allowed the United States to stay out of squabbles in Europe and Asia, while selling goods to all sides. However, in what can be seen a marked shift in presidential doctrine, 1917 would see the United States finally drop its long-held refusal to become involved in European affairs.

The defining element of the Wilson Doctrine was the conviction that a leading priority of U.S. foreign policy should be the promotion of democratic government, or as Wilson himself put it, "national self-determination." Original as this conviction was with Wilson, many believed that the U.S. should be careful so as to see it more as a development out of an American tradition rather than as a wholly new departure. For as Wilson himself said, what he was calling for was the "globalization of the Monroe Doctrine." Put differently, international order should be based on a politically plural world, a situation where self-determination would be the rule of the day. As the evocation of the Monroe Doctrine (1823) indicates, and as the Open Door Notes with respect to China confirmed at the turn of the century, Wilson understood that his call to dismember the Ottoman, Austro-Hungarian, and Russian empires in 1918–1919 was long-standing U.S. policy. This same reliance on globalizing the Monroe Doctrine would be reflected later, during and after World War II, when the administrations of Franklin D. Roosevelt and Harry

Truman denounced great power spheres of influence, subsequently supported the de-colonization of European empires, and criticized the expansion of Soviet influence in Eastern Europe by use of the Red Army. If Wilson's dedication to a politically plural world was in the established tradition of American foreign policy, his call for the democratization of this political plurality most certainly was not. Here was this president's single most important contribution to the American foreign-policy tradition and the essence of his doctrine—the notion that in an era of nationalist passion, the blueprint for state construction should be of a liberal democratic sort. [1]

WOODROW WILSON AND THE GREAT WAR

Though informed Americans had been aware of the growing tensions in Europe, the actual outbreak of war took the American public and government by surprise. The assassination of Archduke Francis Ferdinand, heir to the Austro-Hungarian throne, at Sarajevo on June 28, 1914, by Gavrilo Princip—a young, ardent Serbian nationalist and member of the terrorist group the Black Hand—unsettled the complex alliance system. For over three weeks, there were few hints of serious trouble brewing. Then on July 23, Austria-Hungary presented to Serbia a 48-hour ultimatum whose terms, if accepted, would have largely extinguished Serbian sovereignty. Rejecting Serbia's partial acceptance as unsatisfactory, Austria-Hungary declared war on July 28. Determined to defend its small protégé, Russia mobilized two days later. On August 1, Germany declared war against Russia; on August 3 against France, Russia's ally, which had refused to give assurance of remaining neutral; and on August 4 against Belgium, which had denied passage to German armies en route to France. On August 4, Britain declared war on Germany, ostensibly as a joint guarantor of Belgian neutrality; more realistically, because of moral commitments to France and Russia and unwillingness to acquiesce in Germany's domination of Western Europe. Subsequently, Turkey and Bulgaria entered the war as allies of Germany and Austria-Hungary—the "Central Powers"—while Italy and Rumania eventually joined the Triple Entente powers—the "Allies." Meanwhile, Japan had declared war on Germany on August 23, 1914, and seized German holdings in China's Shantung peninsula and the German islands in the North Pacific. Eventually no fewer than 32 nations—including the British Dominions and India—were involved in the war against Germany. As if prompting Wilson to produce the doctrine that would become the "seeds of democracy," Winston Churchill's proclamation that "business carried on as usual during the alterations on the map of Europe" was certainly an affirmation that the old world needed to change. [2]

While the war in Europe seemed remote to most Americans, others saw the struggle much differently and as one that held a deep ideological significance for the United States. Elihu Root, secretary of state under Theodore Roosevelt and proponent of Wilson's decision to enter the war, wrote to an English friend: "Underlying all the particular reasons and occasions for the war, the principle of Anglo-Saxon liberty seems to have met the irreconcilable conception of the German State, and the two ideas are battling for control of the world."[3] Robert Lansing, who in July 1915 became Wilson's secretary of state, took a view similar to Root's and drew from it a practical conclusion: "Germany must not be permitted to win this war or to break even, though to prevent it this country is forced to take an active part. . . . American public opinion must be prepared for the time, which may come, when we will have to cast aside our neutrality and become one of the champions of democracy."[4] Still, other Americans foresaw a danger to the United States in Germany's upsetting the European balance of power. Britain and France were "satisfied" powers; so long as they dominated the eastern Atlantic, the United States had nothing to fear. However, should their place be taken by imperial Germany, "unsatisfied" and hungry for colonies and colonial markets, Americans might have to surrender the Monroe Doctrine or fight to defend it.[5] Notwithstanding such sentiments, they were only shared by a select few. Although Americans may have sympathized with one side or the other, the war was a European affair. However, it was German submarine attacks on American ships with the loss of American lives—inhumane and illegal in American eyes—that finally persuaded the United States to intervene.

President Wilson issued a formal proclamation of neutrality on August 4, 1914. Fifteen days later, reminiscent of Washington's Farewell Address, he appealed to his countrymen to avoid taking sides in the European struggle. Otherwise, he warned, Americans might "be divided in camps of hostile opinion, hot against each other, involved in the war itself in impulse and opinion if not in action." Over the next two and a half years Wilson attempted to keep the United States "neutral in fact as well as in name," though consciously or unconsciously American interpretations of international law consistently favored the Allies. The American people could not really be persuaded to be "impartial in thought," nor was the president's official family impartial.[6] If William Jennings Bryan, secretary of state until July 1915, saw little to commend the British case over the German, Robert Lansing, his successor, believed that the United States must enter the war if necessary to prevent a German victory. Walter H. Page, ambassador to Britain, saw the war as a crusade, while Edward M. (Colonel) House, Wilson's close unofficial adviser, was almost as pro-Ally. Wilson, impartial at first, had come by May 1915 to believe that "England is fighting our fight," yet a year later certain British practices drove him back to a relatively impartial attitude.

Public opinion from the beginning tended to be pro-Ally. Americans had ties of race, language, culture, and political ideals with England and bonds of ancient friendship with France, which had no substantial counterpart in their relations with Germany. In communities where the German or Irish heritage was strong, there was likely to be a pro-German (or anti-British) sentiment. Both sides in the war made their propaganda appeals to American public opinion. The British had the advantage of controlling the cables and thus of shaping news about the war. German atrocities were magnified, even invented, and often accepted as sober truth. German propaganda, on the other hand, was more often spotted as such and discounted accordingly.

Economic Impact

Inevitably the war would bind the United States to France and Britain. The initial effect on the American economy was disastrous as the British navy cut off German markets while Allied ships were often away from their customary routes. American business, already floundering in minor cyclical depression, was further impacted by these disruptions. Relief soon came, however, with large munitions orders from the Allies; by the end of 1915, America was enjoying a war-born prosperity. The sale of munitions to the Allies raised questions of neutral obligations. German sympathizers complained that such sales, being made exclusively to the Allied side, were not neutral. To such critics Lansing answered: "If one belligerent has by good fortune a superiority in the matter of geographical location or of military or naval power, the rules of neutral conduct cannot be varied so as to favor the less fortunate combatant."[7] Law and precedent held that the sale of war matériel to England and France did not violate America's neutrality. The sale of munitions and other supplies continued at an increasing rate—$6 million in 1914, jumping to $467 million in 1916.

It became readily apparent that the Allies, if their purchases were to continue over a long period of time, would need to finance them in the American money market. In August 1914, the New York firm of J. P. Morgan inquired of Secretary Bryan the government's position regarding such transactions. Bryan replied that loans by bankers to belligerent governments were "inconsistent with the true spirit of neutrality."[8] Whatever the ethics of Bryan's position, it had no legal standing. Both North and South had borrowed in Europe to finance the American Civil War. Japan had borrowed extensively in England and the United States to pay for its recent war with Russia, and Russia had fought with money borrowed in France. Bryan retreated from his untenable position by distinguishing between loans and credits. In October 1914, Morgan granted the first "credit" to the French and other credits followed.[9] "Loans" were still banned when Bryan resigned, but in late 1915, Secretary of State Lansing and Secretary of Treasury William

G. McAdoo changed Wilson's position, arguing Allied purchasing would taper off without large-scale loans and the United States would face a depression. Before American entry into the war, in 1917, the Allies had borrowed more than $2.25 billion in the United States—London requiring $1.5 billion.

The German Threat

British maritime practices, which drew an occasional U.S. protest, violated only property rights and endangered no lives. In contrast, Germany's use of submarines to disrupt commerce differed significantly and became a major American grievance. On September 2, 1916, Wilson clarified the different grievances, stating that when American rights became involved our guiding principle was that "property rights can be vindicated by claims for damages when the war is over, and no modern nation can decline to arbitrate such claims; but the fundamental rights of humanity cannot be. The loss of life is irreparable."[10] German submarines violated "the fundamental rights of humanity." On February 4, 1915, Berlin declared the waters around the British Isles to be a "war zone" in which German submarines would sink enemy merchant vessels on sight. Since the British ships frequently flew neutral flags, Germany could not guarantee the safety of neutral vessels in the war zone.[11] Washington promptly replied that Berlin would be held to a "strict accountability" for any loss of American ships or lives "due to the new policy." So began the controversy that would involve the United States in the war.

Submarines could not easily conform to traditional maritime rules. Recognized practice called for the enemy warship to visit and search a commercial vessel and, if possible, bring the suspected ship into a home port of the captor for adjudication by a prize court. If this procedure was impossible, international law permitted destruction of the prize at sea, but only if adequate provision was made for the safety of crew and passengers. A fragile submarine, however, was vulnerable when surfaced to challenge a resisting merchant ship.

The State Department pondered how to meet the new German strategy. Fearing that challenging Germany on this issue might lead to war, Bryan warned American citizens that travelling on belligerent ships was at their own risk. That said, his deputy, Lansing, argued that American citizens had a right to travel even on armed British ships and that the United States must defend these citizens. Lansing erred on two counts: (1) persons of whatever nationality on a British ship could expect only the British government's protection; and (2) an armed merchant vessel, even with defensive armament, forfeited its immunity from armed attack.[12] Wilson, nevertheless, accepted Lansing's position. Two compromises were offered. Initially, Washington proposed that German submarines legally visit and search merchant vessels, in return for a relaxation of the British food blockade and a British promise to stop using neutral flags. This attempt failed when Berlin demanded free access to raw industrial materials as well as food. Then in early 1916, Lansing proposed the British halt arming their merchant ships in return for a German agreement that submarines would not attack unarmed ships without warning, taking precautions for the safety of those aboard. London and Paris rejected this proposal. Wilson blocked a Congressional effort to warn American citizens against travel in armed ships, insisting that he could not "consent to any abridgment of the rights of American citizens in any respect."[13]

Long before this second proposal, German-American relations confronted their first serious crisis, brought on by the torpedoing of the British liner *Lusitania* off the Irish coast on May 7, 1915, with 1,198 persons losing their lives, including 128 American citizens. Despite the German embassy's published warnings for Americans to avoid the *Lusitania*, there was no deliberate German plot to "get" that particular ship. The big liner was sighted, steaming with culpable disregard of the British Admiralty's prescribed precautions. Lansing and some others wished for a declaration of war against Germany but could not arouse public support. Despite Bryan's resignation, the president demanded Berlin officials disavow the sinking, provide reparations, and take "immediate steps to prevent the recurrence" of such acts. The German government, unwilling to publicly surrender but not ready to break with Washington, secretly ordered submarine commanders not to attack passenger ships without warning. In Washington, the German ambassador Count von Bernstorff offered this assurance: "Liners will not be sunk by our submarines without warning and without safety of the lives of non-combatants, provided that the liners do not try to escape or offer resistance." Later, Berlin conceded its liability for the sinking of the *Lusitania*.[14]

In March 1916, another crisis arose when the unarmed French passenger steamer *Sussex* was torpedoed in the English Channel. The *Sussex* made port and no American passengers were lost, though some were injured. Although the submarine commander mistook the *Sussex* for a British mine-layer that it closely resembled in silhouette,[15] to Washington it appeared a deliberate violation of recent assurances. Lansing and House advised breaking off diplomatic relations with Germany, but Wilson hesitated. "Unless the Imperial Government," the president told Berlin, "should now immediately declare and effect an abandonment of its present methods of submarine warfare against passenger and freight-carrying vessels, the Government of the United States can have no choice but to sever diplomatic relations with the German Empire altogether."[16] Again, the German government yielded, with assurances on May 4, 1916, that merchant vessels would "not be sunk without warning and without saving human lives, unless these ships attempt to escape or offer resistance."[17] Berlin, in return, expected that the United States insist

England abandon its allegedly illegal practices; should London refuse, "the German Government would then be facing a new situation, in which it must reserve [to] itself complete liberty of action."[18]

Testing Wilson's Fortitude

During the following eight months, German submarines impacted Allied commerce, albeit within the threshold of international maritime rules. The British, on the other hand, proved increasingly uncooperative when early in 1916 Wilson permitted Colonel House to seek an end to the war. Wilson proposed to invite the belligerents to a peace conference. If the Allies were to accept, but if Germany declined, as expected, or if, after accepting, refused a peace on "reasonable" terms (already agreed on by Wilson and the Allies), the United States would enter the war against Germany. The plan, accepted by House and Britain's Sir Edward Grey, was cabled to Wilson. The president, constitutionally unable to promise a declaration of war, inserted "probably" in the clause predicting American action. Whether because of this uncertainty or because they hoped for victory, the Allies never signified their readiness for the president's proposed invitation. Wilson, like House, was chagrined at this cool treatment and intensely annoyed at the British government's July 1916 blacklisting of nearly 100 American firms or individuals for supposed German connections. The blacklist, coupled with the British government's ruthless suppression of an Irish rebellion, in April 1916, aroused anti-British feelings. "I am . . . about at the end of my patience with Great Britain and the Allies," Wilson wrote House. "This blacklist is the last straw." Wilson also noted that earlier public sympathy for England and the Allies "had greatly changed."[19] His supporters campaigned for his reelection with the slogan "He kept us out of war," implying he would continue to do so. Yet he endorsed U.S. military preparedness, strengthening the army and significantly increasing the navy.

Had Berlin acted with a modicum of wisdom and moderation, it might have ensured the continued neutrality of the United States. Chancellor von Bethmann-Hollweg and other civilian officials desired to continue appeasing the United States, but they also faced mounting pressure from the military and naval leaders: an immediate peace on their terms or else a submarine fleet capable of starving Britain into surrender. Victorious against Russia and Rumania, and holding their own on the western front in France and Belgium, Germany and its allies urged Wilson to invite the belligerents to a peace conference. When he procrastinated, on December 12, 1916, Germany announced that it was ready for peace negotiations. In London, the new prime minister, David Lloyd George, responded that only Germany's defeat could ensure a lasting peace. If the Allies rejected the German invitation, Wilson, still seeking a compromise, asked both sides to state their peace terms. The

Central Powers stated a conference was the proper place for announcing such terms, while the Allies simply referred to an extravagant list of demands.[20] Realizing failure of these efforts meant unrestricted submarine warfare, undoubtedly a prelude to hostilities, Wilson made one last effort at peace. For months he had been considering a league of nations that would guarantee world peace from future wars.[21] Addressing the Senate on January 22, 1917, Wilson stated the conditions under which the United States "would feel justified in asking our people to approve its formal and solemn adherence to a League for Peace." His conditions included: "a peace without victory" based on the equality of rights of all nations, the principle of government by the consent of the governed, the access to the sea for "every great people," the freedom of the seas, and a general reduction of armaments.[22] Wilson's proposal would come too late.

The German Assertion

Three days earlier, the German government decided to resume unrestricted submarine warfare. Ambassador von Bernstorff urged them to reconsider their decision. Wilson had promised, he reported, that if Germany adhered to the *Sussex* pledge and offered reasonable peace terms, the president would bring the Allies into line. His plea unheeded, the ambassador informed Lansing on January 31 that because Britain continued its illegal practices, Germany would resume the "freedom of action" reserved in the *Sussex* note and, beginning the next day, would sink all vessels encountered in the seas adjacent to the British Isles and the coasts of France and Italy. Neutral ships at sea prior to the notification would be spared, and one American steamer weekly, carrying no contraband and painted with red and white stripes, could proceed uninhibited from New York to Falmouth, England.

On February 3, 1917, von Bernstorff was given his passport and Ambassador Gerard was recalled from Berlin, diplomatic actions Wilson hoped might deter Germany from carrying out its threat.[23] But Germany's military leaders expected a submarine blockade to crush England before America took a significant role in the war. Meanwhile on February 24, the State Department had received from London an intercepted note from German foreign minister Arthur Zimmermann to the German minister in Mexico, proposing if the United States entered the war, Mexico should ally itself with Germany and persuade Japan, Britain's ally, to do the same. For its cooperation, Mexico would regain its "lost provinces" of Texas, New Mexico, and Arizona. Publication of Zimmermann's absurd proposal on March 1 outraged Americans, particularly in the Southwest.[24] Meanwhile, two American women died when a German submarine sank the Cunard liner *Laconia* on February 25.[25] Addressing a special session of Congress on April 2, 1917, Wilson reviewed the history of the submarine controversy. After denouncing the current submarine campaign as "warfare against mankind" and "war against all nations," Wilson advised Congress to "accept the status of belligerent which has thus been thrust upon it." He also declared that the United States' goal was "to vindicate the principles of peace and justice."[26] In his final paragraph, he declared:

> We shall fight for the things which we have always carried nearest our hearts—for democracy, for the right of those who submit to authority to have a voice in their own Government, for the rights and liberties of small nations, for a universal dominion of right by such a concert of free peoples as shall bring peace and safety to all nations and make the world itself at last free. [27]

Four days later, Congress resolved: "That the state of war between the United States and the Imperial German Government which has been thrust on the United States is hereby formally declared." The vote was 373 to 50 in the House, 82 to 6 in the Senate.[28] Following the United States' declaration of war, Austria-Hungary and Turkey broke off diplomatic relations. Bulgaria did not do so, nor did the United States sever relations with Bulgaria or declare war against Turkey. On December 7, 1917, after the Italian army's disaster at Caporetto, Congress declared war against Austria-Hungary to bolster Italian morale. With the British and French and their various allies, the United States became an "associated power"—and in real terms, merely a gesture in adhering to the Americans' tradition against "entangling alliances."

In the spring of 1918, the United States accepted French general Foch as supreme commander of all armies on the western front. General John J. Pershing, commander of the American Expeditionary Force, successfully resisted the Allied demand that American troops be merged with British and French, insisting they be deployed as a distinct U.S. army. The withdrawal of Russia from the war after the Bolshevik revolution of November 1917[29] enabled Germany to shift large forces from the eastern to the western front and to launch a succession of formidable offensives in the spring of 1918. With France and England near exhaustion, the timely arrival of American forces prevented a German victory. The German drives were halted, and after the last one in July failed, their armies were pushed back. Its allies succumbed one by one: Bulgaria surrendered September 29; Turkey, a month later. An Austrian proposal of September 16 for a peace conference was rejected. Finally, on October 6 and 7, Germany and Austria-Hungary offered to accept the terms previously set forth by Wilson.

The Fourteen Points

Shortly after the United States entered the war, Wilson felt that a clear statement of war aims was necessary. Such a statement might commit the

Allied governments to a peace of justice rather than a peace of vengeance. Immediately after seizing power on November 7, 1917, the Bolshevik leaders exposed the Allies' secret treaties and appealed to all the belligerents to make peace based on universal self-determination, a peace without annexations or indemnities. Only Germany and its allies responded favorably to this proposal, offering the prospect of a separate Russian-German peace. Colonel House urged Allied leaders to meet the Soviets' declaration of war aims, hoping to induce the Russians to stay in the war. When French and Italian premiers refused to disavow their nationalistic objectives, Wilson addressed Congress on January 8, 1918, outlining U.S. peace terms in his famous Fourteen Points.

The address referred particularly to Russia. The president discussed current negotiations between the new Soviet government and the Central Powers, and assured the Russian people of the United States' sympathy. "It is our heartfelt desire and hope," he declared, "that some way may be opened whereby we may be privileged to assist the people of Russia to attain their utmost hope of liberty and ordered peace." Wilson then stated American war aims, the object of which was "that the world be made fit and safe to live in; and particularly that it be made safe for every peace loving nation." The Fourteen Points encompassed "open covenants of peace, openly arrived at;" freedom of the seas; removal of economic barriers; limitation of armaments; recognition of the interests of native populations in the adjustment of colonial claims; evacuation and restoration of Allied territory invaded by the Central Powers; readjustment of the boundaries of Italy, the Balkan States, and Turkey on lines of nationality; an independent Poland; opportunity for autonomous development for the peoples of Austria-Hungary; and the creation of "a general association of nations."

Point 6 called for the evacuation of all occupied Russian territory and a sincere welcome of Russia "into the society of free nations under institutions of her own choosing. . . . [T]he treatment accorded Russia by her sister nations in the months to come," the president continued, "will be the acid test of their good will, of their comprehension of her needs as distinguished from their own interests, and of their intelligent and unselfish sympathy." Wilson appealed directly to the Russian people to continue fighting, but to no effect. In the harsh Treaty of Brest-Litovsk, March 3, 1918, the Soviets surrendered title to Finland, the Baltic provinces, Lithuania, Russian Poland, and the Ukraine and withdrew from the war. Although Wilson's Fourteen Points failed to keep Russia in the war, they did offer an idealistic peace platform that gained a popular worldwide hearing. Because the Allies did not at the time take exception to them, the Fourteen Points were accepted as a statement of the war aims of the Allies and became the basis on which Germany offered to make peace.[30]

Allied Involvement in Russia

Conservative leaders in the Allied ranks, including President Wilson and Secretary Lansing, strongly disapproved of the new Bolshevik government of Russia because of the vast ideological differences. When the Bolsheviks repudiated all previously accumulated debts, Wilson insisted these obligations be met before the United States would recognize the new government, a policy that continued until November 1933. During the spring of 1918, officials in London and Paris sought a way to intervene in Russian affairs and, as they informed Wilson, to maintain an eastern front. Lacking the troops to intervene, they turned to the United States and Japan. Initially, he was not convinced an Allied intervention in Russia was justified, but in July, Wilson changed his mind and sent 7,000 American troops to northern Russia and 9,000 to assist the Japanese in Siberia. Czechoslovakia's leader Thomás Masaryk convinced Wilson that the marooned Czech Legion in Siberia required U.S. assistance, while the objective of sending forces to Murmansk was to secure 160,000 tons of military supplies. If the president did not believe the intervention was intended to topple the Russian government or gain territorial concessions, the British, French, and Japanese saw the episode differently.

U.S. troops joined British and French forces at outposts around Archangel and Murmansk, but because freezing weather had closed the ports they had to wait seven months after the armistice to withdraw in June 1919. The French, instructed by Premier Georges Clemenceau to eliminate Russian Bolshevism, also intervened at Odessa in the Ukraine, joining former tsarist and local nationalist forces. In April 1919, however, domestic politics led Clemenceau to bring French forces home without accomplishing their mission. This venture was the clearest example of Allied efforts to overthrow the Bolsheviks. Tokyo sent some 72,000 troops to seize the Trans-Siberian Railway inland as far as Irkutsk, where they met the Czech forces and secured positions in Manchuria and eastern Siberia. U.S. forces, after limiting the impact of the Japanese presence, left in April 1920 with the Czech units, while the Japanese reluctantly departed in October 1922. The Bolshevik revolution and Allied intervention long influenced Soviet and American attitudes. In the United States, Bolshevik successes spurred fears of communist agitation that with official approval launched the nation's first Red Scare from 1919 to 1920. In the Soviet Union, the interventions heightened suspicions of the West's policies during and after the Second World War.

A Resolution

President Wilson acted as spokesman for "the principal Allied and Associated Powers" in answering the Austrian and German peace overtures. As far as

Austria was concerned, the president replied that Point 10, calling for the autonomous development of the peoples of Austria-Hungary, was no longer wholly applicable. Since the United States had recognized the Czechoslovak National Council, it was for the other nationalities to determine what concessions would satisfy them. To Germany, Wilson specified the following conditions: acceptance of the Wilsonian terms; evacuation of Allied territory; abandonment of illegal practices on sea and land; assurance that the German officials conducting the negotiations represented the people; and the abdication of the kaiser. The kaiser left on November 9, 1918, and there was organized the same day a provisional German People's Government. Germany meanwhile had accepted Wilson's other conditions. It soon became apparent that Wilson's idealism had outdistanced the interests of his European allies, for only after a protracted argument, and even a threat of a separate peace, did Colonel House secure England, France, and Italy's acceptance of the Fourteen Points, with two reservations. On Wilson's second point, "freedom of the seas," a phrase open to varied interpretations, they reserved complete freedom of decision. Wilson's statement that territory occupied by the enemy should be "restored" as well as freed was construed as meaning that Germany must pay compensation. Wilson accepted this second reservation, which would serve as the basis of the large reparations bill presented to Germany. The Germans were also informed that Marshal Foch would formulate the military terms of an armistice that would render Germany incapable of renewing the conflict. While German armies were still intact and on foreign soil, morale in both the civilian population and the armed forces had nearly collapsed. Since the high command feared to continue the war, the German government accepted Marshal Foch's terms. In a railway car near Compiegne, the German commissioners signed the armistice on November 11, 1918. Austria and Italy agreed to an armistice on November 3.

WILSON AND PEACE NEGOTIATIONS

Wilson's participation in the peace negotiations led to the following objectives: (1) a just peace based, with respect to territorial adjustments, on the principle of self-determination, a settlement eliminating centers of infection productive of future wars; and (2) the creation of a league of nations to ensure preservation of peace. Adherence to the principles of the Fourteen Points, Wilson believed, would accomplish these objectives. His eloquent statements of idealistic aims had led war-weary and/or oppressed populations throughout the world to hail him as their deliverer. This moral leadership faded as ideals clashed with practical considerations and as incompatible aspirations. One obstacle pertained to the secret agreements that the Allies had arranged among themselves before the United States had even entered the war. In this regard, France had been promised by Russia, although not by Britain, not only the return of Alsace-Lorraine, but also possession of the Saar Valley and the conversion of German territory west of the Rhine into an independent "buffer state." Italy had been assured of large accessions of Austrian territory in the Trentino or southern Tyrol and about the head of the Adriatic, while Japan had been promised the German islands in the North Pacific and the inheritance of German rights in Shantung, China. Russia had been promised Constantinople and other Turkish territory, and still other portions of the Ottoman Empire had been apportioned respectively among France, Britain, Italy, and Greece. The Bolsheviks renounced Russian claims, but other Allies pushed on. The French and Italian claims in Europe and Japan's claim to Shantung were destined to be Wilson's major dilemmas. The secret claims conflicted with the principle of self-determination and, specifically, with Wilson's declaration that "peoples and provinces are not to be bartered about from sovereignty to sovereignty as if they were mere chattels and pawns in a game."[31]

Wilson made no effort to have the secret treaties set aside and rejected a French proposal that they be suspended. In the end, the principle of self-determination was often sacrificed to claims based on these treaties. His second obstacle was the vindictive attitude prevalent among the Allied publics, not excluding the United States. Britain's Lloyd George, France's Clemenceau, and Italy's Vittorio Orlando had promised that Germany would pay for the war. Now, often against their better judgment, they felt public pressure to make good on these promises. A third obstacle to Wilson's planned objectives was that the other negotiators had become very aware of his dip in domestic popularity. When a recent midterm election gave majorities in both houses to the Republicans, Theodore Roosevelt exulted in a public statement that "Mr. Wilson has no authority whatever to speak for the American people at this time."[32] The electorate's decision inevitably lessened his bargaining power.

Treaty of Versailles

Wilson arrived in Paris on December 13, 1918, but it was not until the following January 12 that representatives of the great powers held their first formal meeting. Since November 1917, the British, French, and Italian prime ministers, with the occasional attendance of Colonel House representing the president, had exercised direction of the war as the Supreme War Council. Now the three—George, Clemenceau, and Orlando—along with President Wilson and the ranking Japanese delegate, representing the Big Five powers and attended by 27 victorious nations and their 70 delegates, dominated the conference and made all crucial decisions. Neither Germany nor its wartime allies were represented since they were expected merely to sign arrived-at agreements. Nor were the Soviets invited to join the conference. If disarming Germany and creating the League of Nations were major concerns, Allied leaders also worried about the influence of Communists amid the chaos and uprisings in Germany and central Europe. Thus, fear of the Bolsheviks disrupted some of the treaty negotiations and often subtly influenced decisions.

Wilson's greatest success at the conference was the adoption of the Covenant of the League of Nations and the decision that it should be an integral part of each peace treaty. Wilson was chairman of the commission that drafted the covenant. On February 14, it was presented to the conference, where, with a few changes, it became the Covenant of the League. His desire to gain support for the league, however, forced him to allow France to draft terms of a peace treaty punishing Germany. With partisan opponents organizing in the Senate, Wilson returned to the U.S. on the steamer *George Washington* with the aim of convincing his own countrymen of the league's value. Wilson had invited the members of the Senate Foreign Relations and House Foreign Affairs committees to the White House on February 26 to discuss the League Covenant, but won no converts. A few hours before Congress adjourned, Senator Henry Cabot Lodge read a statement signed by 37 Republican senators or senators-elect, declaring that "the constitution of the league of nations in the form now proposed . . . should not be accepted by the United States" and that peace with Germany should be made as soon as possible, after which "the proposal for a league of nations to insure the permanent peace of the world should then be taken up for careful and serious consideration."[33]

Before returning to Paris, Wilson gave a speech in New York City and informed his opponents that the treaty of peace would be tied with so many threads to the League Covenant that it would be impossible to separate them. It did not occur to him, apparently, that such organic union might result not in acceptance of the covenant, but in rejection of the treaty. On the advice of Democratic and Republican friends of the league who warned that without certain changes the covenant would never receive Senate approval, Wilson reconvened the League of Nations Commission and asked that the covenant be amended. The changes deemed essential to ensure Senate approval were: (1) recognition of the right of members to withdraw from the league; (2) exemption of domestic questions (such as tariffs and immigration) from league jurisdiction; (3) a statement that no member would be required, against its will, to accept a mandate over a former enemy colony; and (4) a declaration safeguarding the Monroe Doctrine. France, Britain, Italy, and Japan each tried to exact a quid pro quo for their consent to the American amendments. France requested an international general staff to direct action against new aggressions. Britain demanded that the United States give up its ambitious naval building program. Italy insisted that its new boundaries include Fiume, a city and port on the Adriatic. Japan revived a proposal for recognition of racial equality in the preamble of the Covenant. Wilson ultimately secured the desired amendments, adopted by the conference on April 28, without accepting the changes in the covenant proposed by others.

Subsequent events suggest that Wilson's most serious failure in Paris was his consent to the reparations clauses in the German treaty. Although they brought little benefit to the victors, and in the end were largely nullified, they imbued Germans with a feeling of grave injustice, a grievance that bode ill for the future. The president had declared earlier that there should be "no contributions, no punitive damages,"[34] which along with the Fourteen Points comprised the basis of Germany's surrender. The Allied reservation to this stipulation was Germany's obligation to "restore" occupied territory while embracing payment "for all damages done to the civilian population of the Allies and their property by the aggression of Germany by land, by sea and from the air." This phrasing would seem to have precluded placing the entire cost of the war on Germany, but Allied statesmen, particularly the British in the parliamentary election campaign of December 1918, had promised to do just that. Lloyd George brought forward the specious contention that pensions and separation allowances paid to Allied soldiers and their dependents could properly be classified as "damages done to the civilian population"[35] —a contention that doubled the aggregate reparations bill, substantially increasing Britain's share. Wilson allowed himself to be persuaded by the British argument, apparently under the impression that the increased British share was taken from a fixed sum based on Germany's capacity to pay.

The claim based on pensions and separation allowances was added to claims for other losses, increasing the total reparations bill to a sum far exceeding Germany's capacity to pay, particularly when the treaty also reduced its resources. These included its colonies, merchant marine, German-owned property in Allied countries, the coal of the Saar, the iron ore of Lorraine, and a substantial fraction of its industrial and agricultural capacity. A Reparations Commission eventually set the reparations figure at $33 billion. Though only a small part of it was ever paid, the enormous bill left Germany with a sense of having been double-crossed. This feeling was aggravated by the imposition of the "war guilt" clause (Article 231) of the treaty by which Germany was required to accept moral and legal responsibility "for causing all the loss and damage" that the Allies and their nationals had suffered "as a consequence of the war imposed upon them by the aggression of Germany and her allies."[36] Those who wrote the treaty may have subscribed to this argument, but Germans accepted it only under duress.

The Germans were summoned to Paris, not to discuss the treaty, but to receive and to sign it. On May 7, 1919, Premier Clemenceau, as president of the conference, handed the lengthy document of 440 articles to the German delegation. The Germans received the treaty with a display of sullenness and discourtesy and made their reply on May 29 in a similar spirit. Many in the

Allied delegations, having at last seen the treaty as a whole, were appalled at its severity. Dissatisfaction with the treaty was especially strong among members of the British delegation. Had the Germans been so inclined, they might have divided their opponents and won concessions; however, by their resentful attitude and attacking all major features of the treaty, they helped consolidate Allied delegations around the rigid Clemenceau. A few concessions were granted: slight modifications of the boundaries between Germany and Poland and Denmark, agreement that the disposition of a part of Upper Silesia should be decided by plebiscite instead of by outright cession to Poland, better German representation on the commissions that were to control German rivers, and assurance that the limitations of armaments imposed on Germany was "also the first step towards that general reduction and limitation of armaments . . . which it will be one of the first duties of the League of Nations to promote." With such changes and assurances, the Germans had to be content.[37] On June 23, 1919, they accepted the treaty.[38]

The U.S. Senate and the League of Nations

In a moment that had the potential to define his presidential doctrine, Wilson presented the treaty to the Senate on July 10, 1919. Weeks earlier, Senator William E. Borah of Idaho, a leading opponent of the league, had procured a copy and read the long text verbatim into the *Congressional Record*. Now, members of Congress and any citizen had the opportunity to peruse it. The League of Nations Covenant had been known since February and had been debated by both friends and foes alike. The amendments subsequently added to the covenant had also been published, and Senator Lodge had indicated that Wilson's changes did not satisfy him. From the time that the Senate met in a special session in May, Republican opponents of the treaty had been planning a strategy. Senator Lodge, who desired to see the treaty defeated despite protestations to the contrary,[39] believed that sentiment for the league was so strong that the treaty could not be defeated by direct attack. The course adopted was: first, delay action via prolonged hearings and debate, giving pro-League enthusiasm time to cool; and second, load the treaty with amendments or reservations and count on Wilson and the Democrats to kill it.[40]

Opposition to the treaty stemmed from varied motives. Some feared the league as a "super-state," which would destroy American independence and drag the United States into endless international quarrels. A resurgent nationalism saw treason in an attempt to subject the will of the American people to any form or degree of international control. The league, Senator Borah said, was "the first step in internationalism and the sterilization of nationalism" that was designed by Wall Street bankers and big business. Others, former supporters of Wilson, charged him with surrendering his principles and selling out to British, French, and Japanese "imperialists." Socialists of nearly all varieties would have none of the league because, as they charged, it enthroned capitalism.[41] While liberals and radicals were damning the league as an invention of big business, other opponents obtained funds from millionaires Andrew W. Mellon and Henry Clay Frick to fight the treaty. The battle produced some strange alliances.

Partisanship and personal feuds also contributed to the opposition. Republicans, with an eye on the 1920 campaign and suspecting Wilson might run for a third term, were reluctant to place such an impressive achievement as the league in Democratic hands. Senatorial jealousy of the executive and personal dislike for Wilson certainly stimulated the fight against the League Covenant and the treaty. Leader and organizer of the Senate opposition, Lodge was chairman of the Committee on Foreign Relations in the Senate, where the Republicans held the slender majority of 49 to 47. Of the 49 Republicans, 15 were determined opponents of the league—"irreconcilables" who would support any reservations Lodge proposed and, at the end, would still vote against the treaty. Thirty-four would vote for reservations and the treaty with reservations that suited them. The Senate Democrats, too, were divided. A few would support the treaty only with strong reservations; others, pro-league but not 100 percent behind Wilson's covenant, would support Lodge at least part of the way. The remaining Democrats were divided equally between those who insisted on the covenant as it was and those who would take it either with or without reservations. The ideals of the Wilson Doctrine proved a difficult ticket to sell.

Additionally, Lodge had seen to it that the Senate Committee on Foreign Relations was "packed" with senators unfriendly to the league.[42] Officially printed copies of the treaty reached the committee on July 14; however, hearings were delayed until July 31. Wilson was heard, the committee meeting with him at the White House on August 19. William C. Bullitt, who resigned at Paris, now bared the rift in the American delegation. He revealed a confidential conversation with Lansing, in which the secretary reportedly described the League of Nations as "entirely useless" and added that "if the Senate could only understand what this Treaty means . . . it would unquestionably be defeated."[43] Though Lansing claimed that his language had been distorted, Bullitt's testimony—along with a long list of witnesses—was nonetheless damaging.

Attempting to Sway the American People

It now appeared that the committee, and perhaps the Senate, would insist on more interpretative reservations than Wilson was willing to accept. Consequently, the president resolved to appeal to the country. His tour was routed through the Old Northwest, the Upper Mississippi Valley, and the Far West, the sections that furnished much of the opposition to the treaty. Despite the rather academic style of his addresses, Wilson garnered much popular enthusiasm for a league that would make unnecessary a repetition of recent sacrifices and future U.S. interventions. Although Wilson captivated popular audiences, he had no success in winning the needed senatorial support. His references to his opponents were tactless and occasionally offensive. He offered no compromise; the Senate, he said, must take the treaty as it was or have no treaty at all. Senators who withheld U.S. support from the peace organization would be, he said, "absolute, contemptible quitters." Isolationist senators trailed his footsteps, giving their side of the argument to the same public.

Ultimately, the trip was a political failure, ending in personal tragedy. The strain of 36 formal addresses, numerous "whistle-stop" back-platform speeches, the intense heat, and unrelenting personal interviews and press conferences was too much for Wilson's health. After the speech at Pueblo, Colorado, on September 29, he was rushed back to Washington, a very ill man. A few days later came the paralytic stroke from which he never fully recovered. Secluded from friends and shielded from sound advice by his solicitous wife, the sick man in the White House clung to his conviction that the treaty must be approved as he had written it or not at all. [44]

Meanwhile, the Foreign Relations Committee had completed hearings on the treaty, and on September 10, the majority report proposed 45 amendments and four reservations. This action was too drastic even for many Republicans, and the idea of amending it was given up. On November 6, Lodge proposed a resolution of advice and consent to ratification subject to 14 reservations. [45] Wilson was not opposed to all compromise. Before setting out on his speaking tour, he had handed to Senate Minority Leader Gilbert M. Hitchcock four reservations that he would accept if necessary to get the treaty approved. These dealt with withdrawal from the league, Article 10, the Monroe Doctrine, and domestic questions, and differed from Lodge's reservations on the same points more in wording than in substance. They were so similar to proposals made by Republican mild reservationists as to suggest that they and the Democrats could have reached a compromise with Wilson's encouragement. But when, in November, Hitchcock introduced the substance of the Wilson reservations, adding a fifth on the British Empire's six votes, [46] the moderate Republicans had committed themselves to the Lodge program and complained with reason that Hitchcock came too late.

Wilson denounced Lodge's reservation on Article 10 as "a rejection of the covenant." As the day approached for the vote on the treaty with the 14 reservations, he wrote Senator Hitchcock that "I trust that all true friends of the treaty will refuse to support the Lodge resolution." [47] Hitchcock and the Democrats heeded the word of their stricken leader, and so on November 19, 1919, all but four of the Democrats joined the Republican irreconcilables to defeat the treaty with reservations. Neither with the Lodge reservations, nor without any, could the treaty command a bare majority of the Senate, not to mention the required two-thirds. The Senate adjourned.

The Last Opportunity

Not all "true friends of the treaty" favored Wilson's uncompromising position. House, no longer in the president's good graces, had urged compromise. Herbert Hoover had urged acceptance of the Lodge reservations, as had former president William H. Taft. When the next session of Congress convened in December, new hope for compromise arose. At the Jackson Day dinner in January 1920, William Jennings Bryan told fellow Democrats that democracy required that the president bow to a majority of the Senate. London indicated that it would welcome American ratification, with or without the Lodge reservations. But Wilson stood firm. Nevertheless, during the same month, Republican and Democratic senators, including Lodge and Hitchcock, met informally, seeking common ground in a modified set of reservations. Lodge, however, reassured a delegation of alarmed, irreconcilable senators "that there was not the slightest danger of our conceding anything that was essential or that was anything more than a change in wording."[48] Agreement was reached on minor points but not on the crucial questions of Article 10 and the Monroe Doctrine.

On February 10, 1920, Lodge again reported the treaty to the Senate, with a few recent changes in the November reservations; the Senate went over the old ground, readopting the Lodge-changed reservations. The resolution of ratification did provide, as Lloyd George had suggested, that failure of the allied and associated powers to object to the reservations should be counted as acceptance. But even this was balanced by giving the right of objection to all or any of the allied and associated powers, rather than only to the Big Four. Yet nothing changed that could have made the reservations more palatable to Wilson. Again, on March 8, he urged supporters to defeat ratification on Lodge's terms. In the final vote on March 19, 1920, the tally for the treaty, with the reservations, fell seven short of the necessary two-thirds for approval.[49] The treaty, together with Wilson's vision of the great departure for America, was dead.

CONCLUSION

Although Wilson in the end defeated what was left of the 1919 treaty, his announcement of the Fourteen Points and the subsequent League of Nations was nevertheless a significant ideological departure from previous foreign policies. The growing proximity of World War I to American interests reached its apex in 1917, putting an end to America's isolationism and hith-

erto non-participation in European affairs. Determined that American participation in the war should not be in vain of another European imperial conquest, Wilson was adamant that, at the very least, a liberal democratic order
would replace the Old World empires. If the Allied powers, at the beginning
of the war, had anything in common with Washington, it was that they, too,
"championed" democracy. Wilson's war aims and his subsequent globalized
vision of the Monroe Doctrine formed the seed that, prompted by the Zimmermann Telegram, promulgated America's foreign policy, and American
entanglement in European affairs.

Wilson's fight to have the Fourteen Points agreed upon, in most of its
entirety, was proof that American diplomacy and foreign policy had achieved
a successful parity with, if not overtaken, their European counterparts. Wilson's perhaps ahead-of-his-time idealism was nevertheless stunted by the
Europeans' stubborn demands for harsh reparations and territory acquisition.
The end result of negotiations with the Europeans left no doubt in the minds
of many American policymakers at home that European vicissitudes of power were likely to continue for some time into the foreseeable future. That the
Germans felt betrayed, abused, and bereft of any hope for a future livelihood
mattered little in the minds of the Allied powers, determined to exact all that
they could. Only for a small few did it seem at the time that such harsh
policies would return to haunt them, some 14 years later. John Maynard
Keynes, writing to British Prime Minister Lloyd George in June of 1919,
perhaps foresaw better than most when he exclaimed that the Treaty of Peace
was a battle lost: "I've gone on hoping even through these last dreadful
weeks that you'd find some way to make of the Treaty a just and expedient
document," but "I can do no more here."[50] The Peace, he exclaimed, was
"outrageous."

The League of Nations, for many in Congress, was the stipulation that
sold future American involvement in European wars as a sure thing, a direction Washington had turned its back on since the days of the founding
fathers. For Wilson, the League promoted American values abroad, directly
influencing the disassembly of the old imperial order. Democracy, as the
argument went, would prevent future conflicts because inevitably the people
would vote against such high costs to economy and life. However, the
Bolshevik revolution meant Wilson's democratic idealism was not the only
ideology competing for European priority—a priority he was willing to protect at the cost of further political and material involvement in Russian affairs
at the behest of Paris and London's insistence. Sensitivity to the rise of
socialism became an anxiety in the minds of not only the European powers,
but discernibly to Americans as well; enough, at least, to break with policy
tradition and become entangled in another European political affair. However, as the ideological threat of socialism pronounced itself within the United
States, it became clear that the traditional vicissitudes of European politics

had become materially, and ideologically, global. Despite Washington's return to isolationism after the war, America's appeal to the prospect of the globalization of its ideals had been stirred. The seeds of democracy promotion had been born.

NOTES

1. Also see Richard Dean Burns, Joseph M. Siracusa, and Jason Flanagan, *American Foreign Relations since Independence*, Santa Barbara, CA: Praeger, 2013.

2. See Winston Churchill, *The World in Crisis, 1874–1965*, Toronto: Macmillan Co. of Canada, 2005.

3. Philip C. Jessup, *Elihu Root*, 2 vols., New York: Dodd, Mead, & Co., 1938, vol. 2, p. 313.

4. Quoted in Joseph M. Siracusa, "Wilson's Image of the Prussian Menace: Ideology and Realpolitik," in John A. Moses and Christopher Pugsley, eds., *The German Empire and Britain's Pacific Dominions, 1871–1919*, Claremont, CA: Regina Books, 2000, p. 68.

5. Walter Lippmann, *U.S. Foreign Policy, Shield of the Republic*, Boston: Little, Brown, 1943, p. 33–39. See also Siracusa, "Wilson's Image of the Prussian Menace," pp. 51–89.

6. See Woodrow Wilson "Message on Neutrality" August 19, 1914, The American Presidency Project, available at: http://www.presidency.ucsb.edu/ws/index.php?pid=65382.

7. See Memorandum by the Counselor for the Department of State (Lansing) on Professor Hugo Münsterberg's Letter to President Wilson of November 19, 1914, U.S. Department of State Office of the Historian, available at: http://history.state.gov/historicaldocuments/frus1914-20v01/d167.

8. See The Secretary of State to President Wilson, Washington, September 6, 1915, U.S. Department of State Office of the Historian, available at: http://history.state.gov/historicaldocuments/frus1914-20v01/d148.

9. See "A Communication from Charles A. Beard," *New Republic* 87, June 17, 1936, p. 177.

10. R. S. Baker and W. E. Dodd, eds., *The Public Papers of Woodrow Wilson: The New Democracy*, 2 vols., New York: Harper & Row, 1926, vol. 2, p. 282.

11. The Germans had begun laying mines in the North Sea. The British had asserted the right to retaliate, and on November 2, 1914, had proclaimed the entire North Sea to be a "war area," which merchant vessels would enter at their own risk. C. C. Tansill, *America Goes to War*, Boston: Little, Brown, 1938, pp. 176–77.

12. E. M. Borchard and W. P. Lage, *Neutrality for the United States*, 2nd ed., New Haven, CT: Yale University Press, 1940, pp. 87–88, 136–37, 77–83.

13. See Woodrow Wilson's letter to Senator Stone cited in Woodrow Wilson, *Selected Addresses and Public Papers of Woodrow Wilson*, BiblioBazaar, LLC, 2009, p. 106.

14. Tansill, *America Goes to War*, chapters 13–14.

15. *Ibid.*, p. 491.

16. See Woodrow Wilson's Address to a Joint Session of Congress on the Severance of Diplomatic Relations with Germany, February 3, 1917, The American Presidency Project, available at: www.presidency.ucsb.edu/ws/?pid=65397.

17. See Wilson, *Selected Addresses and Public Papers of Woodrow Wilson*, p. 180.

18. Howard Jones, *Crucible of Power: A History of U.S. Foreign Relations since 1897*, New York: Rowman & Littlefield, 2001, p. 83.

19. Arthur S. Link, *Woodrow Wilson and the Progressive Era, 1910–1917*, New York: Harper & Row, 1954, pp. 219–22.

20. Arthur S. Link, *Wilson: Campaigns for Progressivism and Peace*, Princeton, NJ: Princeton University Press, 1965, pp. 221–25.

21. Wilson and Henry Cabot Lodge had spoken to this effect to the League to Enforce Peace, in Washington, May 27, 1916.

22. See Address to the Senate of the United States: "A World League for Peace," January 22, 1917, The American Presidency Project, available at: http://www.presidency.ucsb.edu/ws/?pid=65396.

23. In hearings on the treaty in 1919, Wilson was asked: "Do you think that if Germany had committed no act of war or no act of injustice against our citizens that we would have gotten into this war?" He replied: "I do think so." *Peace Treaty Hearings*, Senate Document 106, 66 Congress 1 sess., p. 536. This later opinion is contradicted in Link, *Wilson: Campaigns*, pp. 277–81.

24. Wilson was particularly indignant because von Bernstorff had been permitted to communicate with his government in cipher through the State Department and the American embassy in Berlin. British Intelligence, having possession of the German code, caught the communication from the cable and also as sent by wireless. R. S. Baker, *Woodrow Wilson, Life and Letters*, 8 vols., Garden City, NY: Doubleday, 1927–1939, vol. 6, pp. 470–79.

25. Samuel R. Spencer Jr., *Decision for War, 1917*, Peterborough, NH: Richard R. Smith, 1953, chapter 2.

26. President Wilson's Address to Congress, April 2, 1917, Library of Congress Internet Archive, available at: https://ia700504.us.archive.org/22/items/presidentwoodrow00unit/presidentwoodrow00unit.pdf.

27. *Ibid.*

28. Daniel M. Smith and Joseph M. Siracusa, *The Testing of America: 1914–1945*, St. Louis: Forum Press, 1979, chapter 2.

29. Joseph M. Siracusa, *Diplomacy: A Very Short Introduction*, Oxford: Oxford University Press, 2010, pp. 42–44.

30. See Thomas A. Bailey, *Woodrow Wilson and the Lost Peace*, New York: Macmillan, 1944, pp. 297–98. The later addresses in R. S. Baker and W. E. Dodds, eds., *The Public Papers of Woodrow Wilson: War and Peace*, 2 vols., New York: Harper & Row, 1927.

31. Most secret agreements are in H. W. V. Temperley, ed., *A History of the Peace Conference of Paris*, 6 vols., London: Henry Frowde and Hodder & Stoughton, 1920–1924.

32. Cited in George Sylvester Viereck, *The Strangest Friendship in History: Woodrow Wilson and Colonel House*, New York: Aware Journalism, 1932, p. 238.

33. Really six more, for two additional senators signed later. U.S. Senate Treaty of Peace with Germany, Hearings before the Committee on Foreign Relations, United States Senate, Senate Document No. 106, 66th Cong, 1st sess., 1919.

34. Siracusa, *Diplomacy*, pp. 48–53.

35. See Treaty of Versailles, The Avalon Project, available at: http://avalon.law.yale.edu/subject_menus/versailles_menu.asp.

36. *Ibid.*

37. The German counterproposals and the Allied reply are in *Foreign Relations of the United States: The Paris Peace Conference*, 13 vols., Washington, DC: U.S. Government Printing Office, 1942–1947, vol. 6: 800 ff. See also J. T. Shotwell, *At the Paris Peace Conference*, New York: Macmillan, 1937, chapter 4; Temperley, *A History of the Peace Conference of Paris*, 2, pp. 1–20.

38. The treaty with Germany took effect—but not for the United States—on January 10, 1920. Treaties with the other Central Powers were signed as follows: with Austria at St. Germain-en-Laye, September 10, 1919; with Bulgaria at Neuilly-sur-Seine, November 27, 1919; with Hungary at the Trianon, June 4, 1920. A treaty with Turkey was signed at Sevres, August 10, 1920.

39. H. C. Lodge, *The Senate and the League of Nations*, New York: Charles Scribner's Sons, 1925, p. 209. For an opposite view, see D. F. Fleming, *The United States and World Organization, 1920–1933*, New York: Columbia University Press, 1938, pp. 19–25; also D. F. Fleming, *The United States and the League of Nations, 1918–1920*, New York: G. P. Putnam's Sons, 1932, pp. 475–87.

40. Lodge, *Senate and the League of Nations*, p. 164.

41. The liberals' break with Wilson is in Selig Adler, *The Isolationist Impulse: Its Twentieth Century Reaction*, New York: Abelard-Schulman, 1957, chapter 3.

42. Lodge, *Senate and the League of Nations*, p. 151.

43. U.S. Senate Treaty of Peace with Germany, Hearings before the Committee on Foreign Relations, United States Senate, Senate Document No. 106, 66th Cong, 1st sess., 1919, p. 1276.

44. Kurt Wimer, "Woodrow Wilson Tries Conciliation: An Effort That Failed," *The Historian*, 25, August 1963, pp. 419–38. Wilson's speaking tour is appraised in Thomas. A. Bailey, *Woodrow Wilson and the Great Betrayal*, New York: Macmillan, 1945, chapters 6–7.

45. On the third reservation, declaring that the United States should accept no mandate without consent of Congress, see Lodge, *Senate and the League of Nations*, p. 185.

46. Wilson and Hitchcock's reservations are in Bailey, *Wilson and the Great Betrayal*, pp. 393–94.

47. Cited in Norman A. Graebner and Edward M. Bennett, *The Versailles Treaty and Its Legacy: The Failure of the Wilsonian Vision*, New York: Cambridge University Press, 2011, p. 64.

48. Lodge, *Senate and the League of Nations*, p. 194. Also see C. O. Johnson, *Borah of Idaho*, New York: Longmans, Green, 1936, pp. 246–48.

49. Graebner and Bennett, *The Versailles Treaty*, pp. 65–66.

50. Gilles Dostaler, *Keynes and his Battles*, Northampton, MA: Edward Elgar Publishing, 2007, p. 146.

Chapter Four

The New Terrain: Containing the "Outside"

The United States' foreign policy after World War II saw a doctrinal shift that would entail a more decisive role in defining international affairs. With the traditional European powers decimated, the U.S. was now in a position where it had both the opportunity and "apparent" responsibility of shaping the post-war order. Of course, the concurrent emergence of the Soviet threat between 1945 and 1947—both perceived and to some extent real—engendered a reassessment of the post-war approach that would also have a profound impact on international relations. In 1947, State Department analyst George F. Kennan penned a highly influential essay on the Soviet Union that transformed fear of the U.S.S.R. into a cohesive policy. Arguing that "insecure" Russians had always had the desire to expand and acquire territory, Kennan wrote that the Soviet Union would take every opportunity to spread Communism into every possible "nook and cranny" around the globe, either by conquering neighboring countries or by subtly supporting Communist revolutionaries in politically unstable states. Kennan also wrote, however, that the United States could prevent the global domination of Communism with a strategy of "containment," a strategy that rapidly became the root of U.S. presidential doctrine for countering Communism. While subsequent presidents interpreted the doctrine differently and/or employed different tactics to accomplish their goals, the overall strategy for keeping Communism in check remained consistent until the Cold War ended in the early 1990s.

In looking at this doctrinal adjustment, this chapter will unpack the key developments in Truman's incorporation of containment into his doctrine, reflected in a special address to Congress in March 1947. Here, Truman announced that the United States would support foreign governments resisting "armed minorities" or "outside pressures"—or more specifically, Communist revolutionaries or the Soviet Union—and would follow this with a congressional appropriation of $400 million to the "susceptible" Greece and Turkey. Critics, both at the time and looking back in retrospect, have charged that Truman's adoption of containment as the key pillar in his doctrine unnecessarily intensified the Cold War polarization between the United States and the U.S.S.R. Indeed, many have claimed that the United States may have avoided fifty years of competition and mutual distrust had Truman sought a more nuanced, diplomatic solution to tensions. Defendants of Truman's policy, however, have argued that the Soviet Union had already begun the Cold War by thwarting Allied attempts to reunite and stabilize Germany. Truman, they contend, merely met the existing Soviet challenge. Other supporters believe that Truman used dichotomous language so as to prevent U.S. isolationists from abandoning the cause in Europe. Whatever the motivations, Truman's adoption of the containment strategy and his characterization of the Communist threat had a marked impact on American foreign policy and set the doctrinal tone for the subsequent four decades.

THE END OF ISOLATIONISM?

The Japanese attack at Pearl Harbor, together with the global war that followed, silenced, if not ended, isolationism in the United States. The elaborate neutrality legislation of the 1930s had failed to insulate the United States from war in Europe and Asia. To many Americans, it appeared that the United States could only hope to avoid war in the future by joining a system of collective security capable of *actually* preventing war. To these citizens who enthusiastically embraced the idea, American membership in an improved and strengthened League of Nations seemed the only hope of peace—and this would come in the form of the United Nations. In spite of much planning and preparing the American people to accept a process of international cooperation, it soon became evident after its inception that the United Nations would not be able to live up to its idealistic promises. Ideologies shaped national perceptions of their vital interests and, as much as anything, bred distrust and alienation between the victors.

Indeed, for a small minority of U.S. officials and writers, well conditioned to distrust the Kremlin, the euphoria of victory and peace in 1945 evaporated quickly. If the Soviet Union's costly victory over Nazi military forces had been a vital contribution to V-E day, these Americans now feared that the historic European balance of power had been upset. The continued Soviet occupation of Eastern Europe enhanced that country's strategic position in the Balkans and rendered bordering regions vulnerable to further Soviet expansion.[1] It required only the Kremlin's post-war demands on Iran and Turkey to unleash visions of Soviet military expansion reminiscent of the Italian, German, and Japanese aggressions. Joseph and Stewart Alsop, writing in the May 20, 1946, issue of *Life*, defined the emerging Soviet threat in Hitlerian terms:

> Already Poland, the Baltic States, Rumania, Bulgaria, Yugoslavia and Albania are behind the Iron Curtain. Huge armies hold Hungary and half of Germany and Austria. Czechoslovakia and Greece are encircled. . . . In the Middle East, the Soviets are driving southward. Iran is in danger of being reduced to puppethood; Turkey and Iraq are threatened. Finally, in the Far East, the Kuriles has been stripped and left in condition to be transformed at will and half of Korea are occupied and Manchuria into another Azerbaijan. The process still goes on. One . . . must also wonder whether they will ultimately be satisfied with less than dominion over Europe and Asia. [2]

In responding to Soviet pressures on Turkey for a new Straits settlement in an August 1946 memorandum, Acting Secretary of State Dean Acheson, Navy Secretary James Forrestal, and Secretary of War Robert Patterson warned that if the Soviet Union were to succeed in its objective of attaining a hold over Turkey, "it will be extremely difficult, if not impossible, to prevent [it] from obtaining control over Greece and over the whole Near and Middle East." This, they argued, would encompass the territory that stood between the Mediterranean and India. "When the Soviet Union has once obtained full mastery of this territory . . . it will be in a much stronger position to obtain its objectives in India and China." [3]

COLD WAR ORIGINS

The rift in the United Nations between the Soviet Union, backed by its satellites, and the United States, generally supported by the other democracies, reflected a mounting antagonism between the two groups. For many U.S. citizens, the growing fear and distrust of the U.S.S.R. did not necessarily pertain to a clear disliking of the Communist ideology, but was more based on the perception of communism being inimical to Western principles of liberal democracy and the "American way of life." However embellished and exaggerated this notion was, the country's emerging anti-Communist elite saw the real Soviet danger in the limitless promise of Soviet ideological expansion. Soviet rhetoric had long predicted communism's ultimate world conquest. For those Americans who took the Soviet rhetoric seriously, the U.S.S.R., as the self-assigned leader of world communism, possessed the power and will to incite or support Communist-led revolutions everywhere, imposing on them its influence, if not its direct control. It mattered little whether Soviet troops or even Soviet officials were present, for ideological expansionism assured future Soviet triumphs without war. This alleged capacity to expand far beyond the reach of its armies seemed to transform the U.S.S.R. into an international phenomenon of unprecedented expansive power. As such, the chaotic economic, social, and political conditions prevailing throughout most of post-war Eurasia were perceived to present an immediate danger to Western security and a vacuum for Soviet ideological exploitation.

Anti-Communist writers and spokesmen, as early as 1946, detected few limits to the Kremlin's external needs and ambitions. In February, Soviet specialist and diplomat George F. Kennan's famed Long Telegram attributed to the Kremlin a paranoia that demanded America's destruction. "We have here," he warned, "a force committed fanatically to the belief that with the United States there can be no permanent *modus vivendi*, that it is desirable and necessary that the internal harmony of our society be disrupted, our traditional way of life destroyed, the international authority of our state broken, if Soviet power is to be secure."[4] Writing in *Life* magazine, foreign policy expert (and future secretary of state) John Foster Dulles warned in June that the Soviets intended "to have governments everywhere which accept the doctrine of the Soviet Communist Party." Should the Soviets achieve that goal, he acknowledged, they would gain world hegemony.[5] The report of Clark Clifford and George Elsey on the Soviet danger, presented to President Truman in September 1946, reflected the convictions of Washington insiders. "The key to understanding of current Soviet policy," the report concluded, "is the realization that Soviet leaders adhere to the Marxian theory of ultimate destruction of capitalist states by Communist states."[6]

Of course, the decades-long superpower confrontation—the "Cold War"—began with Washington's refusal to accept the Soviet Union's expansionism in Central and Eastern Europe. In the final days of World War II, the Red Army overran this region and fostered post-war indigenous Communist governments that relied on Moscow and, often, the Soviet military for survival. Washington desired a return to the pre-war status quo in this region, with the re-creation of independent, freely elected, democratic governments as proclaimed at wartime conferences. As a matter of first importance for the future European peace, the Allied governments undertook to determine the fate of Germany. At Yalta, no decision had been reached. What was certain, however, was that Germany would be "de-Nazified" and demilitarized, and forced to pay a large (as yet undetermined) amount of reparations. Wartime arrangements called for temporary military occupation by the victors. Following Germany's surrender, a European Advisory Commission drew the boundaries of the occupation zones into segments of Russian, British, American, and later, French control. The zone assigned to Russia—including Mecklenburg-Pomerania, Brandenburg, Saxony-Anhalt, Thuringia, and all eastward—contained 40 percent of the territory, 36 percent of the population, and 33 percent of the productive resources of pre-1937 Germany. This no doubt seemed a fair division at the time, but it had placed Berlin far within the Soviet zone, a hundred miles or more distant from the British zone. The consequence was that, except by air, American and British access to Berlin was at the option of the Russian occupiers.

The unexpectedly rapid advance of the Anglo-American armies brought them into the Soviet zones of Germany and Austria and also into western Czechoslovakia, which the Russians viewed as within their sphere. Prime Minister Churchill wished to take advantage of Western military success by seizing Berlin and holding all the territory occupied until Stalin could be induced to live up to the promises made at Yalta.[7] Otherwise, Churchill warned, an "iron curtain," which the Russians had already "drawn down upon their front," would descend over a much wider area, and "a broad band of many hundreds of miles of Russian-occupied territory will isolate us from Poland."[8] But Eisenhower, supported by Roosevelt and then by Truman, declined what he thought was a useless advance to Berlin, and Truman refused to postpone the withdrawal of American troops from the Russian zone beyond July 1. The Russians took Berlin, Prague, and Vienna—the three great ancient capitals of Central Europe.

The "Big Three" heads of government held their last wartime meeting at Potsdam, just outside the ruins of Berlin, from July 17 to August 2, 1945. Truman had replaced Roosevelt, and midway through the conference the Labour Party's victory in the British elections saw Churchill and Eden replaced with Clement Attlee and Ernest Bevin as prime minister and foreign secretary, respectively. The atmosphere was friendly, and the discussions were generally good-tempered. Many controversial issues, however, remained unresolved: the West complained of one-party domination in Bulgaria and Rumania, while the Soviets requested British and American recognition of these governments[9]; the Soviets desired control of the Dardanelles and a trusteeship over former Italian possessions in the Mediterranean; and the Americans had interest in the internationalization of such waterways as the Dardanelles and the Danube. On other important matters there was agreement. The task of drawing up treaties with Italy and with the Axis satellites Hungary, Bulgaria, Rumania, and Finland[10] was assigned to a Council of Foreign Ministers, which was to meet in London.

The three leaders agreed that supreme authority in Germany should rest in the hands of the commanders of the four occupying armies, each in his own zone, and acting together in Berlin as a Control Council in matters affecting Germany as a whole. Germany was to be demilitarized, de-Nazified, and democratized; war criminals were to be punished; local German governments were to be established; and certain central administrative departments were to be set up in such fields as finance, transport, communications, foreign trade, and industry. It was expected that Germany would be administered as an economic unit, with common policies in all major fields of economic activity. Production policies were to be adjusted to meet the needs of the occupying forces and displaced persons, and to maintain for the German population a certain (although limited) standard of living. The United States and Britain accepted the Polish occupation of German territory up to the Oder-Neisse line (except the Königsberg area of East Prussia, which was claimed by the Soviets) and the expulsion of the German population from that area, though nominally the fixing of Germany's eastern boundary was reserved for the future treaty of peace. For reparations, the Potsdam agreement authorized each occupying power to remove property from its own zone and to seize German assets abroad. In order to balance the predominance of industry in the Western zones against that of agriculture in the East, Russia was entitled to 10 percent of industrial equipment taken from the Western zones, plus another 15 percent that was to be exchanged for products of the East, chiefly coal, raw materials, and foodstuffs. What remained of the German merchant marine and navy was to be divided equally among the United States, the United Kingdom, and the Soviet Union.

THE SATELLITE TREATIES

The ongoing succession of post-war negotiations and disagreements would ultimately spur the U.S. towards its doctrine of containment. Testament of such fora was the Council of Foreign Ministers that met in London in September 1945, Moscow in December 1945, Paris in April-May and June-July 1946, and New York in November-December 1946, all to work out treaties with the former so-called Axis satellites. The first meeting of the council, to which Secretary of State James Byrnes went "with the atomic bomb in his pocket," produced nothing but an unseemly wrangle. Though the agenda was limited to Europe, Molotov complained repeatedly of the exclusion of the Soviets from a share in the control of Japan. The post-war control of occupation decision-making was a persistent area of disagreement beginning when Italy surrendered in September of 1943. The United States and Britain established and dominated the commission that controlled occupation decisions despite Soviet resentment at being excluded. Moscow, in turn, followed the same pattern when it occupied the countries in Eastern Europe, this time with the West complaining. In Moscow, three months after the initial meeting in London, the Soviet Union consented to the holding of a conference of the Big Five with the 16 other nations that had made more than nominal contributions to the war in Europe. This conference sat in Paris from July 29 to October 15, 1946. Agreement was finally reached in New York in December 1946, and the treaties were signed in Paris on February 10, 1947.

The treaties imposed monetary indemnities on all the former Axis satellites, Finland, Hungary, Rumania, and Bulgaria, as well as on Italy. They required Finland and Rumania to cede territory to the Soviet Union and Italy to surrender its African conquests, and imposed strict limits on their armed forces. Unable to agree on the disposition of Italy's former African possessions—although the Soviets dropped their demand for a Libyan trusteeship—the foreign ministers turned over the problem to the UN General Assembly, which put Libya and Italian Somaliland on the path to independence and federated Eritrea with Ethiopia. The most difficult problem the foreign ministers faced was the conflict between Yugoslavia and Italy over Trieste. The Yugoslav claim was backed by the Kremlin; the Italian claim, by the Western powers. Until 1954, the territory remained under military occupation, the city and northern portion (Zone A) by Anglo-American forces, the remainder (Zone B) by the Yugoslav army. Through an agreement signed on October 5, 1954, Italy received Zone A, with slight adjustments in the boundary; Zone B was retained by Yugoslavia. The Soviet Union, more flexible since Stalin's death in 1953, announced that it approved the settlement. The United States was a party to, and in due time would come to ratify, all these treaties except that with Finland. (The United States had never declared war on Finland, which fought with Germany against the Soviet Union.) As in the case of Rumania, the United States recognized the Communist-dominated government of Bulgaria. At Moscow, in December 1945, Stalin had promised a relaxing of one-party control in Rumania and Bulgaria. The United States had recognized Rumania without waiting for the promise to be fulfilled, and Bulgaria, after waiting a year in vain.

Austria presented further complexities. At Moscow in 1943, the Big Three foreign ministers had promised that Austria—as "the first free country to fall a victim to Hitlerite aggression"—should be "liberated from German domination" and reestablished as "free and independent," and that the way should be opened for the Austrian people to find "political and economic security."[11] At Potsdam, Austria was exempt from the payment of reparations. Yet, like Germany, it was subjected to a four-power occupation, with Vienna a divided city. In November 1945, the Austrians were permitted to elect their own parliament, which was, and remained thereafter, overwhelmingly anti-Communist and pro-Western. Negotiations for a treaty that would liberate the country from military occupation began in 1946, and were only completed in the spring of 1955 when Soviet objections were met. On May 15, 1955, a treaty was signed that ended the occupation and reestablished Austria as a free and independent state. Separate agreements with the Soviet Union and the Western powers guaranteed its neutralization.

THE BREAKDOWN OVER GERMANY

The U.S. doctrinal shift toward containment was further punctuated during the Four-Power Control Council negotiations. Established in Berlin as a means to resolve the apparent differences, the council soon reached a condition of chronic deadlock, resulting from the requirement that all decisions be determined by unanimous vote. While the French, annoyed at their exclusion from Yalta and Potsdam, were guilty of some of the most flagrant obstructionist tactics in the early months of the occupation, ultimately it was the Soviets who thwarted attempts at a common policy for the four zones by repudiating in practice the Potsdam agreement, which specified that Germany should be treated as an economic unit. The consequence was that each of the four powers applied *its* own "ideas" in its zone. In this regard, the Americans vied for democracy that would start from the grass roots and combine with a system of free enterprise. The Soviets forced a union of Communists and Social Democrats to form the Socialist Unity Party, which became their instrument of government. Large landed estates were broken up, and large industries were nationalized. The French and British were less zealous for democracy than the Americans, and the British, under a Labour government, talked little of free enterprise and much of nationalizing the giant Ruhr industries located in their zone. Notwithstanding some differences in policies, the three Western zones were sufficiently alike to make their economic and political union compatible. The Soviets' independent course on reparations—taking from their zone freely whatever they wished in capital goods and current production—and their refusal to send food and raw materials to the Western zones led to an abandonment of the reparations policy in the latter in the spring of 1946 and, a few months later, to the economic union of the American and British zones. Additionally, the Soviets refused an invitation to merge their zone with the "Bizonia" thus formed, denouncing it as a step toward a permanent division of Germany. France also held aloof.

In order to prevent Germany's permanent division and lessen the Western powers' economic support, Secretary of State Byrnes, in a speech at Stuttgart, September 6, 1946, proposed that Germany be reunited, not only economically but politically, with a central government on a federal pattern. To quell French or Russian fears of a revived and rearmed Germany, Byrnes repeated an earlier offer on the part of the United States to sign a 25- or even 40-year four-power treaty to keep Germany disarmed and have American troops in Germany as long as deemed necessary.[12] The Soviet government rejected this offer, and again in March 1947 when George Marshall, then secretary of state, went to Moscow for another meeting of the Council of Foreign Ministers. Insofar as economic unity, the Soviets would only agree to a union on two conditions: a share in control of the industry of the Ruhr and recognition by the West of Russia's claim to $10 billion in reparations. On neither point did Western powers yield. As for political organization, Western allies proposed a relatively loose federal system, while the Russians insisted on a strong centralized government. The former, it was believed, would be a barrier against communism; the latter might facilitate the "communizing" of the entire German state.[13] Not surprisingly, both camps could not resolve their differences, which ultimately led to West Germany becoming a unified entity.

THE CONTAINMENT STRATEGY BEGINS

A mutual antagonism between the two powerhouses had been building up since early 1946. On February 9, Stalin began preparing Soviet citizens, who had suffered incredible wartime hardships, for the sacrifices required to rebuild the devastated countryside. Drawing on Marxist-Leninist predictions of an inevitable war between communism and capitalism, he called for three five-year plans to prepare the Soviet Union for the struggle. Stalin followed his speech with a tightening of the Kremlin's hold on the governments of Eastern Europe and a propaganda campaign directed against the West, especially the United States. According to John Gaddis, Stalin's speech outlined the coming ideological "new pre-war period" of Soviet-U.S. relations.[14] A month later, Winston Churchill—not then a member of the British government—also employed the element of fear at Fulton, Missouri, in delivering his famous denunciation of the "iron curtain" and urged "a fraternal association of English-speaking peoples" to defend the free world.[15] Standing beside Churchill and applauding, President Truman endorsed the growing political chasm. Of course, actions on both sides contributed to the growing tension. These included Washington ignoring the Soviets' application for an American loan; Soviet rejection of Secretary Byrnes's Stuttgart offer; disruption of the reparations program; pressures of Soviets or Soviet satellites on Greece and Turkey; and replacement of negotiations with mutual propagandist oratory in the meetings of the Council of Foreign Ministers. Notwithstanding these developments, toward the end of 1946 there was some hope when the satellite treaties were made and ratified. Soviet troops, whose presence in Iran delayed wartime promises, were finally withdrawn, and Stalin's affable demeanor with visitors from the West presented some optimism for peaceful relations between the opposing systems.

As early as 1945 Truman had been impressed with Stalin, if only in conversation, and would go on to remark in his notes of July 17 that "[he] is honest—but smart as hell," noting yet that he could "deal with Stalin if necessary."[16] Stalin's amiable nature during wartime and post-war conferences, however, was replaced with the machinations of Soviet policy advancement afterwards that would ultimately embolden Truman's doctrine. According to Byrnes, the difference between 1945 and 1946 was that Washington was in fact "facing a new Russia, totally different than the Russia we dealt with a year ago."[17] Any progress that had been attained in the immediate post-war context had now given way to the polarizing situation in Eastern Europe and the broken promises of Yalta. Thus, by the spring of 1947, with the failure of the Moscow Conference and associated Soviet deceptions, combined with the hardening of U.S. policy recommendations with the likes of the Long Telegram, the Clifford-Elsey Report, and Churchill's popular "iron curtain" speech, the Cold War was under way. The new American policy of containment was based on the thesis that the Soviet Union had a persistent tendency to expand the boundaries of its empire wherever possible but would not undertake to do so at the risk of major war. The United States, therefore, in exerting counter pressure to contain the U.S.S.R. and its Communist satellites within their existing bounds, hoped that time and internal strains would eventually sap the strength of the Soviet empire.[18]

While the foreign ministers were wrangling in Moscow, President Truman went before Congress on March 12, 1947, to ask for $400 million in military and economic aid for Greece and Turkey. Since 1945, the royal government of Greece had been struggling against local Communist forces, aided by assistance from Greece's three northern neighbors, satellites of the Soviet Union. Moscow, authorized by the 1936 Montreux Convention, requested a revision of Turkey's role in controlling the straits and the surrender of the districts of Kars and Ardahan at the eastern end of the Black Sea, which Russia had lost at the end of World War I. Britain, which had been aiding both Turkey and Greece, informed Washington in February 1947 that it would no longer be able to do so. The British had in fact been adamant that America play a larger and more direct role in the countering of the Soviet machine, a policy Truman had been hitherto reluctant to take. While England was no doubt in financial troubles following the conclusion of the war, the manner in which it conducted the handover of Greek patronage to the U.S., according to Robert Frazier, was highly suspicious.[19] Whether or not it was Britain's intention for the U.S. to take over in the manner the administration adopted, Truman's doctrine nevertheless made it policy to compete with Soviet expansionism. The president's address to Congress of the Soviet threat and the subsequent dilemma in Greece and Turkey was thus coincidentally also the announcement of the Truman Doctrine: "I believe that it must be the policy of the United States to support free peoples who are resisting attempted subjugation by armed minorities or by outside pressures."[20]

While Truman's proposal met a generally favorable response in the United States, some critics thought that its scope was too broad. It had shifted the narrow concept of assisting a state dealing with an external invasion to include the unlimited prospects of intervening in internal strife. Despite this, and after two months of debate, Congress authorized on May 22, 1947, the expenditure of $100 million in military aid to Turkey and, for Greece, $300 million to be equally divided between military and economic assistance. The act also empowered the president to send military and civilian experts as advisers to the Greek and Turkish governments.

After the Greece and Turkey aid package, the Truman administration moved quickly to expand the doctrine's impact into other areas. In Western Europe, it was viewed that the danger from communism lay principally in the economic stagnation that had followed the war. By the spring of 1947, many of these states were facing a potentially catastrophic situation after an exceptionally severe winter. Food and fuel were in short supply, and foreign exchange—notwithstanding the large dollar loan to England—would be exhausted by the end of the year. Large Communist parties in France and Italy stood ready to benefit from the impending economic collapse caused by unemployment, wartime devastation, and general human suffering. From Washington's perspective, the best chance in halting the spread of indigenous communism appeared to be economic recovery. In this regard, Secretary of State George Marshall, speaking at the Harvard Commencement, June 5, 1947, offered American aid to those European nations that agreed to coordinate their efforts for recovery and present the United States with a program and specifications of their needs. Marshall drew no distinction between Communist and non-Communist Europe, but the Soviet Union spurned the proposal as a new venture in "American imperialism." The satellite governments obeyed the dictum from Moscow, as did Finland and Czechoslovakia, which dared not offend the Soviet giant. While they had been tempted by Marshall's proposal, all three declined with regret.

The other 16 states of Europe (excluding Franco's Spain, which was not invited, and Germany, which as yet had no government) formed a "committee of European Economic Cooperation," which in September 1947 proposed to the United States the achievement by 1951 of a self-sufficient European economy, at an estimated cost of $19.3 billion. In December, President Truman laid the proposal before Congress with a request for $6.8 billion for the first 15 months of the program and $10.2 billion for the succeeding three years, a total of $17 billion. In explaining his request, the president said: "I am proposing that this Nation contribute to world peace and to its own security by assisting in the recovery of sixteen countries which, like the United States, are devoted to the preservation of free institutions and enduring peace among nations."[21] While Congress adjusted the figure, on April 3, 1948, it established the Economic Cooperation Administration to handle the program and at the end of June appropriated an initial $4 billion for the program. (Almost all of the money was spent in the United States to purchase industrial equipment and supplies, thus stimulating the host country's economy.) The European Recovery Program, which continued for three years, ultimately cost the United States $13 billion and contributed to an impressive European economic recovery.

The Marshall Plan was designed to aid in the recovery of nations with advanced economies that had been dislocated by the war. By increasing production and trade, and alleviating unemployment and poverty, its authors expected it to stymie the expansion of communism among the working classes of Europe. However, Washington was also worried about the threat of communism among the poverty-stricken masses in countries of Asia, Africa, and Latin America who were also without a stable economic foundation. As such, the global containment of communism in Truman's doctrine would now call for measures to raise the standard of living in these states. In an address on January 20, 1949, the president proposed a "Point Four," or technical assistance, program in which the United States would "embark on a bold new program for making the benefits of our scientific advances and industrial progress available for the improvement and growth of underdeveloped areas."[22] While the Point Four program was launched in 1950 with a modest appropriation of $35 million, it increased authorized expenditures for 1951–1954 to nearly $400 million. In 1953, the program was placed, with other forms of foreign aid, under the Foreign Operations Administration (FOA).

THE GERMAN DICHOTOMY

Further definition to the Truman Doctrine would also emanate from key developments in Germany. Failure of the foreign ministers to reach agreement on Germany's future in 1947 (discussed earlier) had led the Western powers to join their three zones and create a unified and self-governing West Germany. Consultations in London in the spring of 1948 by representatives of France, Britain, and the United States, as well as the three Benelux countries (Belgium, the Netherlands, and Luxembourg), resulted in agreements on June 7, proposing the creation of a West German government. As a safeguard, an international authority representing the six states and West Germany would control the Ruhr industries. The Germans of the Western zones would elect members of a constituent assembly. This body would then draw up a constitution for a federal state, which might eventually include the Eastern zone. The new government would exercise sovereignty over its domestic affairs and limited control over foreign relations; however, the ban on rearmament would remain, and the military occupation would continue "until the peace of Europe is secured."[23] The West German Constituent Assembly met at Bonn, on September 1, 1948, and proceeded to prepare a constitution. A German Federal Republic, comprising the three Western zones, was inaugurated at Bonn in September 1949. While occupation forces remained, military government ended and Allied authority would be exercised through a High Commission to which the United States, France, and the United Kingdom each appointed one member. The Federal Republic was soon made eligible for Marshall Plan aid and was given a voice in the international control of the Ruhr. Under its first chancellor, Konrad Adenauer (1949–1963), it showed a spirit of willing cooperation with the West.

Not surprisingly, the Soviets criticized these Western moves. They interpreted the Marshall Plan as an aggressive U.S. scheme and were concerned with the ambitions of the new West German government. In response, they held a conference of nine East European states in Warsaw during September 1947, which resolved to do everything possible to defeat the program of "American imperialism." Communist-inspired strikes in France and Italy sought in vain to deter these states from accepting Marshall Plan aid. The Communist Information Bureau (Cominform), a successor of the Comintern, was established at Belgrade. Defensive alliances linking the Soviet Union with Bulgaria, Finland, Hungary, and Rumania were added to treaties previously negotiated with Czechoslovakia, Poland, and Yugoslavia. As the West moved toward the unification of West Germany, Moscow tightened its grip on its satellite states. In February 1948, a Communist coup overthrew the democratic government of Czechoslovakia and installed one firmly attached to Moscow. The Soviets encountered resistance when Yugoslavia, under Tito's leadership, broke with the Cominform and with Moscow. Tito's government remained firmly Communist, but it ceased to take orders from the Kremlin and assumed a neutralist position in the Cold War.

When the six-power talks on Germany opened in London, the Soviets complained that the Western powers were destroying the four-power control of Germany that had been agreed to three years earlier and, hence, that they must leave Berlin. The Western Allies, on the other hand, maintained that they were in Berlin by virtue of their role in the defeat of Germany. Stalin attempted to squeeze the Western forces out of Berlin, which lay well within the Soviet zone and with no guaranteed connecting surface corridor. Restrictions on movement to and from the city were first imposed in April 1948, and by June all surface transportation between Berlin and the Western zones was halted. The Western powers faced either withdrawing their garrisons from Berlin or finding means of supplying them and the 2 million people of West Berlin. Rejecting advice that he "call the Russian bluff"—opening the roads by military force—President Truman and the British resorted to air transport, authorized by signed agreements with the Soviets. The airlift started at once, and by September 1, American and British planes were flying into Berlin 4,000 tons of supplies daily. Soviet aircraft occasionally harassed the American and British cargo planes but were instructed not to attack. Allied persistence and patience eventually paid off. In May 1949, the Soviet Union ended the blockade.

In October 1949, after the inauguration of the German Federal Republic at Bonn, the People's Council in Berlin proclaimed a new government for the

Soviet zone of Germany. The new German Democratic Republic, East Germany, rested on a constitution designed, like that at Bonn, to unite all of Germany. Two Germanys had come into being and would wait several decades for unification.

COLLECTIVE DEFENSE AGREEMENTS

The Communist coup in Czechoslovakia and the Berlin blockade alarmed the Western powers and would play a significant role in emboldening the Truman Doctrine. Though the blockade had been ended, there was no guarantee that the Soviets might not make a new attempt to oust the West from Berlin or to prevent the formation of the German Federal Republic. While the Soviets had reduced their armed forces from 11.5 million men to fewer than 3 million,[24] they still far outnumbered those available in the West. Their numerical superiority, it was feared, might tempt Moscow to commit some form of an aggressive act. Up until this stage, containment of the Soviets had been dependent chiefly on economic and political means, but now, containment via military power was also being considered an option. Indeed, if the Soviet Union could be warned that an act of aggression against any one of the free nations of Western Europe would mean hostilities with the others, and also with the United States, it might well be deterred. Notwithstanding the United Nations' inability—based on the Soviet veto—to provide such a deterrent, Article 51 of the UN Charter legalized "collective self-defense" by groups within the United Nations. In the Americas, the Rio Pact of September 2, 1947, had already invoked Article 51 in a hemispheric collective security agreement. In Europe, a beginning was made in March 1948, when Britain, France, and the Benelux states signed at Brussels a 50-year treaty of economic, social, and cultural collaboration and collective self-defense. However, as a means to bolster the treaty, it needed the backing of the United States.

The military arm of the doctrine came to the fore on March 17, 1948, when President Truman proposed to "restore the strength" of the United States' forces in an address to Congress. After warning of the Soviet danger, he urged the adoption of a universal military training program and temporary reenactment of selective service legislation. The United States had also greatly reduced its military after the war. The build-up of American armed strength began with the enactment by Congress of a new selective service, or draft, law in June 1948. With the draft and under the stimulus of war in Korea, which began in June 1950, the strength of the army, navy, and air force grew from 1,350,000 in 1948 to 3,630,000 in June 1952. For the first time in nearly a century and a half, the Vandenberg Resolution of June 11, 1948, agreed that the United States should, among other measures for promoting peace, associate itself, "by constitutional process, with such regional and other collective arrangements as are based on continuous and effective self-help and mutual aid, and as affect its national security." The United States would also, the resolution declared, make clear "its determination to exercise the right of individual or collective self-defense under article 51 should any armed attack occur affecting its national security."[25]

The Vandenberg Resolution would become the prelude to the North Atlantic Treaty, an ambitious venture in search of collective security. The treaty—a pronounced departure from the doctrinal principle of "no entangling alliances"—was signed on April 4, 1949, by 12 states of the North Atlantic and Western Europe. This number increased to 15 by the accession of Greece and Turkey in 1952 and West Germany in 1955.[26] The parties agreed to settle peacefully all disputes between themselves and to develop their capacity to resist armed attack "by means of continuous and effective self-help and mutual aid." But the heart of the treaty was Article 5, which declared that an armed attack on any one of the members in Europe or North America would be considered an attack on all, and pledged each member in case of such an attack to assist the party attacked "by such action as it deems necessary, including the use of armed force."[27] Thus began the North Atlantic Treaty Organization, or NATO, with the North Atlantic Council, consisting of the foreign, defense, and finance ministers of the member states, as its directing body.

NATO AND NSC-68

The United States took the lead in providing and organizing the military deterrent envisaged by the framers of the North Atlantic Treaty. The American position in the superpower struggle was aggressively defined in a top-secret document labeled NSC-68, prepared by the State and Defense Departments in the spring of 1950. NSC-68 started from a vastly overstated assumption as to Soviet intentions, which, as Secretary of State Dean Acheson admitted, was opposed by some of the more prominent Soviet experts in the State Department. In this analysis, the Russian threat, in Acheson's words, "combined the ideology of Communist doctrine and the power of the Russian state into an aggressive expansionist drive, which found its chief opponent, and, therefore, target in the antithetical ideas and power of our own country." The threat to Western Europe, he thought, seemed "singularly like that which Islam had posed centuries before, with its combination of ideological zeal and fighting power."[28] With such an extravagantly perceived threat to Western Europe and ultimately to the United States, NSC-68 recommended that the United States "strike out on a bold and massive program of rebuilding the West's defensive potential to surpass that of the Soviet world, and of meeting each fresh challenge promptly and unequivocally."[29] With the security of the free world at stake, costs of such a program were immaterial. The country could afford to spend, if necessary, 20 percent of its gross national product on defense. President Truman quietly approved NSC-68 in September 1950. This was the first of several U.S. government overstatements of Soviet goals issued during the ensuing decades, designed to arouse what was perceived as a flagging public to the need for more militant and expensive Cold War policies. In essence, according to Ernest R. May, NSC-68 was the prototype for Truman's militarization of the Cold War, while the escalation of the situation in Korea supported the ambitious funding the document prescribed.[30]

The assumption of NSC-68 as to Moscow's aggressive purposes seemed to Acheson and others to be borne out by events in the Far East and by the revelation, in August 1949, that the Soviet Union had successfully exploded its first atomic bomb. Of course, this dimension of horror was exacerbated when the Chinese Communists' conquest of the mainland was complete in the summer of 1949, and the government of the People's Republic of China was proclaimed in Beijing on October 1. The Chinese Communists were, incorrectly as it turned out, regarded as puppets of Moscow and their victory as a major triumph in the Kremlin's program of world revolution. Additionally, on June 25, 1950—with the approval of Stalin and several months before the approval of NSC-68—Communist North Korea forcefully attempted to unify the state. Korea was in essence divided into two zones until a peaceful unification could be negotiated, the North under the influence of the Soviet Union and the South occupied by the United States. Unable to resolve their ideological disagreements, the North attacked the South in 1950, which was perceived by Washington to be yet another Soviet attempt at enlarging its empire.[31] Here was a "fresh challenge" of the kind that NSC-68 had said should be met "promptly and unequivocally," and this North Korean "action" made the task of selling NSC-68 to the American public a much easier proposition.

With the Korean War under way, the United States, working now through NATO, began building the military defenses in Western Europe against supposed Soviet plans for an attack. Early in 1951, the North Atlantic Council set up military headquarters near Paris, known as SHAPE (Supreme Headquarters, Allied Powers in Europe), with General Dwight Eisenhower as Supreme Commander. Its purpose was to build a defense force in Western Europe, not equal to the army maintained by the Soviet Union (175 Russian divisions and 60 or more divisions from the satellite states), but strong enough to hold the Soviet forces in check until the United States' strategic airpower could, with atomic bombs, destroy the centers of Soviet strength. Thus, American aid to Europe—a significant strand of the doctrine—shifted from the economic to the military. From October 1949 to the end of 1953, the

United States supplied nearly $6 billion worth of arms and military equipment to its European allies, as well as $1.7 billion worth to other states. The United States also increased its divisions stationed in Germany and Austria from two to six, following an extensive debate in which the Senate approved this increase but advised against sending additional troops abroad without the consent of Congress. European allies in the same period spent more than $35 billion in building up their military forces and installations. The overall result saw a marked increase in troops, planes, and airfields available for NATO responses.

Throughout this period, the United States strongly urged the inclusion of West German units in the defense forces. The prospect of a rearmed and nationalistic Germany was almost as alarming to France and the Benelux states as the Soviet danger. The French government proposed a European Defense Community (EDC) that would make it possible to use and yet control German troops by integrating them with those of France, Italy, and the Benelux states. Despite urgent pleas by U.S. secretary of state John Foster Dulles, however, the French Assembly in August 1954 finally rejected the proposal. A substitute was found in a set of treaties constituting Western European Union (WEU)—an alliance rather than the EDC's organic union—that became effective on May 6, 1955. Under this arrangement, Italy and the Federal Republic of (West) Germany were admitted to the Brussels Pact alliance of 1948 with Britain, France, and the three Benelux states. West Germany recovered its sovereignty and was permitted to rearm, though pledging itself not to manufacture atomic, chemical, or bacteriological weapons. U.S., British, and French troops were to remain in West Germany for its defense and that of the North Atlantic area until the Bonn government could provide its own defense forces. Additionally, West Germany would become a member of NATO and the armed forces of the Western European Union, and—with certain exceptions—became subject to the NATO supreme command. Of course, to lessen French fears of a rearmed Germany, Britain and the United States agreed, in principle, to maintain substantial military forces on the continent.

But despite such plans for a substantial NATO army, it was evident by 1955 that these would never fully materialize based on state considerations and priorities. Indeed, even with the strength garnered from the addition of the West German army to NATO forces, this too was largely offset by losses elsewhere. The nationalist rebellion against the French in Algeria, which had begun in 1954, drew off the greater part of the French forces that had been committed to NATO. Pressure for economic well-being, doubt as to the efficacy of conventional forces in an age of nuclear weapons and long-range ballistic missiles, and occasional relaxation in East-West tensions led to reductions in other national contingents. The goal of 96 divisions set at the Lisbon meeting of the North Atlantic Council in 1952 was abandoned, and the "irreducible minimum" of 30 divisions, announced year after year by American Supreme Commanders at SHAPE, was never attained. Shortages of manpower, indeed, were compensated for by increases in firepower, as NATO troops in Europe were gradually equipped with tactical (low-yield) atomic weapons. These were supplied by the United States, and their atomic warheads were kept under American custody as required by the U.S. Atomic Energy Act. Any satisfaction afforded by this modernization of weaponry was qualified, however, by the reflection that the Soviets would feel it necessary to make similar improvements.

As for the Kremlin, it had watched with misgivings the formation of NATO and the Western European Union, and in particular, the plans for rearming West Germany. It tried to stymie the process through threats, persuasion, and offers of compromise, but was largely ignored. What the Soviets feared most was the rearming of West Germany, especially the possibility that German troops, under the NATO umbrella, might acquire atomic weapons. Having failed in their attempts to block these measures of the West, they turned to countermeasures. At Warsaw on May 14, 1955, the Soviets negotiated an alliance of eight Communist states—the Warsaw Pact—for defense against any aggressive intentions of NATO.

AN INCREASE IN ARMS ON BOTH SIDES

Weapons postures had been slowly changing since the end of the war. Since 1945 the United States had held a monopoly on atomic weapons, including an increasing fleet of long-range bombers under the Strategic Air Command (SAC), capable of destroying Soviet centers of population and industry. In 1949, however, the Soviet Union at considerable expense exploded its first atomic bomb to reestablish a balance of power. Four years later, it followed the United States by only a few months in setting off its first hydrogen—or thermonuclear—device, thus closing the gap between the nuclear-weapon capabilities of the two superpowers. The Soviet success in launching the rocket-propelled satellites Sputnik I and Sputnik II (October 4 and November 3, 1957) and the Americans' development of the Atlas and Titan missiles ushered in the age of the intercontinental ballistic missile (ICBM), with its no less potent relative in the form of the intermediate-range ballistic missile (IRBM) and the less vulnerable submarine-launched ballistic missiles (SLBMs). These missiles soon became the primary carriers of nuclear destruction, although the slower and more vulnerable bombers remained one leg of the U.S. nuclear triad. While the Soviets lagged behind in numbers of ICBMs in the 1960s, by the 1970s they had all but secured parity in nuclear weaponry.

Since each had achieved the unquestioned power to destroy the other, the prospect of a nuclear war had become unthinkable. Although terms such as the "balance of terror" or "mutual deterrence" described the relationship, each government continued to search for more powerful and reliable weapons. Initially, this search involved the decision to explode test nuclear devices in the atmosphere, with the resulting fallout of radioactive particles that created worldwide hazards to health. An unofficial moratorium on such tests was instituted in 1958, but the Eisenhower administration was unable—some officials even unwilling—to agree to a formula to terminate this hazard. As such, in 1961 the testing resumed. Shortly after the nerve-racking Cuban missile crisis, the Kennedy administration, aided by the British prime minister and a more cooperative Soviet leader under Nikita Khrushchev, temporarily resolved the issue. On August 5, 1963, the three powers signed the Limited Test Ban Treaty (LTBT), by which they agreed to abstain from exploding nuclear devices in the atmosphere, in outer space, and underwater; although underground tests were still permitted. The treaty was promptly ratified by the signatories and adhered to by most of the governments, excluding France, Israel, Communist China, and Cuba.[32] The quest for a comprehensive nuclear test ban, which many believed would reduce the proliferation of nuclear weapons, remained moribund at the negotiating table.

CONCLUSION

The economic and technological superiority of the U.S. following the war provided the Truman administration with a bundle of policy options previously unobtainable in American history. Combined with the threat of Soviet expansionism, as expounded by George Kennan's famous telegram, and Stalin's failure to live up to the agreements set down in wartime conferences, Washington feared that a domino effect would engulf Western Europe if it did not attempt to affect the outcome. The Truman Doctrine was thus an offset of the U.S.'s new economic and technological superiority and the animosity it drew from the Soviet Union's policies against liberal democracy, circumstances the Truman administration would attempt to exploit.

Washington's responsibilities in Europe as the creator of the atomic bomb and guarantor of the status quo boosted the appearance that it held the upper hand in diplomacy with the Soviet Union. Post-war Europe was Washington's chance to diplomatically undo Europe's underlying antagonisms, including the threat of communism. However, the bomb in the pocket refused to show diplomatic dividends, marking instead a greater distrust between the opposing ideological forces. According to Kissinger "[b]y the end of the [Postdam] conference it was clear that the atom bomb had not made the Soviets more co-operative—at least not in the absence of more threatening diplomacy."[33] Washington's acceptance of the containment thesis further added to the increasing volatility of relations. Truman was convinced enough that if economic aid wasn't enough to discourage Soviet aggression from communist expansion in Europe and elsewhere, military supremacy would need to be a consideration. Yet, with Russia's advancements in atomic and hydrogen weaponry, NSC-68, and the Korean War, it became apparent in Washington that further integration of democratic forces was necessary if the status quo was to be upheld. The North Atlantic Treaty Organization answered this issue. Washington's departure from non-entangling alliances came at the expense of further polarization of the two ideological camps. The ensuing rise of the security dilemma provided the impetus for further developments in technological and weaponry capacities, beginning the largest and most destructive arms race in history. The resulting new terrain of international relations had clearly become bipolar, and would ultimately see American presidential doctrine consequently embroiled in regional conflicts and "transitions" on a global scale for the next four decades.

NOTES

1. Early predictions of Soviet expansionism included Joseph C. Grew, *Turbulent Era: A Diplomatic Record of Forty Years, 1904–1945*, Walter Johnson, ed., Boston: Houghton Mifflin, 1952, vol. 2: 1446; Mark Ethridge's memorandum on Bulgaria and Rumania, December 7, 1945, *Foreign Relations of the United States, Diplomatic Papers* (hereafter *FRUS*), 1945, Washington, DC: U.S. Government Printing Office, 1967, vol. 5: 637; John D. Hickerson to James Byrnes, December 10, 1945, *ibid.*, Washington, 1968, vol. 4: p. 407; Joint Chiefs of Staff quoted in Melvyn P. Leffler, *A Preponderance of Power*, Stanford, CA: Stanford University Press, 1992, p. 50. Also see Richard Dean Burns, Joseph M. Siracusa, and Jason Flanagan, *American Foreign Relations since Independence,* Santa Barbara, CA: Praeger, 2013.

2. Joseph and Stewart Alsop, "Tragedy of Liberalism," *Life* 20, May 20, 1946, p. 69.

3. Edwin G. Wilson to Byrnes, March 18, 1946, *FRUS*, 1946, Washington, DC: U.S. Government Printing Office, vol. 7, 1969, pp. 818–19; George Lewis Jones to Loy Henderson, August 9, 1946, *ibid.*, p. 830; Acheson to Byrnes, August 15, 1946, *ibid.*, pp. 840–41.

4. For Kennan's Long Telegram of February 22, 1946, see George F. Kennan, *Memoirs: 1925–1950*, Boston: Little, Brown, 1967, p. 547–59.

5. On the fears of U.S. officials, see John Lewis Gaddis, *The United States and the Origins of the Cold War, 1941–1947*, New York: Columbia University Press, 1972, p. 319; and John Foster Dulles, "Thoughts on Soviet Foreign Policy and What to Do about It," *Life*, June 3, 1946, pp. 113–26; June 10, 1946, p. 19–20.

6. The Clifford-Elsey Report, "American Relations with the Soviet Union," in Arthur Krock, *Memoirs: Sixty Years on the Firing Line*, New York: Funk & Wagnalls, 1968, pp. 427, 431.

7. Winston S. Churchill, *Triumph and Tragedy*, vol. 6 of *The Second World War*, Boston: Houghton Mifflin, 1953, p. 456.

8. *Ibid.*, p. 573.

9. At the end of May, Truman sent Harry Hopkins to Moscow to seek agreement on Poland. Stalin consented to the admission of Mikolajczyk and other non-Communist Poles to the Provisional Government of National Unity, recognized by the United States and the United Kingdom.

10. Finland, defeated and having lost part of her territory to Russia in 1939–1940, had joined Germany in the war against the Soviets after June 1941.

11. See the "Declaration on Austria," The Moscow Conference, October 1943, The Avalon Project, available at: http://avalon.law.yale.edu/wwii/moscow.asp.

12. *Documents on American Foreign Relations*, vol. 8: 210–18. This was a startling offer in light of President Roosevelt's statement to Stalin that American troops would remain in Europe no longer than two years.

13. *U.S. in World Affairs*, 1947–1948, p. 78.

14. Cited in John L. Gaddis, *We Now Know: Rethinking Cold War History*, New York: Oxford University Press, 1997, p. 23.

15. See Winston Churchill's speech "Sinews of Peace," 1946, Fulton, Missouri. National Churchill Museum, available at http://www.nationalchurchillmuseum.org/sinews-of-peace-iron-curtain-speech.html.

16. Robert H. Ferrell, *Off the Record: The Private Papers of Harry S. Truman*, New York: Harper and Row, 1980, p. 44.

17. Cited in Henry Kissinger, *Diplomacy*, New York: Simon and Schuster Paperbacks, 1994, p. 437.

18. Authorship of the "containment" policy is attributed to George F. Kennan, a Foreign Service officer who became head of the new Policy Planning Staff in the State Department in the spring of 1947. Kennan expounded "containment" in an anonymous article (signed "X"), "The Sources of Soviet Conduct," in *Foreign Affairs* 25, July 1947, pp. 566–82; republished in G. F. Kennan, *American Diplomacy, 1900–1950*, Chicago: University of Chicago Press, 1951, pp. 107–28; he and his staff also played a part in the Marshall Plan. See George. F. Kennan, *Memoirs, 1925–1950*, Boston: Atlantic Monthly Press, 1967, chapters 14–15; Joseph M. Jones, *The Fifteen Weeks*, New York: Viking Press, 1955, pp. 154–55, 255; Dean Acheson, *Present at the Creation: My Years in the State Department*, New York: W. W. Norton, 1969, chapters 24–26.

19. Robert Frazier, "Did Britain Start the Cold War? Bevin and the Truman Doctrine," *The Historical Journal* 27, No. 3, 1984, pp. 715–727.

20. President Harry S. Truman's address before a joint session of Congress, March 12, 1947, The Avalon Project, available at: http://avalon.law.yale.edu/20th_century/trudoc.asp.

21. Harry S. Truman Special Message to Congress on the Marshall Plan, December 19, 1947, The American Presidency Project, available at: http://www.presidency.ucsb.edu/ws/?pid=12805.

22. *Documents on American Foreign Relations*, vol. 11: 10.

23. *Documents on American Foreign Relations*, vol. 10: 106–27.

24. Adam B. Ulam, *Expansion and Coexistence: The History of Soviet Foreign Policy, 1917–1967*, New York: Praeger, 1968, p. 404.

25. *Documents on American Foreign Relations*, vol. 10: 302; A. H. Vandenberg Jr., ed., *The Private Papers of Senator Vandenberg*, Boston: Houghton Mifflin, 1952, pp. 403–11.

26. The 12 original signers were the United States, Canada, Iceland, the United Kingdom, France, Belgium, the Netherlands, Luxembourg, Denmark, Norway, Portugal, and Italy.

27. The North Atlantic Treaty, Washington DC, April 4, 1949, available at: http://www.nato.int/cps/en/natolive/official_texts_17120.htm.

28. Acheson, *Present at the Creation*, pp. 375–77, 752–53. Also see Joseph M. Siracusa, "NSC 68: A Reappraisal," *Naval War College Review* 33, 1980, pp. 4–14.

29. National Security Council document 68: United States Objectives and Programs for National Security, April 14, 1950, Federation of American Scientists, available at: http://www.fas.org/irp/offdocs/nsc-hst/nsc-68.htm.

30. See Ernest R. May, *American Cold War Strategy: Interpreting NSC-68*, New York: Bedford Books, 1993.

31. For a different view, see Norman A. Graebner, Richard Dean Burns, and Joseph M. Siracusa, *America and the Cold War, 1941–1991: A Realist Interpretation*, 2 vols., Santa Barbara, CA: Praeger, 2010, vol. 1, pp. 194–209.

32. The treaty was open to other nations for signature, and 124 states had acceded to it by 2003. Richard Dean Burns, *The Evolution of Arms Control: From Antiquity to the Nuclear Age*, Santa Barbara, CA: Praeger, 2009, p. 125.

33. Cited in Henry Kissinger, *Diplomacy*, New York: Simon and Schuster, 1994, p. 437.

Chapter Five

Maintaining the "Outside"

With the communist "threat" clearly articulated under Truman, American presidential doctrine maintained a tradition of ensuring that containing such a threat—albeit at varying levels—would now be a significant component of U.S. foreign policy. Beginning with Eisenhower, this chapter will illustrate the quest to thwart any advance of "creeping socialism" in U.S. domestic policy, while also rolling back the advances of communism abroad. After taking office in 1953, Eisenhower devised a new foreign policy tactic to contain the Soviet Union and even win back territory that had already been lost. Devised primarily by Secretary of State John Foster Dulles, this so-called "new look" at foreign policy proposed the use of nuclear weapons and new technology—rather than ground troops and conventional bombs—in an effort to threaten "massive retaliation" against the U.S.S.R. or communist advances abroad. Announced by the president in a message to the United States Congress on January 5, 1957, the Eisenhower Doctrine also signified that a country could request "aid against overt armed aggression from any nation controlled by international communism . . . to secure and protect" its "territorial integrity and political independence."[1]

Of course, all this was partially in response to the Soviet Union's attempt to use the Suez War as a pretext to enter Egypt. Coupled with the power vacuum left by the decline of British and French influence in the region after their failure in the said war, Eisenhower felt that a strong position was needed to address the complications presented by Egypt's Gamal Abdel Nasser. Nasser, who had rapidly built up a local power base, was using Soviet-American tensions to extract concessions from either power using the so-called policy of "positive neutrality." The military action provisions of the Eisenhower Doctrine were applied in the Lebanon Crisis the following year, when America intervened in response to a request by that country's presi-

107

dent. Additionally, the doctrine endorsed the restoration of Mohammed Reza Shah Pahlavi in Iran and demonstrated the growing importance of oil in American foreign-policy decision-making.

As a corollary to Eisenhower's policy attempt to roll back the communist threat abroad, Kennedy's doctrine similarly answered the threat to maintain those challenges on the "outside." While not fully articulated, the Kennedy Doctrine became evident in the months just after the president took office when Soviet premier Nikita Khrushchev threatened to sign a treaty with East Germany that would cut off the city of Berlin from the United States and Western Europe. Although the Soviet Union never signed any such treaty, it did construct a massive wall of concrete and barbed wire around West Berlin in 1961 to prevent East Germans from escaping to the Western-controlled part of the city. Over the years, guard towers were installed, and the "no man's land" between the inner and outer walls was mined and booby-trapped, making it near impossible for East Germans to escape to West Berlin without being killed or captured. Over the ensuing decades, the Berlin Wall came to be the most famous symbol of the Cold War.

In addition to European developments, this chapter considers the issue of decolonization and how it posed a particularly difficult problem for a U.S. government committed to halting the spread of communism. As new independent states were formed from old European colonies in Africa, Asia, and the Middle East, Kennedy faced an increasingly difficult task of ensuring that communists did not seize power.

Complicating the situation was the fact that Eisenhower's stated policy of "massive retaliation," which threatened to use nuclear weapons to halt communist expansion, effectively impeded the president. On one hand, Kennedy would lose credibility if he allowed communism to take root in any of these newly decolonized states. At the same time, however, he wanted to do anything he could to avoid using nuclear weapons. The growing communist power in the Southeast Asian country of Laos made this catch-22 very real. After carefully considering his options, Kennedy finally decided not to use military force and instead convened a multinational peace conference in Geneva in 1962 to end the civil war that had erupted in Laos. Additionally, hoping never to have to decide between nuclear war and political embarrassment again, Kennedy devised a new strategy of "flexible response" to deal with the U.S.S.R. Crafted with the aid of Defense Secretary Robert S. McNamara, the flexible response doctrine was meant to allow the president to combat Soviet advances around the world through a variety of means. In other words, Kennedy could send money or troops to fight communist insurgents, authorize the CIA to topple an unfriendly government, or, as a last resort, use nuclear weapons.[2]

FROM UNEASY COEXISTENCE TO DÉTENTE

The death in March 1953 of Marshal Josef Stalin was the prelude to the rise to power in Moscow of more flexible leadership in the form of Nikita S. Khrushchev. In March 1958, he took over the premiership from Nikolai A. Bulganin, who was a close ally of Khrushchev's at the time. At the Twentieth Congress of the Communist Party of the Soviet Union meeting in Moscow, during February 1956, Khrushchev secretly condemned Stalin's bloodthirsty methods and outdated policies. He enunciated a policy of "peaceful coexistence," repudiating the Leninist doctrine of inevitable war between the communist and capitalist societies, declaring rather that communism could achieve its victory by peacefully demonstrating its superiority. The Soviet government, meanwhile, having negotiated the Warsaw Pact in response to NATO, signed a treaty on May 15, 1955, ending the occupation of Austria and accepting on the same day an invitation from the United States, Britain, and France for a summit meeting of the Big Four heads of government at Geneva in July.

At Geneva, July 18 to 23, 1955, President Eisenhower, British prime minister Anthony Eden (who had recently succeeded Winston Churchill), French premier Edgar Faure, Soviet premier Bulganin, their foreign ministers, and other dignitaries (including, of course, Party Secretary Khrushchev) met face to face in an effort to resolve critical East-West difficulties. The meeting had been heralded by Moscow and Washington as a promising development, and its sessions were conducted in a tone of cordiality. On substantive matters, however, no agreement was achieved as neither side was ready to offer concessions. Richard Immerman, who wrote of the summit in "'Trust in the Lord But Keep Your Powder Dry': American Policy Aims at Geneva," argued that the outcome was preconceived. Washington's pretense at the summit, he argues, was rather "to steer the talks away from substantive issues" that might reveal a lack of consensus among the allies.[3] Moscow's summit rigidity, according to Vladislav Zubok, was maintained by internal power struggles and the esoteric goal of dealing with the West "without being intimidated."[4]

Thus it was in this climate that Eisenhower's ambitious proposal that East and West exchange "blueprints" of their armed forces and permit mutual "open skies" aerial inspection of their territory was rejected as being a form of espionage. (No similar objection was raised when orbital "spy" satellites were introduced.) On disarmament, the West considered effective inspection essential; the Soviets held it inadmissible, often because they did not wish to expose their weaknesses. It was only on "freer cultural exchanges" that there was any meeting of minds. An important characteristic of Soviet policy after Stalin was a relaxation of Moscow's control of communist parties and governments in neighboring states. The dissident Marshal Tito of Yugoslavia, after playing host to Khrushchev, was welcomed on a visit to Moscow and assured that the Kremlin accepted the principle of "national Communism," which Tito espoused. Encouraged by this display of conciliation toward Yugoslavia, the Polish Communists installed a pronounced anti-Stalinist, Wladyslaw Gomulka, as party secretary and dissuaded Khrushchev from interfering. Still communist and continuing to adhere to the Warsaw Alliance, the Polish regime had successfully defied the dictatorship of the Kremlin.

From 1955 to 1963, relations among the United States and its NATO allies with the Soviet bloc, so far as Europe was concerned, were in a state of fluctuating crises. The first serious crisis after the Geneva summit meeting of 1955 was a dual predicament produced by Soviet suppression of Hungary's attempted anti-communist revolution, and by Israel, France, and Britain's attack on Egypt.

In Hungary, anti-Soviet and anti-government riots in Budapest led to the formation of a new government on October 24, 1956, headed by Imre Nagy. A few days later, Nagy, though a communist, admitted non-communists to his government. On November 1, the government repudiated the Warsaw Alliance, declared Hungary a neutral state, and appealed to the United Nations for assistance. Moscow reacted violently to Hungary's secession from the communist bloc. After temporarily withdrawing its tanks and troops from Budapest, it sent them back in force, suppressed the popular uprising in the city, and installed a new communist government headed by Janos Kadar. Initially taking refuge in the Yugoslav embassy, Nagy was enticed out by hints of office in the new government, and quickly seized, abducted to Rumania, and executed. Despite weeks of fighting that followed, a virtually unarmed populace was no match for Soviet tanks. No aid came from the West, for doing so would likely have been considered by Moscow as an act of war. The collapse of the insurrection was inevitable.

In Washington, Dwight D. Eisenhower had been elected to the presidency in 1952 after a Republican campaign condemning the "containment" policy of the Democrats. The Republicans had slammed the policy as "negative, futile, and immoral" and promised to "again make liberty into a beacon light of hope that will penetrate the dark places."[5] "Liberation" of peoples under the communist yoke was to replace containment of communism. Whether the Hungarians had been encouraged to hope for aid by these campaign declarations and by the official Voice of America and unofficial Radio Free Europe broadcasts is impossible to say. Dulles was accused by some commentators of giving false hope to the Hungarian movement.[6] However, it was neither President Eisenhower nor the secretary of state's intention to encourage a popular rebellion against impossible odds or to assist such a rebellion at the risk of war with the Soviet Union. Action by Washington was limited to the expression of sympathy for the Hungarian people and the offering of asylum in the United States to Hungarian refugees.

The next serious crisis concerned Berlin. In a speech on November 10, 1958, and in notes to the United States, Britain, and France on the 27th, Khrushchev demanded an end to the occupation of West Berlin by the three Western powers. He insisted on a solution within six months, threatening otherwise to make a separate peace treaty with East Germany and leave the Allies to negotiate their rights in, and their access to, Berlin with an East German government they did not recognize. Any attempt to maintain their position by force, Khrushchev warned, would be met by the full power of the Warsaw Alliance. The Soviet ultimatum received a unified response from the Western powers. In Paris, on December 14, the foreign ministers of the United States, Britain, France, and West Germany joined in an unqualified rejection of the Soviet ultimatum, and the NATO Council endorsed their position two days later. Briefly stated, the Western argument was that the Soviet Union had no right by unilateral action to cancel the rights of the Western Allies in West Berlin, which were theirs by virtue of the common victory over Germany. The Allies also emphasized their obligation to maintain the freedom of the more than two million people of West Berlin. They expressed their desire to see the Berlin question settled as a part of the German question as a whole and repeated their proposal that Germany be unified through the holding of free elections in both parts of the divided country.

Faced with determined and united Western opposition, Khrushchev first withdrew his time limit. From May 11 to June 30 and again from July 13 to August 5, 1959, the foreign ministers met at Geneva, but reached no agreement on this or on any of the other major issues. Eisenhower, who had at first made some preliminary agreement a prerequisite of another summit meeting, now waived that requirement. He invited Nikita Khrushchev—now chairman of the Council of Ministers of the U.S.S.R., or premier—to visit him at Camp David, the presidential retreat in Maryland. The Camp David meeting, from September 25 to 27, 1959, climaxed 10 days later when Khrushchev toured the United States and proposed to the United Nations General Assembly a plan for general and complete disarmament. His conversations with Eisenhower were marked by a similar cordiality to the Geneva summit. Their joint communiqué stated that the talks had been useful in mutually clarifying the positions of the two leaders and should thus contribute "to the achievement of a just and lasting peace." The two had agreed that the question of general disarmament was "the most important one facing the world today." On the Berlin question they agreed that, subject to the approval of the other parties concerned, negotiations should be reopened in the hope of reaching a satisfactory solution. It was also agreed, Eisenhower told a news conference, with Khrushchev's concurrence, "that these negotiations should not be prolonged indefinitely but there could be no fixed time limit on them." The leaders rejected the use-of-force in settling "outstanding international questions."[7]

In December, after the Camp David meeting, Britain and France joined the United States in proposing a summit meeting of the Big Four. The Russians accepted and agreed to meet on May 16, 1960, in Paris. In the months prior to the meeting, however, the "spirit of Camp David" was clearly deteriorating. There were renewed threats from Khrushchev of drastic action if the Berlin question was not settled soon, and equal assurances from Washington that the United States would never desert the people of West Berlin. Of course, prospects of agreement were completely destroyed by the U-2 incident early in May.

On May 1, a high-flying U.S. reconnaissance airplane, a U-2, was shot down while on a flight across Russia, and the pilot, Francis Gary Powers, was captured unharmed, along with his photographic and other equipment. Khrushchev adroitly held back details while the State Department tried to explain that the presence of the U-2 over Soviet territory was a result of navigational error. Secretary of State Christian A. Herter admitted that the U-2 flight was but one of a number of such flights, conducted to photograph Soviet installations. The president confirmed Herter's admission, and both men defended this type of espionage as a means of guarding against surprise attack, necessitated by Soviet secretiveness. Khrushchev arrived at Paris and refused to negotiate unless President Eisenhower apologized for the U-2 flight and agreed to punish those responsible for it. He was not mollified by the president's assurance that there would be no more U-2 flights during his term of office or by the conciliatory efforts of President de Gaulle and Prime Minister Macmillan. Eisenhower walked out and the summit abruptly ended on May 17, one day after its opening.[8]

Chairman Khrushchev temporarily put aside his threat to conclude a separate peace treaty with the East German regime, hoping to find Eisenhower's successor more yielding. In June 1961, Khrushchev and President John F. Kennedy met for a two-day conference at Vienna that the American found difficult; the Soviet chairman lectured the young president on the German situation, repeating his earlier ultimatum with the six-month time limit. Unless within that time the four governments could agree on a peace treaty or treaties with Germany, united or divided, the Soviets would conclude a separate treaty with the German Democratic Republic, and occupation rights in West Berlin would end. West Berlin might continue as a "free city," and either neutral UN troops or "token forces" of the three Western powers and the Soviet Union might be stationed there, but it seemed clear that the city's contacts with the West would be at the mercy of the East German authorities.[9] Kennedy replied, attaching himself to Eisenhower's doctrine, that the United States had, together with its British and French Allies, "a fundamental political and moral obligation" to "maintain the freedom of over two million people in West Berlin." Any attempt to hinder the fulfillment of that obligation "would have the gravest effects upon international peace and security and endanger the lives and well-being of millions of people."[10]

In a nationwide broadcast on July 25, Kennedy told the country: "We cannot and will not permit the Communists to drive us out of Berlin, either gradually or by force." Although, he concluded, "we do not want to fight . . . we have fought before." Kennedy announced that he would ask Congress for a $3.25 billion increase in the defense budget for army, navy, and air force manpower, and for authority to call various reserve units to active duty. By increasing the conventional forces at home and in Europe, the president intended "to have a wider choice than humiliation or all-out nuclear action."[11] Congress gave Kennedy what he asked for, and an additional force of 45,000 troops was sent to Europe. France and West Germany also strengthened their NATO forces. Whether or not he expected these warlike gestures, Khrushchev again dropped the time limit for a Berlin settlement. On August 13, 1961, the East German regime began construction of the wall separating East from West Berlin, thus effectively putting an end to West Berlin's important role as an escape hatch from Communist East Germany. The United States protested, but did not press the issue. At the end of August, since the Eisenhower administration could not find a formula to end nuclear testing, Khrushchev announced a new series of atmospheric nuclear tests, ending an informal moratorium begun in 1958. The United States and Britain hesitated little in conducting their own tests.

THE CENTRAL AND LATIN AMERICAN COMPONENT OF THE KENNEDY DOCTRINE

On March 13, 1961, President Kennedy proposed his Alliance for Progress to Latin American ambassadors assembled at the White House. Described by Michael Dunne as Kennedy's Cold War Monroe Doctrine,[12] the Alliance for Progress program implemented the Act of Bogota, signed by 19 nations in September 1960, which established a cooperative program—including a 10-year American pledge of $20 billion—for Latin American economic development. Thus by 1970, "the need for massive outside help will have passed" and each American state would be "the master of its own revolution of hope and progress."[13] The Alliance for Progress, like the Act of Bogota, attached to the promise of aid the requirement for Latin American economic and political reform. A point of concern in the alliance was its lack of a standard in determining when recipient states had taken adequate steps towards implementing reform. Additionally, U.S. special interests placed a variety of obstacles before Latin American nations' exports and imports. These roadblocks, combined with the unwillingness of established Latin American elites to give up their privileged positions, undermined the program from the outset.

Notwithstanding American efforts to establish task forces on education, land and tax reform, and low-cost housing—the essential ingredients in social progress—the alliance produced little social change and less democracy. Further, military coups in Brazil, Argentina, and Peru during the first year further eroded the impact of the alliance. On October 6, 1963, Edwin A. Martin, assistant secretary of state for Latin American affairs, regretfully reported that the fundamental principle of the alliance was beyond attainment and acknowledged that military coups were a traditional part of Latin American politics. Latin Americans understood that the alliance had come in response to the administration's fear of Cuban-based communism. They soon discovered that such economic and technical assistance programs as the Peace Corps and the Alliance for Progress, despite their humanitarian overtones, embraced Cold War objectives by seeking to render the hemisphere more resistant to revolutionary pressures. [14]

A combination of Fidel Castro's dictatorial methods including his nationalization program, ties to the Soviet bloc, support of revolutionary movements in Latin America, and intemperate denunciations of U.S. "imperialism" brought Cuban-American relations to the breaking point in April 1961. The Eisenhower administration in 1960 had ended diplomatic relations with Cuba and handed Kennedy a poorly planned counter-revolutionary movement designed to overthrow the Castro regime in the spring of 1961. At the time of Kennedy's inauguration, some 2,000 to 3,000 rebel Cuban refugees were training in the United States and Guatemala for an invasion of the island. [15] With the Cuban people living under the duress of "communist domination," it was envisaged that the guerrilla invasion would assuredly ignite a revolution and free the state. Several American officials had doubts about these plans of the CIA. General Edward Lansdale, the government's leading expert on counterinsurgency, told an uneasy Paul Nitze, now the assistant secretary of defense for International Security Affairs, that the operation was too poorly managed to succeed. Yet Nitze supported the project, as he explained in his memoirs: "The Soviet Union had inserted itself in our backyard . . . in the form of the Castro regime in Cuba. Like a spreading cancer, it should, if possible, be excised from the Americas." [16] For Nitze and many others, the Cuban assault finally amounted to an objective military target for Eisenhower's rolling-back doctrine. Kennedy doubted the wisdom of the invasion, but grudgingly consented after insisting that he would never commit American forces to the assault. [17] On April 17, 1961, the Cuban refugee assault brigade struck the Cienaja de Zapata swamps of Las Villas Province (Bay of Pigs) on the south coast of Cuba. There was no popular uprising. Kennedy's refusal to back the invasion with U.S. airpower assured Castro's control of the skies. Cuban regulars quickly defeated the vastly outnumbered invading forces; the brigade's losses were 114 dead and 1,189 captured.[18] The Castro regime was now firmly implanted.

The president accepted blame for the fiasco, but lamented to his special counsel, Theodore C. Sorensen, "How could I have been so stupid to let them go ahead?"[19] Yet so favorable was the public response to such executive candor that Kennedy's popularity soared. Upon reflection, Kennedy believed that any unilateral aggression "would have been contrary to our traditions and to our international obligations." However, "should it ever appear that the inter-American doctrine of non-interference merely conceals or excuses a policy of non-action . . . then I want it clearly understood that this Government will not hesitate in meeting its primary obligations which are to the security of our nation."[20] Whether Cuba merited Washington's concern was questionable; other threats to hemispheric stability pertained to the 200 million Latin Americans who lived in misery, a potential source of revolutionary pressure. Despite such potential, the Kennedy administration continued to embark on a variety of maneuvers to weaken the Castro regime.[21] The administration sent sabotage units of Cuban émigrés into Cuba under a covert action plan called Operation Mongoose. After the necessary internal preparations, guerrilla operations would begin in August and September 1962, and during October, an open revolt would establish the new government. Attorney General Robert Kennedy, determined to remove Castro after the Bay of Pigs, was the driving force behind Mongoose.[22]

Operation Mongoose was orchestrated as a means to do what the Bay of Pigs invasion had been unable to achieve: remove the Communist Castro regime from power in Cuba. Put together by the CIA and Department of Defense under the direction of Edward Lansdale, Operation Mongoose constituted an assortment of tactics with wide-ranging purpose and scope. Lansdale articulated the project's six-tiered plan to Attorney General Kennedy on February 20, 1962, and President Kennedy received an outline of the operation on March 16, 1962. Encompassed in the briefing was a program of political, psychological, military, sabotage, and intelligence operations, as well as planned termination attempts on key political actors, including Castro. Key components of the plan were to be instituted as a means to significantly undermine the Communist regime, including the delivery of arms for militant opposition forces, the release of anti-Castro propaganda, and the formation of "asymmetrical" bases throughout the state, all of which would ultimately lay the groundwork for an October 1962 military intervention. Despite some of the Operation Mongoose actions taking place in 1962, the military intervention did not occur, and the Castro regime remained in power. Of course, with the revelation of Soviet weapons being introduced into Cuba—including ballistic missiles with nuclear warheads—the Kennedy administration suspended Operation Mongoose to focus on one of the most

dangerous Cold War episodes involving both the United States and the Soviet Union.[23]

THE CUBAN MISSILE CRISIS

Khrushchev's decision to send intermediate- and short-range missiles to
Cuba was based on the desire, among others, to establish a superpower
strategic nuclear balance prior to the fielding of Soviet intercontinental ballistic missiles. While adjusting the "balance" was Khrushchev's primary
goal, the Russians were also motivated by their dissatisfaction with Berlin's
divided status, U.S. missiles based in Turkey across the Black Sea from
Khrushchev's summer residence, and the Sino-Soviet contest for leadership
of the worldwide communist movement. Later, it was suggested that the
Soviet missile deployment in Cuba was designed primarily to defend Cuba
and, secondarily, to correct the (im)balance of power. Explaining to his con-
temporaries why he sent missiles to defend Cuba after the ill-fated Bay of
Pigs episode, Khrushchev elaborated: "We didn't want to unleash a war, we
just wanted to frighten them, to restrain the United States in regard to Cuba."
When the Americans finally discovered the missiles, Khrushchev could not
comprehend why Washington became so upset, given that the United States
had military bases next door to the Soviet Union.[24]

If the Americans attempted to invade Cuba to destroy the missile sites,
Khrushchev explained to his colleagues, they would be met with dozens of
short-range, nuclear-armed missiles capable of annihilating an invading
force. "The tragic thing is that they can attack us, and we will respond," he
worried. "This could all end up in a big war." Khrushchev was concerned
that some American leader "might think" that given "a seventeen-to-one
superiority" in intercontinental ballistic missiles (ICBMs), a "first strike was
possible." To Moscow, this was an "impossible" situation.

Of course, American commentators have viewed the episode differently.
"I do not know what insanity caused the Soviets to send missiles to Cuba,"
one later wrote, "after showing commendable caution about the deployment
of this gadgetry in far less dangerous locations." But he neglected to point
out that such caution was "not paralleled" by Washington and NATO when
they located tactical nuclear weapons in Europe and Jupiter missiles on Turkish soil. Kennedy's advisers promoted the thesis that Khrushchev was testing
Kennedy and America's willingness to respond to an aggressive Soviet
move. Much later a Khrushchev aide acknowledged that Kennedy was often
perceived as "weak."[25]

The president secretly called together a small group of high-level advisers, a group known as ExCom: the Executive Committee of the National
Security Council. ExCom immediately rejected the notion that the Soviets

merely meant to protect Cuba. Some concluded, logically enough, that Khrushchev mainly sought to redress the Soviet Union's exposed strategic inferiority. While the Joint Chiefs accepted that judgment, the close proximity of Cuba *was* sufficient to change the strategic balance. Other ExCom members detected little increase in Soviet first-strike or retaliatory capabilities from Cuban-based missiles, for as Secretary of Defense Robert McNamara declared, "A missile is a missile. It makes no difference whether you are killed by a missile fired from the Soviet Union or from Cuba."[26] What *was* at stake, the ExCom finally agreed, was the nation's will and credibility, a rationale that appeared frequently in Washington. Neither friends nor enemies, at home or abroad, it was argued, would take Washington's pledges seriously if the Soviets were permitted, uncontested, to place offensive missiles in Cuba. At first, several members of ExCom—including bankers, lawyers, and diplomats—advocated an air strike to eliminate the missile bases or an actual invasion of the island.

While Joint Chiefs confidently insisted that an invasion of Cuba could be undertaken without embarking on a general war with the Soviet Union, Kennedy wasn't as convinced based on their ill-prepared, poorly planned Bay of Pigs intervention. He was particularly uneasy with the air force chief of staff, General Curtis LeMay, and his often assertive briefings about how to deal with America's enemies. In response to the president's misgivings, LeMay derided the president's fear that a miscalculation could end in a nuclear holocaust, stating that the president's concerns in essence advocated a form of appeasement. As such, the general's resolution to the strategic dilemma was simple: since the United States possessed overwhelming nuclear superiority, the Kremlin would not launch a nuclear conflict that it would likely lose. Kennedy, however, found it difficult to understand that the Soviets would just stand by and ignore the deaths of hundreds of their soldiers. "These brass hats have one great advantage in their favor," Kennedy said. "If we listen to them and do what they want us to do, none of us will be alive later to tell them that they were wrong."[27]

Kennedy's nationwide telecast on October 22 embodied the official assumption that the Soviet missiles endangered the hemisphere, and, unlike U.S. missiles in Europe, their mission was offensive, not defensive. He had gradually endorsed the ExCom concept of a stop and search blockade or quarantine to isolate the Soviet forces in Cuba. The president's central warning was clear: "It shall be the policy of this Nation to regard any nuclear missile launched from Cuba against any nation in the Western Hemisphere as an attack by the Soviet Union on the United States, requiring a full retaliatory response upon the Soviet Union."[28] In Europe, the alliance held firm as Britain, France, and West Germany pledged their support. In a display of common sense, Khrushchev agreed to withdraw his missiles, while Kennedy authorized removal of the obsolete U.S. Jupiter missiles from Turkey and pledged that the United States would not invade Cuba. The resolution of the missile crisis, without a nuclear exchange, was a close-run affair. Shortly afterward, President Kennedy and Chairman Khrushchev agreed to a limited nuclear test ban and instituted a "hot line" to allow them to communicate with each other directly, instead of through intermediaries.

DÉTENTE AND THE DOCTRINAL IMPACT

After the settlement of the Cuban missile crisis, the United States and the U.S.S.R. accepted the nuclear stalemate as a reality—and for all intents and purposes, nuclear "developments" were to remain an embedded consideration in all presidential doctrines from here on in. While the questions of Germany and Berlin remained unsettled, Chancellor Adenauer's successors were less insistent on immediate German reunification, while the Soviets refrained from creating further crises over Berlin. Under these circumstances, Presidents Lyndon B. Johnson (1963–1969), Richard M. Nixon (1969–1974), Gerald R. Ford (1974–1977), and Jimmy Carter (1977–1980) sought to improve relations with the Soviet Union and, as Johnson phrased it, to "build bridges" of trade and understanding with the smaller nations of Eastern Europe.

Of course, the Vietnam War and the Arab-Israeli wars of 1967 and 1973 kept tensions alive between the superpowers. Moscow viewed the war in Vietnam as a "war of national liberation" and a war of U.S. "aggression" and "imperialism." Premier Alexei Kosygin, who together with Communist Party chief Leonid I. Brezhnev replaced Khrushchev in 1964, told the editors of *Life* that "we [the Soviets], for our part will do all we can so that the U.S. does not defeat Vietnam." "American aggression," he added, "will be met with growing rebuff."[29] Accordingly, attempts by both Johnson and Nixon to persuade Moscow and Beijing to assist in bringing Hanoi to accept United States peace terms provided, on the whole, limited results. President Nixon ended America's commitment to South Vietnam in 1973 with the signing of the Paris Peace Accords, but the North Vietnamese military successfully unified the country in 1975 as the Americans withdrew from Indochina. In other parts of the world, the superpowers were frequently drawn to conflicts in the Middle East, especially the Arab-Israeli wars, during which the Soviets established a large naval presence in the Mediterranean, and shadowed the movements of the American Sixth Fleet.

Where the United States and the Soviet Union *did* succeed in reducing Cold War tensions was in their efforts to employ diplomacy and political agreements to slow the arms race and to dampen the impact of weapons of mass destruction. President Kennedy and Soviet Chairman Khrushchev initiated the process with the 1963 treaty banning nuclear tests in the atmosphere that removed a threat to global health; however, it did not halt the proliferation of nuclear weaponry or the superpowers' quest for more sophisticated versions. "I am haunted," President Kennedy posited in 1963, "by the feeling that by 1970, unless we are successful, there may be 10 nuclear powers instead of four, and by 1975, 15 or 20."[30] In addition to the original four nuclear weapons states—the United States, Britain, Russia, and France—six other states—China, Israel, India, Pakistan, North Korea, and South Africa—would develop nuclear weapons. South Africa would later relinquish its weapons and means of producing them, while a number of states that at one time had considered a nuclear weapons program, or had even begun one, subsequently halted their efforts.

President Johnson reenergized the doctrinal and diplomatic efforts to reduce the prospects of global proliferation of nuclear weaponry. Following the People's Republic of China's first nuclear test on October 16, 1964, Washington and Moscow responded to the UN General Assembly's 1965 call to prevent nuclear proliferation. Each cooperated with the Eighteen Nation Disarmament Committee in drafting the Non-Proliferation Treaty (NPT) of 1968 that drew widespread adherence. The non-nuclear states argued that the pact must not divide the world into nuclear "haves" and "have-nots," but rather balance obligations. Non-nuclear weapons states pledged not to acquire nuclear weapons in exchange for access to peaceful nuclear technology and a pledge from the nuclear weapons states to pursue nuclear disarmament. The task of inspection was placed under the International Atomic Energy Agency (IAEA), which supervised the peaceful use of nuclear energy and the exchange of necessary technology. At the same time, Washington and Moscow reluctantly agreed "to pursue negotiations in good faith on effective measures relating to cessation of the nuclear arms race at an early date" and "to nuclear disarmament, and on a treaty on general and complete disarmament under strict and effective international control."[31]

In time, the NPT emerged as the main component of a "regime" encompassing the IAEA, negotiations for a comprehensive nuclear test ban, and regional Nuclear-Weapons-Free Zones. While never materializing, early proposals for the latter originated from Polish foreign minister Rapacki, in 1957 and 1962, who sought to eliminate nuclear weapons from Poland, Czechoslovakia, and West and East Germany. The multilateral Antarctic Treaty of 1959 excluded a specific geographical area from major power competition and, at the same time, provided the confidence for future such pacts. The Treaty of Tlatelolco of 1967 to denuclearize Latin America was the first of several such agreements. The significant Outer Space Treaty of 1967, a UN-sponsored, multilateral pact, committed its signatories "not to place in orbit around the Earth any objects carrying nuclear weapons" or "any other kinds of weapons of mass destruction, install such weapons on celestial bodies, or station such weapons in outer space in any other manner." In addition, the

article prohibited "the establishment of military bases, installations and for-
tifications, the testing of any type of weapons and the conduct of military
manoeuvres on celestial bodies." In related developments, the Seabed Treaty
of 1971 prevented the installation of nuclear weapons on the ocean floor
beyond national territorial waters. [32]

The first multilateral efforts that sought to bring an entire range of nuclear
weaponry under control—the Baruch Plan (1946)—and Soviet and American
proposals for General and Complete Disarmament (1962) were unsuccessful.
Following their embarrassment from a lack of offensive missiles during the
Cuban missile crisis, the Soviets launched an intense effort to build a fleet of
intercontinental ballistic missiles (ICBMs) to offset the United States' superiority. At the same time, both superpowers were in the early phase of developing defensive antiballistic missile (ABM) systems. In the United States,
the Nixon administration constructed a primitive "light" ABM system,
known as "Safeguard," for defense of missile sites; however, it was disman-
tled shortly after becoming operational. To lessen the dangers of an unintentional nuclear conflict, the superpowers turned to diplomacy while continuing to seek more efficient weapons.

The major impediment to any treaty limiting or reducing weaponry was
Washington's insistence on "on-site inspections" to verify compliance. How
could an adversary be reasonably confident that the other was faithfully
honoring its agreements? After all, the increasingly sophisticated nuclear
weapon systems fostered a mutual fear of a surprise attack, or "first strike."
Early in the 1950s, Presidents Truman and Eisenhower were so desperate to
gain information regarding Soviet military capabilities that they authorized
the U.S. Air Force to overfly Soviet territory. Ignoring international law,
Washington officials on one occasion sent RB-47Es on 156 missions over
Soviet territory from March 21 to May 10, 1956. With the intelligence-
gathering missions completed, the Eisenhower administration dispatched a
diplomatic note to Moscow expressing regret that navigational errors had led
to the intrusion into Soviet airspace. Nevertheless, the United States employed the U-2 airplane to continue attaining information and photographing
Soviet military installations until 1960, when Francis Gary Powers was shot
down.

Technology finally resolved the issue. In August 1960, an American
"spy" satellite began operating on a regular basis, while the Soviet Union
launched its own space reconnaissance vehicles in 1962. Both superpowers
now embraced the age of national technical verification—the Soviets perhaps
less enthusiastically—which opened the way to arms-control agreements on
strategic weaponry. With the advent of modern electronics, photography,
space vehicles, and other devices, "national technical means" added to the
effectiveness of self-monitoring. Such devices could verify, with reasonable
accuracy, both the quantitative and qualitative features of strategic weaponry,

particularly the numbers and characteristics of ballistic missiles, providing information vital to negotiations and to the monitoring of actual agreements. In ironic fashion, the sophisticated technologies developed by the superpowers as part of their military competition had contributed greatly to progress in verification techniques. The "billions of dollars and rubles" that had been invested, according to Allan Krass, "gave each side a remarkably accurate picture of the military capabilities of its adversary."[33] By early 1965, satellite cameras could count antiballistic missile systems, land-based strategic ballistic missiles, aircraft on the ground, and submarines in port with reasonable accuracy. Some minor evasions might take place, but a major violation would be detected, as the Central Intelligence Agency proved that it could monitor Soviet missile deployments with a substantial degree of accuracy. In an October 1967 speech, Assistant Secretary of Defense Paul Warnke urged the Soviets to discuss limiting strategic weapons, stipulating that the United States would consider an agreement that would be verified by "our own unilateral capability" rather than on-site inspections.[34]

Having witnessed the difficulty of reaching a multilateral agreement, the superpowers shifted their focus to a series of bilateral agreements. From these negotiations gradually emerged limits on nuclear weapons systems and, much later, their actual reduction. The first was the 1972 Interim Agreement on Strategic Offensive Weapons (SALT I), establishing, among other restrictions, a quantitative limit on both intercontinental ballistic missiles—the United States' 1,054 ICBMs, the Soviets' 1,618 ICBMs operational and under construction—and submarine-launched ballistic missiles (SLBMs). SALT I focused on the numbers of missiles or launchers rather than on warheads, and allowed the deployment of multiple independently targeted reentry vehicles (MIRVs) that eventually expanded greatly the number of warheads in both states' arsenals. SALT I did not secure reductions, and its ceilings were higher than existing forces, thereby allowing the deployment of additional ballistic missiles. Article V of the SALT I pact declared that "Each Party shall use national technical means of verification at its disposal in a manner consistent with generally recognized principles of international law"; that "Each Party undertakes not to interfere with the national technical means of verification of the other Party"; and that "Each Party undertakes not to use deliberate concealment measures which impede verification by national technical means."[35]

The 1972 Anti-Ballistic Missile Treaty, negotiated concurrently with SALT I, stipulated that each side could deploy up to 100 ABM interceptors at each of two sites, later reduced to one site. Although both parties had spent substantial funds to develop ABM systems, their efforts spurred minimal traction because of doubtful operational technology and the increasing numbers of warheads, especially on MIRVed missiles. The ABM Treaty also endorsed national technical means for verification purposes. Significantly, this was the first mention in any arms control treaty of prohibitions on hindering or limiting verification efforts. Noteworthy was the creation of the Standing Consultative Commission to quietly examine questions regarding the treaty's implementation. In 1974, President Gerald Ford and General Secretary Brezhnev at Vladivostok, agreed to the formula for SALT II, which was eventually signed in Vienna on April 18, 1979. Negotiated by President Jimmy Carter, SALT II was a mix of an engineering document and a lawyer's brief; the text was extraordinarily complex, with extensive definitions and elaborate "counting rules" appended. The treaty limited each side to 2,400 ICBMs, SLBMs, and heavy bombers, to be reached within six months after the treaty entered into force, followed by a further reduction to 2,250 strategic nuclear launch vehicles by 1981. Each side was limited within this ceiling to no more than 1,320 ICBMs, SLBMs, and long-range bombers equipped with MIRVs or multiple cruise missiles. The 78-page treaty required both parties to dismantle some systems so as to make room for new deployments and included an extensive list of qualitative restrictions. [36]

The Soviet-American negotiations produced several other agreements, some dealing with "arms control," a relatively new concept. Earlier, Kennedy and Khrushchev had initiated the "hot line"—frequently modified—to connect the chiefs of state in Moscow and Washington directly to lessen the prospect of an unintended conflict. Several similar bilateral pacts followed, including: the Accidents Measures Agreement (1971) to improve the safety and security of each party's nuclear weapons, the High Seas Accord (1972) to regulate the "shadowing" of each other's warships, and the Prevention of Nuclear War Accord (1973). The latter pact was instigated by Moscow's unsuccessful effort to obtain a U.S. commitment of "no-first-use" of nuclear weapons; the Soviets did make this pledge in 1982, though not before it was recommended by the Chinese.

Meanwhile, Nixon on November 25, 1969, reaffirmed the United States' chemical warfare "no-first-use" policy (dating back to World War II), while he unilaterally renounced the United States' use of bacteriological or biological weapons, closed all facilities producing these offensive weapons, and ordered existing stockpiles of biological weapons and agents to be destroyed. In April 1972, the United States and the Soviet Union joined other nations in signing the Biological Convention. In 1974, the two countries also signed a Threshold Test Ban pact, limiting the yield of underground tests of nuclear weapons to the upper limits of 150 kilotons for single detonations. These agreements, together with progress in commercial and economic relations, peaceful uses of atomic energy, and cultural exchanges, seemed to augur well for Soviet-American relations. [37]

Nixon and Brezhnev, at the June 1973 Washington summit, regarded their agreements on arms limitation and the avoidance of nuclear war as defining achievements. Washington and Moscow understood the risks and costs of their perennial disagreements and the advantages of a stable relationship. That said, the 1973 Basic Principles of Relations agreement, initiated by the Kremlin but largely ignored by American leadership, might have substantially reduced tensions between the superpowers if this effort to institutionalize détente had been better defined and realistically explained to the American public. Moscow thought that this pact could provide the basis for superpower cooperation in resolving basic differences. Thus, Soviet officials considered it "an important political declaration" that they wished, as Ambassador Anatoly Dobrynin recalled, would be the basis of a "new political process of *détente* in our relations." Moscow hoped the agreement would recognize the Soviet doctrine of peaceful coexistence (or détente) and acknowledge the "principle of equality as a basis for the security of both countries." However, the Soviets could not escape their ideological past and the expectations it placed on their actions. Similarly, the Nixon Doctrine could not satisfy those Americans who believed the Soviet threat too immediate and pervading to permit any lasting agreements or relaxation of tension. Failure to develop détente's boundaries and to gain public acceptance for it clearly undermined the idea.[38]

THE TRANSITION OF NATO IN U.S. PRESIDENTIAL DOCTRINE

In its second and third decades, NATO had lost much of its cohesiveness and at least some of its importance. As the apparent danger of Soviet aggression declined, so did the bond that held the diverse members of the alliance together, and rifts appeared in the structure. Europeans, understandably, resented Washington's habit of making unilateral decisions on defense and other matters, while Americans, in turn, felt that the NATO states of a newly prosperous Europe were carrying less than their share of the burden of common defense. Some Americans deplored the failure of most of the NATO allies to sympathize with, not to mention support, American policy in Vietnam, Communist China, Cuba, and the Middle East. The United States, furthermore, found its neighbor to the north, Canada, less than cooperative in continental defense policy during the tenure of Prime Minister John Diefenbaker (1957–1963), though this trend reversed itself somewhat under Pierre Trudeau. Portugal resented its allies' fault-finding with its colonial policy in Africa and threatened to deny them the use of bases in the Azores. In the mid-1970s, Portugal's domestic upheavals caused the United States no small concern. Greece and Turkey continued to quarrel over Cyprus, thereby rendering NATO's right flank vulnerable. And Italy, which increasingly relied on the support of the Italian Communists to function,[39] caused NATO to worry about bringing local communists into policymaking with its classified material.

These misunderstandings and problems were of minor importance compared with the aftermath of France's defection. Assuming power in France in June 1958 after a succession of weak governments, Charles de Gaulle quickly restored stability to French political life and ended the exhausting colonial war in Algeria. But he was dissatisfied with France's relatively minor role in world politics compared with that of the "Anglo-Saxons." When President Eisenhower rejected his proposal for a three-power directorate—France, Britain, and the United States—to guide the policies of NATO, de Gaulle repeatedly took positions antagonistic to the United States: recognizing Communist China, condemning American policy in Vietnam, catering to anti-Americanism in Latin America, encouraging French separatism in Quebec, siding with the Arabs against Israel in the Six-Day War of 1967, and rebuffing the United States as well as England in temporarily barring the United Kingdom from the European Economic Community (Common Market).

More serious, however, was de Gaulle's nationalistic policy toward NATO. In opposition to American policy, he insisted that France must have, at great expense, its own independent nuclear force, or *force de frappe*. To justify the enormous costs involved, he warned the French people and their European allies that the United States probably would not sacrifice its cities to defend Western Europe in a nuclear exchange with the Soviet Union.[40] While France would fulfill its obligations under the North Atlantic Treaty, de Gaulle rejected the idea of a unified command, a fundamental concept of NATO.

Measures of partial withdrawal from the command structure—detachment of the French Mediterranean fleet, denial of base and air rights to nuclear-armed American planes, and so forth—climaxed in March 1966 when the French president declared that all NATO military installations, including its headquarters, and U.S. soldiers must leave French soil by April 1, 1967. President Lyndon B. Johnson, furious with de Gaulle, demanded that Secretary of State Dean Rusk ask the French president "about the cemeteries." What Johnson was asking, as Rusk more eloquently put it, was did the order to remove all U.S. troops "include the bodies of American soldiers in France's cemeteries?"—which added up to more than 60,000 soldiers from two world wars.[41] Taken aback, de Gaulle allegedly stormed out of the room without reply.

Before April 1, French officers had in fact been withdrawn from all of the headquarters' planning committees. NATO headquarters, civil as well as military, moved to Belgium. France continued as an ally and made no move to withdraw, but its armed forces, the geographical and military keystone to the defense of Western Europe, could no longer be counted on to take orders from the supreme commander in the event of an attack from the East. De Gaulle's passing from the scene failed to improve matters, as his successors continued to pursue an independent nuclear force replete with atomic bombers, second-generation ICBMs, and a modest nuclear submarine fleet. Furthermore, the French made no secret that they would respond to a threat of Soviet invasion with the immediate use of tactical nuclear weapons, in contrast to NATO's policy of "flexible response," which relied initially on conventional warfare rather than on nuclear weapons. [42]

By the late 1960s, other NATO states followed France's example, not in detaching their forces but in reducing the number of forces readily available. The United States, whose 350,000 troops stationed in Europe contributed to a chronic foreign exchange deficit, transferred 35,000 troops from Europe to American soil in 1967 (though these troops were still committed to NATO and could be returned to Europe on short notice). Britain took similar action with 6,500 of its 51,000 troops on the continent; Canada, two years later in 1969, announced that it would cut its ground troops and air force in Europe by almost 50 percent; and West Germany reduced its projected contribution to NATO forces from 508,000 to 400,000 men. [43] Democratic Senate leader Mike Mansfield called year after year for a "substantial reduction" of American forces in Europe, a move successfully resisted by Johnson and Nixon. By mid-1976, and in the face of a new set of circumstances—the steady buildup of Soviet military power—the United States pledged to increase its army in Europe from 13 to 16 divisions.

THE U.S., THE PRC, AND DOCTRINAL ADJUSTMENTS

Although there was considerable evidence of the Sino-Soviet rift after 1960, the Kennedy and Johnson administrations made few attempts to reexamine their previous assumptions and policies regarding China. This was partly due, according to Kochavi, to Washington's preoccupation with Mao Zedong's aggressive and fundamentalist Chinese Communist Party, an image Eisenhower, Kennedy, and Johnson shared. [44] Throughout the terms of the three aforementioned presidents doctrinal containment was still fresh, international communism was a big issue, and memories of the Korean War were still warm. Despite the beginnings of a Sino-Soviet break in the late 1950s and early 1960s, officials in Washington continued to see a dangerous Moscow-Beijing axis. In practice, their anti-Beijing attitudes resulted in charges of misbehavior, non-recognition, and trade restrictions. Richard Nixon, however, had early identified with the critics' arguments that the United States' China policies—to isolate 700 million Chinese diplomatically and economically—served no useful purpose and antagonized much of the world. Indeed, Nixon wrote in the October 1967 issue of *Foreign Affairs* that "any American policy toward Asia must come urgently to grips with the reality of China." As president, his doctrine established the need to improve relations with China as one essential component of a new American foreign policy. "I was fully aware," he recalled, "of the profound ideological and political differences between our countries. . . . But I believed also that in this era we could not afford to be cut off from a quarter of the world's population. We had an obligation to try to establish contact . . . and perhaps move on to greater understanding." Nixon understood that China posed a lesser danger than two decades of apocalyptic rhetoric had suggested. [45]

In 1969, the Nixon administration, working through third states, opened some discussion with Beijing, but its initial efforts were largely unilateral—allowing Americans to purchase Chinese goods; validating passports after March 1970 for travel in China; and licensing, after April 1970, of certain non-strategic American goods for export to China. During a visit to Rumania in October 1970, Nixon, for the first time, deliberately used Beijing's official title, the People's Republic of China. No American initiatives toward China would succeed unless they were received with some graciousness. When, in October 1970, President Yahya Khan of Pakistan carried a Nixon overture to Beijing, the Beijing government responded: "We welcome the proposal from Washington for face-to-face discussions. We would be glad to receive a high-level person for this purpose, to discuss withdrawal of American forces from Taiwan." Nixon welcomed the invitation, but could not accept the Chinese objective. During April 1971, in Nagoya, Japan, the Chinese ping-pong team invited the American team, competing for the world champion-ships, to visit the Chinese mainland. Prime Minister Chou En-lai addressed the American team: "[W]ith your acceptance of our invitation, you have opened a new page in the relations of the Chinese and American people." Then, on July 15, the president announced that earlier Kissinger and Chou had held secret talks in Beijing. The premier invited the president to visit China, and Nixon accepted the invitation. [46]

Washington's new opening to China culminated in the president's trip to Beijing in February 1972. Minutely prepared, the venture became one of the greatest media events of the decade. By acknowledging the legitimacy of the Chinese government—which four preceding administrations had refused to do—Nixon expected Beijing to accept the legitimacy of the existing international order and the limits of proper political and diplomatic conduct. Late in 1971, the Beijing government, facing only an adverse vote from the United States, replaced the Republic of China in the United Nations. In 1973, the United States established a permanent liaison office in Beijing, and Nixon's informal recognition of the Beijing regime was met with the American people's almost universal approval.

Clearly, the Asia of the 1970s presented opportunities for new policies. The changes to Washington's doctrinal image to incorporate a more benign relationship with the People's Republic of China—less focus on international, non-Soviet Union communism—engendered a relaxation of East-West tension in Asia. In response to such developments, Moscow offered defense pacts to the countries of Southeast Asia against an allegedly aggressive China. Beijing retaliated in 1972 by inviting the United States to maintain its bases in Southeast Asia as a guarantee against Soviet encroachment. Nothing dramatized more effectively the revolution in the U.S. perception of Asia than the president's recognition of a new regional balance of power. "We must remember," he declared in early 1972, "the only time in the history of the world that we have had any extended period of peace is when there has been a balance of power. . . . I think it will be a safer world and a better world if we have a strong, healthy United States, Europe, Soviet Union, China, Japan—each balancing the other." Thereafter, the new American outlook toward Asia set the stage for a limited, ordered relationship with China.[47]

CONCLUSION

Extending the communist threat from Truman's doctrine of containment, Eisenhower and later Kennedy's version of "maintaining the outside" promulgated the power relations of U.S.-Soviet polarization into newer and more dangerous grounds. With the Republican takeover of the presidency in 1953, Eisenhower was given a mandate to pursue a more proactive policy of "liberating" countries from the communist threat, something not all that dissimilar to Woodrow Wilson's promotion of "national self-determination." Eisenhower's concept of massive retaliation was the attempt to replace containment with the notion that the U.S. had overwhelming strength in nuclear arms. Indeed, more than that, the Americans had nuclear weapons close to Soviet-controlled borders. That Khrushchev's policy towards Berlin and the West was somewhat antagonistic, given that he was also considerably more moderate than Stalin, added to Washington's belief that the Russians could only be dealt with by American military power. Yet, as the test of Soviet recalcitrance played out, bold threats of nuclear preponderance risked the perception that massive retaliation was no better than Truman's containment. President Kennedy's escape from the choice of humiliation or nuclear war over the question of Laos was enough to convince the president that not all aspects of the doctrine were going to work. Kennedy's doctrine of "flexible response," largely an adaptation of the Eisenhower doctrine, was the proposed answer.

The Cuban missile crisis of 1962 became the preamble to a new balance-of-power politics. Flexible response allowed the Kennedy administration to steer away from the impending doom of a military strike against Russian and Cuban troops; however, it also paved the way for a freer interpretation of executive powers in dealing with any new perceived threat. Though the question of nuclear weapons in Cuba had been dealt with, the prospect of further communist insurrections in Latin America proved difficult to shake from the Washington mindset. The ability of the Johnson administration to take the full force of Kennedy's restructured doctrine to South America was the result of this newfound insecurity in the balance of power. Johnson's actions in Latin America demonstrated a still-significant Monroesque thinking in that communism in South America was far too close to American interests to be comfortable. As it was, Cuba was trouble enough.

Additionally, if "maintaining the outside" proved all but impossible, Washington's trouble with maintaining the internal cohesion of allied and domestic support proved no small deed. All three doctrines since Truman were hugely costly not only in military terms but also to the economy. Additionally, French President de Gaulle's nationalist turn against American support exacerbated the perception that America's position had weakened. Whether NATO's declining forces added to the Soviet or American relaxation of tensions with détente is a question worth exploring further. Indeed, the irrationality of the situation was a constant question both sides would often ask. Regardless, the perception that the United States and its allies' fight against communism might unravel at the seams was very real, enough at least to keep alive the significance of the Eisenhower and Kennedy doctrines. That eventual détente came about when it did can thus be attributed more to the technological progress that began with the arms race itself, than the mutual realization that an arms race of such magnitude was indeed irrational.

NOTES

1. President Eisenhower's Speech on the U.S. Role in the Middle East, 1957, Council on Foreign Relations, available at: http://www.cfr.org/middle-east-and-north-africa/president-eisenhowers-speech-us-role-middle-east-eisenhower-doctrine-1957/p24130.

2. Also see Richard Dean Burns, Joseph M. Siracusa, and Jason Flanagan, *American Foreign Relations since Independence,* Santa Barbara, CA: Praeger, 2013.

3. Richard Immerman, "'Trust in the Lord but Keep Your Powder Dry': American Policy Aims at Geneva," in Günter Bischof and Saki Dockrill, eds., *Cold War Respite: The Geneva Summit of 1955*, Baton Rouge: Louisiana State University Press, 2000, pp. 35–54.

4. Vladislav M. Zubok, "Soviet Policy Aims at the Geneva Conference, 1955," in Günter Bischof and Saki Dockrill, eds. *Cold War Respite: The Geneva Summit of 1955*, Baton Rouge: Louisiana State University Press, 2000, p. 62.

5. Republican Party Platform, July 7, 1952, The American Presidency Project, available at: http://www.presidency.ucsb.edu/ws/?pid=25837.

6. Wayne Bert, *American Military Intervention in Unconventional War*, New York: Palgrave Macmillan, 2011, p. 22.

7. Dwight D. Eisenhower, *Public Papers of the Presidents of the United States: Dwight D. Eisenhower, 1959*, New York: Best Books, 1960, p. 696.

8. Francis Gary Powers and Curt Gentry, *Operation Overflight: The Story of U-2 Sky Pilot Francis Gary Powers*, New York: Holt, Rinehart and Winston, 1970.

9. *Documents on American Foreign Relations, 1961*, pp. 137–41.

10. The Summit Conference at Vienna, June 3–4, 1961, U.S. Department of State Archive, available at: http://2001-2009.state.gov/r/pa/ho/frus/kennedyjf/xiv/15856.htm.

11. The note of July 17 and the broadcast of July 25 are printed in *Documents on American Foreign Relations, 1961*, pp. 1411–49 and 95–105.

12. Michael Dunne, "Kennedy's Alliance for Progress: Countering Revolution in Latin America. Part I: From the White House to the Charter of Punta del Este," *International Affairs* 89, no. 6, 2013, pp. 1,389–1,409.

13. Cited in Jeffrey Taffet, *Foreign Aid as Foreign Policy: The Alliance for Progress in Latin America*, New York: Routledge, 2012, p. 201.

14. "Address . . . for Members of Congress and for the Diplomatic Corps of the Latin American Republics," March 13, 1961, in Woolley and Peters, The American Presidency Project, available at: http://www.presidency.ucsb.edu/ws/?pid=8531; see also Teodoro Moscoso, "Progress Report on the Alliance for Progress," *New York Times Magazine*, August 12, 1962, pp. 11, 59–63; Jerome Levinson and Juan de Onís, *The Alliance That Lost Its Way*, Chicago: Quadrangle Books, 1970, pp. 77–87, 166.

15. See Peter Wyden, *Bay of Pigs: The Untold Story*, New York: Simon & Schuster, 1979.

16. Paul H. Nitze, *From Hiroshima to Glasnost: At the Center of Decision—A Memoir*, New York: Grove Weidenfeld, 1989, pp. 183–84.

17. Lawrence Freedman, *Kennedy's Wars: Berlin, Cuba, Laos, and Vietnam*, New York: Oxford University Press, 2000, pp. 134–35.

18. Wyden, *Bay of Pigs*, chapters 5–7.

19. Quoted in *ibid.*, p. 8.

20. *New York Times*, September 9, 1962; "Address Before the American Society of Newspaper Editors," April 20, 1961, in Woolley and Peters, The American Presidency Project, available at: http://www.presidency.ucsb.edu/ws/?pid=8076.

21. "Lessons of Cuba," *New York Times*, September 9, 1962.

22. Taylor Branch and George Crile III, "The Kennedy Vendetta: How the CIA Waged a Silent War against Cuba," *Harper's* 251, August 1975, pp. 49–63; see "Mongoose," in Freedman, *Kennedy's Wars*, pp. 153–60.

23. "The Bay of Pigs Invasion and its Aftermath, April 1961–October 1962," U.S. Department of States, Office of the Historian, available at: https://history.state.gov/milestones/1961-1968/bay-of-pigs.

24. See Michael Dobbs, *One Minute to Midnight: Kennedy, Khrushchev, and Castro on the Brink of Nuclear War*, New York: Knopf, 2008; Lester H. Brune, *The Cuba-Caribbean Missile Crisis of October 1962*, Claremont, CA: Regina Books, 1996; Michael Beschloss, *The Crisis Years: Kennedy and Khrushchev, 1960–63*, New York: Harper Collins, 1991; James G. Blight and David A. Welch, *On the Brink: Americans and Soviets Reexamine the Cuban Missile Crisis*, New York: Noonday, 1989; A. A. Fursenko and Timothy J. Naftali, *One Hell of a Gamble: Khrushchev, Castro, and Kennedy, 1958–1964*, New York: Norton, 1997.

25. *Ibid.*

26. Barton J. Bernstein, "The Week We Almost Went to War," *The Bulletin of American Scientists* 2, No. 2, February 1976, p. 16.

27. Dobbs, *One Minute to Midnight*, pp. 26–30, 109, 125, 179, 249, 282–84; McNamara quoted in Ned Lebow and Janice Gross Stein, *We All Lost the Cold War*, Princeton, NJ: Princeton University Press, 1994, p. 98; Freedman, *Kennedy's Wars*, pp. 127–46, 171.

28. John F. Kennedy, "Radio and Television Report to the American People on the Soviet Arms Build-up in Cuba," October 22, 1962, The American Presidency Project, available at: http://www.presidency.ucsb.edu/ws/?pid=8986.

29. "Blunt and Bristling Talk Inside the Kremlin: A Private Interview with Aleksei Kosygin," *Life Magazine*, Vol. 64, No. 4, February 2, 1968, p. 28.

30. The President's News Conference, March 21, 1963, The American Presidency Project, available at: http://www.presidency.ucsb.edu/ws/?pid=9124.

31. Treaty on the Non-Proliferation of Nuclear Weapons (NPT), United Nations Office for Disarmament Affairs, available at: http://www.un.org/disarmament/WMD/Nuclear/NPTtext.shtml.

32. William Epstein, "The Non-Proliferation Treaty and the Review Conferences" in Richard Dean Burns, ed., *Encyclopedia of Arms Control and Disarmament*, 3 vols., New York: Scribners, 1993, vol. 2: 855ff; John R. Redick, "Nuclear Weapons-Free Zones," in *ibid.*, vol. 2:

1079–92; see also Richard Dean Burns, *The Evolution of Arms Control: From Antiquity to the Nuclear Age*, Santa Barbara, CA: Praeger, 2009, chapters 2, 4.

33. Allan S. Krass, *The United States and Arms Control: The Challenge of Leadership*, Westport, CT: Praeger, 1997, p.14.

34. Burns, *The Evolution of Arms Control*, chapter 8; David F. Winkler, *Cold War at Sea: High-Seas Confrontation between the United States and the Soviet Union*, Annapolis, MD: Naval Institute Press, 2000, p. 20; Krass, *The United States and Arms Control*, pp. 14–15.

35. Interim Agreement Between The United States of America and The Union of Soviet Socialist Republics on Certain Measures With Respect to the Limitation of Strategic Offensive Arms, Signed at Moscow, May 26, 1972, U.S. Department of State, available at: http://www.state.gov/t/isn/4795.htm.

36. Joseph M. Siracusa, *Nuclear Weapons: A Very Short Introduction,* Oxford: Oxford University Press, 2008, pp. 112–15; John Newhouse, *Cold Dawn: The Story of SALT*, New York: Holt, Rinehart & Winston, 1973; Gerard C. Smith, *Doubletalk: The Story of SALT I*, Garden City, NY: Doubleday, 1980; Strobe Talbott, *Endgame: The Inside Story of SALT II*, New York: Harper & Row, 1979, chapter 5.

37. Charles C. Flowerree, "Chemical and Biological Weapons and Arms Control," in Burns, *Encyclopedia of Arms Control and Disarmament*, vol. 2: p. 1,005; see also Thomas Graham Jr., *Disarmament Sketches: Three Decades of Arms Control and International Law*, Seattle: University of Washington Press, 2002, chapter 2.

38. Henry Kissinger, *White House Years,* Boston: Little, Brown, 1979, pp. 1,132, 1,150–51; Anatoly Dobrynin, *In Confidence: Moscow's Ambassador to America's Six Cold War Presidents*, New York: Random House, 1995, pp. 251–52.

39. See Vincent P. DeSantis's "Italy and the Cold War," in Joseph M. Siracusa and Glen Barclay, eds., *The Impact of the Cold War: Reconsiderations*, Port Washington, NY: Kennikat Press, 1977, pp. 26–39.

40. "Today, in the world of freedom, the proudest boast is '*Ich bin ein Berliner.*'" Joseph M. Siracusa, ed., *The Kennedy Years*, New York: Facts on File, 2004, pp. 592–93.

41. Thomas J. Schoenbaum, *Waging Peace and War: Dean Rusk in the Truman, Kennedy, and Johnson Years*, New York: Simon and Schuster, 1988, p. 421.

42. *New York Times*, December 23, 1973.

43. *U.S. in World Affairs*, 1967, 201–4; *New York Times*, September 20, 1969, pp. 1, 4.

44. Noam Kochavi, "Limited Accommodation, Perpetuated Conflict: Kennedy, China, and the Laos Crisis, 1961–1963," *Diplomatic History* 26, no. 1, 2002, p. 98.

45. Richard M. Nixon, "Asia after Viet Nam," *Foreign Affairs*, October 1967, p. 121; Richard Nixon, *RN: The Memoirs of Richard Nixon*, New York: Grosset & Dunlap, 1978, p. 344.

46. Nixon, *RN*, pp. 545, 548; Marvin Kalb and Bernard Kalb, *Kissinger*, Boston: Little, Brown, 1974, pp. 239–40, 251.

47. Richard Nixon, *Third Annual Report to Congress,* Washington DC: February 8, 1972.

Chapter Six

Variations and Continuities in Cold War Approaches

While there are some definitional criteria as to what constitutes a "doctrine" insofar as resolute language, a definitive speech or set of speeches, or a formal policy release, there is no absolute consistency in terms of its makeup or conception. What *is* consistent is that all doctrines in some shape or form have embodied the exceptional American swagger and the belief—at times exploited and exaggerated—in the principles of democracy and freedom. As this chapter will illustrate, while the Nixon, Carter, and Reagan doctrines at times seemingly veered from interventionist to expansionist, from defensive to offensive, from a preparedness to negotiate to wielding their respective power unchecked, all maintained what they deemed to be the requisite response in mitigating the communist "threat" and creating an international order that would ultimately best advance American interests, an order that would encompass self-determining/democratic states, and ultimately open free markets in which the U.S. could benefit and "navigate" unimpeded.

This chapter will begin its evaluation by looking at the Nixon Doctrine, often linked to a press conference the president gave on July 25, 1969. Nixon stated that the United States henceforth expected its allies to assume primary responsibility for their own military defense, thereby beginning the "Vietnamization" of the Vietnam War. The doctrine also argued for the pursuit of peace through a partnership with American allies. In his "Address to the Nation on the War in Vietnam," on November 3, 1969, Nixon stated that the United States would keep all of its treaty commitments; provide a shield if a nuclear power threatened the freedom of a nation allied with the U.S. or of a nation whose survival was considered vital to U.S. security; and in cases involving other types of aggression, would provide military and economic assistance when requested in accordance to its treaty commitments. Notwithstanding these security qualifications, it would look to the nation directly threatened to assume the primary responsibility of providing the manpower for its defense. The doctrine was also applied by the Nixon administration in the Persian Gulf region—with military aid to Iran and Saudi Arabia—so that these U.S. allies could undertake the responsibility of ensuring peace and stability in the region. According to Michael Klare, author of *Blood and Oil: The Dangers and Consequences of America's Growing Petroleum Dependency*, application of the Nixon Doctrine "opened the floodgates" of U.S. military aid to allies in the Persian Gulf, and helped set the stage for the Carter Doctrine and for the subsequent direct U.S. military involvement in both the Gulf War and the Iraq War.

In assessing Carter, this chapter argues that while the Soviet invasion was the contiguous spur for his doctrine, impetus for the president's policy shift had been building over the previous two years. Much of that energy emanated from concern over internal developments in Iran. As one of the United States' key allies in the Middle East for more than two decades, its position in the context of regional affairs was significant to say the least. Despite the country being defined by Carter himself as "an island of stability" as late as January 1978, Iran's shah would be toppled within the year, and Ayatollah Ruhollah Khomeini would transform the state into an Islamic republic. But concerns of regional instability were only partially attributable for Carter's apparent shift toward a new strategic posture. According to the president, a combination of three divergent forces had unified in prompting his declaration of U.S. policy. As stated: "[T]he steady growth and increased projection of Soviet military power beyond its own borders; the overwhelming dependence of the Western democracies on oil supplies from the Middle East; and the press of social and religious and economic and political change in the many nations of the developing world, exemplified by the revolution in Iran."[1] Because Carter believed that American interests in the Persian Gulf were under significant threat, it would require a more forthright adjustment so as to redress the regional and—in the administration's assessment—global balance of power.[2]

This chapter also considers the Carter Doctrine's approach to the Soviet Union, particularly given the divergent views of his Secretary of State Cyrus Vance and National Security Adviser Zbigniew Brzezinski. For Brzezinski, instability in both Central America and Africa came out of Moscow's ongoing desire for ideological competition and involvement in these regions. Détente, he argued, had simply permitted the Russians to continue their expansionist drive in these developing regions under the guise of superpower cooperation. In contrast to Vance's predilection for conciliation, Brzezinski vied for a more assertive approach toward Moscow. With a succession of developments—including the discovery of Soviet soldiers in Cuba and the Soviet invasion of Afghanistan—his position evidently became the administration's preference in Carter's State of the Union address in January 1980.[3]

The last section of the chapter evaluates the Reagan Doctrine's Cold War strategy of opposing Soviet influence through the backing of anti-communist guerrillas against the governments of Soviet-backed client states. It was created partially in response to the Brezhnev Doctrine and was a centerpiece of American foreign policy from the mid-1980s until the end of the Cold War in 1991. Reagan first explained the doctrine in his 1985 State of the Union address: "We must not break faith with those who are risking their lives . . . on every continent, from Afghanistan to Nicaragua . . . to defy Soviet aggression and secure rights which have been ours from birth. Support for freedom fighters is self-defense."[4] The doctrine called for American support of the Contras in Nicaragua, the Mujahideen in Afghanistan, and Jonas Savimbi's UNITA movement in Angola, among other anti-communist groups.

Upon first look, the Reagan Doctrine appears to sit comfortably alongside the United States' 40-year quest for containment of the Soviet Union. However, unlike Presidents Truman, Eisenhower, Nixon, and Carter, whose names defined previous doctrines through *defensive* containment in mitigating the further spread of Soviet power, the Reagan Doctrine emphasized an *offensive* form. In responding to a third wave of newly declared or alleged Marxist states—following the earlier waves launched by the two wars, with South Vietnam, Cambodia, and Laos falling to communism, and traditional Western positions lost in Angola, Mozambique, Ethiopia, South Yemen, Nicaragua, Grenada, Suriname, and Afghanistan—Reagan instituted his forthright approach. Indeed, such responses were based on the integrated and consequential reflection of a new global imbalance engendered by a default of American will—the "Vietnam syndrome"—and by Moscow's assertive orchestration of Soviet troops, arms, and surrogates. Thwarting the further development of this would become a defining pillar of the Reagan Doctrine.

THE PRECEDING STALEMATE AND THE SEARCH FOR PEACE

The Nixon Doctrine was synonymous with the developments of the Vietnam War. Campaigning against the Democratic presidential nominee, Vice President Hubert Humphrey, Nixon's aim was to use the war to drive a wedge through the Democratic base. Already fractured by the loss of Robert Kennedy, and two months prior Martin Luther King Jr., the Democratic 1968 nomination was further mired by internal disunity and struggle by anti-Vietnam forces, culminating in the Chicago riots at the conclusion of the Democratic Convention. Upon receiving the Republican presidential nomination, Nixon wasted no time lambasting the Johnson administration as the destroyer of American unity, engendering a nation of "unprecedented lawlessness" and "racial violence," and committing America to a war "with no end in sight." "The first priority foreign policy objective," Nixon announced in his acceptance speech for the Republican presidential nomination in Miami, "will be to bring an honorable end to the war in Vietnam."[5] Adding the preamble to his eventual doctrine, Nixon also argued that "the time has come for other nations in the free world to bear their fair share of the burden of defending peace and freedom around this world." Nixon was cognizant of the Vietnam struggle that had defined Johnson's administration and wasn't prepared to wait for the perfect truce that would bring Vietnam's North and South forces together.

Indeed, despite the enormous American effort, supplemented by the operations of some 700,000 South Vietnamese troops and the smaller contingents from other allies, the war by 1968 had reached a stalemate. While the Viet Cong and North Vietnamese troops could not drive the Americans out or destroy the Saigon government, the Americans and their allies' forces were not able to defeat their adversaries, nor could they protect South Vietnamese cities and villages. Yet, in most concerning fashion, in November 1967, General William C. Westmoreland, commander of U.S. troops in Vietnam, stated, "We are winning a war of attrition," predicting a slow withdrawal of U.S. forces beginning in two years with a progressively larger share of the security responsibility falling to the Vietnamese.[6] The Tet (Lunar New Year) offensive of January-February 1968 illustrated the vulnerability of South Vietnam. On January 31, Viet Cong and North Vietnamese forces simultaneously assaulted 26 or more unsuspecting provincial capitals and, as the *New York Times* reported, "uncounted numbers of district towns and American and Vietnamese air fields and bases."[7]

The most dramatic episodes were the six-hour occupation by 20 Viet Cong of the American embassy compound in Saigon and the capture of Hue, the old Annamese capital. Decimated Viet Cong forces were eventually expelled from all the towns and cities that they had seized, allowing President Johnson to proclaim the Tet offensive "a complete failure." While this was true in military terms, it had all but destroyed the optimism conveyed by Westmoreland, set back the pacification program, and largely ended talk of "victory." A negotiated peace in South Vietnam became the objective; however, this was thwarted by Washington's failure to understand Vietnamese nationalism and the Hanoi leadership's inability to grasp U.S. motives in Southeast Asia. Hanoi's Communist Party secretary Le Duan tried from May to August 1962 to interest the Kennedy administration in developing a neutralist coalition government for Vietnam to be staffed exclusively by southerners. French president Charles de Gaulle publicly supported a "neutral solution," but Washington had serious doubts about neutralization based on what they believed to be serious Hanoi violations. Moreover, Hanoi failed to develop its views on how the coalition would function with the Americans because "(1) it feared appearing weak; and (2) it feared the wrath of the Chinese," who opposed negotiations with Washington. Even though the president's thinking was beginning to focus on "How do we get out?" neither Kennedy nor his staff ever "probed or even carefully examined Hanoi's interest in a neutral solution."[8]

President Johnson stated the essence of America's peace terms at Johns Hopkins University on April 7, 1965: "[A]n independent South Vietnam—securely guaranteed and able to shape its own relationships to all others—free from outside interference—tied to no alliance—a military base for no other country." If peace were assured, he added, the United States would be ready to invest a billion dollars in development of the Mekong River delta.[9] Hanoi responded the next day with a four-point proposal: (1) Complete withdrawal of all U.S. troops from South Vietnam and cancellation of the alleged U.S.-South Vietnam military alliance; (2) observation of the 1954 Geneva agreement pending the unification of Vietnam; (3) settlement of the internal affairs of South Vietnam by the people of South Vietnam in accordance with the program of the NLF (National Liberation Front); and (4) peaceful unification of Vietnam "to be settled by the Vietnamese people in both zones, without any foreign interference."[10] Later Hanoi imposed a fifth requirement or precondition: all bombing of North Vietnam must stop before negotiations could begin.

Ho Chi Minh, Le Duan, and Prime Minister Pham Van Dong doubtlessly presumed they had designed flexibility into their proposal, especially on point 3, which recognized the southern resistance for a neutral coalition government to last at least 10 years. However, Washington focused on point 4, declaring it would not negotiate on these terms because of the presumption that the NLF was Hanoi's puppet. Under pressure at home and abroad to pave the way for negotiations, Johnson experimented with a bombing halt, although a five-day cessation in May 1965 was criticized as being too short. Then from Christmas Eve 1965 to January 31, 1966, Johnson sent Vice President Hubert Humphrey, UN ambassador Arthur Goldberg, Ambassador-at-Large W. Averell Harriman, and others to 40 foreign capitals, seeking to enlist their aid in bringing Hanoi to the conference table. When this appeal failed, the bombing was resumed.

The bombing continued through 1966 and 1967, hitting targets in North Vietnam and along the Ho Chi Minh Trail in Laos where the Joint Chiefs of Staff sought to inhibit the movement of supplies and men from North Vietnam to the scene of fighting. Although Secretary of Defense Robert McNamara was skeptical about its efficacy, Johnson now took the position that he could not halt the bombing without some corresponding de-escalation. In a speech at San Antonio, Texas, on September 29, 1967, he set forth his "San Antonio formula": "The United States is willing to stop all aerial and naval bombing of North Vietnam when this will lead promptly to productive discussions. We, of course, assume that while discussions proceed, North Vietnam would not take advantage of the bombing cessation or limitation."[11]

On November 2, UN ambassador Arthur Goldberg stated—and the State Department concurred—that the United States would not resist participation of the NLF as a party in a peace conference. Hanoi's response was the Tet offensive, which produced deep disillusionment with the war in the United States. Secretary of Defense Clark M. Clifford, who succeeded McNamara on March 1, 1968, became convinced that pressing for military victory in Vietnam was useless and that the bombing should be halted as a step toward a negotiated peace. His arguments ultimately prevailed. In a television address on March 31, 1968, Johnson announced that the bombing of North Vietnam would largely end on the following day. He also announced that he would neither seek nor accept his party's renomination for the presidency.

The Hanoi government responded by agreeing to negotiate. Eventually both sides met in Paris on May 10, 1968, with delegations headed by Harriman for the United States and Xuan Thuy for North Vietnam. The results were disappointing, though not surprising, for the North Vietnamese refused to discuss terms of settlement until *all* bombing of the North stopped. The United States had refused to stop bombing the supply routes that threatened the security of U.S. troops, and it was only on October 31 that Johnson ended all bombing of North Vietnam, thereby allowing the opportunity for future negotiations. By this stage, the new Republican administration of Richard M. Nixon would be in office.

THE NIXON ADMINISTRATION

When the delegations met on January 25, 1969, Henry Cabot Lodge, who had replaced Harriman, proposed as an eventual goal the withdrawal of all foreign (including North Vietnamese) troops from South Vietnam, but as an immediate objective the restoration of the neutralized character of the Demilitarized Zone (DMZ). Five days later, the North Vietnamese and NLF delegations rejected Lodge's proposal in a seven-hour session in which, as described by a *New York Times* reporter, "most of the proceedings were devoted to propaganda, recriminations and occasionally rough language."[12]

In March, President Nixon endorsed secret talks with Hanoi, while at the same time President Thieu revealed a willingness to begin private talks with the NLF or Viet Cong.[13] On May 8, the NLF made public a 10-point peace proposal and six days later in a television address to the nation, Nixon stated the American objectives.[14] A comparison of these two sets of proposals revealed the points of incompatibility that were for many months to stand in the way of any agreement. In a few words, President Nixon demanded, as the Johnson administration had insisted, that Hanoi withdraw its troops from

South Vietnam and leave the South Vietnamese people to settle their own affairs in peace. Hanoi refused and with the NLF called for the unilateral withdrawal of allied troops and the creation of a South Vietnamese coalition government that excluded Thieu and Ky and their factions. Ho Chi Minh's death on September 3, 1969, failed to bring significant changes. Finally, on July 1, 1970, after the military campaign in Cambodia, Nixon replaced Lodge with David K. E. Bruce, a distinguished diplomat and a Democrat, as head of the American negotiating team in Paris with "great flexibility."[15]

Nguyen Thi Binh, the chief Viet Cong negotiator, returned to the peace table on September 17, 1970, bringing an eight-point formula. The new proposal, like those before it, called for the unilateral withdrawal of all American and allied troops. There were some concessions, including a possible cease-fire and a willingness to discuss exchange of prisoners prior to a general settlement. There was a sufficient degree of "give" here, thought the *New York Times*, to warrant exploration through submission of new proposals by the United States.[16] On October 7, Nixon presented a five-point plan for a "standstill" cease-fire, immediate exchange of prisoners, a widened peace conference to include Cambodia and Laos (tacit admission that the war had become an "Indochina war"), and a promise to withdraw all American troops as part of an overall settlement. Although the actual proposal did not repeat the insistence that withdrawal of troops be mutual, it became evident that this demand still stood.[17] If the new formula favorably impressed Nixon's former critics at home and abroad, the response from the enemy camp was disappointing. Moscow promptly described the offer as "a great fraud," while it was totally rejected by the Hanoi and Viet Cong negotiators in Paris.

"Vietnamizing" the Doctrine

In maintaining the hope to end the war through negotiations, President Nixon attempted to quiet criticism by adjusting the doctrine through "Vietnamization" of the conflict: a gradual withdrawal of U.S. forces and their replacement by better trained and equipped South Vietnamese troops. An announcement on June 8, 1969, that 25,000 U.S. troops would be withdrawn during July, to be replaced by South Vietnamese, was followed a few days later by the hope that more than 100,000 could be withdrawn before the end of 1970. Then on September 16, it was announced that by the end of 1969 an additional 35,000 would be brought home. All U.S. combat ground forces, Nixon said on November 3, 1969, would be withdrawn from Vietnam and replaced by Vietnamese forces "on an orderly scheduled timetable." The rate of withdrawal depended on three variables: (1) progress of the peace negotiations, (2) "the level of enemy activity," and (3) progress in training the South Vietnamese forces. He warned Hanoi that any increase in violence would be met with "strong and effective measures."[18] While the Vietnamization plan focused specifically on the withdrawal of U.S. ground combat forces, other elements—air, logistics, and artillery—would presumably remain as needed to support Vietnamese forces.[19] Nixon's program added up to a reduction of 265,000 troops by the spring of 1971.

Notwithstanding persistent doubts, the president's plan appeared effective in placating some of his critics, albeit momentarily. On December 2, the Democratic-controlled House of Representatives adopted by a vote of 333 to 55 a resolution supporting the president "in his efforts to negotiate a just peace in Vietnam."[20] Nixon's promise to begin withdrawing American troops seemed to take some steam out of the anti-war movement until he announced on April 30, 1970, that American and South Vietnamese forces were carrying the war into Cambodia. The declared purpose of the intrusion into Cambodia was to capture the Communist command headquarters for operations in South Vietnam and to destroy Viet Cong and North Vietnamese sanctuaries in areas adjoining South Vietnam, which for years had been used with the tacit consent of nominally neutralist Prince Norodom Sihanouk, Cambodia's chief of state. The United States had long tolerated this breach of neutrality rather than risk driving Sihanouk into the enemy camp. In March 1969, however, the U.S. Air Force began a series of secret, illegal bombing raids in eastern Cambodia that lasted until Sihanouk was ousted on March 18, 1970, by pro-West premier General Lon Nol. Described as long on ambition but short on ability, Lon Nol believed his country was threatened by the presence of North Vietnamese troops. Not only was the enemy threatening to take over Cambodia, Nixon declared, he was "concentrating his main forces in the sanctuaries where they are building up to launch massive attacks on our forces and those of South Vietnam." In view of this dual threat, the president argued it was necessary "to go to the heart of the trouble. That means cleaning out major North Vietnamese and Viet Cong–occupied sanctuaries which serve as bases for attacks on both Cambodia and American and South Vietnamese forces in South Vietnam."[21]

The move into Cambodia produced a new, more intense round of demonstrations on some 1,350 college and university campuses, some turning violent. At Kent State University, Ohio National Guard troops fired on demonstrators, killing 4 students and wounding 9, and at Jackson State University in Mississippi, police killed 2 students and wounded 12. Senators introduced several resolutions designed to prevent the president from expanding the area of war without consent of Congress. Upon completion of the sweep on June 30, limited to 30 kilometers within Cambodia, the president issued a long report claiming dubious successes for the operation, since the "key control center" of the Communist command had not been found.[22] The American public had had enough. According to a Gallup poll taken in May 1971, 6 out of 10 Americans now thought it had been a mistake for the United States to get involved in Vietnam. While this signified a complete reversal of public opinion since August 1965, the poll also revealed that Republicans had changed their views of the war almost as drastically as Democrats. [23]

Vietnamization and Other Doctrinal Actions

In the November following the Cambodian invasion, the Nixon administration began to increasingly concern itself with a large buildup of supplies in North Vietnam, and the problem of how to prevent them from moving southward. To meet the challenge and to test Vietnamization, in February 1971, two of South Vietnam's best divisions launched a major offensive (Lam Son 719) aimed at cutting the Ho Chi Minh Trail in Laos. Without American advisers but with American air cover, the outmanned South Vietnamese were challenged by four veteran North Vietnamese divisions, resulting in a disaster for Saigon's forces. Thereafter, the intensified fighting of 1971 was met with increased U.S. bombing, albeit within the framework of continued American withdrawals. In the spring of 1972, perceiving that President Nixon's hands would be tied in an election year, and persuaded of the vulnerability of the Thieu regime, Hanoi launched a major offensive in the south, this time abandoning its guerrilla tactics in favor of a conventional alignment led by Soviet-supplied T-54 tanks. Initial results were striking as entire South Vietnamese divisions panicked. In less than a month, Hanoi had captured the northern capital of Quantri and imperiled Saigon itself, but did not destroy the South Vietnamese army. Although some southern units disintegrated, others fought well, but it was U.S. airpower that played the decisive role in stopping the Easter Offensive. Despite his proposed trip to Moscow in May, Nixon ordered the heaviest bombing raids of the war thus far. Major facilities and installations were struck. The president then authorized the mining of the entrances of North Vietnamese ports, thus setting the stage for a potentially direct confrontation with either the Soviet Union or China or both. While nothing of the sort eventuated, the war was again stalemated, with the North Vietnamese forces holding stronger positions in the south. [24]

Anxious to secure peace before the coming presidential election in November, Nixon let it be known that he would accept a cease-fire in place rather than the complete withdrawal of North Vietnamese troops. With the American counter-offensive partially successful and in the face of a strengthened Thieu government, Hanoi opted for the peace table. Nixon suspended the bombing of North Vietnam, north of the 20th parallel. Negotiations took place at the formal meetings in Paris, but presidential adviser Henry Kissinger and North Vietnamese representative Le Duc Tho privately worked on preliminary terms of a final agreement. President Thieu balked, however, at the terms of the agreement and demanded that they be renegotiated. In the end, Nixon issued Thieu with an ultimatum, and he acquiesced. [25] Meanwhile, when Hanoi began to stall, the president on December 18 resumed the bombing of the north with a vengeance. The North Vietnamese capital and Haiphong were bombed more heavily than at any previous stage of the conflict. In response to worldwide protests, Washington again restricted the bombing on December 30 to the area south of the 20th parallel and on January 15, 1973, ended all bombing of North Vietnam. Private talks between Kissinger and Le Duc Tho resumed in Paris on January 8 and five days later resulted in the conclusion of the elusive peace agreement, signed on January 27.

The Paris cease-fire agreement, as it came to be called, provided for, among other things: a standstill cease-fire to take place immediately; the withdrawal of all U.S. forces from South Vietnam; the release of all American prisoners of war within 60 days; the formation of a four-party joint military commission to enforce these provisions; the establishment of an International Commission on Control and Supervision; the formation by agreement between the South Vietnamese parties of a National Council of National Reconciliation and Concord, which would set about the task of organizing general elections; and the holding of an international conference on Vietnam within 30 days of the signing of the agreement. American fighting on the ground terminated with the withdrawal of the last U.S. troops in March 1973, two months after the cease-fire and eight years after the first formal commitment of military forces. Thus ended, until then, the longest war in U.S. history.

The Nixon Doctrine's Vietnam drive was, by any standard, a most costly episode. The loss in national treasure and blood was staggering. According to Pentagon estimates, from 1961 until late April 1975, U.S. expenditures in Indochina came to more than $141 billion or, to put it another way, $7,000 for each of South Vietnam's 20 million people. The war produced many dubious precedents, including U.S. chemical operations, defoliation, and crop destruction that consumed some 5,229,484 acres; bombing tonnage (more than three times the total amount dropped in World War II); and the first known use of weather warfare, all of which left lasting ecological damage. The loss of life was equally staggering. From the 1961 death of Specialist 4 James Thomas Davis of Livingston, Tennessee, whom President Lyndon Johnson later called "the first American to fall in defense of our freedom in Vietnam," until the Paris Peace Accords of 1973, American casualties alone reached 350,000 with 59,000 killed (40,000 in combat).[26] Casualty figures for the Vietnamese (North and South), at best an estimate, may have reached a million deaths (including civilians), with more than 224,000 South Vietnamese combat deaths, and perhaps 660,000 combined North Vietnamese and Viet Cong combat deaths. Vietnam also had an impact at home: the "television war" turned *napalm* and *free-fire zones* into household words; severe inflation affected the economy as early as 1965; university campuses grew highly politicized; draft resisters fled to Canada and foreign lands; and presidents were made and unmade. Vietnam shaped and reshaped all who survived it—from political leaders and military chiefs to the proverbial person in the street.

The Breakdown of American Policy

While the negotiated peace settlement allowed the United States an opportunity to extricate itself from Indochina with what the Nixon administration regarded as a semblance of "peace with honor," the reality of the situation was vastly different for those who remained behind. In view of the almost irreconcilable nature of the conflict between President Thieu and his opponents and the potential threat of 150,000 North Vietnamese regulars and Viet Cong poised on South Vietnamese soil, it seemed to most observers that it would be only a matter of time before the south would be overrun, perhaps as few as five years. As it turned out, it only required three. Hanoi was utterly undeterred by the peace agreement and soon set out to reunify the two Vietnams by force of arms. Correctly gauging the mood of the American public, the North Vietnamese General Staff, according to the most authoritative sources,[27] carefully laid the groundwork for the next offensive. In the spring of 1975, a combined North Vietnamese and Viet Cong attack proved too much for the poorly led South Vietnamese army. Saigon, renamed Ho Chi Minh City, fell on April 30.

The United States' covert activities in Laos were for years conducted by the Hmong, who were supplied and directed by the Central Intelligence Agency. Backed by U.S. airpower from 1962 to 1973 and by special Thai units, these mountain warriors, despite suffering very heavy casualties, conducted guerrilla operations that slowed the advance of Pathet Lao and North Vietnamese forces in Laos. The Vientiane Agreement of February 1973 ended U.S. bombing, required the withdrawal of Thai forces, and created a new coalition government. In December 1975, the Hanoi-backed Pathet Lao established the Lao People's Democratic Republic. The United States provided military support for Lon Nol's Cambodian regime from 1970 to 1973, especially in channelling American airpower to help slow the advancing Khmer Rouge. After Congress halted aid shipments in late 1974, resistance collapsed and the Khmer Rouge seized Phnom Penh on April 17, 1975, renamed Cambodia as Democratic Kampuchea, renounced ties with North Vietnam, and set about killing and torturing nearly one million Cambodians by the end of 1978.[28] The collapse of South Vietnam, together with the defeat of the pro-Western forces in Laos and subsequently in Cambodia, marked the end of an American era in Southeast Asia.

An enduring legacy of the Vietnam War has been the extraordinary number of accounts by participants and critics of all sorts—a virtual cottage industry—that continue to present arguments without end. U.S. military officers, writing after the war, often felt that they had been denied victory. These professional soldiers have often held President Johnson responsible for refusing to mobilize the nation for war, for placing limitations on the forces in the field, for gradually escalating hostilities instead of launching a knockout aerial blow, and for not invading North Vietnam. However, as Pulitzer Prize–winning author Stanley Karnow points out, "Such autopsies, like war games, often bear little resemblance to actual war. In reality, the Communists were almost fanatical in their resolve to reunify Vietnam under their control. They saw the struggle against America and its South Vietnamese allies as another chapter in their nation's thousands of years of resistance to Chinese and, later, French rule. And they were prepared to accept unlimited losses to achieve their sacred objective."[29] In pursuit of their paramount patriotic mission, the Vietnamese Communists obviously were willing to spend much more blood and treasure than was the United States to achieve its ill-defined, broadly conceived objective of staving off a possible domino debacle.

THE CARTER DOCTRINE

Fighting the same battles as his predecessors before him, Jimmy Carter, the 39th president of the United States, exhibited a new, updated, and adapted corollary of the Cold War doctrines that went before him. Smartened by the upset of the Vietnam War and the general public fatigue of Cold War posturing, Carter's doctrine emphasized a renewed effort to fight Soviet expansionism but with a number of important changes. In his State of the Union speech on January 23, 1980, Carter reiterated the events of the Cold War that had since "shaped our challenges" and were now reasserting themselves in the form of the invasion of Afghanistan. "The steady growth and increased projection of Soviet military power beyond its own borders" was once again threatening the balance of power.[30] More importantly, as the State of the Union address would unveil, access to the Persian Gulf's oil fields had become "vital" to American interests, and as such, invaders would be "repelled by any means necessary, including military force." President Carter's National Security Advisor Zbigniew Brzezinski's aforementioned addition to the address was intended to clearly outline to the Soviets that America would not tolerate interruptions to its oil supply. Brzezinski would later go on to state in *Power and Principle: Memoirs of the National Security Adviser* that the introduction of the Carter Doctrine was to act as the "immediate deterrent," an "awareness in Moscow and elsewhere of America's engagement" while U.S. forces were recouping.[31] Subsequently, given the dependence of the U.S. on Middle Eastern oil in the decades to come, Carter's addition to the Cold War repertoire of U.S. presidential doctrines would be the only one to survive the fall of the Soviet Union and the end of the Cold War.

The origins of the Carter Doctrine can best be understood as a mixture of initial optimism followed by a series of destabilizing foreign-policy concerns in the Middle East. The president's foreign-policy assessment at the beginning of his tenure displayed a strong desire to move beyond the tribulations of the Cold War. Representing this optimism, Carter announced in a May 1977 speech that the "unifying threat of conflict with the Soviet Union ha[d] become less intensive" and that détente and cooperation could be achieved.[32] This assessment was shaped by the major economic and political dissent infecting the Soviet Union's domestic environment at the time. However, if Carter wasn't particularly concerned by the demonstrations erupting in Iran in 1977, by 1978 Washington's mood was somber. Demonstrations against the shah of Iran, America's greatest ally in the Middle East, had been increasing in intensity every month, climaxing in January of 1979 when the shah was forced into exile. Ten months later Iranian students belonging to the Muslim Student Followers of the Imam Line stormed the U.S. embassy, taking 52 American hostages. The students demanded the return of the shah, who had been admitted to the U.S. on the grounds of health since October, for trial and execution. In all, the Iranian hostage crisis, as it came to be known, would last for a total of 444 days.

The main driver of President Carter's new Middle East policy came a month after the Tehran embassy invasion. On December 24, Soviet officials ordered the 40th Army into Afghanistan, and within weeks occupying Russian army personnel would rise to more than 100,000. Russian military personnel had in fact been deployed in Afghanistan since April under a pseudo-military security task force invited by then Afghanistan President Nur Muhammad Taraki. Taraki's rule in Afghanistan had been mired in controversy and political sabotage.[33] Following the fallout between Taraki and Hafizullah Amin, chairman of the Council of Ministers and one-time close friend of Taraki, the political situation in Kabul became tenuous. With Taraki's assassination in September, Amin wasted no time in establishing his own rule. The Amin government, however, was poorly equipped to deal with the increasingly deteriorating interest the public had in socialism. An attempt to win the support of the Afghan people through the introduction of new investment and reforms also failed to dissuade public discontent. The repressive Amin government was in a state of irremediable disposition. The assessment of the Special Commission on Afghanistan, comprising KGB chief Yuri Andropov, Central Committee member Boris Ponomarev, and Defense Minister Dmitriy Ustinov, was that the decay was far-reaching and as such would require Soviet assistance. On December 27, 1979, the Soviets carried out Operation Storm-333 and took control of the country, killing Amin and his son in the storming of the Tajbeg Palace and placing Babrak Karmal as head of Russia's new puppet government in Afghanistan.

Washington's reaction was to adopt a series of restrictions that would subsequently end any hope of a détente. Almost immediately the U.S. ambassador to Moscow was recalled, SALT II negotiations were put on hold, cultural and economic exchanges were deferred, Soviet Union fishing privileges in American waters were severely curtailed, the 1980 Moscow Olympic Games were boycotted, 17 million tons of grain were diverted to other nations and livestock feeding programs, and any trade of strategic value including high-technology leases was halted. At the United Nations, Washington personnel had been ratcheting up international support to put pressure on the Kremlin. Despite Russia's power of veto status in the UN Security Council, additional pressure was added through resolutions in the General Assembly, though these proved largely unsuccessful. Additionally, in 1980 the Carter administration commenced a CIA program aimed at arming Mujahideen fighters to fight Soviet forces. This was done covertly, buying Soviet-made weapons through Egypt and China and supplying fighters through Pakistan.[34]

Whether or not Middle Eastern security had been high on Carter's radar before the Soviet invasion of Afghanistan, the volatility in the region after 1979 gave new focus to the strategic vulnerability the United States faced in its oil supply. Brzezinski in fact had been trying to bring the president's attention to the issue as early as 1978 with the idea of developing force projection capabilities for the region, but his message wasn't received.[35] He tried again a few weeks later, this time with the Comprehensive Net Assessment 1978 (CNA-78), which otherwise described the extent to which U.S. interests remained discernibly vulnerable.

Carter's eventual decision to make the region "vital to American interests" was thus framed by the threat of Soviet Afghanistan to both Iran and Pakistan as a "steppingstone to possible control over much of the world's oil supplies."[36] Moreover, Carter did not want to run into the same impediments to which his predecessors had been subjected, namely Eisenhower's "massive retaliation" and in the 1960s the Americanization of the Vietnam conflict. The State of the Union speech was therefore specific enough to threaten any Soviet plans in the Persian Gulf but also ambiguous enough to allow multiple options in its strategic response, including the possibility of a coalition of forces. This omission of specificity would later provide the basis for the first Gulf War and, more significantly, the invasion of Iraq in 2003.

THE REAGAN DOCTRINE

Long before the cultivation of his doctrine, Reagan had developed a well-crafted anti-communist litany in a succession of speeches. Addressing the Phoenix, Arizona, Chamber of Commerce in 1961, he stated, "Wars end in victory or defeat. One of the foremost authorities on communism in the world today has said we have ten years. Not ten years to make up our minds, but ten years to win or lose—by 1970 the world will be all slave or free." Two decades later, Reagan still approached the Cold War much as other strident anti-communists: "We are faced with the most evil enemy mankind has known in his long climb from the swamp to the stars." After castigating American liberals for seeking agreements to limit strategic nuclear weapons, he insisted, "We are being asked to buy our safety from the threat of the Bomb by selling into permanent slavery our fellow human beings enslaved behind the Iron Curtain." Reagan charged his opponents with "encouraging them to give up their hope of freedom because we are ready to make a deal with their slave masters."[37]

Concern pertaining to Soviet military power and global expansionism dominated the outlook of the Reagan administration. The president defined these dangers at a White House news conference in late January 1981: "From the time of the Russian revolution until the present, Soviet leaders have reiterated their determination that their goal must be the promotion of world revolution and a one world socialist or Communist state. . . . They have openly and publicly declared that the only morality they recognize is what will further their cause; meaning they reserve unto themselves the right to commit any crime; to lie [and] to cheat in order to obtain that." Echoing this view, secretary of state designate Alexander Haig at his confirmation hearings warned members of the Senate Foreign Relations Committee the years ahead would "be unusually dangerous. Evidence of that danger . . . [was] everywhere." The nation needed to be vigilant and be prepared to expend the resources necessary to control future events. "Unchecked," he said, "the growth of Soviet military power must eventually paralyze Western policy altogether." Three months later, Haig declared that Washington needed to concentrate its policies on the Soviet Union because the Kremlin was "the greatest source of international insecurity today. . . . Let us be plain about it: Soviet promotion of violence as the instrument of change constitutes the greatest danger to world peace."[38] Of course, it was Reagan's "evil empire" speech, on March 8, 1983, to the National Association of Evangelicals that, despite not being the first occasion he employed that term to describe the Soviet Union, represented one of the defining points in his hostile rhetoric.

The Reagan administration's rhetoric also sought to distance itself from previous presidential diplomatic efforts in seeking limits to the nuclear arms race, although this would progressively change over his two-term tenure in office. The president was on record opposing the 1963 Test Ban pact (Kennedy), the 1968 Non-Proliferation Treaty (Johnson), the 1972 Strategic Arms Limitation (SALT I) pact and the Anti-Ballistic Missile (ABM) agreements (Nixon), and the Helsinki Accords (Ford). He now insisted the SALT II treaty (Carter) was "fatally flawed." Indeed, he argued, SALT II allowed the

Soviet Union a "window of vulnerability" through which its missile superiority would threaten U.S. long-range missile forces. Despite his anti-Soviet rhetoric, Reagan would periodically weave in the potential to improve relations with the Kremlin. His inaugural address emphasized the American people's desire for peace: "We will negotiate for it, sacrifice for it, [but] we will not surrender for it, now or ever." Notwithstanding these sentiments, the new president's doctrine quickly exhibited a determination to negotiate from strength and to build up before building down.[39]

U.S. Military Buildup

During the presidential campaign, Reagan and his supporters repeatedly pledged to rebuild America's military forces to reverse what they perceived as a national malaise. Consequently, the new administration eventually set in motion the costliest defense program in the nation's peacetime history. Reagan's military advisers, pushing for higher levels of defense expenditures, ignored traditional review procedures and refused to reconsider the military utility of a project once authorized. Even Defense Secretary Caspar W. Weinberger, who had arrived with a well-earned reputation for cost cutting, endorsed the Pentagon's "wish list," with its requirement of nothing less than an annual 7 percent budget increase. Reagan agreed and included the inflated figure in his new budget, not recognizing that his staff had confused budget calculations and actually increased military expenditures by 10 percent per year. The fiscally conservative president would consequently triple the national debt from slightly under $1 trillion to more than $3 trillion by the end of the decade.

With new, technologically advanced weapons, Washington expected to deal from a position of greater strength, reassure allies, and perhaps force Moscow to agree to a disadvantageous reduction of its nuclear weaponry. The proposed expenditures—$1.6 trillion in five years—would be used to acquire new missile systems, especially the mobile MX; underwrite the nation's most ambitious naval program ever; update air force planes and facilities; and create a stronger, more mobile conventional force prepared for any global challenges. The immediate dilemma, not always resolved, required distinguishing weapons that were necessary, effective, and manageable from those that were merely expensive. Reiterating a long-held Pentagon truism, Secretary Weinberger nevertheless insisted that Soviet intervention in Afghanistan demonstrated the United States must always be ready to fight several conventional wars simultaneously: "We must be prepared for waging a conventional war that may extend to many parts of the world."[40]

The massive new military buildup component of the Reagan Doctrine was not without its critics. To informed observers the administration's claim of overwhelming Soviet military power was a significant embellishment.

According to James Fallows, symbols unquestionably play a part in international politics. As he stated, "The Russians have derived incalculable mileage from the impression that they have built a world-conquering military force, an impression they have been fostering, overtly and covertly, since 1945. But why should we help them create that impression," he questioned, "when it is at such variance with the facts? . . . If the problem is the perception of American strength, why not assess that strength coolly rather than create exaggerated fears?" The administration's avoidance of readily available facts was evident. As Christopher Paine pointed out in a fall 1982 edition of *Bulletin of the Atomic Scientists*, "85 percent of the Soviet submarine-launched ballistic missile force [is] usually in port on any given day," while only one-third of U.S. submarines were similarly in port. The New York *Daily News* reported in February 1982, that "morale among Soviet troops stationed in East Germany is so bad that some units are close to mutiny."[41] Not surprisingly, the Pentagon's public relations office used overly generous annual assessments of the Soviet armed forces to justify its budgets during the early Reagan years.

There were many in the commercial sector, though, and even some Pentagon officials, who questioned whether the projected military spending exceeded the requirements of national security. Could Defense Secretary Weinberger reduce the military's wasteful habits? Could the Pentagon be accountable—perhaps even balance its books? Congressmen, equally troubled by the perennial rise in the cost of national defense, had difficulty arguing that specific expenditures were excessive when the experts, with their control of essential information, insisted that they were not. Moreover, most Congressional representatives benefited from the monies spent in their districts and recognized substantial reductions of defense expenditures would result in the loss of jobs at home. There existed in Washington, in any case, a strange lack of concern for an effective distribution of allocated defense funds. Nonetheless, the expenditures themselves were somehow expected to send a message to the Kremlin.

The president and his advisers expected far more than the perpetuation of the status quo from the country's costly defense efforts; indeed, some thought the higher levels of U.S. preparedness would bring about long-desired changes in Soviet behavior. "We have a right, indeed a duty," Secretary Haig echoed, "to insist that the Soviets support a peaceful international order, that they abide by treaties, and that they respect reciprocity."[42] Another senior administration official announced that a Soviet withdrawal from Afghanistan and Angola was not sufficient as a precondition for moderating the United States' posture; he would demand nothing less than an extensive reduction in Soviet military spending. Others in Washington anticipated that when the United States achieved overwhelming nuclear supremacy, the Soviet Union would be coerced into accepting conditions that conformed to

American design. In some measure, Reagan's approach to the U.S.S.R. was a reaffirmation of the Eisenhower administration's concept of massive retaliation with its underlying assumption that the Soviets could not, in the long run, survive American competition. [43]

A New Cold War?

For some analysts and commentators, however, the Reagan Doctrine's ideological crusade inexcusably heightened tensions between Washington and Moscow. Writing in the *New Yorker* on October 3, 1983, Soviet expert George F. Kennan noted that public discussion of Soviet-American relations seemed to point to a military showdown. "Can anyone mistake, or doubt," he asked, "the ominous meaning of such a state of affairs? The phenomena just described . . . are the familiar characteristics, the unfailing characteristics, of a march toward war—that, and nothing else." [44] This grim assessment suggested that America was bent on creating a second, more dangerous Cold War. Yet nowhere did the administration's alleged toughness result in diplomatic achievements that improved America's security. Reagan's ideological approach, Stanley Hoffmann argued in *Dead Ends*, "has turned out to be utterly deficient as a strategy because it fails to address many real problems, it aggravates others, it provides no priority other than the anti-Soviet imperative, and precious little guidance even in connection with the new Cold War." [45] The character of the Soviet power structure was irrelevant to the requirement of dealing openly and frankly with the Kremlin. "Like Mount Everest," wrote *Newsweek*'s Meg Greenfield in September 1983, "the Russians are there. And, like Mount Everest, their features are not exactly a mystery. We need to stop gasping and sighing and exclaiming and nearly dying of shock every time something truly disagreeable happens. We have to grow up and confront them, as they are." [46]

However exaggerated the Soviet threat may have been, on September 1, 1983, the downing of a Korean commercial airliner (KAL 007) that had strayed into Soviet territory provided Washington officials with defining evidence on what they saw as the Soviets' preparedness to undermine security. While the State Department called the disaster "brutal and unprovoked," the president's statement for the media declared: "What can we think of a regime that so broadly trumpets its vision of peace and global disarmament and yet so callously and quickly commits a terrorist act? What can be said about Soviet credibility when they so flagrantly lie about such a heinous act?" [47]

In perhaps the most comprehensive and categorical top-level Soviet denunciation of any U.S. administration since the early Cold War, Soviet premier Yuri Andropov condemned Reagan's attitude on September 28. The president's ideological challenges risked the prospect of actual war, the Soviet leader declared. "To turn the battle of ideas into military confrontation would be too costly for the whole of mankind. But those who are blinded by anticommunism are evidently incapable of grasping this," Andropov continued. "Starting with the bogey of a Soviet military threat, they have now proclaimed a crusade against socialism as a social system."[48]

The reality of Andropov's warning came two months later. Without notifying Warsaw Pact states, NATO had scheduled a command post exercise test involving nuclear release procedures (code-named Able Archer) for November 2–11, 1983. Uncertain of the exercise's purpose, the Soviet Union went on a strategic intelligence alert. Days passed, and the attack did not come; the Soviets had apparently exaggerated the danger. Throughout the crisis—although they were aware of the turmoil in Moscow—Washington offered the Soviets no explanation. On November 16, Alexander Bovin, *Izvestia*'s political commentator, accused American leaders of ignoring the security interests of the Soviet Union and compelling the two countries to walk "the edge of the missile precipice." From mid-1983 into 1984, according to CIA reports, senior officials in Moscow took "very seriously" the threat of a U.S. preemptive nuclear attack. Former diplomat W. Averell Harriman warned Reagan on January 1, 1984, that his program of emphasizing military strength while denigrating diplomacy could lead to disaster. Blaming the Kremlin for the world's current instabilities was, he wrote, "not a strategy or a policy. . . . It will not reshape the Russian nation; it will not bring down the Iron Curtain; and, above all, it will not reduce the nuclear threat that hangs over every American."

The Rationale of the Reagan Doctrine

While the Soviet Union would define broader strategic thought, U.S. incursions into specific "domains of concern" would also become a key doctrinal plank of the Reagan administration. In his 1985 State of the Union address, the president declared: "We must not break faith with those who are risking their lives on every continent from Afghanistan to Nicaragua to defy Soviet-supported aggression and secure rights which have been ours from birth."[49] In an apparent adjustment of the Truman Doctrine, which ultimately justified intervening to protect governments threatened by communists, the Reagan Doctrine proclaimed the right, indeed an obligation, to subvert existing communist regimes. Ignoring the Helsinki Agreement, Reagan told Polish Americans at the White House on August 17, 1984, that he rejected "any interpretation of the Yalta agreement" indicating "American consent for the division of Europe into spheres of influence." Cold Warriors saw Reagan's doctrine as the antithesis of the Brezhnev Doctrine's assertion that Soviet gains were irreversible. To Charles Krauthammer, Reagan's doctrine rested on America's support of justice, necessity, and tradition: justice because anti-communist revolutionaries were fighting tyranny; necessity because any defeat for "freedom fighters" assigned a country irrevocably to Soviet dominance; and tradition because the United States had always supported the cause of freedom abroad. [50]

Critics pointed to Washington's usual habit of exaggerating the dangers posed by communist regimes, as well as available capacity to eliminate them. Robert Tucker questioned the doctrine's core tenet that all Marxist-Leninist governments lacked legitimacy and that the United States had a moral responsibility to support rebels who opposed them. The Nicaraguan government, he noted, served its people far better than several of those in Central America supported by the United States. "What the Reagan Doctrine requires, in theory," political scientist Kenneth Thompson warned, "is indiscriminate intervention to overturn communist regimes regardless of calculations of interest and power." In practice, the Reagan Doctrine unleashed limited war by proxy. It provided the rationale for Washington's economic and military assistance to the Mujahideen resistance in Afghanistan, to rebel factions in Cambodia, and, following the repeal of the Clark Amendment in 1985, to Jonas Savimbi's guerrilla forces in Angola. Here the United States' contribution was the risk-free funding of low-cost mercenaries, whose devotion to democratic principles and prospects of success remained highly questionable. [51]

But the doctrine's main thrust, of course, sought to justify Reagan's obsession with the Nicaraguan contras. "They are our brothers, these freedom fighters, and we owe them our help," he observed on March 1, 1985. "They are the moral equivalent of the Founding Fathers and the brave men and women of the French Resistance. We cannot turn away from them. For the struggle is not right versus left, but right versus wrong." Unfortunately, few contra leaders possessed democratic credentials; some ultimately faced trial and execution for murder and other crimes. When support in Congress stalled, Wyoming's Dick Cheney, anticipating his later position as vice president, criticized those who held back: "You can't have foreign policy carried out by 435 House members and 100 Senators. There are times when the president needs strong support, and debate has to stop at the water's edge." [52]

Indeed, the administration endorsed notoriously oppressive authoritarian governments in Argentina, Chile, Guatemala, El Salvador, Haiti, and the Philippines. The Republican platform of 1980 had warned of the growing power of communism in Central America as demonstrated by the Marxist takeover of Nicaragua and Marxist attempts to destabilize El Salvador, Guatemala, and Honduras. "As a result," noted the platform, "a clear and present danger threatens the energy and raw material lifelines of the Western world." [53] Reagan resurrected the domino theory to emphasize the nature of the Soviet challenge. "What we're doing," he told newsmen, "is [to] try to halt the infiltration into the Americas, by terrorists and by outside interference, and those who aren't just aiming at El Salvador but, I think, are aiming at the whole of Central America and possibly later South America and, I'm sure, eventually North America." Lawrence Eagleburger, Reagan's undersecretary of state for political affairs, worried: "[I]f the Sandinistas and the Salvadoran guerrillas are successful in overthrowing the Government in El Salvador, that's the beginning, not the end, of the problem. The Costa Ricans, the Hondurans and the Guatemalans are certainly going to face the same sort of threat. I can't even say that the Mexicans wouldn't have a problem."[54] Secretary Haig insisted that the Kremlin must control its clients in Cuba, Nicaragua, and El Salvador or assume responsibility for their activities. El Salvador was merely a single item on "a priority target list, a hit list, if you will, for the ultimate takeover of Central America," he informed the House Foreign Affairs Committee in mid-March. If the spread of this Soviet-sponsored terrorism was not halted, the secretary warned, "[We] will find it within our own borders tomorrow." With Nicaragua already under Moscow's influence, El Salvador, Guatemala, and Honduras would surely follow.[55] To many observers, however, the administration had overplayed its hand and officials were subsequently forced to recognize that the political realities of Central America were far more complex than Haig's list suggested.

The so-called Iran-Contra affair not only embarrassed the administration and tarnished the president, it wrote the concluding chapter to Reagan's Central American crusade and confused Washington's intervention in the Iran-Iraq War. Iraq's invasion of Iran on September 22, 1980, went well until the Iranians regrouped. Fearing Iraq was in danger of losing the war, the United States, the U.S.S.R., France, and England provided sophisticated military equipment and financial aid. Yet while the administration was openly assisting Iraq, it also secretly sold arms, especially anti-aircraft weapons, to Iran in the hope of gaining funds to help the Nicaraguan contras and, at the same time, achieving the release of Americans held hostage by radical Islamist groups. After the Iran-Contra affair became public, Congressional investigations began, in May 1987, to focus on National Security Adviser John Poindexter and staff member Lieutenant Colonel Oliver North. Over initial objections by Secretary of State Shultz and Defense Secretary Weinberger, North directed a parallel, largely secret, foreign policy apparatus, with its own sources of funds, communications systems, secret envoys, leased ships and airplanes, and Swiss bank accounts. Testifying in July, decorated and unrepentant, Colonel North blamed Congress for the loss of Vietnam and the failure to confront enemy aggression in Central America. Similarly, Poindexter declared that the security of the United States was not safe in the hands of the State Department, the Defense Department, or Congress. Both men were convicted and later pardoned.[56]

But the fallout did not end there. The administration's long crusade to eliminate the Sandinistas and subdue the Salvadoran guerrillas was about to end. An independent Costa Rican peace process emerging in 1987 found more in common among the Marxist-oriented Sandinistas and the other Central American governments than in Washington's anti-Soviet crusade. The Reagan administration failed to recognize that Central Americans had minds, wills, and interests of their own. Nicaragua ceased to be an issue when, in 1990, a free election drove the Sandinistas from power.[57]

The Pursuit of Arms Control and Limitation

With early emphasis on increasing America's nuclear armaments, lack of interest in arms control, and harsh anti-Soviet rhetoric, the doctrinal drive and its proponents significantly spurred the anxieties of anti-nuclear movements from the United States across Western Europe. The administration's ardent anti-communists openly acknowledged the possibility of hostilities. As Reagan's arms control chief, Eugene Rostow, stated, "We are living in a pre-war and not a post-war world." Even Defense Secretary Weinberger, who believed nuclear wars were not winnable, nevertheless insisted: "We are planning to prevail if we are attacked." Echoing this opinion, White House adviser Thomas C. Reed added, "Prevailing with pride is the principal new ingredient of American foreign policy."[58] In the spring of 1982, four distinguished Americans—McGeorge Bundy, George Kennan, Robert McNamara, and Gerard Smith—argued in *Foreign Affairs* that the United States, to limit the possibilities of nuclear war, should reverse its policy of three decades and promise never to use nuclear weapons first. This did not happen and the nuclear option would remain intact for decades to come.

Of immediate concern was Moscow's deployment in Europe of SS-20s, a significantly upgraded intermediate missile carrying three nuclear-tipped warheads. The United States began planning in 1979 to counter with 108 Pershing II and 464 ground-launched cruise missiles (GLCMs) in West Germany, Belgium, Britain, the Netherlands, and Italy. Fear of a renewed nuclear arms race by the superpowers set off the powerful European peace movement of 1981, as more than two million Europeans joined anti-nuclear, and largely anti-American, demonstrations. West Germans, at the potential center of any European firestorm, were understandably upset with the apparent nonchalance in Washington about the talk of fighting and "winning" a nuclear war.

Pressure from anti-nuclear protesters in NATO states and the nuclear freeze movement at home prompted the administration, in late 1981, to review the unsuccessful arms control negotiations. Attempting to pacify European demonstrators, the Reagan administration offered a "zero option" concept; the United States would cancel its deployment of intermediate-range missiles, scheduled for two years in the future, in exchange for the Soviets' prompt withdrawal of its deployed SS-20s carrying some 1,100 warheads. In

May 1982, Reagan unveiled his two-phased proposal for the promised Strategic Arms Reduction Talks (START) that emphasized a "practical phased reduction" of strategic nuclear systems. This plan would require the Soviets to substantially reduce their force of land-based ICBMs—their most effective strategic weapons—and to reduce by almost two-thirds the aggregate throw weight of their missiles. In response the United States would retain most of its land-based Minutemen, deploy a hundred new large MX missiles, expand its cruise missiles, and modernize its submarine and bomber fleets. Knowledgeable observers found the START formula, like the earlier "zero option," so one-sided it was nonnegotiable. "This proposal is so stacked against the Soviets," the sponsor of the House's nuclear freeze resolution, Congressman Edward J. Markey, complained, "there is little chance they will accept it." Not surprisingly, Moscow ignored both proposals.[59]

Neither beltway insiders nor Kremlin leaders were prepared for Reagan's March 23, 1983, proposal for a defense against nuclear-tipped ballistic missiles. After noting that America's security currently depended on nuclear deterrence, he offered his vision of a better future to a television audience: "It is that we embark on a program to counter the awesome Soviet military threat with measures that are defensive." With little or no understanding of the technological challenges or the history of previous failures, Reagan called "upon the scientific community in this country, who gave us nuclear weapons . . . to give us the means of rendering these weapons impotent and obsolete." The official program was named the Strategic Defense Initiative (SDI) in January 1984, while critics quickly dubbed it "Star Wars." It mattered little that SDI ignored reality, for Reagan, although he never analyzed SDI's complicated problems, became emotionally and politically attached.[60] If many U.S. military leaders and most scientists believed a successful Star Wars program lay far in the future, its existence initially posed problems to Moscow. Soviet leader Yuri Andropov viewed SDI as a program to bury the 1972 Anti-Ballistic Missile (ABM) treaty and unleash an arms race in offensive and defensive weapons. "Engaging in this is not just irresponsible, it is insane," Andropov charged in a March 27 *Pravda* interview, "Washington's actions are putting the entire world in jeopardy." Of course, the SDI project would raise questions about the status of the 1972 ABM Treaty and haunt future arms control negotiations.[61]

Reagan, Gorbachev, and Revitalizing Arms Control

As early as February 12, 1983, Reagan lamented that he had not visited Moscow. After Secretary Shultz explained such trips would require a significant improvement in Washington's relations with leaders of the communist powers, the president began exchanging messages with Soviet premier Andropov. In his July 11 letter, Reagan emphasized his long-held antipathy toward nuclear weapons and noted that both leaders shared "an enormous responsibility for the preservation of stability in the world."[62] In October, Robert McFarlane, who had succeeded Clark as head of the National Security Council, advised the president that it was time for the United States to exploit its military buildup by negotiating arms limitations with the Soviet Union. At Georgetown University on April 6, 1984, the president commented that the United States' increased military power paved the way for successful negotiations. "If the new Soviet leadership is devoted to building a safer and more humane world, rather than expanding armed conquests," he stated, "it will find a sympathetic partner in the West." Both countries should focus on reducing the risk of nuclear war because, he warned, "a nuclear war cannot be won and must never be fought."[63] Reagan ended his successful campaign for a second term determined to pursue closer ties with Moscow.

Of course, it was the rise of Mikhail Gorbachev to the head of the Soviet state that would prove to be the game-changer. When Gorbachev visited London in mid-December 1984, Prime Minister Margaret Thatcher detected in Gorbachev's predictable elevation new diplomatic opportunities. "I can do business with this man," she informed the press. Following Chernenko's death in March 1985, Gorbachev emerged as secretary general of the party, with a better grasp of the realities of international life than his predecessors. His basic challenges lay in maintaining the U.S.S.R.'s international status while rescuing it from its debilitating global role—especially in Afghanistan—and stimulating a stagnant economy. As Gorbachev, a dedicated socialist, struggled with the Kremlin's internal troubles, his "new thinking" on foreign affairs began to emerge. During 1985–1986, Gorbachev intensified military operations, installed a stronger Afghan leader, and sought to save "Soviet credibility" before withdrawing. If Gorbachev focused less on Third World issues, he nevertheless was annoyed by what he saw as Reagan's hypocrisy. In an April 23, 1985, speech, he pointed to Washington's criticism of Moscow's intervention in Afghanistan, while asserting its "right to interfere" in Grenada and Nicaragua.[64]

Notwithstanding these disparities, in the summer of 1985 it was evident that Reagan had found someone in the Kremlin willing to discuss the possibility of curbing the nuclear arms race. Gorbachev believed that "the policy of total, military confrontation has no future," and that the "arms race, as well as nuclear war, cannot be won." Equally significant, Gorbachev saw that "the task of building security appears to be a political task, and it can be resolved only by political means." This approach evoked criticism from veteran Soviet policymakers, one of whom stated, "Are you against force, which is the only language that imperialism understands?" Following eight months of long-range discussions, Reagan and Gorbachev finally prepared to meet at a Geneva Summit in November 1985. At this time, historian Raymond Garthoff noted, "a limited but interesting transformation occurred in [Reagan's] statements on the source and nature of the difficulties in American-Soviet relations." Departing for Geneva, the president hoped both nations would "seek to reduce the suspicions and mistrust that had led us to acquire mountains of strategic weapons." He even conceded that nuclear weapons, not an evil opponent, posed "the greatest threat in human history to survival of the human race."[65]

At Geneva, Gorbachev pressed for limiting the Strategic Defense Initiative, maintaining SALT II and new arms reductions, but found Reagan refusing to offer concessions on any contested point. The president, however, saw Gorbachev as one with whom he shared "a kind of chemistry." The most significant outcome of the summit undoubtedly was the growing rapport that developed between the two heads of state. In January 1986, Gorbachev offered the United Nations a grand plan for arms reductions. He would eliminate medium-range missiles altogether, set aside the issue of French and British nuclear forces, and cut strategic weapons by 50 percent, including the SS-18 heavy missiles. Gorbachev's ambitious economic modernization program, endorsed by the 27th Party Congress in February–March, required the reduced military spending that would follow arms reductions. The Soviet objective had become the attainment of mutual security at the lowest possible strategic balance.[66]

In May 1986, Reagan announced that by the year's conclusion the United States would no longer be bound by the SALT II formula unless the Kremlin undertook undefined "constructive steps." Critical European reaction followed. *Le Figaro* complained that Washington had not bothered to ask Europe's opinion. "It's a disaster," fumed Helmut Kohl. *The Economist* noted that half the Britons polled distrusted Reagan's judgment and considered Americans equal to the Soviets as a threat to peace. In Washington, officials insisted that the president was justified in his action because of alleged Soviet "cheating," but also conceded that they had not anticipated Europe's reaction. Gorbachev recognized Europe's anxiety and offered a series of new arms proposals, which Pentagon officials routinely rejected. *New York Times* columnist James Reston noted the preference for "ideological confrontation and warrior diplomacy . . . at the Pentagon and the White House." To columnist Andrew J. Glass, "[T]he national security apparatus in the White House remains thoroughly fractionated. With so many hawks and pseudo-hawks flapping about in the Reagan aviary, it will muster all the administration's ability in diplomatic falconry merely to fashion a cogent response to the latest Soviet initiative." Meanwhile, Gorbachev topped European polls as the man of peace, while Reagan put aside a decision on the SALT II treaty until their October meeting.[67]

The two leaders met briefly at Reykjavik, Iceland, in October, with Gorbachev proposing to scrap all SS-20s in Europe while retaining 100 in Asia and allowing the United States 100 similar missiles in Alaska. At the final session, Reagan presented what appeared to be sweeping U.S. proposals to eliminate all nuclear warheads by 2000, which his advisers were confident Gorbachev would reject. Startling everyone, the Soviet leader responded with a resounding "Yes." He would accept Reagan's proposal if the president agreed to limit SDI research to "laboratories" for at least five years. Reagan rejected Gorbachev's counteroffer, declaring he would not compromise his missile defense project. For some analysts, while Reagan pointed to the elimination nuclear weapons, he clung to the strategic defense despite questions pertaining to its working viability. Thus, he rejected an opportunity that may have satisfied his frequently professed desire to *actually* eliminate the nuclear threat. Reagan and Gorbachev departed Reykjavik disappointed and exhausted. Not surprisingly, however, Western military strategists and political leaders—and most certainly Soviet marshals—were shaken by news of a near-agreement to abolish nuclear weapons. Prime Minister Margaret Thatcher hurried to Washington, warning Reagan that the nuclear deterrence strategy had been the bedrock of almost 40 years of U.S. and European security.[68]

But despite such opposition, Gorbachev's strategy of ending the Cold War by reducing the nuclear threat found widespread popular approval. He surprised Pentagon hard-liners on February 28, 1987, by accepting their proposal to eliminate all intermediate-range nuclear missiles in Europe and, later, in Asia: the United States' "zero option." Secretary of State Shultz immediately accepted Gorbachev's offer, which saw negotiators subsequently agree to destroy 2,611 intermediate-range missiles with flight ranges from 300 to 3,440 miles (500 to 5,000 kilometers), including U.S. Pershing IIs and cruise missiles, and Soviet SS-4s, SS-12s, SS-20s, and SS-23s. When Defense Secretary Weinberger and other hard-liners demanded on-site inspections, Gorbachev agreed to an "intrusive verification" plan where each power would inspect the other's facilities to fulfill Intermediate Nuclear Force (INF) Treaty terms. Soviet enthusiasm for intrusive inspections gave pause to the Pentagon, the National Security Agency, and the CIA—all of whom had for decades made this a fundamental requirement for substantial reductions. Now they feared the prospect of Soviet inspectors prowling U.S. defense plants, nuclear-armed submarines, and missile sites. As Weinberger's replacement, Frank Carlucci, admitted, "[V]erification has proven to be more complex than we thought it would be. The flip side of the coin is its application to us. The more we think about it, the more difficult it becomes." The United States *now* desired less intrusive procedures.

The Washington summit of December 1987 led to the signing of the INF Treaty and was regarded to be a Reagan-Gorbachev triumph with hugely favorable media coverage. The Soviet leader and his wife were so enthusiastically greeted in the normally blasé capital that it prompted *Washington Post* columnist Tom Shales to observe the city was seized by "Gorby fever."

When Gorbachev expressed concern about the criticism that Reagan was receiving from hard-liners, Shultz reassured him, "[T]he vast majority of Americans support what President Reagan is doing." "For the first time in history," Reagan declared when signing the INF treaty on December 8, "the language of 'arms control' was replaced by 'arms reduction'—in this case, the complete elimination of an entire class of U.S. and Soviet nuclear missiles." The treaty offered "a big chance at last to get onto the road leading away from the threat of catastrophe," Gorbachev added. "It is our duty . . . to move forward toward a nuclear-free world . . . [that is] without fear and without a senseless waste of resources on weapons of destruction." Although the INF pact eliminated only 4 percent of the superpowers' nuclear arsenal, it would eventually launch other serious arms reductions. [69]

That said, the INF treaty initially failed to spur the talks toward a broader strategic arms reduction treaty. Although the Soviets offered several concessions, interminable bureaucratic delays hampered Washington's attempts to modify its initial START proposal substantially—and as such, an agreement would not be reached until 1991. Meanwhile, the intractability of various American bureaucracies over the specific terms was frequently more intense than the negotiations with Moscow. As a member of the National Security Council stated, "Even if the Soviets did not exist, we might not get a START treaty because of disagreements on our side." If the Soviets "came to us," another high-ranking U.S. official complained, "and said, 'You write it, we'll sign it,' we still couldn't do it." [70] In the context of the Kremlin, concerns pertaining to Reagan's strategic missile defense program gradually dissipated. Russian scientist Andrei Sakharov persuaded Gorbachev there was no defense capable of stopping a barrage of intercontinental ballistic missiles carrying decoys and multiple warheads. He argued that SDI was a kind of "Maginot line in space," a line that could not defeat a concentrated missile attack any more than the French Maginot defense line stopped the German blitzkrieg in 1940. Soviet scientists recognized that the SDI program was a "fuss about nothing." As Roald Z. Sagdeyev, the head of the Soviet Institute for Space Research told Strobe Talbott, "We came to realize that we had not helped ourselves by screaming so much about SDI. . . . [W]e had overestimated how much damage SDI could do to strategic stability in the short run and even in the medium term." [71]

With the vast majority of the Senate favoring the INF Treaty and Reagan's assurance that he was negotiating from strength, ratification came on May 29, 1988, as the president left for the Moscow summit. The significance of this triumphant meeting was the reintroduction of détente and perhaps the end of the Reagan Doctrine's ideological crusade. On Sunday, May 29, 1988, as Reagan received a warm welcome at the Kremlin, Gorbachev declared, "[H]istory has objectively bound our two countries by a common responsibility for the destinies of mankind." On Tuesday, as Reagan walked through

Red Square, he commented publicly that the two leaders had "decided to talk to each other instead of about each other. It's working just fine." In the Kremlin, when asked by a reporter what became of the 1983 "evil empire," the president replied, "I was talking about another time, another era." Gorbachev and Reagan signed the INF ratification documents at the final ceremony.[72] If short on achievement, the summit was long on goodwill.

Predictably, the neo-conservatives once again criticized Reagan's actions, asserting that the Soviet Union, with its human rights violations, remained the "evil empire." George Will's judgment of the Moscow summit served for most hawks: "Ronald Reagan's foreign policy has produced much surprise but little delight. His fourth and, one prays, final summit is a suitable occasion for conservatives to look back with bewilderment and ahead with trepidation." In his final White House years, as Will saw it, the president had ruined his earlier, superb foreign and military policy. Despite such criticism from the right, it seemed apparent that moderates were gaining the ascendancy in the administration's turf wars over foreign policy. Secretary of State Shultz had organized the State Department into an effective group for conducting negotiations with the Soviets. Together with Frank Carlucci as the new secretary of defense and General Colin L. Powell as national security adviser, the Reagan administration finally had three top advisers who were in general agreement. As one administration spokesman phrased it in March 1988, "Over the past three years we have established a broad, active, and quietly developing relationship, almost from a cold start in '85." For the president, the move toward moderation appeared to be a slow, pragmatic evolution of policy. The pragmatists understood that there was no choice but to coexist on the planet with the U.S.S.R. and regarded Gorbachev as a durable Soviet leader. They agreed with his December 7, 1988, address before the United Nations where he criticized the reliance on nuclear arms. Gorbachev, at this time, reached the high point of his global leadership by pledging the unilateral reduction of Soviet military forces by 500,000 men and withdrawing forces from Afghanistan.[73]

Leaving Washington hours after George H. W. Bush was inaugurated, Reagan declared flatly: "The Cold War is over." Weeks ahead of most policymakers, the American public had grasped that the Cold War was over after hearing Gorbachev's UN speech. Public opinion polls revealed that 54 percent of Americans now considered the Soviets to be either "no threat" or "only a minor threat," while 60-odd percent believed the Soviets were now essentially focused on their own security and only 28 percent thought they were still seeking world domination. Frances Fitzgerald summed it up best: "Gorbachev launched a political revolution in the Soviet Union. Few in Washington understood what he was doing or where he was going, and the Cold War was over before the American policy establishment knew it."[74]

CONCLUSION

As the only military defeat America had suffered (at that point in time), the Vietnam War would see a reevaluation in U.S. foreign policy. The American public, baffled, sober, and ambivalent, demonstrated a distinct lack of enthusiasm to undertake another overseas military venture. They, much like the U.S. military leadership, were infected with the "Vietnam Syndrome." Out of this reluctance to send U.S. troops anywhere to engage in hostilities emerged the so-called Weinberger Doctrine. In a November 28, 1984, speech, President Reagan's secretary of defense, Caspar Weinberger, outlined six points that had to be met before the Pentagon would again recommend sending U.S. forces into combat: (1) armed force would be used only to protect vital interests of the U.S. or its allies; (2) when the U.S. commits itself to the use of force it must do so wholeheartedly, with the clear intention of winning; (3) troops should be committed only in pursuit of clearly defined political and military objectives, and we should know in advance precisely how the forces committed can accomplish those clear objectives; (4) the relationship between the forces committed—their size, composition, etc.—and the objectives must continually be reassessed and adjusted if necessary; (5) before the U.S. commits combat forces abroad, there must be some reasonable assurance we will have the support of the American people and their representatives in Congress; and (6) the commitment of U.S. armed force should be the last resort.[75]

The Vietnam Syndrome influenced the American public and the Pentagon until the United States' overwhelming military victory in the first Gulf War. According to Nixon, writing in 1986 in *Richard Nixon, No More Vietnams*, "The psychological impairment [of the Vietnam war] was such that the United States retreated, like a traumatised individual, into a five-year, self-imposed exile."[76] Similarly, Geoffrey Simons wrote that the resulting loss of confidence produced by the Vietnam War led to a years-long hiatus in Cold War doctrine as developing countries Angola, Eritrea, and the territory of Ogaden were left to fend for themselves against communist threats from the Cubans and Soviet-aligned Ethiopians.[77] Immediate results of the Vietnam syndrome, and impending recession, were nevertheless that American armed forces and CIA operations were scaled back significantly, affecting the end of Nixon's term and the subsequent years of President Gerald Ford's tenure. Not until the Iranian revolution in the Middle East during President Jimmy Carter's term in office would U.S. Cold War doctrine snap back into its original containment form. Framed in the terms of vital interests, the subsequent threat to America's oil supply ended the wilderness years of the Vietnam Syndrome and engendered the creation of the Carter Doctrine.

After the Carter years, presidential doctrine took a marked shift with the election of Ronald Reagan. Entering the White House in January 1981, Reagan promptly launched what some historians have labeled "The Second Cold War." The Republican Party platform had detected "clear danger signals indicating that the Soviet Union was using Cuban, East German, and now Nicaraguan, as well as its own, military forces to extend its power to Africa, Asia and the Western Hemisphere."[78] During the presidential campaign, Reagan condemned the Carter administration for the humiliation caused by Iran's seizure of American hostages, its failure to act while the Soviets intervened in Afghanistan, and for permitting the Soviet Union to gain military supremacy over the United States. "We're already *in* an arms race," Reagan replied to doubters, "but only the Soviets are racing."[79] Even though America's economic and military strength continued to stabilize a divided Europe, to Republicans the Carter administration failed to halt Soviet expansionism. In pressing the ideological doctrine over the first five years of his administration, Reagan rode the United States precariously close to what would have been a catastrophic World War III. It was only the rise of the moderate Mikhail Gorbachev that saw Reagan adjust his doctrinal drive, engaging and concluding some defining agreements, particularly in relation to arms control and reductions. While there is ample discourse that points to Reagan's firm approach as being the catalyst in spurring such changes, more weight perhaps need to be given to Gorbachev's dual program of "perestroika" ("restructuring") and "glasnost" ("openness") in redefining economic practice and internal affairs, and in the context of this chapter, providing the real circuitbreaker in redefining superpower relations and international security.

NOTES

1. Jimmy Carter, "The State of the Union Address Delivered Before a Joint Session of the Congress," Washington D.C., January 23, 1980, available at: http://www.presidency.ucsb.edu/ws/?pid=33079.

2. "The Carter Doctrine," *New American Nation*, 2015, available at: http://www.americanforeignrelations.com/A-D/Doctrines-The-carter-doctrine.html#ixzz3alW427pn.

3. *Ibid.*

4. Ronald Reagan, "Address Before a Joint Session of Congress on the State of the Union," February 4, 1986, The American Presidency Project, available at: http://www.presidency.ucsb.edu/ws/index.php?pid=36646%20.See also Richard Dean Burns, Joseph M. Siracusa, and Jason Flanagan, *American Foreign Relations since Independence*, Santa Barbara, CA: Praeger, 2013.

5. Richard Nixon, "Address Accepting the Presidential Nomination at the Republican National Convention in Miami Beach, Florida," August 8, 1968, The American Presidency Project, available at: http://www.presidency.ucsb.edu/ws/index.php?pid=25968.

6. *New York Times*, November 26, 1967, Sec. 4, 2.

7. *Ibid.*

8. Robert S. McNamara, et al, *Argument without End: In Search of Answers to the Vietnam Tragedy*, New York: Public Affairs, 1999, pp. 99, 403.

9. Department of State *Bulletin*, 52, April 26, 1965, pp. 606–10.

10. M. G. Raskin and B. B. Fall, eds., *The Viet-Nam Reader: Articles and Documents of American Foreign Policy and the Viet-Nam Crises*, New York: Vintage Books, 1965, pp. 342–43. Matters included in the NLF program and not mentioned in that of Hanoi were

removal of the Saigon government, agrarian and educational reform, improved living conditions, and equal treatment of the minorities in Vietnam. Text in *ibid.*, pp. 216–21.

11. *New York Times*, September 30, 1967, p. 8.

12. *Ibid.*, January 26, 31, 1969, p. 1.

13. *Ibid.*, March 26, 1969, p. 3. See also Henry A. Kissinger, "The Viet Nam Negotiations," *Foreign Affairs*, January 1969, pp. 211–234.

14. *New York Times*, May 9, 1969, pp. 1, 6; May 15, 1969, p. 16.

15. *Ibid.*, July 2, 1970, pp. 1, 14; John Osborne, "Why Cambodia?" *New Republic*, June 11, 1970, pp. 7–9.

16. *New York Times*, September 18, 1970, p. 2; September 27, 1970 (sec. 4), p. 14.

17. *New York Times*, October 8, 1970, 1, 18; *The New Republic*, October 17, 1970, pp. 5, 6.

18. *New York Times*, November 4, 1969, p. 16. The president's address on Vietnamization came 19 days after a nationwide peaceful demonstration at which hundreds of thousands of people called for an "immediate" pullout of all U.S. forces in Vietnam. For Vietnamization efforts, see James H. Willbanks, *Abandoning Vietnam: How America Left and South Vietnam Lost its War*, Lawrence: University Press of Kansas, 2004.

19. *New York Times*, January 11, 1970, Sec. 4, 5.

20. Cited in Andrew Johns, *Vietnam's Second Front: Domestic Politics, the Republican Party, and the War*, Kentucky: University Press of Kentucky, 2010, p. 274.

21. *New York Times*, May 1, 1970, pp. 1–2.

22. *New York Times*, May 31, 1970 (sec. 4), p. 3; see Tom Wells, *The War Within: America's Battle over Vietnam*, New York: Holt, 1994.

23. *New York Times*, June 6, 1971. Publication of the "Pentagon Papers" later reinforced the American public's belief that the war indeed had been a mistake. *New York Times*, June 13, 1971, pp. 1, 35–38. This was the first in a series of articles.

24. See Dale Andradé, *Trial by Fire: The 1972 Easter Offensive, America's Last Vietnam Battle*, New York: Hippocrene Books, 1995.

25. President Nixon's letter of proposal for postwar support to Thieu came to light after the fall of South Vietnam, *New York Times*, May 1, 1975, pp. 1, 16.

26. Joseph M. Siracusa and David G. Coleman, *Depression to Cold War: A History of America From Herbert Hoover to Ronald Reagan*, Portsmouth, NH: Greenwood Publishing Group, 2002, p. 190.

27. Hanoi's chief of staff, General Van Tien Dung, candidly recounted these and subsequent events of the war's final battles in two official North Vietnamese newspapers, excerpts of which are found in *New York Times*, April 26, 1976, p. 16.

28. See Timothy N. Castle, *At War in the Shadow of Vietnam: United States Military Aid to the Royal Lao Government, 1955–1975*, New York: Columbia University Press, 1993; and William Shawcross, *Sideshow: Kissinger, Nixon and the Destruction of Cambodia*, New York: Simon & Schuster, 1979.

29. Stanley Karnow, *Vietnam: A History*, Vol. 122, New York: Random House, 1994, p. 19.

30. Jimmy Carter, "State of the Union Address Delivered before a Joint Session of the Congress," January 23, 1980, The American Presidency Project, available at: http://www.presidency.ucsb.edu/ws/?pid=33079.

31. Zbignew Brzezinski, *Power and Principle: Memoirs of the National Security Adviser*. New York: Farrar, Strauss, Giroux, 1983, pp. 443–54.

32. Jimmy Carter, "Address at Commencement Exercises at the University of Notre Dame," May 22, 1977, The American Presidency Project, available at: http://www.presidency.ucsb.edu/ws/?pid=7552.

33. Hafizullah Emadi, *State, Revolution, and Superpowers in Afghanistan*, New York: Praeger, 1990.

34. L. Britt Snider, *The Agency and the Hill: CIA's Relationship with Congress, 1946–2004*, Center for the Study of Intelligence, Central Intelligence Agency, 2008.

35. Jeffrey Macris and Saul Kelly, eds., *Imperial Crossroads: The Great Powers and the Persian Gulf*, Annapolis, MD: Naval Institute Press, 2012, p. 117.

36. Jimmy Carter, "Address to the Nation on the Soviet Invasion of Afghanistan," January 4, 1980, The American Presidency Project, available at: http://www.presidency.ucsb.edu/ws/?pid=32911.

37. Frances Fitzgerald, *Way Out There in the Blue: Reagan, Star Wars and the End of the Cold War*, New York: Simon & Schuster, 2000, pp. 27–31.

38. Reagan quoted in *Newsweek*, February 9, 1981, p. 45; Opening Statement at Confirmation Hearings, January 9, 1981, U.S. Department of State, Bureau of Public Affairs, *Current Policy No. 257*; *New York Times*, May 3, 1981.

39. *Public Papers of the Presidents: Ronald Reagan, 1981*, Washington, DC: Government Printing Office, 1981, vol. 1, pp. 957, 958; also see Joseph M. Siracusa and David G. Coleman, *Depression to Cold War: A History of America from Herbert Hoover to Ronald Reagan*, Westport, CT: Praeger, 2002, pp. 249–50.

40. Richard Rhodes, *Arsenals of Folly: The Making of the Nuclear Arms Race*, New York: Knopf, 2007, pp. 148–49; Drew Middleton, *New York Times*, June 21, 1981, January 3, 1982, February 14, 1982; Richard Halloran, *New York Times*, April 11, 1982.

41. James M. Fallows, *National Defense*, New York: Random House, 1981, pp. 70–71, 163; Christopher Paine, "A False START," *Bulletin of the Atomic Scientists*, 38, August/September 1982, p. 13; *New York Daily News*, "Report from Munich," February 20, 1982, p. 6.

42. "Haig Calls Moscow the Primary Source of Danger to the World," *New York Times*, April 25, 1981.

43. U.S. Department of State, Bureau of Public Affairs, *Current Policy No. 275*, p. 2; Seweryn Bialer and Joan Afferica, "Reagan and Russia," *Foreign Affairs*, 61, Winter 1982–83, p. 71; "Promoting Democracy and Peace," U.S. Department of State, Bureau of Public Affairs, *Current Policy No. 399*, pp. 3–5.

44. George F. Kennan, "Breaking the Spell," *The New Yorker*, October 3, 1983, p. 49.

45. Lawrence T. Caldwell and Robert Legvold, "Reagan through Soviet Eyes," *Foreign Policy*, 52, Fall 1983, p. 5; Stanley Hoffmann, *Dead Ends: American Foreign Policy in the New Cold War*, Cambridge, MA: Ballinger, 1983, pp. 154–55.

46. Cited in Norman A. Graebner, "The Soviet-American Conflict: A Strange Phenomenon," *VQR: A National Journal of Literature and Discussion*, Vol. 60, No. 4, Autumn, 1984.

47. Transcript of Reagan's statement on Airliner, *New York Times*, September 3, 1983.

48. Reagan's Address to Congress, September 5, 1983, *American Foreign Policy: Current Documents, 1983*, Washington, DC: Government Printing Office, 1985, pp. 544–47; Strobe Talbott, *The Russians and Reagan*, New York: Vintage, 1984, pp. 122, appendix.

49. Ronald Reagan, "Address Before a Joint Session of Congress on the State of the Union," February 4, 1986.

50. George P. Shultz, "Shaping American Foreign Policy: New Realities and New Ways of Thinking," *Foreign Affairs*, Spring 1985, p. 713; George Will, *Washington Post*, December 12, 1985, A19.

51. Robert W. Tucker, "Intervention and the Reagan Doctrine," *Intervention and the Reagan Doctrine*, New York: The Council on Religion and International Affairs, 1985, pp. 16–17.

52. Christopher Dickey, *With the Contras: A Reporter in the Wilds of Nicaragua*, New York: Simon & Schuster, 1987, pp. 10–11; *The Sandinista Military Build-Up*, Inter-American Series 119, Washington, DC: Department of State, 1985; and *The Soviet-Cuban Connection in Central America and the Caribbean*, Washington, DC: Department of State and Department of Defense, 1985; Cheney quoted in Steven V. Roberts, *New York Times*, May 25, 1986, E1.

53. Republican Party Platform of July 15, 1980.

54. Lawrence S. Eagleburger, "The State of Things as Seen from State," *New York Times*, April 22, 1984, available at: http://www.nytimes.com/1984/04/22/weekinreview/the-state-of-things-as-seen-from-state.html?pagewanted=1.

55. Reagan quoted in Alexander Cockburn, *Wall Street Journal*, March 12, 1981; other quotes in Siracusa and Coleman, *Depression to Cold War*, pp. 260, pp. 261–64; Karen de Young, *Washington Post*, March 8, 1981; *Newsweek*, March 16, 1981, pp. 34–38; *Newsweek*, March 30, 1981, pp. 20–21.

56. Michael T. Klare, "Fueling the Fire: How We Armed the Middle East, *Bulletin of the Atomic Scientists*, 47, January/February 1991, pp. 19–26; Theodore Draper, *A Very Thin Line: The Iran-Contra Affairs*, New York: Hill and Wang, 1991, pp. 333, pp. 344–45.

57. George Black, *The Good Neighbor: How the United States Wrote the History of Central America and the Caribbean*, New York: Pantheon Books, 1988, pp. 179–80.

58. Richard J. Barnet, *The New Yorker*, October 17, 1982, p. 153; Christopher Paine, "A False START," *Bulletin of the Atomic Scientists*, 38, August/September 1982, p. 14; see also Douglas C. Waller, *Congress and the Nuclear Freeze*, Amherst: University of Massachusetts Press, 1987.

59. Barnet, *New Yorker*, p. 156; Fitzgerald, *Way Out There in the Blue*, pp. 83–96; Waller, *Congress and the Nuclear Freeze*, pp. 14, 94–97, 99; Thomas Graham Jr., *Disarmament Sketches: Three Decades of Arms Control and International Law*, Seattle: University of Washington Press, 2002, p. 103; Lou Cannon, "Dealings with the Soviets Raise Uncomfortable Questions," *Washington Post*, July 2, 1984, A13.

60. Edward Reiss, *The Strategic Defense Initiative*, New York: Cambridge University Press, 1992; McGeorge Bundy, *Danger and Survival: Choices about the Bomb in the First Fifty Years*, New York: Random House, 1988, p. 571; Ronald Reagan, *An American Life: The Autobiography*, New York: Simon & Schuster, 1990, pp. 571–72; Rhodes, *Arsenals of Folly*, pp. 178–80; also see Richard Dean Burns, *The Missile Defense Systems of George W. Bush: A Critical Assessment*, Santa Barbara, CA: Praeger, 2010, chapters 1 and 2.

61. John Tirman, "The Politics of Star Wars," in John Tirman, ed., *The Empty Promise: the Growing Case against Star Wars*, Boston: Beacon, 1986; Union of Concerned Scientists, *The Fallacy of Star Wars*, New York: Vintage, 1984; and Burns, *The Missile Defense Systems of George W. Bush*, pp. 34–35.

62. Reagan, *An American Life*, p. 576.

63. Ronald Reagan, "State of the Union Address," January 25, 1984, *American Foreign Policy: Current Documents, 1984*, Washington, DC: Government Printing Office, 1986, p. 28; "Address at Georgetown University," April 6, 1984, *American Foreign Policy*, 8; "Address on U.S.-Soviet Relations," January 16, 1984, *Public Papers of the Presidents: Ronald Reagan, 1984*, vol. 1, Washington, DC: Government Printing Office, 1986, p. 42; John Newhouse, "Annals of Diplomacy: The Abolitionist—II," *The New Yorker*, January 9, 1989, p. 51.

64. For Gorbachev in London, *New York Times*, December 16, 1984, pp. 1, 5; see Robert D. English, *Russia and the Idea of the West: Gorbachev, Intellectuals & the End of the Cold War*, New York: University of Columbia Press, 2000, chapter 6; and Vladislav M. Zubok, *A Failed Empire: The Soviet Union in the Cold War from Stalin to Gorbachev*, Chapel Hill: University of North Carolina, 2007, pp. 278–84.

65. Gorbachev quoted in Zubok, *A Failed Empire*, p. 286; Reagan in George P. Shultz, *Turmoil and Triumph: My Years as Secretary of State*, New York: Charles Scribner's Sons, 1993, p. 598; Raymond L. Garthoff, *The Great Transition: American-Soviet Relations and the End of the Cold War*, Washington, DC: Brookings Institution, 1994, pp. 235–38.

66. *See*, Shultz, *Turmoil and Triumph*, pp. 596–607; Jack F. Matlock Jr., *Reagan and Gorbachev: How the Cold War Ended*, New York: Random House, 2004, chapter 6; English, *Russia and the Idea of the West*, 206; Philip Taubman, *New York Times*, April 6, 1986.

67. On compliance, see John Newhouse, *The New Yorker*, January 9, 1989, pp. 59–61; James Reston, *New York Times*, April 6, 1986, E23; Michael R. Gordon, *New York Times*, June 7, 1987, p. 7; *New York Times*, August 29, 1986.

68. Garthoff, *The Great Transition*, pp. 252–67; Shultz, *Turmoil and Triumph*, pp. 751–755; Mikhail Gorbachev, *Reykjavik: Results and Lessons*, Madison, CT: Sphinx Press, 1987; see also "The Reykjavik File: Previously Secret Documents from U.S. and Soviet Archives on the 1986 Reagan-Gorbachev Summit," posted October 13, 2006, by the National Security Archive, George Washington University, available at: http://nsarchive.gwu.edu/NSAEBB/ NSAEBB203; on Thatcher see David K. Shipler, "The Week in Review," *New York Times*, October 26, 1986, E1.

69. Garthoff, *Transition*, p. 327, n. 64; Shultz, *Turmoil*, pp. 1,009–15; Newhouse, *The New Yorker*, January 9, 1989, pp. 65–66; Lou Cannon, *President Reagan: The Role of a Lifetime*,

New York: Public Affairs, 1991, p. 694; Fitzgerald, *Way Out There in the Blue*, pp. 426, 444–45.

70. Fitzgerald, *Way Out There in the Blue*, p. 431.

71. Fitzgerald, *Way Out There in the Blue*, p. 445; Andrei Sakarov, *Moscow and Beyond*, New York: Alfred A. Knopf, 1991, pp. 21–42; Strobe Talbott, *Master of the Game: Paul Nitze and the Nuclear Peace*, New York: Alfred A. Knopf, 1988, p. 306.

72. Lou Cannon and Gary Lee, *Washington Post*, May 30, 1988, A1, A21; Don Oberdorfer, *Washington Post*, June 1, 1988, A1.

73. Will in *Washington Post*, June 7, 1988, A23; *Ibid.*, May 29, 1988, C7; *New York Times*, July 10, 1988, E30; see David K. Shipler, *Ibid.*, May 29, 1988, E1, E3.

74. Fitzgerald, *Way Out There in the Blue*, pp. 17–18, 466–71. See also Richard Dean Burns, Joseph M. Siracusa, and Jason Flanagan, *American Foreign Relations since Independence*, Santa Barbara, CA: Praeger, 2013.

75. "Excerpts from Address of Weinberger," *New York Times*, November 29, 1984, A5.

76. Richard Nixon, *No More Vietnams*, London: W. H. Allen, 1986, pp. 12–13.

77. Geoffrey Leslie Simons and G. L. Simons, *Vietnam Syndrome: Impact on US Foreign Policy*, Basingstoke: Macmillan, 1998, p.12.

78. Republican Party Platform of 1980, July 15, 1980, The American Presidency Project, available at: http://www.presidency.ucsb.edu/ws/?pid=25844.

79. *Newsweek*, September 1, 1980, p. 18.

Chapter Seven

Prevention for the 21st Century

The formal articulation of the Bush Doctrine, under the administration of George W. Bush, was encompassed in the 2002 release of the *National Security Strategy of the United States of America*. In emphatic terms, the document asserted that "WMD—nuclear, biological, and chemical—in the possession of hostile states and terrorists represents one of the greatest security challenges facing the U.S." and "Our enemies have openly declared that they are seeking WMD. . . . [T]he U.S. will not allow these efforts to succeed. . . . [A]s a matter of common sense and self defense, America will act against such emerging threats before they are fully formed."[1] Through these two points, the Bush administration argued that the most significant danger to the national security of the United States was the fusion of "radicalism and technology" and that the U.S. would now counter these "before they are fully formed."[2] The charged rhetoric of the document would come to dominate American security debates as political leaders, academic scholars, analysts, and the general public wrestled with the potential ramifications that this could have on U.S. foreign policy. Advocates contended that a pressing and unparalleled threat insurrection was well under way that required new and proactive approaches to using force. In contrast, critics of the Bush Doctrine viewed its promotion of preventive war to fight the proliferation of WMD as further demonstration of American unilateralism, and perhaps most importantly, an excessive departure from the traditional, well-worn strategies of deterrence and containment that featured so prominently in overcoming the Soviet Union during the Cold War.[3] Their political predispositions notwithstanding, both "ends" of the equation agreed that the Bush Doctrine was "candid," "bold," and "perhaps the most sweeping reformulation of U.S. strategic thinking in more than half a century."[4]

PRELIMINARY INDICATORS OF PREVENTION

It was evident in statements made well before the publication of the *National Security Strategy of 2002* that the George W. Bush administration was contemplating a stronger foreign policy and security approach. For instance, on September 23, 1999, then presidential candidate Bush hinted that should he secure the role of president, he would undertake a preventive/"preemptive" form of action to impede America's adversaries: "When direct threats to America [emanating from the "troubled frontiers of technology and terror"] are discovered, I know that the best defense can be a strong and swift offense—including the use of Special Operations Forces and long-range strike capabilities."[5]

Of course, it was the 9/11 attacks on U.S. home soil that truly brought the preemptive option into clearer focus. The administration's first unequivocal reference to "preemption" came in the statement of the chairman of the Joint Chiefs of Staff in the Quadrennial Defense Review Report released just nineteen days after 9/11.[6] The report stated that "defense of the U.S. homeland is the highest priority for the U.S. military. . . . The U.S. must deter, prevent and defend against aggression targeted at U.S. territory sovereignty, domestic population, and critical infrastructure."[7] In building upon these sentiments, Secretary of Defense Donald Rumsfeld argued that there needed to be a shift in U.S armed forces that necessitated "prevention, self-defense and sometimes pre-emption." While this approach could not possibly "defend against every conceivable kind of attack in every conceivable location at every minute of the day or night" it was now imperative to defend "against terrorism and other emerging 21st century threats" by taking "the war to the enemy."[8]

The preventive trajectory was now a key feature in all of the administration's rhetoric. In a teleconference broadcast to the Warsaw Conference on Combating Terrorism on November 6, 2001, Bush told the assembled audience that "we will not wait for the authors of mass murder to gain the weapons of mass destruction."[9] Encompassed in this approach was a preparedness to act proactively in mitigating the spread of WMD, and in his State of the Union address on January 29, 2002, Bush included specific reference to what he referred to as "rogue" states. The address argued that the second objective in the global war on terror was to prevent state sponsors of terror—specifically, the "axis of evil" states of North Korea, Iran, and Iraq—from procuring WMDs.[10] Bush cautioned his audience, stating that in "seeking weapons of mass destruction, these regimes pose a grave and growing danger," and "could provide these arms to terrorists, giving them the means to match their hatred" and "attack our allies or attempt to blackmail the United States."[11] In this regard, he promised those in attendance that the U.S. would not allow the world's most dangerous regimes to threaten the U.S. with the world's most destructive weapons.[12]

Of course, it was President Bush's seminal speech to the West Point graduating class on June 1, 2002, that unambiguously elevated the prospect of prevention in the global war on terror. He declared that the U.S. must "confront the worst threats before they emerge"[13] and warned that "if we wait for threats to fully materialize, we will have waited too long."[14] Bush argued that while "homeland defense and missile defense are part of stronger security" and "essential priorities for America," the "war on terror will not be won" if the U.S. remains defensive: *We must take the battle to the enemy, disrupt his plans, and confront the worst threats before they emerge. In the world we have entered, the only path to safety is the path of action. And this nation will act.*"[15] He again postulated the need for assertive options that included those of a military preemptive means so as to—should it be necessary—prevent attacks from either states or terrorist groups using weapons of mass destruction: "Our security will require modernizing domestic agencies such as the FBI, so they're prepared to act, and act quickly, against danger. Our security will require transforming the military you will lead—a military that must be ready to strike at a moment's notice in any dark corner of the world. And our security will require all Americans to be forward-looking and resolute, to be ready for pre-emptive action when necessary to defend our liberty and to defend our lives."[16]

Augmenting this leitmotif, administration officials highlighted that conventional military technologies were being developed as part of a Joint Stealth Task Force that could launch "no warning" preemptive incursions on suspected nuclear, biological, and chemical weapons facilities, and did not rule out using nuclear weapons themselves against biological weapons where the extreme heat of a nuclear blast could vaporize toxic biological agents.[17] The administration's interest in emboldening its preventive suite also considered the development of a new, low-yield nuclear weapon (including in the sub-kiloton range) that could be used with earth-penetrating missiles to destroy underground command and control bunkers and hidden facilities used for developing or storing weapons of mass destruction. Of course, these innumerable components aimed at elevating preemption (or in reality, preventive war) to a more protuberant role in American defense strategy became further evident in the president's *National Security Strategy* report, made public on September 20, 2002.[18]

THE FORMALIZATION OF THE DOCTRINE

As indicated earlier, it was the *National Security Strategy of 2002* that provided the formal enunciation of a strategy of preventive war against antagonistic states and terrorist actors developing weapons of mass destruction. The text stated that the United States would destroy such subterranean organizations and recalcitrant state actors through direct and incessant action using all the "elements of national and international power."[19] Specifically, its emphasis would be on those terrorist organizations of global influence and any terrorist or state sponsor of terrorism that attempted to gain or use WMDs, including their "precursors." Bush argued that the identification and destruction of the threat before it "reached borders" was crucial in defending the United States, the American people, and U.S. interests at home and abroad. In connecting his doctrine to Iraq and the need to impede a "rogue proliferator," Bush highlighted what he defined as "irrefutable proof" that Iraq's weapons stockpiles were not limited to the chemical types it had used against Iran and its own people, but also extended to those of a nuclear and biological level.[20] As such, he argued, the United States was prepared to obstruct such rogue states and their terrorist clients before they were able to threaten or use weapons of mass destruction against the United States and its friends. Again referring to the administration's inclination to undertake a preventive option, Bush stated that "minimizing the effects of WMD" use against "our people" necessitated a forthright response to mitigate potential WMD use against U.S. forces abroad.[21] Here, the United States could no longer exclusively depend on a "reactive posture" as it had done in the past. To deter a potential attacker, the United States would now be proactive so as to avoid a position where "our enemies strike first."[22]

Until the end of the 19th century, the United States was generally disinclined to use military force abroad, with limited exceptions, to defend American interests and expand the national territory. As the U.S. became a great power during the 20th century, it became more prepared to conduct what it defined as "appropriate" military interventions around the world, with policymakers generally maintaining—though not always following—a preference only to use force as a last resort. According to Richard Betts, even when faced with imminent threats, policymakers have seldom used preemption—defined as the use of U.S. military force to eliminate credible and imminent threats to U.S. interests before enemy attacks occur—due to "organizational and political obstacles."[23] In fact, Betts continues, the U.S. has arguably undertaken only three preemptive actions in the last century. Notwithstanding these very debatable figures, it is evident that the shifting landscape of the international system in the Cold War's absence redefined the calculus of action and the desirability of traditional forms of preemption.[24] In cultivating his more assertive strategy, Bush was quick to juxtapose the new post-9/11 phase with the Cold War period of deterrence. During the bi-polar era, especially following the Cuban missile crisis, the United States was faced with a "status quo, risk-averse adversary,"[25] and as such, deterrence was an effective form of defense. In contrast, the post–Cold War era threat of retaliation was "far less likely to work against leaders of rogue states" who had no fixed address, and who were "more willing to take risks, gambling with the lives of their people, and the wealth of their nations."[26]

Indeed, the increasing number of failing states, the proliferation of weapons of mass destruction (WMD), and the rise of non-state terrorism as a synchronized, global phenomenon augmented the level of threat to American security. Concurrently, the demise of the Soviet Union and the non-existence of any countervailing power or bloc clearly diminished the perceived costs of employing force and intervention abroad.[27] As Bush further explained, during the Cold War, weapons of mass destruction were considered weapons of last resort whose use risked the destruction of those who used them. In the post-9/11 context, "enemies see weapons of mass destruction as weapons of choice," while rogue states view such weapons as "tools of intimidation and military aggression against their neighbors." The acquisition of such weapons would "allow these states to attempt to blackmail the United States" and could potentially "prevent us from deterring or repelling the aggressive behavior of rogue states" who also see "these weapons as their best means of overcoming the conventional superiority of the United States."[28] For Bush, the threat confronting the U.S. in the 21st century was based in the nexus of transnational terrorism and WMD proliferation. In again emphasizing the significance of "today's threats," he argued that the "deadly challenges" and "motivations" of these "rogue states and terrorists," combined with "their determination to obtain destructive powers hitherto available only to the world's strongest states, and the greater likelihood that they will use weapons of mass destruction against us, make today's security environment more complex and dangerous."[29] In response, the administration believed that using traditional concepts of deterrence would not be effective against actors whose affirmed strategies were "wanton destruction and the targeting of innocents; whose so-called soldiers seek martyrdom in death and whose most potent protection is statelessness."[30]

DELINEATING BETWEEN PREVENTION AND PREEMPTION

At the time of its release, many scholars and analysts argued that the most defining assertion of the Bush Doctrine was the statement that the U.S. would now "act against such emerging threats before they are fully formed,"[31] evidently suggesting that the U.S. would sanction a type of proactive response, or, "anticipatory self-defense." In international relations discourse, anticipatory self-defense has often been aligned to the concepts of "preemption" or "prevention," and while they have been occasionally used interchangeably, the terms are actually two distinct strategic conceptions. As such, in truly coming to terms with the central theme of the Bush Doctrine, it is imperative to understand the delineation between these two concepts, where the explicit dichotomy centers on the relative timing of their application and the propinquity of the perceived threat. Indeed, it is the extended understanding of what constitutes an imminent threat that logically connects to the consideration of preemption (or preventive war) as a potential strategic option so as to confront *that* threat.

In terms of the concept of preemption, it is in the most rudimentary sense, nothing more than a quick response. Upon substantiating that an antagonist is about to attack—conventionally a visible mobilization of armies, navies, and air forces preparing to attack—the endangered state beats the opponent to the punch and attacks first so as to impede the approaching strike.[32] It is wielded in a "downstream" fashion in response to a more specific, direct, and immediate threat where "the necessity of self-defense becomes so instant and overwhelming that it leaves no choice of means and no moment for deliberation."[33] As Jack S. Levy conveyed, "Pre-emption involves the initiation of military action because it is perceived that an adversary's attack is imminent and that there are advantages to striking first or at least in preventing the adversary from doing so." It is a strategic response to a direct threat, "designed to forestall the mobilization and deployment of the adversary's existing military forces."[34] Similarly, according to Jon Rosenwasser, "Pre-emption constitutes a 'war of necessity' based on credible evidence of imminent attack against which action is justified under international law as enshrined in the self-defense clause (Article 51) of the UN Charter."[35] An example often cited is the 1967 Six-Day War, in which Israel launched an "unprovoked" attack upon the Egyptian, Syrian, and Jordanian armies massing on its borders, and which, thereby, is regarded in the most purest sense a preemptive war.[36]

Conversely, prevention is the strategy executed by states as a means to redefine long-term tensions stemming from hostile and/or powerful adversaries. Like preventive medicine, preventive war is utilized in an "upstream" fashion so as to address "dynamics" that are likely to contribute to the materialization of a threat before they are able to become specific, direct, or immediate. The preventive stimulus for conflict or war is set on the foundation that military conflict, while not necessarily imminent, is probably inevitable, and that the best option is to initiate the conflict while the costs and/or risks are low(er) than at a later period when the costs are high(er). In most occurrences, a preventive war is undertaken in order to prohibit the diminishing level of an individual state's power in relation to an ascending adversary. The dominant state endeavors to take advantage of an apparent opportunity gap—"a period during which a state possesses a significant military advantage over an adversary"—before a gap of vulnerability—"a window of opportunity from the perspective of the disadvantaged side"—appears likely to open.[37] As Levy again emphasized, "prevention involves fighting a winnable war now in order to avoid the risk of war later under less favourable circumstances. . . . [It] is a response to a threat that will generally take several years to develop . . . [and] aims to forestall the creation of new military assets." Additionally, he argues, "the consequence of non-action . . . is the gradual deterioration of . . . relative military power and the risk of a more costly war from a position of inferiority."[38] In reaffirming this line of thinking, Jon Rosenwasser contends that "in choosing preventive wars," policymakers essentially believe "that waging a war, even if unprovoked, against a rising adversary sooner is preferable to an inevitable war later when the balance of power no longer rests in their favor." Of course, the legitimacy in this proposition garners the requisite "traction when that enemy state is arming itself with WMD, or credibly threatens the supply of a critical resource such as oil, and national intelligence indicates that the enemy intends to harm one's own state."[39] Simply put, "preventive wars are essentially 'wars of choice' that derive mostly from a calculus of power, rather than the precedent of international law, conventions and practices."[40]

ADJUSTING THE INTERPRETATION OF PREVENTION AND PREEMPTION

It was clear from the outset that the Bush administration was keen to blur, distort, and ambiguously redefine the preemptive option. Indeed, Bush's *National Security Strategy of 2002* began with the events of September 11, 2001, as a means to articulate and legitimize what would be his preemptive adjustment. He pointed to the mass civilian casualties as being the defining objective of terrorists and that these fatalities could rise to an incomprehensible level if they "acquired and used weapons of mass destruction."[41] It was this emotionally charged reference that provided Bush with the ultimate platform on which to formally unveil his reinterpretation of what constituted preemptive war.

As stated, the United States has "long maintained the option of preemptive actions" to impede or "counter a threat to their national security." However, in this new security epoch, there was now a more convincing argument for taking "anticipatory action" to defend the United States, even if, he argued, "uncertainty remains as to the time and place of the enemy's attack." In an age of rampant technological exchange, where non-actors move seamlessly across porous borders, and where the compression of "time and space" was becoming more intensified, the doctrine demanded a newer prescription of preemption "to forestall or prevent such hostile acts" reaching American shores.[42] To do this, "we must adapt the concept of imminent threat to the capabilities and objectives of today's adversaries."[43] In building upon this technological claim, Jon Rosenwasser argues that the Bush administration justified his expanded definition of preemption with the constant, and embellished, referral to "today's circumstances." The nature of modern ordnance, from long-range missiles to information warfare, has transgressed the once robustly secured borders of the United States, and terrorist cells could once again surface near or within close proximity to wreak havoc. Of course, the covert nature of these plans and capabilities truly came to the fore after 9/11, and presented the administration with the most "glaring example of the need to adopt a more forward-leaning posture"[44] that can "adapt" to this new type of "imminent threat." In other words, "in today's world of stateless terrorists and rogue states with potential access to dangerous technologies, the length of the fuse has shortened, rendering the difference between preemption and prevention moot."[45]

In this new era, Bush signified that the United States would not use force in all cases to preempt emerging threats, nor should nations use preemption as a "pretext for aggression." However, "in an age where the enemies of civilization openly and actively seek the world's most destructive technologies," the United States could not remain idle while threatening actors organized and planned their attacks.[46] As a means to support his preemptive option, Bush articulated what he deemed to be essential for the future of U.S. national security: the creation of improved and more integrated intelligence capabilities to provide timely, accurate information on threats, wherever they may emerge; the close coordination with allies to form a common assessment of the most dangerous threats; and "the transformation of our military forces to ensure our ability to conduct rapid and precise operations to achieve decisive results."[47] As will be discussed later in the chapter, the attack on Iraq was the manifestation of the Bush Doctrine's form of preemption—or in reality, preventive war—formalized in the *National Security Strategy of 2002*. Here, the Bush administration identified rogue states seeking to attain nuclear weapons—in conjunction with "their terrorist clients"—to validate the promotion of preventive military intervention from a last-resort option to one that many critics argued was the new direction in U.S. security policy.[48] Indeed, the introduction of a policy legitimizing preventive attack on sovereign states for the purposes of self-defense spurred contentious debate, as well as an array of associated political and diplomatic implications.

Critics argued that attacking potential enemies before a threat had fully materialized potentially increased the specter and probability of inadvertent ramifications, and as such, made it imperative that action necessitated a high degree of accuracy in any first move. Additionally, others suggested the U.S. risked inaugurating a precedent of defensible inter-state preventive attacks in which the actual use of preventive force could inspire other international actors to also integrate "preventive approaches" into their security planning. In simple but damning terms, preventive military intervention was a form of vigilante justice in which a state preventively attacking another contravened both the UN Charter and the NATO Charter and raised the capacity to engender nuclear proliferation amongst weaker states instead of deterring them.[49] Finally, critics argued that the *National Security Strategy of 2002* advocated violence instead of attempting to mitigate it. As John Steinbruner stated, the document "appears to neglect and indeed to disdain international legal restraint. In the judgment of much of the world, that formula is more likely to generate violence than to contain it."[50]

Of course, this is not to say that preventive military intervention in some shape or form has not been an option for states. However, the version included in the *National Security Strategy of 2002*—combined with the U.S. preventive intervention actually undertaken in Iraq—elevated its legitimacy (in the eyes of the Bush administration) as a viable, defensible approach that other states could potentially consider in the pursuit of their own foreign policy goals.[51] This scenario would not necessarily translate into stability and order as some in the administration were clearly sold on, but would actually engender an environment in which more states themselves could consider preventive action as a potential option in addressing their own irritants. As articulated in a policy brief from the Brookings Institution, "[T]oday's international system is characterized by a relative infrequency of interstate war. Developing doctrines that lower the threshold for pre-emptive action could put that accomplishment at risk, and exacerbate regional crises already on the brink of open conflict."[52]

In contrast, some analysts have argued that in the instance of WMD "movements," the extent to which the nonproliferation regime alone would "be capable of preventing the further proliferation of WMD or weapon-related technologies or expertise, let alone be capable of rolling back existing capabilities in key states of proliferation concern," was highly questionable.[53] They argue that a reactive, diplomatic-oriented, multilateral approach that would actually deter the possibility of a rogue state or non-state actor from attacking the United States would be distinctly limited at best. In advocating the Bush call to adapt preemption to the 21st century, many proponents thereby subscribed to an approach that was proactive, militarily operational, and unilaterally balanced. As stated by Ellis and Kiefer, rather than being a "recipe for further proliferation, the Bush National Security Strategy of 2002 is a direct outgrowth of an existing post-proliferated and terror-prone security environment." In this regard, "it is both the logical culmination of more than a decade's worth of experience with recalcitrant proliferants in key regions and a sound premise on which to base U.S. national-security planning in the years ahead."[54]

Indeed, as reflected in the NSS, "the greater the threat, the greater is the risk of inaction—and the more compelling the case for taking anticipatory action to defend ourselves, even if uncertainty remains as to the time and place of the enemy's attack."[55] The Bush Doctrine hastened to add that preemption would not necessarily be the first or the only option considered when confronting these threats. Nor, it warned, should other states use this option as an excuse for aggression. But from now on in, it contended, the U.S. reserved the option of acting preemptively when the cause was just—in other words, preemption if necessary, but not necessarily preemption. In reaffirming this bold approach, forestalling or stymying hostile acts of state or non-state actors, the United States would be prepared to "act pre-emptively (preventively) . . . [t]o support pre-emptive actions (preventive war)" and "will . . . continue to transform its military forces."[56]

REAFFIRMING THE DOCTRINAL DRIVE

In reiterating the preventive strategy, senior administration officials followed up the release of the document with statements intended to reaffirm, cultivate, and, to some extent, qualify the central tenets of this option. In the first instance, many in the administration stipulated that that the U.S. had not completely discarded preceding strategic doctrines in favor of prevention/preemption, nor had it enshrined this strategy as the fundamental component in its overall national security policy. In October 2002, National Security Adviser Condoleezza Rice maintained that prevention/preemption was only one of a variety of strategic choices available to the U.S. in the global war on terror. She argued that the formalization of the strategy articulated in the *National Security Strategy* did not supplant five decades of doctrine and abandon containment or deterrence. These strategic concepts, she argued, would continue to be employed where appropriate; however, in instances when potential catastrophic threats were covertly fermenting elsewhere, a more proactive approach would be undertaken. As stated, "extremists who seem to view suicide as a sacrament are unlikely to ever be deterred. And new technology requires new thinking about when a threat actually becomes 'imminent.' So as a matter of common sense, the United States must be prepared to take action, when necessary, before threats have fully materialized."[57]

Additionally, Rice emphasized that preemption (preventive war) was an option of last resort, to be utilized only when the threat was critical and all other means of opposing it had been considered. In this regard, however, she also qualified that the approach "must be treated with great caution" and that it "does not give a green light" to the United States—or any other state—to act first without exhausting other options, including diplomacy. Indeed, preemptive action does not come at the fore of security proceedings, but only when "the threat" is "very grave . . . and the risks of waiting . . . far outweigh the risks of action.[58] In echoing these sentiments, Secretary of State Colin Powell argued that preemption's scope was more applicable to "the undeterrable threats that come from non-state actors such as terrorist groups," and was never meant to "displace deterrence, only to supplement it. . . . As to its being central, it isn't."[59]

State Department legal adviser William H. Taft IV also emphasized the dual requisites for preventive/preemptive action—i.e., a credible imminent threat and the exhaustion of peaceful remedies. In a memorandum presented to the Council on Foreign Relations, he stipulated that after all peaceful options had been considered and the deliberation of the ramifications had been undertaken, in the face of defining evidence that an imminent threat (in the administration's expanded understanding of that term) was "evolving," a state may take preemptive action to defend itself from "unimaginable harm."[60] These statements from senior administration officials, sought to qualify what they maintained was the misconception that the Bush approach represented the explicit adoption of a use-of-force doctrine in which preventive/preemptive action would now be the core strategy in the administration's fight against international terrorism and WMD proliferation.[61] Notwithstanding these attempts by the administration to soften and assure their audiences that the doctrine was a mere adjustment set for the ambiguous adversaries of the 21st century, a newer form of unilateralism was clearly under way—presenting challenges to global governance and international law.[62]

THE DOCTRINE'S REINTERPRETATION OF INTERNATIONAL LAW

Indeed, if the foundation of the United Nations Charter *jus ad bellum* regime—right to war or a just war—embodies the general prohibition on the use-of-force found in Article 2 (4)—coupled with the self-defense exception found in Article 51—to what extent was Bush's preventive or preemptive use-of-force lawful under the regime anchored on these two requirements? First, it is evident from other provisions of the charter that the Security Council can resort to the preventive or preemptive use-of-force under its Chapter VII powers.[63] As per Article 39, the council may pursue forcible measures in response to "any threat to the peace, breach of the peace, or act of aggression."[64] The reference to "threat to the peace" suggested that the Security Council may act (or authorize members to act) before a breach of the peace or an act of aggression had actually taken place. This is confirmed in rhetoric used elsewhere in Chapter VII, Article 50, for example, that referred specifically to "preventive or enforcement measures against any state . . . taken by the Security Council."[65] The question, however, was as to whether states are permitted to act unilaterally (i.e., without prior and explicit Security Council authorization) in a preventive or preemptive military capacity as a measure of self-defense. The answer to this of course depended upon the interpretation of Article 51, and specifically, as to whether the article permitted the anticipatory use-of-force in self-defense.

The debate over the legitimacy of anticipatory self-defense, that is, unilateral measures of military force taken by a state to prevent an expected armed attack, has been one of the most controversial and extensive disputes connected with the charter *jus ad bellum* regime. On a general level, there have been two competing interpretations of Article 51 of the Charter of the United Nations, which defines the inherent right of individual or collective self-defense in the event of an armed attack against a UN member. The restrictive or *narrow* interpretation posits that a state may exercise its right of self-defense *only in response* to an actual armed attack. The non-restrictive or *broad* interpretation, conversely, emphasizes that a state may also undertake this strategy in *anticipation of* an impending armed attack. Both sides of the equation have articulated and conveyed powerful arguments in support of their respective positions. But while there may be a substantial and admittedly controversial basis for preemptive counter-proliferation strategies in international law, there is much less so for preventive strategies. It seems reasonable to recognize the legitimacy of anticipatory self-defense in the face of a clearly defined imminent threat. As has often been said, international law in general—and the UN Charter regime, in particular—is not a suicide pact. No state can be expected to sit passively and absorb an aggressor's impending attack. At the same time, however, active defense does not necessarily imply that preemptive action should be taken in all circumstances against all threats.

Nevertheless, there is a place for preemption both in a state's national security policy and, more to the point of this section, in international law. This does not extend, however, to the brand of prevention/preemption set out in the Bush Doctrine, in so far as it does not meet the conditions of necessity and proportionality that regulate the anticipatory use of defensive force under the current interpretation of the charter *jus ad bellum* regime. The reason is, quite simply, that the strategic option enshrined in the doctrine—as argued extensively throughout the above—is not preemption but, rather, prevention cloaked in the rhetoric of preemption. This is more than just semantics. As also demonstrated in the above, the international community had serious reservations concerning preventive military action. Such action, based often on ambiguous evidence of potential long-term threats, engendered greater scope for abuse—that is, for the pursuit of aggressive ends under the guise of anticipatory self-defense, as well as for major informational mistakes in which thousands die as a result.

In order to make its preventive strategy more palatable to the international community—and hence lessen its instinctive opposition to the strategy—the Bush administration attempted to convey this strategic option as preemption. It drew the conceptual link to preemption through its emphasis on an expanded notion of imminence, a key element in the condition of necessity as it related to preemption. Here again, the Bush Doctrine embellished the concept of imminence beyond the semantic breaking point. The doctrine pushed imminence back to the early research and development stage of the nuclear threat cycle, where the time to develop an operational nuclear weapons capability was measured not in days, weeks, or even months but, rather, in years. Nuclear activities at this stage of the threat cycle do not pose an imminent threat in the true meaning of the word. This is not to argue for complacency in the face of such a potential long-term threat, and it may call for determined non-military action in order to prevent its realization. But it is not an imminent threat in the sense of a clear and impending attack, the basis for truly preemptive action.[66]

This leads to the second component of the necessity condition on which the Bush Doctrine's brand of preemption faltered. Traditionally, necessity requires that force be used as a last resort after all reasonable non-military alternatives have been exhausted. It is difficult to credibly make the argument that there is no alternative to the use-of-force when dealing with a WMD capability whose emergence to the point where it actually poses an existential threat to the target state is measured in years. In such circumstances, the target state certainly has time for "a hundred visions and revisions" of its counter-proliferation efforts. The Bush Doctrine attempted to bypass the issue of time by portraying conflict with the adversary as inevitable. It assumed that the irrational hostility of the leaders of rogue proliferators was such that, once they acquired nuclear weapons, they would—not might—use them against the U.S. and its friends either directly or through their terrorist proxies. That being the case, it was better to "impede now" when there was a better chance of success at relatively low cost, than later when the threat was more fully developed.[67]

The last point where the Bush Doctrine's version of preemption faced limitations pertained to the second condition of regulating the defensive use-of-force on proportionality. The target state should not, for example, incinerate an aggressor's city in response to a rifle shot at a border post. For preemption of a perceived nuclear threat, in particular, the severity of the response turns critically on the characterization of that threat. In its public pronouncements, the Bush Administration focused on the worst-case scenario imaginable—a nuclear holocaust unleashed on American cities at the cost of hundreds of thousands, if not millions, of lives—to underpin its preventive/preemptive strategy. Can this scenario be completely ruled out? Obviously not. It was not only the consequences of a catastrophic event but the likelihood of that event that must be assessed in order to place a particular threat scenario in its proper perspective among the panoply of other possible threats to the nation's security. This was particularly important when the threat response under consideration was preventive military action, with all the intended—and unintended—consequences that can flow from such action. The target state must have the ability to gather and assess accurate, reliable, and timely intelligence on the capabilities and intentions of the adversary.

As several American committees studying the 9/11 and Iraqi WMD intelligence failures have revealed, the U.S. intelligence system did not demonstrate that it had this capacity, certainly to the degree necessary to underpin a strategy of prevention. In the absence of such a capacity, falling back on worst-case-scenario planning to "cover the bases" had the associated consequence of rendering the concept of proportionality irrelevant. The hypothesized demise of millions of innocents effectively served to justify any level of preventive military action. It is here that while there may have been grounds, at least in principle, under the UN Charter *jus ad bellum* regime for a counter-proliferation strategy of preemption that satisfied the conditions of necessity and proportionality, the Bush Doctrine's brand of preemption—prevention by any other name—was extensively limited in this context of international law. [68]

CONNECTING THE DOCTRINE'S PREVENTIVE STRATEGY TO IRAQ

The decision to go into Iraq under the preemption pretext gathered further traction when Dick Cheney, in August 2002, argued that Saddam Hussein's possession of a nuclear arsenal presented a serious threat to the U.S. because Iraq possessed 10 percent of the world's oil reserves. In this regard, Cheney argued, Iraq was looking to become the dominant power of the entire Middle East, taking control of a significant portion of the world's energy supplies, directly threatening America's friends throughout the region, and subjecting the United States or any other nation to nuclear blackmail. The fact that Hussein "definitely" had weapons of mass destruction left Cheney with "no doubt he is amassing them to use against our friends, against our allies, and against us."[69] Despite his over-embellishment of the security threat, Cheney's emphatic posture on Iraq was supported by many in the administration—including Bush himself. Only a month after Cheney's bold pronouncements, Bush pointed to Hussein's breaking of "every pledge he made to the United Nations and the world since his invasion of Kuwait was rolled back in 1991," while also making the defining link to their supposed WMDs capabilities: "[S]hould his regime acquire fissile material, it would be able to build a nuclear weapon within a year."[70] Bush also made the other crucial connection in which Hussein had apparent relations with sub-national groups. Through the support of such actors, Bush argued, "Hussein's regime has proven itself a grave and gathering danger. To suggest otherwise is to hope against evidence. To assume this regime's good faith is to bet the lives of millions and the peace of the world in a reckless gamble."[71] Because they both "work in concert," the security threat was that al Qaeda would become "an extension of Saddam's madness and his hatred and his capacity to extend weapons of mass destruction around the world. . . . [Y]ou can't distinguish between al Qaeda and Saddam when you talk about the war on terror."[72]

In the fall of 2002, the Bush administration's securitization of Iraq and the Hussein regime further escalated. The rhetoric of the foreign-policy team became quite shrill and often made the assertion that the only way to disarm Iraq was to oust Saddam Hussein through a proactive military intervention. Cheney continued on with his Iraq "definitely has" WMD narrative in which "the United States may well become the target of those activities."[73] Likewise, Rice told CNN's Wolf Blitzer that "there will always be some uncertainty to obtaining a nuclear weapon," but "we don't want the smoking gun to be a mushroom cloud."[74] While appearing somewhat more restrained, Colin Powell emphasized the preventive-war line of thinking, stating that the best way to resolve the Iraq security threat was via regime change.[75]

Of course, once the preventive doctrine became both definitively public and formalized in the *National Security Strategy of 2002*, Bush was able to convince many in the American public that the threat Saddam Hussein presented—should he use nuclear weapons—would be an attack similar to, but significantly more overwhelming than, the events of 9/11. In laying the preventive platform, Bush's rhetoric clearly illustrated that war was on the administration's agenda in the not too distant future.[76] In specific nuclear-related terms, Bush argued that if Iraq was able "to produce, buy, or steal an amount of highly enriched uranium a little larger than a softball, it could have a nuclear weapon in less than a year." As such, he continued, it "must not be permitted to threaten America and the world with horrible poisons and diseases and gases and atomic weapons. America must not ignore the threat gathering against us. Facing clear evidence of peril, we cannot wait for the final proof of the smoking gun that could come in the form of a mushroom cloud."[77] To again remind Americans that Hussein had supposed links with al Qaeda, Bush was prepared again to rely on shaky evidence to make his assertion. As stated:

> We know that Iraq and al Qaeda have had high-level contacts that go back a decade. Some al Qaeda leaders who fled Afghanistan went to Iraq. . . . We've learned that Iraq has trained al Qaeda members in bomb-making and poisons and deadly gases. And we know that after September the 11th, Saddam Hussein's regime gleefully celebrated the terrorist attacks on America.[78]

Aside from the American public, Bush also had to persuade Congress that the use-of-force was the required option in quelling the Iraq security threat. In pointing to how they voted for a policy of regime change in 1998, Bush reminded key Senate and House members that "doing nothing is not an option."[79] In response, they requested more information on Iraq's WMD program from the CIA. The October 2002 National Intelligence Estimate (NIE) concluded in its key judgments that "Iraq has continued its weapons of mass destruction programs in defiance of UN resolutions and restrictions. . . . [I]f left unchecked, it probably will have a nuclear weapon during this decade." Moreover, "[S]ince inspections ended in 1998, most analysts assess Iraq as reconstituting its nuclear weapons program." Lastly, the intelligence community concluded, "if Baghdad acquires sufficient weapons-grade fissile material from abroad, it could make a nuclear weapon within a year. . . . Without such material from abroad, Iraq probably would not be able to make a weapon until the last half of the decade."[80]

The most significant dissenting opinion to the Bush drive came from the Department of State's Bureau of Intelligence and Research (INR), which argued that the "activities we have detected do not . . . add up to a compelling case that Iraq is currently pursuing what INR would consider to be an integrated and comprehensive approach to acquire nuclear weapons. Iraq may be doing so, but INR considers the available evidence inadequate to support such a judgment."[81]

Conversely, three days prior to the congressional vote that was to be held on October 7, 2001, Director of Central Intelligence George Tenet provided information on the alleged links between Iraq and al Qaeda and permitted its use in unclassified discussions. In a letter to the Senate on Baghdad's intentions, he argued that there *was* ample information pointing to: senior-level contacts between Iraq and al Qaeda going back a decade; credible information indicating that Iraq and al Qaeda had discussed safe havens and reciprocal non-aggression; plausible evidence of the presence in Iraq of al Qaeda members, including some that had been in Baghdad; and credible reporting that al Qaeda leaders had sought contacts in Iraq who could help them acquire WMD capabilities, including that Iraq had provided training to al Qaeda members in the areas of poisons and gases and making conventional bombs.[82]

Notwithstanding this information, however, Tenet did not classify the threat from Iraq as immediate or imminent, and even contended that Saddam Hussein would likely restrain himself from undertaking attacks against the U.S. as long as it did not attack Iraq. Here, Baghdad appeared to be drawing a line short of conducting terrorist attacks with conventional or chemical/biological weapons against the United States. "Should Saddam conclude that a U.S.-led attack could no longer be deterred, he probably would become much less constrained in adopting terrorist actions."[83] Simply put, if the U.S. didn't attack Saddam, he was unlikely to attack the U.S., signifying the CIA's view that Saddam Hussein's Iraq was not an immediate or even intermediate threat to the U.S. . . . . unless *it was* attacked. Nevertheless, the preventive wheel was clearly in motion, and on October 10 and 11 both houses of Congress authorized President Bush to "use the armed forces of the United States as he determines to be necessary and appropriate . . . against the continuing threat posed by Iraq."[84]

THE DOCTRINE AND IRAQ

In coming to a decision on how and where to execute its preventive war, the Bush administration chose to preventively attack Iraq, an unequivocally weaker state than the other "rogues" of choice (Iran and North Korea). In adhering to the sentiments of Richard Ned Lebow, perhaps the most defining consideration in circumventing the drive toward war can be its expected costs. In some conditions they may be high enough to deter policy-makers from using force irrespective of the scale of the projected gains. In this regard, while Bush was still choosing a risky option, "the absolute cost of war . . . was probably an important restraining factor for American policy-makers," where "as the absolute cost of war increases, the importance of relative gains diminishes and may ultimately become irrelevant to the decision for war or peace."[85]

While many opinions have been posited to explain the U.S. decision to attack Iraq—rather than Iran or North Korea, given the vast connections between them—it is evident that the foremost plausible difference between these "threatening" states at the time was their comparative military strength. Nonetheless, it was apparent that Bush's regular public exhortation about the threat from Iraq was focused more on the risks inherent in "doing nothing" to impede the alleged Iraqi WMD programs, and Saddam Hussein's determination to use them against the U.S., that would ultimately win out. In simple terms, the president outlined the options in public on Iraq as being twofold: preventive war or "trusting in the sanity and restraint of Saddam Hussein."[86] In looking for ways to obviate future losses similar to the one suffered by the U.S. on 9/11, Bush took a worst-case-scenario standpoint and accordingly gave little weight to moderate alternatives involving weapons inspections or sanctions that might have actually worked to disarm Iraq, but not necessarily unhinge Hussein from power.

The sheer fact that Bush ordered the incursion before inspections had been completed illustrated that when it came to Iraq, preventive military force was not a last resort. The propensity to disregard data both from the intelligence community and from his advisers—specifically Powell—that was divergent to his objective of regime change also suggested that Bush pursued conflict with Iraq as a way to reestablish the pre-9/11 standing and avoid a future loss to U.S. national security. A March 2005 White

House–commissioned report on NBC (nuclear, biological, chemical) intelligence was extremely critical of American intelligence on Iraqi NBC prior to the 2003 Iraq War, "noting the thin body of information."[87] Similarly, Greg Thielmann, former head of the Office of Strategic Proliferation and Military Affairs in the State Department's Office of Intelligence and Research, argued that the efficacy of any first-strike military doctrine rests on dependable intelligence. The U.S. intelligence community's incapacity to yield accurate information on enemy threats "renders such a doctrine feckless and reckless."[88] Essentially, the administration disregarded intelligence analysts whose deductions did not adhere to their own, while concurrently, they challenged intelligence that interrogated the actual existence of Iraqi WMD or Saddam's links to al Qaeda, and ultimately, questioned the definitive goal of regime change in Iraq. Powell, who believed disarmament could be accomplished without war, was recurrently "outvoted" by Cheney, Rumsfeld, and Wolfowitz, all of whom agreed with the Bush view that war was necessary to permanently disarm Iraq. Exemplifying just how detached Powell became from influencing the "final" decision, Bush selected a preventive version of war that contradicted Powell's doctrine of overwhelming force. Instead, Rumsfeld's rapidity and flexibility won out and the post-Saddam occupation occurred with no clear vision for the future, nor an exit strategy.

THE BUSH DOCTRINE IN ACTION

On March 19, just hours after he had ordered the first attacks on Iraq, Bush reaffirmed his rationale to the American public and once again spoke of the Iraqi threat. As stated, "[W]e meet that threat now, with our Army, Air Force, Navy, Coast Guard and Marines, so that we do not have to meet it later with armies of fire fighters and police and doctors on the streets of our cities."[89] Even as he announced what would be the main plank of his doctrine in action, the president reconnected with 9/11—an event that logistically was considered by many to be quite distinct from Iraq—to justify the action. Bush chose the preventive option because he believed it could allow him, and America for that matter, to recover the pre-9/11 eminence of American imperviousness and this could be attained by banishing Saddam Hussein, disarming Iraq, and, overall, forestalling impending attacks that he painted to his audiences as being similar but extensively more noxious than 9/11. While the preventive option had the highest outcome value if it succeeded, it also posed one of the lowest outcome values if it failed. Nonetheless, Bush selected the riskiest option and gambled on recouping previous losses, reestablishing the previous status quo, and averting future losses.[90] According to Cheney, after the United States suffered the worst attacks on mainland soil, "the President said 'no more'" and enunciated the Bush Doctrine so as to ensure "states that sponsor terror, that provide sanctuary for terrorists to account . . . will be treated as guilty as the terrorists themselves of whatever acts are committed from bases on that soil."[91]

As the main architect of the *National Security Strategy of 2002*, Condoleezza Rice's decision-making process was also significantly defined by the events of 9/11. Like the president, Rice believed that the loss on 9/11 impacted America's sense of security and that future threats of this nature must be averted with more forthright actions: "[S]ince 9/11, our nation is properly focused as never before on preventing attacks against us before they happen."[92] As such, the *National Security Strategy of 2002* provided a framework for foreign policy which Rice arguably believed would allow the U.S. to recoup the pre-9/11 status quo. Using 9/11 as context, Rice asserted that adopting the Bush Doctrine did not necessarily mean abandoning containment or deterrence; it was more that these traditional concepts needed to be emboldened to prevent future losses caused by terrorist attacks. Twenty-first century threats, she contended, were "so potentially catastrophic—and can arrive with so little warning, by means that are untraceable—that they cannot be contained. Extremists who seem to view suicide as a sacrament are unlikely ever to be deterred." In adapting the fusion of radicalism and the greater imminence of new technology, the United States must be primed to take action, when necessary, before threats have come to fruition and are under way.[93]

In authoring the *National Security Strategy of 2002*, Rice essentially unified the threat and dangers of terrorism, with warnings about Saddam Hussein and his drive to procure weapons of mass destruction, in a prescription ostensibly intended to recoup the pre-9/11 status quo of security and to forestall future losses. As stated:

> Terrorists allied with tyrants can acquire technologies allowing them to murder on an ever more massive scale. Each threat magnifies the danger of the other. . . . For these reasons, President Bush is committed to confronting the Iraqi regime, which has defied the just demands of the world for over a decade. . . . The danger of Saddam Hussein's arsenal is far clearer than anything we could have foreseen prior to September 11th. And history will judge harshly any leader or nation that saw this dark cloud and sat by in complacency or indecision.[94]

In the context of deciding on the available options, Rice was not entirely opposed to pursuing a UN resolution on Iraq or reintroducing inspections. In fact, she initially supported going to the UN to obtain a new resolution on Iraq and encouraged the president to at least try new weapons inspections, likely because, even if they failed, U.S. efforts at the UN could validate and possibly garner international support for a war in Iraq. However, Rice ultimately believed that the only way to eliminate the professed threat of Iraqi

WMD was to launch a preventive war. At a meeting at the White House on February 5, 2003, she informed House minority leader Nancy Pelosi that "we tried sanctions, we tried limited military options, we tried resolutions. At some point, war is the only option."[95] While Rice arrived in the Bush administration as a renowned realist who encouraged a foreign policy that focused on big, powerful states in pursuit of the national interest, after the 9/11 terrorist attacks, she began to redefine outside threats to the U.S. differently. When asked by Bush if he ought to pursue war, Rice answered, "Yes, because it isn't American credibility on the line, it is the credibility of everybody that this gangster can yet again beat the international system. . . . To let this threat in this part of the world play volleyball with the international community this way will come back to haunt us someday. That is the reason to do it."[96] On this basis, Rice made the case for going after Iraq as part of the war on terror and set the doctrine on its major "action" trajectory.[97]

CONCLUSION

In terms of the "choice" of Iraq, the cultivation of the preventive-war doctrine (rhetorically and formally in the context of the *National Security Strategy of 2002*) and the alignment of the preventive-war option to Iraq, as well as the orchestration and lead-up to the preventive war itself—it appears that the Bush Doctrine could be deemed as overzealous, extreme, and unprecedented. In fact, when looking at Bush's unrestrained determination to execute its war with Iraq, this seems to be nothing short of the truth. In response to the September 11, 2001, terrorist attacks, the previous structures of U.S. security strategy were replaced with a strike policy that advocated both the identification and destruction of terrorist threats "before" they were able to "reach" the United States' "borders," even if this entailed acting alone and using what was referred to as preemptive force.[98] Indeed, the increasing possibility that chemical, nuclear, and biological weapons could fall into the hands of stateless terrorists, coupled with the al Qaeda attack in the United States, signalled the cessation of the strategy that had served the United States military throughout the Cold War and the first phase (1991–2001) of the post–Cold War period. Having observed firsthand the terrible devastation wrought by a comparatively small and unsophisticated attack upon New York, Washington DC, and rural Pennsylvania, the Bush administration unanimously asserted that keeping the "world's worst weapons out of the hands of the world's worst people" would henceforth become Washington's uppermost national security priority for the foreseeable future.[99]

Of course, the Bush Doctrine's ideologically driven framing of the Iraq issue, and the attitude that regime change in Iraq was necessary to prevent another 9/11, resulted in an inclination to overlook nuance and to condense multifaceted questions to simple, black and white choices that fashioned an *all* or *nothing* perspective on the decision regarding Iraq. Even before he went to the UN, Bush publicly conveyed the decision on Iraq as a choice between two options—doing nothing or toppling the regime—while overlooking any alternatives in the middle. By being convinced regime change was the only viable option for achieving Iraqi disarmament, and thus making the U.S. more secure, the president approached the UN, *not* to prevent a war with Iraq, but to justify one. In making the choice on how to address the apparent proliferation of nuclear weapons in Iraq, Bush gave small prudence to options other than preventive war on the basis that they had been tried to no avail, although not during his administration. The president also chose the preventive option despite the absence of substantive evidence that Saddam Hussein was actually complicit in 9/11, had ties to al Qaeda, or that Iraq's suspected nuclear program was close to producing a nuclear weapon. Bush made repeated pronouncements pertaining to the existential nature and propinquity of threat from Iraq, and punctuated these declarations with images of a nuclear attack coordinated by Saddam Hussein. That he viewed the 9/11 attacks as a type of forerunner to the extreme ramifications that could follow if he did not act to avert it also likely played a role in his decision to vie for preventive war. True to his word, President George W. Bush and his administration formalized and put into action a doctrinal strategy designed to recompense for America's newfound discernment of vulnerability and, more importantly, prevent the possibility of a "nuclear 9/11."[100]

NOTES

1. George W. Bush, *The National Security Strategy of the United States of America*, Washington DC: The White House, 2002, Opening Letter.

2. *Ibid.*; George W. Bush, *National Strategy to Combat Weapons of Mass Destruction (NSCWMD)*, Washington DC: The White House, December 2002, p. 1.

3. Jeffrey Record, "The Bush Doctrine and the War with Iraq," *Parameters*, 2003, 33, p. 9.

4. John L. Gaddis, "A Grand Strategy of Transformation," *Foreign Policy*, 2002, 133, pp. 50–57. See Aiden Warren, *Prevention, Pre-emption and the Nuclear Option: From Bush to Obama*, Routledge, NY, 2011, p. 2.

5. George W. Bush, "A Period of Consequences," address at The Citadel, South Carolina, September 23, 1999, available at: http://www.citadel.edu/pao/addresses/pres_bush.html.

6. M. Elaine Bunn, "Pre-emptive Action: When, How, and to What Effect?" *Strategic Forum*, 2003, 200, pp. 1–8.

7. U.S. Department of Defense, *Quadrennial Defense Review* Report, September 30, 2001.

8. Donald H. Rumsfeld, "Secretary Rumsfeld Speaks on '21st Century Transformation' of the U.S. Armed Forces," January 31, 2002.

9. George W. Bush, "Remarks by the President to the Warsaw Conference on Combating Terrorism," November 6, 2001.

10. George W. Bush, "State of the Union Address," 2002.

11. *Ibid.*

12. *Ibid.* See Warren, *Prevention, Pre-emption and the Nuclear Option*, p. 34.

13. George W. Bush, Graduation Speech at West Point, June 1, 2002.

14. *Ibid.*

15. *Ibid.*
16. *Ibid.*
17. See Thomas E. Ricks and Vernon Loeb, "Bush Developing Military Policy of Striking First," *The Washington Post*, June 10, 2002, A01.
18. See Warren, *Prevention, Pre-emption and the Nuclear Option*, p. 35.
19. Bush, *The National Security Strategy of the United States of America*, 2002, p. 6.
20. *Ibid.*, p. 14.
21. *Ibid.*
22. *Ibid.*, p. 15.
23. For an examination of these obstacles, see Richard K. Betts, 1982. Surprise Attack: Lessons for Defense Planning . Washington DC: Brookings Institution, 1982.
24. Jon Rosenwasser, "The Bush Administration's Doctrine of Pre-emption (and Prevention): When, How, Where?" Council on Foreign Relations, February 1, 2004, available at: http://www.cfr.org/world/bush-administrations-doctrine-preemption-prevention-/p6799.
25. Bush, *The National Security Strategy of the United States of America*, 2002, p. 15.
26. *Ibid.*
27. Rosenwasser, "The Bush Administration's Doctrine of Pre-emption (and Prevention)."
28. Bush, *The National Security Strategy of the United States of America*, 2002, p. 15.
29. *Ibid.*, p. 13.
30. *Ibid.*, p. 15.
31. *Ibid.*, p. 3.
32. James Wirtz and James Russell, "U.S. Policy on Preventive War and Pre-emption," *The Non-proliferation Review*, 2003, Spring, p. 116.
33. Anthony C. Arend, "International Law and the Pre-emptive Use of Force," *The Washington Quarterly*, 2003, 26, p. 91.
34. Jack S. Levy, "Declining Power and the Preventive Motivation for War," *World Politics*, 1987, 40, pp. 90–91.
35. Rosenwasser, "The Bush Administration's Doctrine of Pre-emption (and Prevention)."
36. See Warren, *Prevention, Pre-emption and the Nuclear Option*, p. 8.
37. Richard N. Lebow, "Windows of Opportunity: Do States Jump Through Them?" *International Security*, 9, 1984, p. 147.
38. Levy, "Declining Power and the Preventive Motivation for War," p. 91. See Warren, *Prevention, Pre-emption and the Nuclear Option*, p. 9.
39. Rosenwasser, "The Bush Administration's Doctrine of Pre-emption (and Prevention)."
40. *Ibid.*
41. Bush, *The National Security Strategy of the United States of America*, 2002, p.2.
42. *Ibid.*
43. *Ibid.*, p. 15.
44. Rosenwasser, "The Bush Administration's Doctrine of Pre-emption (and Prevention)."
45. *Ibid.*
46. Bush, *The National Security Strategy of the United States of America*, 2002, p. 16.
47. *Ibid.*
48. Joseph Cirincione, Jessica T. Mathews, George Perkovich, and Alexis Orton, *WMD in Iraq: Evidence and Implications*. Washington DC: Carnegie Endowment for International Peace, 2004, p. 60.
49. Glenn Frankel, "New U.S. Doctrine Worries Europeans," *The Washington Post*, September 30, 2002, I(A) and 15(A).
50. John Steinbruner, "Confusing Ends and Means: The Doctrine of Coercive Pre-emption," *Arms Control Today*, January/February, 2003. See Warren, *Prevention, Pre-emption and the Nuclear Option*, p. 10.
51. Michael O'Hanlon, Susan E. Rice, and James B. Sterling, "The New National Security Strategy and Pre-emption," Policy Brief #113, The Brookings Institution, December 2002.
52. *Ibid.*, p. 7.
53. Jason D. Ellis and Geoffrey D. Kiefer, *Combating Proliferation: Strategic Intelligence and National Policy*, Baltimore, MD: Johns Hopkins University Press, 2004, p. 203.
54. *Ibid.*

55. Bush, *The National Security Strategy of the United States of America*, 2002, p. 16.

56. *Ibid.* See Warren, *Prevention, Pre-emption and the Nuclear Option*, p. 186

57. Condoleezza Rice, "A Balance of Power That Favors Freedom," The Walter Wriston Lecture of the Manhattan Institute, Office of the Press Secretary, New York, Washington DC: White House, October 1, 2002.

58. Rice, "A Balance of Power That Favors Freedom."

59. Colin L. Powell, "A Strategy of Partnerships," *Foreign Affairs*, January/February 2004, 83(1), pp. 22, 24. Powell's contention that preemption applied only to non-state actors such as terrorist groups was disingenuous, to say the least. The most prominent example of the administration's use of preventive military force was the invasion of Iraq in March 2003 to overthrow the regime of Saddam Hussein. This was clearly not an instance of preemptive action against a non-state actor.

60. William H. Taft IV, "The Legal Basis for Pre-emption," *Council on Foreign Relations Journal*, 2002.

61. As Secretary of State Powell commented in his *Foreign Affairs* article:"Some at home have distorted the NSS for partisan reasons, attempting to make the Bush Administration look bad by turning fear of pre-emption into an early twenty-first-century equivalent of the Cold War era's 'rocket rattle.' Some abroad, meanwhile, have distorted U.S. intentions through an apparent exercise in mirror imaging. Using their own mottled political histories as a reference point, they have asked what they would do with the power that the United States possesses and have mistakenly projected their own Hobbesian intentions onto our rather more Lockean sensibilities. But however it has happened, the distortion of U.S. foreign policy strategy requires repair. This distortion does a disservice to honest observers trying to understand U.S. Policy, and it contributes to irrational partisanship."

62. See Warren, *Prevention, Pre-emption and the Nuclear Option*, pp. 37–38

63. David M. Ackerman, *International Law and the Pre-emptive Use of Force Against Iraq*, CRS Report for Congress RS21314 (2003), and Michael N. Schmitt, "Pre-emptive Strategies in International Law," *Michigan Journal of International Law*, 2002, 24, pp. 513, 526.

64. UN Charter Article 39, United Nations Charter, 26 June 1945, available at: http://www.un.org/en/charter-united-nations/index.html.

65. UN Charter Article 50, United Nations Charter, 26 June 1945, available at: http://www.un.org/en/charter-united-nations/index.html.

66. Josef L. Kunz, "Individual and Collective Self-Defense in Article 5I of the Charter of the United Nations," *American Journal on International Law*, 1947, 41, pp. 872, 878; Ian Brownlie, *International Law and the Use of Force by States*, Oxford: Oxford University Press, 1963; Hans Kelsen, *The Law of the United Nations: A Critical Analysis of Its Fundamental Problems*, New York: Frederick A. Praeger, 1964, pp. 797–8; and Michael B. Akehurst, *A Modern Introduction to International Law*, 6th Edition, London: Routledge, 1987, p. 261.

67. Akehurst, *A Modern Introduction to International Law*, p. 261.

68. Derek W. Bowett, *Self Defence in International Law.* Manchester: Manchester University Press, 1958, pp. 193–195; and James L. Brierly, *The Law of Nations: An Introduction to the International Law of Peace*, 6th Edition, edited by Sir Humphrey Waldock, New York: Oxford University Press, 1963, p. 419. According to Akehurst it was expected in 1945 that all states would eventually join the UN. Therefore, the failure to mention protection of non-members from armed attack was "probably due to an oversight." See Michael Akehurst, *A Modern Introduction to International Law*, 1987, p. 261.

69. Richard B. Cheney, "Vice President Speaks at VFW 103rd National Convention," The White House Archives, August 26, 2002, available at: http://georgewbush-whitehouse.archives.gov/news/releases/2002/08/20020826.html.

70. George W. Bush, "President Discusses Growing Danger Posed by Saddam Hussein's Regime," Radio Address by the President to the Nation, The White House Archives, September 14, 2002, available at: http://georgewbush-whitehouse.archives.gov/news/releases/2002/09/20020914.html.

71. *Ibid.* See Warren, *Prevention, Pre-emption and the Nuclear Option*, p. 39.

72. Walter H. Pincus, "CIA learned in '02 That Bin Laden Had No Iraq Ties, Report Says," *The Washington Post*, September 15, 2006, A14.

73. "Top Bush Officials Push Case Against Saddam," *Inside Politics*, CNN.com, September 8, 2002.

74. *Ibid.*

75. *Ibid.*

76. See Warren, *Prevention, Pre-emption and the Nuclear Option*, p. 40.

77. George W. Bush, "Address to the Nation on Iraq," October 7, 2002.

78. *Ibid.*

79. Bob Woodward, *Plan of Attack*, New York: Simon & Schuster, 2004, p. 69.

80. National Intelligence Council, *Iraq's Continuing Program for Weapons of Mass Destruction: Key Judgments*, October 2002, p. 8.

81. *Ibid.*

82. George J. Tenet, "CIA Letter to Senate on Baghdad's Intentions," Globalsecurity.org, October 7, 2002. See Warren, *Prevention, Pre-emption and the Nuclear Option*, New York: Routledge, 2011, p. 41.

83. *Ibid.*

84. Text of congressional joint resolution, published in *The Washington Post*, October 11, 2002, A12.

85. Lebow, "Windows of Opportunity," p. 155.

86. George W. Bush, "President Outlines Priorities," Presidential Hall, Dwight D. Eisenhower Executive Office Building, November 7, 2002, available at: http://georgewbush-whitehouse.archives.gov/news/releases/2002/11/20021107-2.html.

87. The Commission on the Intelligence Capabilities of the United States Regarding Weapons of Mass Destruction, Report to the President, March 31, 2005, available at: http://govinfo.library.unt.edu/wmd/report/wmd_report.pdf.

88. Greg Thielmann, "Preventive Military Intervention: The Role of Intelligence," Ridgway Center Policy Brief 04-1, October 2004.

89. Bush, "State of the Union Address," 2003.

90. See Warren, *Prevention, Pre-emption and the Nuclear Option*, p. 46.

91. Interview with Dick Cheney, *Meet the Press*, NBC, March 16, 2003.

92. *Ibid.*

93. *Ibid.*

94. *Ibid.*

95. Woodward, *Plan of Attack*, p. 308.

96. *Ibid.*, p. 251.

97. See Warren, *Prevention, Pre-emption and the Nuclear Option*, p. 50.

98. Bush, *The National Security Strategy of the United States of America*, 2002, p. 2.

99. See Warren, *Prevention, Pre-emption and the Nuclear Option*, pp. 50–52.

100. Brian M. Jenkins, "A Nuclear 9/11?" This commentary appeared on CNN.com on September 11, 2008, and was republished on the RAND Corporation website, available at: http://www.rand.org/commentary/2008/09/11/CNN.html.

Chapter Eight

Pragmatic Realism and the Use of Force

The Obama administration came into office determined to reverse what it saw as the Bush administration's mistakes and to "rebalance [the United States'] long-term priorities so that we successfully move beyond today's wars, and focus our attention and resources on a broader set of countries and challenges."[1] Under the leadership of his predecessor, George W. Bush, the U.S. had witnessed the first attack upon its soil since Pearl Harbor, and in response, waged a "War on Terror" that would ultimately become the defining legacy of the president's tenure in office. Of course, within this war, the Bush administration aggressively contested and debunked the enduring mainstays of international law, including the legal rationalization for military engagement via its interchangeable use and interpretation of preemption/prevention, and the disposition in which recidivists of war could be captured, questioned, and tried.[2] In contrast, Obama sought to restore the U.S. position *away* from what he saw as debatable expeditions and—as a key focus of this chapter—the legal obfuscation pertaining to the way it wielded its unilateral use-of-force.[3]

In enunciating the broad terms of his foreign-policy transformation early in his first term, Obama stated that he would work to reestablish America's international standing, particularly in the Muslim world, encourage multilateralism, increase cooperation with China on global issues, end the wars in Iraq and Afghanistan, participate in dialogue with Iran and North Korea as part of his nonproliferation goals, establish lasting peace in the Middle East, address climate change through innovative legislation and international agreements, and help assuage global poverty. While covering a broad and ambitious canvas, it was clear that the new president "sought nothing less than to bend history's arc in the direction of justice, and a more peaceful, stable global order."[4] For many analysts, the election of Obama appeared to be a long-delayed "straightening up" of America. Having dissipated the "world's sympathy" in the period after 9/11, making the securitization of terrorist threats the centerpiece of its foreign policy, coercing other states to support its agenda in Iraq and beyond, and disregarding its mission to rebuild failing states, the United States needed to reinstate its international integrity. The 2008 electoral victory was an opportunity to do so, regardless of the situation inherited from the predecessor. Without a doubt, part of Obama's appeal to the rest of the world was his apparent denunciation of the Bush administration's effort to proselytize about the American model or the unilateral "democracy agenda."[5]

For the Bush administration, the international order was centered solely on U.S. unipolar preeminence, with America exercising its unimpeded power to keep others in check. In the Obama prescription, the international order would ascend from the connection of America's preeminence with its formation principles, in which the United States would use its power to shape consensual and legitimate mechanisms of global governance.[6] This ostensible transition, Obama argued, necessitated a move in which the United States would reassert its "soft power" and attract support through ethical leadership.[7] In pursuing this line, the dual preservation of American security and ideals during Obama's time in office would reciprocally underpin and feature regularly in his speeches and public declarations.

However, despite these marked sentiments, this chapter will argue that while the Obama Doctrine has encountered very distinct challenges in pursuing such ambitious goals—the departure from Iraq and Afghanistan, the Arab Springs and subsequent instability in those states, the Syrian crisis, the Ukraine crisis, the P5+1 negotiations with Iran, the emergence of ISIS, deterioration of bilateral relations with Russia, to name a few—it has also demonstrated a tendency to be ambivalent, at times prevaricative, compromising, and cautious in its doctrinal approach. And while Obama's disposition was initially greeted by many as a refreshing departure from the unrestrained unilateralism of Bush, the aforementioned tendencies have often led the president into vacillating waters. In examining the Obama Doctrine's ambivalence, this chapter will specifically assess its use-of-force approach. It will argue that despite rhetoric suggesting that the administration would move decisively *away* from the Bush position, it has continued and—in specific instances—even expanded force (i.e., drones), while also displaying a degree of inconsistency in dealing with Libya, Syria, and the non-state actor, ISIS.

DOCTRINAL DUALISM

The election of Barack Obama as the 44th president of the United States pledged important vicissitudes to U.S. foreign policy and the overall approach to international affairs. Not surprisingly, the new president's first concern was to address the financial crisis, and to some extent he has been able to get the economy in decent working order. As stated by John Cassidy, "[E]ven accounting for the roughly five million jobs that were lost during the Great Recession and its aftermath, about seven million more Americans now have work than when the President took office, in January, 2009." Additionally, the budget deficit "sits at 2.8 per cent of G.D.P., less than it was in the last year of the Bush Administration, when it was 3.1 per cent. Stock prices and corporate profits, as Obama pointed out, have never been higher."[8] In the United States' core security areas, however, things have not fared as well.

In Iraq, Obama replaced the delicate stability attained via the "surge" with a methodical and comprehensive military withdrawal in late 2011, taking a major risk that the inroads made could continue on indefinitely without a significant U.S. presence or prominent U.S. involvement. Iraq's sectarian and ethnic divisions—subdued toward the end of the 2003–2011 U.S. military intervention in Iraq—have reemerged to spur a significant challenge to Iraq's stability and to U.S. policy in Iraq and the broader Middle East region. The antipathy of Iraq's Sunni Arabs toward the Shiite-dominated central government contributed to the seizure in 2014 of nearly one-third of Iraqi territory by the Sunni Islamist extremist group Islamic State (also known as the Islamic State of Iraq and the Levant, or ISIL). Iraq's Kurds have been separately entangled in political and territorial disagreements with Baghdad, although those differences have been somewhat deflected with the focus on the mutual fight against the Islamic State.[9]

In Afghanistan, at the end of 2014, the United States and allied states completed a transition to a smaller mission comprising mainly training and advising the Afghanistan National Defense and Security Forces (ANDSF). However, based on assessments that the ANDSF was having difficulty thwarting advances by the Taliban and other militant groups (exemplified by the insurgent overrunning of the northern city of city of Kunduz in late September 2015), President Obama announced on October 15, 2015, that approximately 10,000 U.S. military personnel would stay on in Afghanistan through 2016.[10]

Not surprisingly, the struggle to secede from these two theaters has deeply impacted Obama's responses to other security situations during his time in the White House. Presented with new and emerging scenarios for major military interventions, the president's doctrine has either repudiated or authorized only the minimum required to achieve what can be deemed as imperfect—and at times unclear—goals. His management of the "red line" on Syria's use of chemical weapons—first proclaiming a significant pledge, then irresolute about living up to it, then frantically deferring to Congress for a decision—was an example "in embarrassingly amateurish improvisation." Additionally, his attempt at an "immaculate intervention" in Libya essential-

ly repeated—albeit on a much smaller scale—the Bush administration's basic error in Iraq: ousting a government without a clear strategy for what
comes next, leaving behind a vacuum for chaos.[11] Indeed, from Syria to
Ukraine, Yemen to Iran, the Obama administration has been resolute in its
drive to avoid another entanglement. However, in avoiding boots on the
ground or even bombers in the air, Obama's national security suite—while
encompassing sanctions and negotiations[12]—has veered in unsettling directions through the amplification of drones or a proclivity to be somewhere "in
the middle."

Indeed, Obama came to office with a belief that reducing the United
States' substantial military and political involvement in the Middle East was
an important national security interest objective. The occupation of Iraq and
the immoderations of the war on terrorism had left the U.S. overstretched,
particularly at a time of economic calamity. "Rightsizing" the United States'
imprint in the region necessitated not only reducing its physical presence but
also undertaking a more restrained diplomacy, seceding back and galvaniz-
ing allies to play a greater role in looking after their own security. Obama has
for the main part adhered steadily to this strategy and has resisted most
efforts to force it off track, particularly from a Washington that is so "hard-
wired for the exercise of American power."[13] Yet for all of Obama's analytic
perspicacity, the application of his policies has often struggled to meet the
promises of his rousing speeches. The administration has not always commu-
nicated its policies effectively to varying publics—at home, in the Middle
East, and in the broader international community—and has more often than
not been viewed by many as embodying ongoing hypocrisies and stark
contradictions. Certainly, efforts to remain balanced and non-intervention-
ist—yet include a preparedness to use force from a distance—have frustrated
"partisans on all sides who wanted unconditional U.S. support rather than an
honest broker."[14]

Of course, the downsizing of the U.S. global role and the withdrawal from
exposed forward positions has led to a situation where instead of being
mollified, the United States' adversaries have become emboldened and
American interests and values have increasingly been challenged. But, as the
administration argues, it has not abandoned traditional U.S. grand strategy; it
has been more willing perhaps "to sacrifice the periphery, both functional
and regional."[15] As Obama stated in 2010, the U.S. "created webs of commerce, supported an international architecture of laws and institutions, and
spilled American blood in foreign lands, not to build an empire, but to shape
a world in which more individuals and nations could determine their own
destiny, and live with the peace and dignity they deserve."[16] In order to get
back to that task, however, the nation needed to "pursue a strategy of national
renewal and global leadership—a strategy that rebuilds the foundation of
American strength and influence."[17] This would require delineating wants

and needs, while putting some issues and areas to the side.[18] Of course, as this chapter will further discuss, in attempting to attain some semblance of balance, the doctrinal pathway has found itself in precarious areas where it has clearly been caught "somewhere in between," evident in its "pick and choose" approach to the use-of-force and its penchant to *partially* partake in new and emerging theaters of conflict.

EARLIER SIGNS OF DUALISM

As indicated thus far, the election of Obama "raised the hopes" that there would be a "dramatic shift in the U.S. attitude towards international law,"[19] the way it conducted its use-of-force approach, and an overall transformation in U.S. foreign policy. The emphasis on U.S. soft power had already been exhibited in many of Obama's campaign public pronouncements and was punctuated during his very first week as president through Executive Orders 13491 and 13492.[20] Executive Order 13491 rescinded the previous Executive Order 13440 that the Bush administration had used to justify its forcible and enhanced interrogation methods by the CIA, and fundamentally, transformed Common Article 3 of the four Geneva Conventions.[21] Executive Order 13491 emphasized legal interrogations and prompted the termination of clandestine CIA detention facilities that elicited extensive criticism during Bush's two terms.[22] When asked about the conditions in which the president may be permitted to disregard international human rights treaties in a campaign questionnaire, Obama responded that "it is illegal and unwise for the President to disregard human rights treaties that have been ratified by the United States Senate, including and especially the Geneva Conventions."[23] In a questionnaire on the role of international law in U.S. foreign policy issued by the American Society on International Law (ASIL), Obama maintained this line in stating that the U.S. "can detain and interrogate suspected terrorists—lawfully and humanely—without amending the laws of war," and should be "championing the Geneva Conventions, instead of looking for ways to evade or rewrite them."[24]

In his thorough evaluation of the first year and a half of the Obama administration, Bob Woodward described the then president-elect's surprised response when informed by the CIA of the six "enhanced" interrogation techniques it was still using.[25] As such, Obama proceeded to eliminate the CIA's enhanced interrogation program and made the organization adhere to the requirements of the Army Field Manual, which abides by the Geneva Conventions in a strict sense.[26] Despite these measures, however, an indication of Obama's doctrinal behavior during the course of his two terms in office quickly came to the fore. That is, Executive Order 13491 did not repeal the controversial practice of rendition (i.e., passing purported terrorists to third states for interrogation and indeterminate detention). Instead, Executive Order 13491 inaugurated a Special Task Force charged with reviewing U.S. interrogation and transfer policies,[27] which published its report in the summer of 2009. While endorsing a closer scrutiny of their detention and interrogation conditions, the report also argued that "when the United States transfers individuals to other countries, it may rely on assurances from the receiving country,"[28] a clear perpetuation of the Bush administration's comparable "assurances" caveat.[29] Notwithstanding the considerable legal condemnation this practice has received in the context of violating basic human rights—prohibition of torture, arbitrary arrest, and forcible transfer, which are preserved in the defining international human rights treaties such as the 1984 *Convention against Torture and Other Cruel, Inhuman or Degrading Treatment or Punishment* and the 1966 *International Covenant on Civil and Political Rights*—rendition is still considered by many administration officials as a viable option[30] and a "practice [that] has continued under President Obama in only cosmetically varied guises."[31]

The policy of relying on the assurances that detainees will not be subject to torture or inhumane treatment raises questions pertaining to the president's position.[32] Why else would the U.S. continue to send individuals to destinations where torture is probable, rather than detaining them themselves, if not because it relies on this practice as a useful means of attaining intelligence? This point has also been highlighted by Stephen Carter, who has argued that the "temptation to torture" has been intrinsic to the demands that the "War on Terror" places on procuring information.[33] In this regard, he defines Obama's policy on coercive interrogation as being "tragically" logical, where in continuing to pursue "the War on Terror, he had no choice but to decide, also, to continue to press, and press hard, for information."[34] In a more forthright fashion, Dan McLaughlin argues that Obama is simply "handing over vastly larger civilian populations to be annihilated by notoriously brutal foreign regimes in the name of keeping America's hands apparently clean of atrocities we intend to wink-and-nudge encourage." By "using unscrupulous allies to do things we dare not do ourselves" this "may explain the Obama administration's foreign policy in ways that go far beyond interrogation and detention policy."[35]

Indeed, the embedded queries and "finer" points of Obama's action against enhanced interrogation *are* very much characteristic of his use-of-force policies, and illustrative of his broader foreign policy/doctrinal position. When looking at his speeches in Prague in April 2009, in which he promoted a nuclear-weapon-free world, and at Cairo University in June 2009, which called for "a new beginning between the U.S. and Muslims around the world,"[36] dualisms abound. While the type of rhetoric used in these speeches exemplifies Obama's ambition and preparedness to undertake the diplomatic route through engagement and multilateral settings, they only tell part of the equation. If one reads between the lines, it is evident that such speeches or responses display another propensity. As noted by Peter Bergen, Obama's fervent criticism of the U.S. intervention in Iraq does by no means make him a pacifist, nor does it necessarily make him opposed to the unilateral use-of-force.[37] Obama's penchant to hedge was on display as far back as 2007 when in a presidential nomination speech he argued that the Bush administration chose to fight the "wrong war" in Iraq at the expense of focusing on the "right war" against al Qaeda and affiliates in Afghanistan/Pakistan. In specific reference to the terrorist safe havens in Pakistan's tribal areas, Obama argued that if "actionable intelligence about high-value terrorist targets" is available "and President Musharraf [then president of Pakistan] won't act, we will. . . . I will not hesitate to use military force to take out terrorists who pose a direct threat to America."[38]

Other signs of then presidential-candidate Obama's stance on the use-of-force were also on display in early 2008. Asked about his views on the preemptive use-of-force doctrine championed by his predecessor, Obama replied that he would "not hesitate to use force, unilaterally if necessary, to protect the American people or our vital interests whenever we are attacked or imminently threatened." In making his case, he pointed to those "circumstances beyond self-defense" where "using force" is an acceptable option, particularly when participating in "stability and reconstruction operations, or to confront mass atrocities." However, "when we do use force in situations other than self-defense, we should make every effort to garner the clear support and participation of others—as President George H. W. Bush did when we led the effort to oust Saddam Hussein from Kuwait in 1991."[39] In this regard, Obama unequivocally emphasized the U.S. prerogative to use force "unilaterally if necessary" in conditions covering self-defense situations in which the U.S. or its "vital interests" are "imminently threatened." Additionally, he seemingly expanded the potential unilateral use-of-force to "circumstances beyond self-defense," in other words, for humanitarian and post-conflict related purposes. Legal scholars such as Christian Henderson highlight the consequences of depicting the use-of-force as "necessary" in this respect.[40] A Security Council decree with regard to using force in these instances is not clearly stated, which suggests that the Obama administration chose to view unilateral humanitarian intervention as a feasible policy option—an option not supported by international law. Further, while Obama references multilateral support as being key when using force in situations other than for self-defense purposes, this is prefixed by a provisional: "[W]e *should* make every effort to garner the clear support and participation of others." Despite choosing to remove the terms "preemptive use-of-force" in letter, the sentiment remained.[41]

THE NATIONAL SECURITY STRATEGY (2010)

It was the Obama administration's *National Security Strategy of 2010* that articulated the doctrine's official position pertaining to the use-of-force and the ongoing conflict with al Qaeda. With continuous allusions to the significance of international cooperation and commitment to international norms and the rule of law, the document appeared to be unequivocally different from the formulations used by his predecessor.[42] Bush's "War on Terror" platform was, for instance, replaced with the more palpable war against the specific al Qaeda network and its affiliates,[43] while a clear break in the context of the detention practices and the goal of promoting constructive relations with Muslim groups across the globe was also conveyed. In simple terms, the *NSS 2010* once again attempted to "connect" U.S. soft power and efficacious global leadership in strengthening its commitment to democracy, human rights, and the rule of law.[44] In emphasizing that such values should not be "compromised in pursuit of security,"[45] nor involve "brutal methods of interrogation,"[46] the document stipulated four key commitments: first, to "principled engagement"; second, to diplomacy; third, to "strategic multilateralism"; and fourth, to the notion that living through its values makes the Unites States stronger and safer, by following rules of domestic and international law, and "following universal standards, not double standards."[47]

In contrast to the 2006 Bush *NSS* where there was not an explicit reference to international law, the *NSS 2010* referred to it on three occasions,[48] giving predilection to the terms "international norms" or "international standards."[49] This was also evident in Obama's Nobel Peace Prize acceptance speech in which he referred to "standards that govern the use-of-force" and the "rules of the road,"[50] although on this point he remained equivocal in the context of where international law sat in the use-of-force domain.[51] As Christine Gray argued, while this "may not seem a significant difference . . . in a policy instrument such as the NSS, this choice of wording must have been deliberate."[52] Moreover, the three references to international law in the *NSS 2010* were made in the context of applying it—which parenthetically is also the most common setting for references that the document makes to international norms: "We are strengthening international norms to isolate governments that flout them and to marshal cooperation against non-governmental actors who endanger our common security."[53] Despite some departure regarding the significance of international law/standards, the *NSS* also argued that military force "may be necessary to defend our country and allies or to preserve broader peace and security, including by protecting of civilians facing a grave humanitarian crisis."[54] While the U.S. would be dependent on an approach encompassing diplomacy, development, and international norms and institutions to help resolve conflicts, and thereby, "mitigating where possible the need for the use-of-force,"[55] the document stated that "we will exhaust other options before war *whenever we can*, and carefully weigh the costs and risks of *action* against the costs and risks of *inaction*."[56] In essence, the administration appeared to opt for a use-of-force approach that would be a last resort and only used if there was a high probability of victory, very much commensurate with the principles of the just war tradition. Qualifications in the wording and the propensity to uphold a hegemonic disposition, where "[the United States] must reserve the right to act unilaterally if necessary to defend the nation and its interests, yet it will also *seek to adhere* to standards that govern the use-of-force," create all sorts of uncertainty. As Gray further laments, "The formulations 'seek to adhere' and 'whenever we can' are indications of a rather weak commitment."[57]

Indeed, as one moves through the *National Security Strategy of 2010* it soon becomes evident that the document is both a redirection and continuum. The redirection is most evident through the type of rhetoric Obama used and the frequent references to the legitimacy of U.S. actions. Here, force would be used "in a way that reflects our values and strengthens our legitimacy and we will seek broad international support, working with such institutions as NATO and the UN Security Council."[58] However, force would be permitted if *necessary*, even on a unilateral basis. For legal scholar Christian Henderson, this necessity-based rationale has been the defining feature of Obama's use-of-force policy,[59] where despite Obama seemingly adhering to standing international law with regard to self-defense, he has often diluted the concept of necessity in the context of humanitarian intervention.[60] In the context of preventive and preemptive use-of-force, the *NSS 2010* did not contain any specific stipulations. While the document did actually include a distinct section entitled "Use-of-Force"[61]—unlike Bush's National Security Strategies—there was little substantive discussion or material, leaving many of the contentious issues of its predecessor unresolved. The only pointers were found in a passage relating to denying safe havens to al Qaeda, where in the context of Yemen, Somalia, the Maghreb, and the Sahel, the U.S. would "disrupt terrorist operations *before they mature* . . . [and] take root."[62] The *NSS 2010* also discussed "new practices to counter evolving adversaries,"[63] offering one of the few references to the administration's amplified drone usage. Aside from stipulating that the use-of-force must be a last resort, the *NSS 2010* remained noncommittal on the extent to which the United States still asserted the right of preemptive self-defense, or whether it was now pronouncing a right of unilateral humanitarian intervention.[64]

Assumptions relating to Obama's ostensible muted prolongation of many of Bush's positions on the use-of-force in counterterrorism are further highlighted when examining the strategic statements of the president himself, as well as government officials. From the day of his inauguration, Obama repeatedly emphasized the enduring nature of the conflict with al Qaeda and the constant threat the organization posed. In an early speech focusing on a new approach for Afghanistan and Pakistan, Obama stated that "multiple intelligence estimates have warned that al Qaeda is actively planning attacks on the U.S. homeland from its safe haven in Pakistan."[65] As such, this imminent threat to the U.S. justified the continued use-of-force in self-defense: "And we will insist that action be taken—*one way or another*—when we have intelligence about high-level terrorist targets."[66] The focus on the continuing imminence of the threat was regularly combined with accentuating that the U.S. did not enter into the Afghanistan war voluntarily, but necessarily had to use force in self-defense. As stated at the time, "We did not choose this war. This was not an act of America wanting to expand its influence; of us wanting to meddle in somebody else's business. We were attacked viciously on 9/11."[67] Although repeatedly championed by Obama as a "war of necessity" in contrast to the "war of [bad] choice" in Iraq, the war in Afghanistan was at best a preemptive war and at worst a preventive war of self-defense. It was certainly not waged in response to an imminent attack but rather a preventive response to an attack that *might* happen sometime in the future, at an unknown time or place.[68]

COMPROMISES AND AMBIVALENCE IN OBAMA'S USE-OF-FORCE DOCTRINE

In building on the seminal foreign-policy speeches, such as in Prague in April 2009 and at Cairo University in June 2009, the Obama administration made many references to its commitment to international law, its predilection for multilateral cooperation, and its strong belief in international organizations, such as the United Nations.[69] However, when it came to interpreting the right to use military force in self-defense, the changeover from the Bush Doctrine to the Obama Doctrine can be more sufficiently defined as a change in style rather than in substance. Despite never articulating an explicit doctrine of preemptive/preventive force similar to that encompassed in the *NSS 2002*, Obama's counterterrorism campaign continued and extended some of the most dubious facets of the Bush administration in practice, particularly in the expanded context of its drones.[70]

While Obama administration officials conveyed a variety of legal arguments in the context of Libya, Syria, and its drone program, these have paradoxically led to more ambiguity. In attempting to argue that military force used was in full accordance with international humanitarian law, officials fused so-called *jus ad bellum* and *jus in bello* self-defense in justifying the use-of-force against terrorist targets inside and outside established theaters of conflict. Interestingly, the second line of argument accounted for much more space than the self-defense arguments—although these worked with an increasingly distant imminence concept, making them clearly preventive in nature. In the context of Libya, the administration came to a relatively quick decision to sanction and use force. In response to Qaddafi's threat to commit atrocities in the rebel stronghold Benghazi in early March 2011, the Security Council authorized a NATO military incursion to "use all necessary means" to protect civilians in Libya via resolution 1973. In contrast, the Syrian crisis saw a rather prolonged response from the administration, and only came to a head when it was discovered the Assad regime had used chemical weapons in the summer of 2013. In this instance, the Obama administration came very close to the use of military force for Syria's violation of a key principle of international law relating to the general prohibition of biological and chemical weapons. Of course, the decision *not* to intervene prompted questions about the subjectivity of intervention conditions, particularly Obama's so-called "red line" on chemical weapons.[71] Because the U.S. would not approve these unilateral use-of-force considerations if assumed by other member states, it is evident that it was supporting an exception to the rules pertinent only to *itself* and *its* own interests.[72]

THE AUGMENTATION OF DRONES

Not surprising, the most contentious aspect of Obama's use-of-force approach relates to the augmentation of drone use. Originally used for surveillance and reconnaissance purposes, armed Predator and Reaper drones have been deployed in Afghanistan since 2001. Targeted killing operations through drone strikes have, however, only become an intrinsic part of U.S. counterterrorism policy since Obama entered the White House in 2009, and have increasingly extended outside of traditional, territorially bound theaters of conflict. While the program's confidentiality makes it difficult to attain precise numbers, it is evident that drone strikes have been targeting "confirmed terrorist targets at the highest level."[73] In Pakistan, the number of drone strikes sanctioned in Obama's first year in office (52) surpassed the number authorized by Bush during his entire two terms in office (41).[74] The number of drone strikes in Pakistan reached the astonishing level of 122 in 2010, although these have somewhat decreased (22 drone strikes in the year 2014) as the administration broadened its strikes to other theaters. Indeed, the same period has seen an increasing number of drone strikes in Yemen, peaking at 47 in 2012, as well as a limited number in Somalia.[75]

While public acknowledgment of drone strikes outside theaters of war only began to garner traction during 2011–2012—when senior administration officials addressed the issue in a series of speeches—the Obama administration has often used the "successes" of its drone program as a selling point for its broader counterterrorist effort.[76] In the context of Obama's legal justifications on the use-of-force in the form of such strikes, it is evident that they are based on a diffused standard of imminence, typical of arguments posited during the Bush administration. Here, the legal rationale championed by senior officials has typically combined "state of non-international armed conflict" with "self-defense" arguments. On one hand, the country is in a state of "armed conflict with al Qaeda, as well as the Taliban and associated forces and may use force consistent with its inherent right to self-defense under international law."[77] Through this reasoning, the use-of-force in self-defense is lawful wherever al Qaeda is in the process of preparing and executing attacks, be it inside or outside declared theaters of conflict.[78] Similar to arguments made by its predecessor, the Obama administration has also justified its targeted-killings campaign with a legally dubious, preventive version of self-defense, which it states is imperative in its quest to "address" terrorists.[79]

Since August 2014, the Obama administration's military operations against the Islamic State in Iraq and Syria have been rationalized in a similar fashion to that of al Qaeda, where the United States "would hunt down terrorists who threaten our country, wherever they are. . . . This is a core principle of my presidency: If you threaten America, you will find no safe haven."[80] In maintaining this approach, the United States has used military force in the forms of air and drone strikes on the sovereign territory of four states with which it was *not* at war: Pakistan, Yemen, Somalia, and Syria. The administration argued that forcible actions against non-state actors who were orchestrating attacks on the territory of a state who was not sponsoring or supporting them was *still* legal if that state consented to the use-of-force or was "unwilling or unable" to fulfill its international counterterrorism obligations. The legality of the subjective "unwilling or unable" formula was questioned during the Bush administration's two terms in office. Additionally, the "quality" of state consent deemed necessary has proven elusive; despite Pakistan's persistent expressions of dissent with the Obama administration's use-of-force on its territory since November 2011, drone strikes continued.[81]

In looking at this approach in rawer terms, Rosa Brooks argues that "when a government claims for itself the unreviewable power to kill anyone, anywhere on earth, at any time, based on secret criteria and secret information discussed in a secret process by largely unnamed individuals, it undermines the rule of law."[82] Notwithstanding the precarious precedents this may establish for other states to follow, it is evident that the Obama administration is not overly perturbed with subjecting its drone program to use-of-force standards enshrined in international law. Aside from the damaging effects U.S. arguments and actions on the use-of-force have on the legitimate and fundamental standards of international law, questions have been asked on whether this approach is the appropriate strategy to follow when the objective in the long run is combating terrorism.[83] While the killing of terrorist actors made for "quick fix" success stories for both administrations, developments on the ground, such as rising membership of al Qaeda in the Arabian Peninsula and surges in the numbers of foreign fighters joining the Islamic State, indicate that this approach has not succeeded in defeating their adversaries, and in fact, has more than likely spurred greater insecurity.[84]

Redefining the Use-of-Force in Response to ISIS

The prevarication in Obama's use-of-force approach is further evident when looking at his administration's use-of-force response to ISIS. In his August 2014 notifications to Congress pertaining to the deployments and airstrikes in Iraq, Obama stated that his powers as commander in chief and chief executive under Article II of the Constitution provided him with the authority to execute military action. In subsequent notifications to Congress for airstrikes and other actions in Iraq and Syria posited in September 2014, however, it was argued that two ratified authorizations for use of military force (AUMFs), the Authorization for Use of Military Force (2001 AUMF; P.L. 107-40) and the Authorization for Use of Military Force Against Iraq Resolution of 2002 (2002 AUMF; P.L. 107-243), in essence, also sanctioned certain types of U.S. strikes against the Islamic State in Iraq and Syria, as well as the Khorasan Group of al Qaeda in Syria. Notwithstanding this authority, the president indicated on November 5, 2014, that he wanted to open the dialogue in Congress so as to develop a newer version of the AUMF that would "right-size and update whatever authorization Congress provides to suit the current fight, rather than previous fights" authorized by the 2001 and 2002 AUMFs. In his January 2015 State of the Union address, the president called on Congress to ratify an AUMF version, and on February 11, 2015, Obama sent through a draft resolution to Congress to authorize the use-of-force against the Islamic State of Iraq and the Levant.[85] According to the Department of Defense, the resolution aimed to provide the United States with the authority to address "the terror group in Iraq and Syria" and updated authorizations last passed after the 9/11 attacks.[86]

In articulating the rationale behind the adjustment, Obama stated that the resolutions would support a strategy of "systemic and sustained . . . airstrikes against ISIS in Iraq and Syria," including "support and training for local forces on the ground . . . [and] moderate Syrian opposition." In thwarting ISIS attacks, the administration sought to continue its support for an inclusive Iraqi government that united the Iraqi people and strengthened Iraqi forces against ISIS. At the core of the Obama pronouncements was the belief that the resolution provided the necessary balance in terms of "flexibility we need for unforeseen circumstances."[87] Specifically, this applied to scenarios where if "actionable intelligence about a gathering of ISIS leaders" was available, the U.S. would be prepared to order its Special Forces to take action so as to preclude terrorists from attaining a safe haven.[88] As stated,

[W]e need flexibility, but we also have to be careful and deliberate. And there is no heavier decision than asking our men and women in uniform to risk their lives on our behalf. As Commander in Chief, I will only send our troops into harm's way when it is absolutely necessary for our national security. [89]

The Authorization for Use of Military Force (AUMF) against the self-declared Islamic State would authorize the president "to use the Armed Forces of the United States as the president determines to be necessary and appropriate against ISIS or associated persons or forces," but with certain restrictions and requirements for reporting to Congress on mission developments biannually, and would only be for a defined period that would "sunset" in three years. While some Washington policy analysts and legal experts argued that the AUMF did not give the president ample tractability, others argued that it was balanced and provided Obama with the requisite authorization to execute the current strikes against ISIL. [90]

To some analysts, however, the new resolution could potentially redefine the AUMF, give greater impetus and legitimacy to *actually* using force, and "broaden the purpose of military force to include unspecified U.S. national security interests." [91] In an apparent stretching of the theaters of conflict, there would be no geographic limitations on where the U.S. could take the fight. While Defense Secretary Ashton Carter described this inclusion as being "wise," given the indications that ISIS had the capability to expand outside of Iraq and Syria, it presented some concerns on where the use-of-force threshold would end up should the U.S. continue on a trajectory of adjustment. [92] Additionally, the definition of "associated persons or forces," particularly the addition of the phrase "fighting . . . on behalf of . . . ISIS," could be interpreted to be lacking in precision, and thereby, possibly lead to confusion in the projected assessments pertaining to what *actually* constitutes a lawfully targeted entity. Further, in contrast to the preceding AUMF proposals, the Obama 2015 version did not specify a purpose or objective for the use of U.S. armed forces against the Islamic State in the authorization rhetoric itself. Again, this created concerns that the authorization did not sufficiently direct the president's actions or provide a definition of victory, and therefore "authorizes military operations without an endpoint or measurable goal." [93]

In attempting to find some semblance of balance, a variety of members of Congress put forward their legislative proposals for the new AUMF in the 113th and 114th Congresses, arguing that prevailing legislation authorizing military force is out of date and inadequate to address the Islamic State. Some articulated the view that a new authorization is essential to prevent the president from becoming embroiled in a large-scale, extended conflict similar to those in Afghanistan and Iraq. Conversely, others have argued that the existing 2001 and 2002 AUMFs, which approved the use of military force against al Qaeda and the Taliban after 9/11 and the incursion in Iraq, respectively, are now too inadequate in their scope and unnecessarily impede Obama's capacity to defeat terrorist and extremist threats to U.S. national security and interests.[94] As stated by Lauren Weatherby, "Congress is clearly divided. Many Democrats and some Republicans fear a fresh AUMF would lead to wider and more extensive military involvement. But many Republicans, and some Democrats, fear an AUMF would be too limited—tying the president's hands in the fight against a significant new enemy."[95] While the dichotomy is not directly related to the Obama administration, it is somewhat symbolic of the congressional paralysis that has hindered his foreign policy approach—leaving many analysts to debate the extent to which Obama has induced these responses, or been unfairly impacted by actions that are politically motivated.

NEW TECHNOLOGIES AND THE USE-OF-FORCE

Not surprisingly, the complexities surrounding the United States' doctrinal ambivalence—both forced and induced—and the way it proposes "new" interpretations of international legal standards governing its use-of-force, may also lead to further global security issues as new technologies emerge. A particular technology to consider in this context is lethal autonomous robots, also called lethal autonomous weapons systems (LAWS) and fully autonomous weapons systems.[96] The term "human out of the loop"[97] has proven uncomfortable for some translators. No one quite knows what the robots of the future will look like, or what actions they might be able to perform, but roboticists, soldiers, politicians, lawyers, and philosophers must ask some very complex and interdisciplinary questions regarding the future use of LAWS. Unlike drones, fully autonomous robots would make their own decisions and act independently from humans. As former UN High Commissioner for Human Rights Navi Pillay has said, "So called 'killer robots'—autonomous weapons systems that can select and hit a target without human intervention—are no longer science fiction, but a reality."[98] While international humanitarian law mandates that the use of violence must be proportional and circumvent indiscriminate damage and killings, the use of "killer robots" has engendered fears that they "will be unable to adequately assess proportionality and precision." That is, discerning decisions of proportionality of force are needed to evaluate "dynamic environments" and "require highly qualitative and subjective knowledge—just the things that robots could lack."[99] The question on how the United States will react to this new area is not very clear, nor is how it will regulate such use or treat international law regulating such force.[100]

For Shirley V. Scott, however, one thing is clear: U.S. decision-makers *will never* consider "surrendering decision-making regarding the use-of-force" and will be even less likely to with the ambiguity deriving from lethal autonomous weapons. As she argues, it is deemed vital that the U.S. retain the freedom to use force when it perceives it as an interest to do so, "and for international law to evolve so as to prevent the United States using force should it wish to do so" would be a severe "incursion on US legal security."[101] Existing armed unmanned aerial vehicles are the precursors to lethal autonomous robotics—devices that could choose targets without further human intervention once they are programmed and activated. While this may appear far-fetched, the Pentagon is already planning for them, "envisioning a gradual reduction by 2036" of the degree of human control over such unmanned weapons and systems, until humans are completely out of the loop. As technology continues to expand and as the human role moves from being "in the loop" of the decision-making process with such devices (making all the key calls) to "on the loop" of the decision-making process, where the role pertains to overseeing operations rather than actually directing, complexities and debate will continue to emerge as the human role moves ultimately to "out of the loop." In considering Scott's argument, it must be noted that in the use-of-force domain, the rise of new forms of technology and shifting security scenarios (e.g. ISIL) may see the United States further reinterpret the rules governing the use-of-force, and continue to challenge the very regime of international law and international order that it played a defining role in creating after World War II.

CONCLUSION

Upon receiving the Nobel Peace Prize in 2009, Obama stated that the United States could not "insist that others follow the rules of the road if we refuse to follow them ourselves" and that "adhering to the standards strengthens those who do, and isolates and weakens those who don't."[102] In examining the doctrinal transition between the Bush and Obama administrations and the extent to which both have legitimized the use-of-force in their efforts to thwart the threat of non-state actors, terrorism, and WMD proliferation, it is evident there have been greater continuities in the "treatment" of the "rules," rather than departures. Additionally, U.S. policies after 9/11 have continued to be defined by long-standing contradictions and opacities that have engendered widespread analysis and new critical questions in international relations and international law discourse. While the dualism is not necessarily unexpected, the ubiquitous themes of uncertainty and inconsistency pose concerns about where this will leave the international legal regime and the broader global order should the United States continue with an approach that has deviated between: stated intentions and tangible outcomes; what it conveys in the context of international rule of law and what it actually does in certain scenarios; its promotion of the principle of sovereign equality and U.S. exceptionalism; what it seems to think other states should do and what it does itself; U.S. engagement at different points in time; and where it stands in regard to adhering to the principles on the use-of-force, compared to what it actually does.

As this chapter has articulated, the apparent contradictions, marked elements of continuity, ongoing dichotomies, and various departures that the Obama administration has undertaken in the context of the use-of-force are emblematic of Obama's overall doctrine. In what was deemed by many to be a marked contrast, President Barack Obama was elected on a platform of change that included a departure from his predecessor in the foreign-policy domain. While this transition in 2009 came with a much-touted reversal of his predecessor's policies, very little has *actually* changed when it comes to the doctrinal pillar pertaining to the use of military force. Given the destabilizing potential such interpretations of otherwise widely accepted use-of-force standards represent—particularly in the absence of an independent judicial system capable of enforcing international law—it is evident that the United States pursues "a general authorization of the use-of-force"[103] *for itself*, when *it* chooses to do so, rather than a pursuit of its general prohibition.

Although Obama's policies in relation to the Arab Spring were cautious, he still, and unsurprisingly, reserved the right to use force unilaterally to defend U.S. security interests and came remarkably close to doing just that after chemical weapons had been used in Syria in the summer of 2013. And notwithstanding the Obama Doctrine's greater reluctance to use large-scale force, as illustrated by his administration's cautious policies toward the conflicts in Libya, Syria, and Syria/Iraq (in the context of ISIS), this has paradoxically led to an even greater reliance and an associated lower threshold for using force in the form of targeted killings through new technologies. Indeed, drones have clearly proven to be alluring for a president interested in keeping American troops out of harm's way, reducing the number of ground forces, and the precise, "dehumanizing" targeting qualities this form of warfare offers.[104] Overall, when appraising the broader Obama Doctrine and its ostensible penchant to adjust, comprise, and hedge, the use-of-force arm within the doctrine provides a case illustration.

NOTES

1. Barack Obama, *The National Security Strategy of the United States of America*, Washington DC: The White House, 2010, p. 9.

2. The estimates for the costs of the wars in Iraq and Afghanistan range from $1.5 to $6 trillion, while a 2010 estimate by the *Washington Post* suggested that "some 1,271 government organizations and 1,931 private companies now work on programs related to counterterrorism, homeland security and intelligence in about 10,000 locations across the United States." National Priorities Project, "Cost of National Security," National Priorities Project, January 24, 2014, available at: http://nationalpriorities.org/cost-of; Ernesto Londoño, "Iraq, Afghan Wars Will Cost to $4 Trillion to $6 Trillion, Harvard Study Says," *Washington Post*, March 29, 2013, available at: http://www.washingtonpost.com/world/national-security/study-iraq-afghan-war-costs-to-top-4-trillion/2013/03/28/b82a5dce-97ed-11e2-814b-063623d80a60_story.html; and Dana Priest and William M. Arkin, "A Hidden World, Growing beyond Control," *Washington Post*, September 2010, available at: http://projects.washingtonpost.com/top-secret-america/articles/a-hidden-world-growing-beyond-control.

3. See Aiden Warren and Ingvild Bode, *Governing the Use-of-Force in International Relations: The Post-9/11 US Challenge on International Law*, Basingstoke: Palgrave Macmillan, 2014, p. 84.

4. Amitai Etzioni and Alexandra Appel, "Book Review: Martin S. Indyk, Kenneth G. Liberthal, and Michael E. O'Hanlon, *Bending History: Barack Obama's Foreign Policy*," *Society*, Volume 49, Number 5, August 21, 2012.

5. David E. Sanger, *The Inheritance*, London: Bantam Publishers, 2009, p. 447.

6. G. John Ikenberry, "America's 'Security Trap,'" in Michael Cox and Doug Stokes (Eds.), *U.S. Foreign Policy*, Oxford: Oxford University Press, 2008, p. 431. See Aiden Warren, *The Obama Administration's Nuclear Weapon Strategy: The Promises of Prague*, New York: Routledge, 2014, p. 3.

7. Joseph S. Nye Jr., "The Decline of America's Soft Power," *Foreign Affairs* 83, no. 3, 2004, available at: http://www.foreignaffairs.com/articles/59888/joseph-s-nye-jr/the-decline-of-americas-soft-power.

8. John Cassidy, "Obama's Well-Earned Victory Lap on the Economy," *New Yorker*, March 19, 2015, available at: http://www.newyorker.com/news/john-cassidy/obamas-well-earned-victory-lap-on-the-economy.

9. Kenneth Katzman and Carla E. Humud, "Iraq: Politics and Governance," Congressional Research Service report, November 13, 2015, available at: https://www.fas.org/sgp/crs/mideast/RS21968.pdf.

10. Kenneth Katzman, "Afghanistan: Post-Taliban Governance, Security, and U.S. Policy," Congressional Research Service report, October 15, 2015, available at: https://www.fas.org/sgp/crs/row/RL30588.pdf.

11. Gideon Rose, "What Obama Gets Right: Keep Calm and Carry the Liberal Order On," *Foreign Affairs*, September/October 2015, p. 10.

12. *Ibid.*, pp. 6–7.

13. Marc Lynch, "Obama and the Middle East: Rightsizing the U.S. Role," *Foreign Affairs*, September/October 2015, pp. 18–19.

14. *Ibid.*

15. Rose, "What Obama Gets Right," pp. 6–7.

16. Lynch, "Obama and the Middle East," pp. 18–19.

17. *Ibid.*

18. Rose, "What Obama Gets Right," pp. 6–7.

19. Shirley V. Scott, *International Law, U.S. Power: The United States' Quest for Legal Security*, Cambridge: Cambridge University Press, 2012, p. 6.

20. President Barack Obama, "Executive Order 13491: Ensuring Lawful Interrogations," The White House, January 22, 2009, available at: http://www.whitehouse.gov/the_press_office/Ensuring_Lawful_Interrogations; President Barack Obama, "Executive Order 13492: Closure of Guantanamo Detention Facilities," The White House, January 22, 2009, available at: http://www.whitehouse.gov/the_press_office/ClosureOfGuantanamoDetentionFacilities.

21. Article 3, shared by all four Geneva Conventions, establishes fundamental rules for all varieties of non-international armed conflicts, such as humane treatment of prisoners without distinction. International Committee of the Red Cross, "Convention (III) Relative to the Treat-

ment of Prisoners of War. Geneva, 12 August 1949," ICRC Treaties and Documents, 1949, available at: http://www.icrc.org/ihl/INTRO/375?OpenDocument.

22. However, Executive Order 13491 does not explicitly revoke the Bush administration's rendition practices. This point is considered in more detail at the end of the chapter.

23. Charlie Savage, "Barack Obama's Q&A," *Boston Globe*, December 20, 2007, available at: http://www.boston.com/news/politics/2008/specials/CandidateQA/ObamaQA.

24. American Society of International Law, "International Law 2008—Barack Obama." As the survey is no longer available on the ASIL website, quoted from Duncan Hollis, "President Elect Obama on International Law," *Opinio Juris*, November 6, 2008, available at: http://opiniojuris.org/2008/11/06/president-elect-obama-on-international-law.

25. Bob Woodward, *Obama's Wars*, New York: Simon & Schuster, 2010, p. 65.

26. *Ibid.*, p. 66.

27. Obama, "Executive Order 13491: Ensuring Lawful Interrogations."

28. Special Task Force on Interrogation and Transfer Policies, "U.S. Task Force Report on Interrogations and Transfers," *The American Journal of International Law* 103, no. 4, October 1, 2009, p. 762.

29. Stephen L. Carter, *The Violence of Peace: America's Wars in the Age of Obama*, New York: Beast Books, 2011, p. 52.

30. Nahal Zamani, "Rendition Program to Continue Under Obama's Watch," *American Civil Liberties Union*, August 27, 2009, available at: https://www.aclu.org/blog/human-rights-national-security/rendition-program-continue-under-obamas-watch; see Warren and Bode, *Governing the Use-of-Force in International Relations*, p. 84.

31. Dan McLaughlin, "The Obama Administration Goes Big on Extraordinary Rendition: It Is More Important that We Pretend to Virtue than that We Practice It," *Red State*, October 6, 2015, available at: http://www.redstate.com/2015/10/06/obama-administration-goes-big-extraordinary-rendition.

32. NYU Center for Human Rights and Global Justice, "Briefing: Torture by Proxy: International Law Applicable to 'Extraordinary Renditions,'" NYU, December 6, 2005.

33. Carter, *The Violence of Peace*, p. 50.

34. *Ibid.*, p. 67.

35. McLaughlin, "The Obama Administration Goes Big on Extraordinary Rendition."

36. President Barack Obama, "Remarks by the President on a New Beginning," The White House, June 4, 2009, available at: http://www.whitehouse.gov/the_press_office/Remarks-by-the-President-at-Cairo-University-6-04-09.

37. Peter L. Bergen, "President Obama, Warrior in Chief," *New York Times*, April 28, 2012, sec. Opinion/Sunday Review, available at: http://www.nytimes.com/2012/04/29/opinion/sunday/president-obama-warrior-in-chief.html.

38. Barack Obama, "Obama's Speech at Woodrow Wilson Center," Council on Foreign Relations, August 20, 2007, available at: http://www.cfr.org/elections/obamas-speech-woodrow-wilson-center/p13974.

39. Quoted from Hollis, "President Elect Obama on International Law."

40. Christian Henderson, "The 2010 United States National Security Strategy and the Obama Doctrine of 'Necessary Force,'" *Journal of Conflict & Security Law* 15, no. 3, 2010, pp. 403–434.

41. See Warren and Bode, *Governing the Use-of-Force in International Relations*, p. 84.

42. Barack Obama, *The National Security Strategy of the United States of America*, The White House, May 2010, available at: http://www.whitehouse.gov/sites/default/files/rss_viewer/national_security_strategy.pdf.

43. *Ibid.*, p. 20.

44. *Ibid.*, p. 2.

45. *Ibid.*, p. 10.

46. *Ibid.*, p. 36.

47. Harold Koh, "The Obama Administration and International Law," U.S. Department of State, March 25, 2010, available at: http://www.state.gov/s/l/releases/remarks/139119.htm; Christine Gray, "President Obama's 2010 United States National Security Strategy and International Law on the Use of Force," *Chinese Journal of International Law* 10, no. 1, 2011, p. 32.

48. Obama, The *National Security Strategy of the United States of America*, pp. 12, 13, 38.

49. "International norms" are mentioned a total number of 15 times, while "international standards" are mentioned twice throughout the *NSS 2010*.

50. Barack Obama, "Remarks by the President at the Acceptance of the Nobel Peace Prize," The White House, December 10, 2009, available at: http://www.whitehouse.gov/the-press-office/remarks-president-acceptance-nobel-peace-prize.

51. Gray, "President Obama's 2010 United States National Security Strategy and International Law on the Use of Force," p. 48.

52. *Ibid.*

53. Obama, *The National Security Strategy of the United States of America*, p. 18; and Gray, "President Obama's 2010 United States National Security Strategy and International Law on the Use of Force," p. 37.

54. Obama, *The National Security Strategy of the United States of America*, p. 22.

55. *Ibid.*

56. *Ibid*, own emphasis.

57. Gray, "President Obama's 2010 United States National Security Strategy and International Law on the Use of Force," p. 48. The 2003 European Security Strategy (ESS) does not contain explicit references to the use of force, but affirms its strong commitment to upholding and developing multilateral institutions and thus the charter's *jus ad bellum* regime, above all the United Nations, in countering global threats: "The United Nations Security Council has the primary responsibility for the maintenance of international peace and security. Strengthening the United Nations, equipping it to fulfil its responsibilities and to act effectively, is a European priority." European Council, "European Security Strategy: A Secure Europe in a Better World," European Union External Action, December 12, 2003, available at: http://www.consilium.europa.eu/uedocs/cmsUpload/78367.pdf. The 2009 Russian Security Strategy contains negative references to the "one-sided use of force in international relations" and explicitly notes that "[o]n the world stage, Russia will act from a position founded on an unchanging course . . . on the unacceptability of use of military force in contravention of the United Nations Charter." President of the Russian Federation, "National Security Strategy to 2020," ETH Zuerich Digital Library, May 2009, available at: http://www.isn.ethz.ch/Digital-Library/Publications/Detail/?id=154915; See Warren and Bode, *Governing the Use-of-Force in International Relations*, p. 88.

58. Obama, *The National Security Strategy of the United States of America*, p. 20.

59. Henderson, "The 2010 United States National Security Strategy and the Obama Doctrine of 'Necessary Force,'" pp. 418–21.

60. *Ibid.*, p. 419.

61. Obama, *The National Security Strategy of the United States of America*, p. 22.

62. *Ibid.*, p. 21, own emphasis.

63. *Ibid.*

64. See Warren and Bode, *Governing the Use-of-Force in International Relations*, p. 90.

65. Barack Obama, "Remarks by the President on a New Strategy for Afghanistan and Pakistan," The White House, March 27, 2009, available at: http://www.whitehouse.gov/the-press-office/remarks-president-a-new-strategy-afghanistan-and-pakistan. Compare also for similar references Barack Obama, "Remarks by the President after the Trilateral Meeting with President Karzai of Afghanistan and President Zardari of Pakistan," The White House, May 6, 2009, available at: http://www.whitehouse.gov/the-press-office/remarks-president-after-trilateral-meeting-with-president-karzai-afghanistan-and-pr; and Barack Obama, "Remarks by the President in State of Union Address," The White House, January 25, 2011, available at: http://www.whitehouse.gov/the-press-office/2011/01/25/remarks-president-state-union-address.

66. Obama, "Remarks by the President on a New Strategy for Afghanistan and Pakistan," own emphasis.

67. Barack Obama, "Remarks by President Obama to the Troops in Afghanistan," The White House, May 1, 2012, available at: http://www.whitehouse.gov/the-press-office/2012/05/01/remarks-president-obama-troops-afghanistan.

68. Carter, *The Violence of Peace*, p. 23. See Warren and Bode, *Governing the Use-of-Force in International Relations*, p. 91.

69. Compare, for example, Zbigniew Brzezinski, "From Hope to Audacity: Appraising Obama's Foreign Policy," *Foreign Affairs* 89, no. 1, 2010, pp. 16–30.

70. See Aiden Warren and Ingvild Bode, "Altering the Playing Field: The U.S. Redefinition of the Use-of-force," *Contemporary Security Policy*, 36:2, p. 182.

71. Glenn Kessler, "President Obama and the Red Line on Syria's Chemical Weapons," *Washington Post*, September 6, 2013, available at: http://www.washingtonpost.com/blogs/fact-checker/wp/2013/09/06/president-obama-and-the-red-line-on-syrias-chemical-weapons.

72. See Warren and Bode, "Altering the Playing Field," p. 184.

73. John F. Kerry, "Remarks at Youth Connect: Addis Ababa Featured by BBC's *Hardtalk*," Washington DC: U.S. Department of State, May 26, 2013.

74. The majority of drone strikes under Bush's leadership, a total of 36, took place during his last year in office in 2008. This indicates the beginning of an emerging trend. New America Foundation, "Drone Wars Pakistan: Analysis," April 12, 2015, http://securitydata.newamerica.net/drones/pakistan/analysis.html.

75. For Yemen see New America Foundation, "Drone Wars Yemen: Analysis," *New America Foundation*, April 22, 2015, available at: http://securitydata.newamerica.net/drones/yemen/analysis.html; for Somalia see General Assembly, *Report of the Special Rapporteur on the Promotion and Protection of Human Rights and Fundamental Freedoms While Countering Terrorism, UN Document A/68/389*, September 18, 2013.

76. See Warren and Bode, "Altering the Playing Field," p. 185.

77. Harold Koh, "The Obama Administration and International Law," Washington DC: U.S. Department of State, March 25, 2010.

78. Compare John O. Brennan, Remarks of John O. Brennan, "Strengthening Our Security by Adhering to Our Values and Laws," Washington DC: The White House, September 16, 2011; Koh, "The Obama Administration and International Law" (note 84); Leon E. Panetta, "Remarks of Director of Central Intelligence Agency, Leon E. Panetta, at the Pacific Council on International Policy," Langley, VA: U.S. Central Intelligence Agency, May 18, 2009.

79. See Warren and Bode, "Altering the Playing Field," p. 185–6.

80. Barack Obama, "Statement by the President on ISIL," The White House, September 10, 2014, available at: http://www.whitehouse.gov/the-press-office/2014/09/10/statement-president-isil-1.

81. Compare Declan Walsh, "Pakistani Parliament Seeks End to Drone Strikes," *New York Times*, March 20, 2012, available at: http://www.nytimes.com/2012/03/21/world/asia/pakistani-parliament-demands-end-to-us-drone-strikes.html; and Ben Emmerson, "Statement of the Special Rapporteur Following Meetings in Pakistan," Office of the UN High Commissioner for Human Rights, March 14, 2013, available at: http://www.ohchr.org/en/NewsEvents/Pages/DisplayNews.aspx?NewsID=13146&LangID=E.

82. Rosa Brooks, "Testimony of Rosa Brooks, US Senate Judiciary Committee, Subcommittee on the Constitution, Civil Rights and Human Rights, Hearing on Drone Wars: The Constitutional and Counterterrorism Implications of Targeted Killing," Washington DC: U.S. Senate Judiciary Committee, April 23, 2013.

83. Audrey Kurth Cronin, "Why Drones Fail: When Tactics Drive Strategy," *Foreign Affairs* 92, 2013, pp. 45–7.

84. Compare Ivan Eland, "United States Accelerates a Counterproductive Drone War in Yemen," *Huffington Post*, April 23, 2014, available at: http://www.huffingtonpost.com/ivan-eland/united-states-accelerates_b_5198396.html; and Jomana Karadsheh, Jim Sciutto, and Laura Smith-Spark, "How Foreign Fighters Are Swelling ISIS Ranks in Startling Numbers," CNN, September 14, 2014, available at: http://www.cnn.com/2014/09/12/world/meast/isis-numbers/index.html.

85. Matthew C. Weed, "A New Authorization for Use of Military Force Against the Islamic State: Issues and Current Proposals in Brief," Congressional Research Service report, February 20, 2015, pp. 1–2, available at: http://fas.org/sgp/crs/natsec/R43760.pdf.

86. Jim Garamone, "Obama Sends Resolution for Use of Force Against ISIS to Congress," *DoD News*, Defense Media Activity, available at: http://www.defense.gov/news/newsarticle.aspx?id=128167.

87. Brookings Institution, "President Obama's Authorization for Use of Military Force (AUMF) against the Islamic State," February 24, 2015, available at: http://www.brookings.edu/events/2015/02/24-obama-aumf-islamic-state.

88. Barack Obama, "Remarks by the President on Request to Congress for Authorization of Force Against ISIL," February 11, 2015, available at: https://www.whitehouse.gov/the-press-office/2015/02/11/remarks-president-request-congress-authorization-force-against-isil.

89. Brookings Institution, "President Obama's Authorization for Use of Military Force (AUMF) against the Islamic State."

90. *Ibid.*

91. Weed, "A New Authorization for Use of Military Force Against the Islamic State," p. 6.

92. Brookings Institution, "President Obama's Authorization for Use of Military Force (AUMF) against the Islamic State."

93. Weed, "A New Authorization for Use of Military Force Against the Islamic State," p. 6.

94. John W. Rollins and Heidi M. Peters, "The Islamic State—Frequently Asked Questions: Threats, Global Implications, and U.S. Policy Responses," Congressional Research Service report, November 25, 2015, p. 5–6.

95. Lauren Weatherby, "Whatever Happened to the Debate over Use of Force Against ISIS?" NPR, June 17, 2015, available at: http://www.npr.org/2015/06/17/415203016/whatever-happened-to-the-debate-over-use-of-force-against-isis.

96. For a summary of the various definitions that have been used, see Fabian Wegmann, "Autonomie unbemannter Waffensysteme. Das CCW-Expertentreffen zum Thema 'Lethal Autonomous Weapons Systems' und der gegenwa"rtige Stand der Technik," IFAR Working Paper, Hamburg: Institute for Peace Research and Security Policy at the University of Hamburg, June 2014), pp. 7–8.

97. Terminology for a man or human "in the loop," "on the loop," and "out of the loop" is used widely in the field of robotics. See Nils Melzer, "Human Rights Implications of the Usage of Drones and Unmanned Robots in Warfare," EU Document EXPO/B/DROI/2012/12, Brussels: Directorate-General for External Policies of the Union, Directorate B, Policy Department, May 2013, p. 6.

98. Navi Pillay, "A 20-20 Human Rights Vision Statement by the UN High Commissioner for Human Rights, Navi Pillay for Human Rights Day," Geneva: Office of the High Commissioner for Human Rights, May 10, 2013.

99. Denise Garcia, "The Case Against Killer Robots: Why the United States Should Ban Them," *Foreign Affairs*, May 10, 2015.

100. See Warren and Bode, "Altering the Playing Field," p. 190–191.

101. Shirley V. Scott, "Looking Back to Anticipate the Future: International Law in the Era of the United States," in Rowena Maguire, Bridget Lewis, and Charles Sampford (eds), *Shifting Global Powers and International Law: Challenges and Opportunities*, London: Routledge, 2013, p. 17.

102. Barack Obama, "Remarks by the President at the Acceptance of the Nobel Peace Prize," Washington DC: The White House, December 10, 2009.

103. Kirsten Schmalenbach, "The Right of Self-Defense and the War on Terrorism," *German Law Journal*, Vol. 3, No. 9 2002, p. 22.

104. James Traub, "U.S. Foreign Policy: What Does Obama Believe? United Nations University Conversations Series," Tokyo, March 11, 2015; compare also James Traub, "When Did Obama Give Up?" *Foreign Policy*, February 26, 2015, available at: http://foreignpolicy.com/2015/02/26/when-did-obama-give-up-speeches.

Conclusion

Despite the ever-changing landscape of international relations, the role and conduct of the United States and the extent to which its actions contribute (or not) to global justice and order remain a source of contested discussion. Undoubtedly, it is difficult to find a point in recent history when the United States and its foreign policy have been the topic of such dichotomous and at times acrimonious reflection, both domestically and internationally. Notwithstanding recent "decline of America as a world power" debates and the rise of emerging states, the fact is that the United States remains the defining holder of all formidable power assets some twenty-plus years since the demise of the Cold War. Few predicted such a situation; many assumed that international affairs would soon return to some kind of symmetry. However, just as the 20th century moved into the 21st, it appeared that U.S. hegemony would remain par for the course—and "the sooner other, lesser actors got used to this not entirely acceptable state of affairs, the better."[1]

This fundamental and ostensibly enduring transformation in the balance of power was one of the reasons why the debate and discourse pertaining to the role of the United States in the world took on a more contested form. The other development that spurred such discussion was the election of George W. Bush in late 2000, and what appeared to be an unbridled exertion on the part of his administration to transform this position of strength into a new U.S. foreign policy that would not only maintain U.S. primacy, but sought its amplification. Indeed, it very soon became clear that the Bush administration and its accompanying doctrine was not only willing to undermine established rules and multilateral fora, but was very much prepared to wield its unchecked power assets as a means to redefine foreign-policy outcomes based on what it deemed to be "appropriate" in the post–Cold War period. While the Bush administration's prescription of power engendered much criticism abroad—particularly its penchant *not* to be constrained by international institutions, international law and norms, or international opinion—it was the events of September 11, 2001, that would truly define its doctrine. The quick and decisive attack on Afghanistan saw the incremental orchestration of Bush's doctrine punctuated via the January 2002 State of the Union speech—in which he defined North Korea, Iran, and Iraq as an "axis of evil"—the West Point speech in June, and its formalization in September 2002 with the release of the *National Security Strategy* (*NSS*).

Almost exactly one year after the 9/11 attacks, the Bush *National Security Strategy* (*NSS*) was met by a vast chorus of critique from scholars and practitioners on both sides of the Atlantic. The most contentious element of what became known as the Bush Doctrine was its apparent sweeping shift on the so-called preemptive use-of-force in self-defense. In pointing to a "new" environment encompassing global terrorist networks, "rogue states," and WMD proliferation, Bush called for radically different responses, including the use of "preemptive" (but really preventive) options to counter long-term, potential threats, "even if uncertainty remains as to the time and place of the enemy's attack."[2] The preemptive version espoused by Bush was a marked departure from accepted interpretations of international law, particularly in regard to the scope of the right to self-defense as expressed in Article 51 of the UN Charter.[3] For Bush, America was now at war with a global adversary every bit as dangerous as—and perhaps even more so than—those it had previously encountered at different intervals during the 20th century. Of course, what became known as the "War on Terror" did not go unchallenged. A lengthy spectrum of analysts and commentators questioned it on many levels: some its strategic rationality; others, its implications for relations with the wider Muslim world; while others pointed to the ramifications it may have on the position of American democracy.[4]

Despite such considerations, it was clear that the United States was moving into an altogether more volatile epoch, similar in broad character—if not unavoidably in specific form—to the Cold War of old with its associated tensions, strain on national security, and the feeling that the state (and the West as a whole) was now having to come to terms with an implacable subversive antagonist whose ultimate determination was the annihilation of the American "order." Simply put, "America had been attacked and America had to respond robustly, even ruthlessly."[5] When the doctrine was turned into practice in March 2003, many of its critics saw their worst fears confirmed with the preventive, "illegal" Iraq War,[6] now considered one of the administration's defining legacies. With the election of President Barack Obama in 2008, "hopes were raised of a dramatic shift in the U.S. attitude towards international law,"[7] and an overall departure in the foreign-policy domain. However, as revealed in the last chapter of this book, while the transition to the Obama administration came with a much-touted reversal of his predecessor's policies, little has *actually* changed when it comes to how the U.S. considers using military force. The Obama administration has continued to embrace and redefine broad self-defense "standards," especially in relation to what constitutes an *imminent* threat.

While the Obama administration has been more open and frequent in offering legal justifications for its use-of-force, the content of these justifications points to a continued stretching of the self-defense article in the direction of mixing preemption and prevention, particularly in regard to the administration's promotion of an increasingly diffused concept of imminence. By separating the imminent threat from immediacy in this way, the Obama administration has, therefore, indirectly condoned one of the Bush Doctrine's disputed aspects. It is such broad self-defense arguments, as well as the congressional authorization to use force (e.g., Authorization for Use of Military Force [AUMF]), that have served as key legitimizers of the Obama administration's drone program and the airstrikes used against the Islamic State (ISIS) in Iraq and Syria in 2014–2015. Indeed, more than a decade after the 9/11 attacks and the alleged al Qaeda affiliation of groups making them "lawful" targets, such arguments for force appear all the more apparent and will likely spur further obfuscation after Obama's tenure in office concludes.

Notwithstanding these defining events of the new millennium, we still need to look at the historical context, and in the context of this book, where the doctrinal drive of previous administrations sits so as to enable us to understand how the United States has attained its position and what key attributes, assets, and limitations it still embodies. Of course, there is the view that the only thing we need to understand about a state is the amount of power assets it has and that other factors such as character are not required in the equation. This non-figurative understanding disregards the specific way in which the United States ascended to power in the first place after winning the revolution in the late 1700s, the impact this trajectory then had upon the United States as an exceptional state as it secured and defined itself during the 1800s, and how this power in turn was translated and interpreted via its doctrinal foreign policy, particularly in the period when it became a superpower after World War II. In the development and arrangement of its substantive assets, America was also transformed as a state, most evidently during the Cold War, when in any typical year it utilized approximately 10 percent of its GNP and 30 percent of its budget conducting its global battle against a perceived communist adversary.[8] While many contemporary analysts feel the Cold War is somewhat "overdone," one would be remiss not to look at the doctrinal drive of this period, how it ultimately concluded on U.S. terms (spurring the "unipolar moment"), and the ramifications it has had on contemporary U.S. conduct and broader international affairs. Despite the U.S. foreign-policy establishment being remarkably consistent in the ways it conceives the world in general and the type of platform that would best suit the United States' national interest imperatives, there has been evidentiary space for doctrinal direction, debate, and discourse. That said, it is also apparent that to a great extent, U.S. policy makers have articulated a global order that would best maintain and enhance national interest objectives via a composition of democratic states, open markets, and self-determining nations (on the assumption that formal empires were not only adversarial to freedom but more likely to reject American influence). As signified through this book, the United States has not always been able to pursue these goals at all times, or in all places together at the same time.[9]

As chapter one illustrated, the Washington Doctrine emerged out of the disorder in the years preceding the American Revolution, and the years thereafter. While the Constitution quickly orchestrated a new supreme government and attained international recognition, the young state would also, for the time being, need to maintain its significant political and commercial ties with European powers. Additionally, in his first years as president, Washington's need to manage European interests along northern, western, and southern borders would remain a significant point of consternation that American foreign policy would have to balance. Washington's ultimate decision for neutrality—after seceding out of the United States' alliance with France—ended the last alliance in which America would involve itself for an extensive period of time, thereby emboldening the legacy of avoiding entangling alliances. As the main progenitor of avoiding "complexities" with foreign nations, Washington implored his successors in his farewell address to be cautious of the "vicissitudes" of European politics he had to balance and to disconnect America from the frequent controversies of European interests. President Adams' anti-Europeanism, as revealed in stations overseas, further cultivated Washington's legacy as a core interest of American foreign policy, while Jefferson's two-term presidency further enhanced "untangling" the affairs of European interests on America's borders. Indeed, by the conclusion of Jefferson's presidency, the Americans had inaugurated a new era in "American-style" diplomacy, while the doctrine of avoiding complex and potentially detracting affairs with "outside states" would become a significant driver of U.S. foreign policy for well over the next hundred years.

As chapter two argued, the transformation of American territory via annexation (at times strategically, often violently) not only came to cultivate American identity, but ultimately provided the state with a defining set of geographical, economic, and security power assets. In "securing" the region not just from the Europeans for the Americas, but also from the Americas for the Americans, the acquisition of territory that would ultimately extend from the Atlantic to the Pacific would be a crucial development in enabling the United Sates to amplify its trajectory toward becoming a superpower in the 20th century. A significant plank in leading to this "moment" was the capacity of administrations to capitalize on the diminishing strength of European powers. The Monroe Doctrine would for all intents and purposes definitively disaggregate European "movements" from what Washington considered an American sphere of influence.

A doctrinal adjustment to this new level of power, articulated in chapter three, would see President Wilson's war aims and his subsequent globalized vision of the Monroe Doctrine promulgate America's foreign policy and American entanglement back *into* European affairs. Despite Washington's brief return to isolationism after the Great War, America's appeal to the prospect of a world conceived through *its* lens and defined by *its* envisaged framework would continue be the doctrinal and foreign-policy determination until December 1941, and definitely at the conclusion of World War II in 1945.

Indeed, as discussed in chapter four, the economic and technological superiority of the U.S. following the war provided the Truman administration with a wide array of policy options previously unobtainable in American history. Combined with the threat of Soviet expansionism and Stalin's apparent inability to adhere to the agreements established in wartime conferences, Washington believed the rippling effect of leftist ideology would manifest itself throughout Western Europe if it did not attempt to impede such movements. As the divergence between the two ideologically opposed superpowers widened, the doctrine would once and for all end Washington's non-entangling alliances with Western states. Additionally, the resultant rise of the security dilemma provided the motivation for further developments in technological and weaponry capacities, and would engender the largest and most destructive arms race in history. As the chapter concluded, the new terrain of international relations and doctrinal accompaniments in articulating American foreign policy had become bipolar—to the extent that newer variations would develop as Washington was now prepared to go global.

As chapter five argued, extending on the Truman Doctrine of containment, Eisenhower and later Kennedy's version of "maintaining the outside" promulgated the power relations of the U.S.-Soviet dichotomy into newer and more insecure domains. Eisenhower pursued a more proactive policy of "liberating" states from the communist threat, while also incorporating the concept of massive retaliation into America's containment suite. While Khrushchev's policies toward Berlin and the West were somewhat provocative—albeit considerably more moderate than Stalin's—Washington affirmed its belief that Russia could only be managed through American military power. Kennedy's doctrine of "flexible response" was an adaptation of the Eisenhower version, while the Johnson variation in Latin America demonstrated "Monroesque" thinking based on its concern that communism was creeping into its regional sphere of influence and need to be impeded.

In chapter six, the Nixon Doctrine "variation" required allies to assume primary responsibility for their own military defense, thereby beginning the

Vietnamization of the Vietnam War. In this regard, the retreat from unconditional defense guarantees to lesser allies was motivated as much by financial
concerns as by policy reexamination of strategic and foreign policy objectives, reflected in Nixon's goals of détente and nuclear arms control with the
Soviet Union, and establishment of formal diplomatic relations with the People's Republic of China.[10] In assessing President Carter, the chapter also
argued that while the Soviet invasion was the contiguous spur for his doctrine, motivation for the president's policy shift had been building over the
previous two years deriving from concern over internal developments in Iran.
That said, in leaning toward National Security Adviser Zbigniew Brzezinski's view, the doctrine maintained the need to address Moscow's desire for
ideological competition and involvement in developing regions, as détente
had merely allowed the Russians to increase their expansionist drive under
the guise of superpower cooperation. The last component of the chapter
evaluated the Reagan Doctrine's Cold War strategy of opposing Soviet influence through the backing of anti-Communist guerrillas against the Communist governments of Soviet-backed client states. Unlike Presidents Truman,
Eisenhower, Nixon, and Carter, whose names defined previous doctrines
through defensive containment in mitigating the (further) spread of Soviet
power, the Reagan variation was a more offensive approach—particularly in
regard to newly declared leftist states. Indeed, such responses were based on
the integrated and consequential reflection of a new global imbalance engendered by a default of American will—the "Vietnam syndrome"—and by
Moscow's assertive orchestration of Soviet troops, arms, and surrogates.
Impeding the further development of this would become a defining driver of
the Reagan Doctrine that would only be tempered with the rise of Gorbachev
and the breaking down of the Soviet economy.

    As briefly discussed above, and assessed in detail in chapter seven, in
response to the events of 9/11 it appeared that the previous structures of U.S.
security strategy were replaced with a preemptive-strike policy. In more
simple terms, it was a policy that advocated both the identification and destruction of terrorist threats "before" they were able to "reach" the United
States' "borders," even if this meant acting in isolation and preventively.[11]
Indeed, the notion that chemical, nuclear, and biological weapons could be
secured by non-state actors and wielded against the United States indicated
the cessation of a doctrinal posture and strategy that had assisted the United
States throughout the Cold War and first phase (1991–2001) of the
post–Cold War period in maintaining security. President George W. Bush
and his administration amplified U.S. doctrine to a newer level and put into
action a strategy designed to compensate for America's newfound perception
of susceptibility and, more importantly, a strategy to mitigate a "nuclear 9/
11."[12] As the chapter illustrated, the core and most contentious strategy of
the doctrine pertained to the concepts of preventive/preemptive military ac-

tion. The international legal foundation of the administration's *jus ad bellum* paradigm in the global "War on Terror" encouraged the early use-of-force in self-defense against imminent (preemptive) and developing (preventive) threats. While there is some justification—at least in principle—under the UN Charter *jus ad bellum* regime for a counter-proliferation strategy of pre-emption that adheres to the balance of necessity and proportionality, the Bush Doctrine's form of preemption was in reality preventive in character, and therefore clearly outside the limits of international law.

Indeed, in the Bush Doctrine's prescription of power, the international order was centered exclusively around U.S. unipolar preeminence, with America utilizing its unchecked power to keep others in line while enforcing an international hierarchy on *its* terms. In the Obama "version," the champined international order would arise from the coupling of America's pre-eminence with its founding principles, the United States using its power to craft consensual and legitimate mechanisms of international governance.[13] This apparent departure, Obama argued, would require a necessary move to preserve the United States' "soft power" and the ability to attract support through leading by moral example.[14] In this light, the safeguarding of American security and ideals under Obama's watch would become mutually reinforcing and feature regularly in his speeches and public pronouncements after taking office. However, as conveyed in chapter eight, there has been much conjecture about the Obama Doctrine in terms of not just meeting such goals, but in the clarity and specific direction of the doctrine. As argued, while Obama has encountered very distinct challenges in meeting his ambi-tious rhetoric, he has also demonstrated a tendency to be ambivalent, cau-tious yet strategic, in his doctrinal approach. As a means to examine the doctrine's ambivalence, the chapter specifically assessed its use-of-force ap-proach and the extent to which it continued the Bush position and expanded force in other areas (i.e. drones), but at times displayed inconsistencies in dealing with Libya, Syria, and the non-state actor ISIS.

As the 9/11 attacks, and the allegations of al Qaeda affiliation of groups making them "lawful" targets, become increasingly distant, arguments legiti-mizing force may become progressively twisted and even more dangerous than their original intent.[15] Given the potential of such elucidations to under-mine otherwise widely accepted use-of-force standards in the absence of an independent judicial system capable of enforcing international law, one is tempted to consider U.S. security policies to be in pursuit of a general author-ization of the use-of-force[16] for *itself*—and on *its* terms—rather than the call for general prohibition.[17] While the Obama Doctrine showed much greater disinclination toward using large-scale force, as demonstrated by his admin-istration's restrained policies toward the conflicts in Libya and Syria, this may paradoxically lead to an even greater dependence and a lower threshold for using force in the context of targeted killings through drones. As the chapter concluded, drones may have proven to be dangerously attractive for a president consumed by not having American troops on the ground, and this tantalizing, and domestically popular, solution has offered a "dehumanized" form of warfare.[18] In the context of the Arab Spring, Obama cautiously reserved the right to use force unilaterally to defend U.S. security interests, and came very close to doing just that when chemical weapons revelations came to the surface in Syria during 2013. Overall, when appraising the broader Obama Doctrine and its apparent penchant to adjust, comprise, hedge, and periodically wield power, the use-of-force component within the doctrine provides an insightful microcosm.

Despite the shifting terrain in international relations, the United States and its doctrinal direction play a significant role in the international order. In defining its vast national security apparatus, remarkably dynamic economy, complex array of alliances, and highly exportable popular culture, U.S. presidential doctrines remain an important driver in cultivating and defining the American outlook. As signified earlier, there is no simple response to the question of what constitutes a presidential doctrine. Although there are parameters as to what may be encompassed in a doctrine insofar as purposeful clear language, a definitive speech, a set of speeches, a formal policy release, or, since 1986, a National Security Strategy that has often been linked to or a component of the doctrine, there is no consistency in terms of its makeup or conception. However, what is consistent is that all doctrines in some shape or form have exuded the exceptionalist belief in the principles and values of democracy and freedom—and while these have at times been exploited and embellished for symbolic purposes, they remain a pervading factor in the mindset and rhetoric of American presidents and policymakers. Additionally, and as conveyed throughout the plethora of examples in this book, while presidential doctrines have at times seemingly veered from isolationist to interventionist to expansionist, all in some form have defined the response and direction conducive to an international order that would best advance American interests: a composition encompassing democratic states (in the confidence that democracies do not go to war with one another), open free markets (on the basis that they elevate living standards, engender collaboration, and create prosperity), self-determining states (on the supposition that empires were not only adversative to freedom but more likely to reject American influence),[19] and overall, a secure and stable international environment that can allow such interests to be pursued unimpeded.

NOTES

1. Michael Cox and Doug Stokes, *U.S. Foreign Policy*, Oxford: Oxford University Press, 2008, p. 1.

2. George W. Bush, *The National Security Strategy of the United States of America*, Washington DC: The White House, September 2002, p. 15.

3. United Nations, "Charter of the United Nations," 1945, available at: http://treaties.un.org/doc/Publication/CTC/uncharter.pdf.

4. Cox and Stokes, *U.S. Foreign Policy*, p. 2.

5. *Ibid.*

6. United Nations News Centre, "Lessons of Iraq War Underscore Importance of UN Charter—Annan," UN News Service Section, September 16, 2004, available at: http://www.un.org/apps/news/story.asp?NewsID=11953&#.VESqNEs2n0s.

7. Shirley V. Scott, *International Law, US Power: The United States' Quest for Legal Security*, Cambridge: Cambridge University Press, 2012, p. 6.

8. Cox and Stokes, *U.S. Foreign Policy*, p. 4.

9. *Ibid.*

10. Francis J. Gavin, "The Gold Battles Within the Cold War: American Monetary Policy and the Defense of Europe, 1960–1963," *Diplomatic History*, Volume 26, Issue 1, pages 61–94, Winter 2002.

11. Bush, *The National Security Strategy of the United States of America*, p. 2.

12. Brian M. Jenkins, "A Nuclear 9/11?" This commentary appeared on CNN.com on September 11, 2008 and was republished on the RAND Corporation website, available at: http://www.rand.org/commentary/2008/09/11/CNN.html.

13. G. John Ikenberry, "America's 'Security Trap,'" in Cox and Stokes (Eds.), *U.S. Foreign Policy*, p. 431.

14. Joseph F. Nye Jr., "The Decline of America's Soft Power," *Foreign Affairs* 83, no. 3 (2004), available at: http://www.foreignaffairs.com/articles/59888/joseph-s-nye-jr/the-decline-of-americas-soft-power.

15. Compare Peter Bergen and Jennifer Rowland, "Drone Wars," *The Washington Quarterly* 36, no. 3 (2013): p. 7–26.

16. Kirsten Schmalenbach, "The Right of Self-Defense and the War on Terrorism," *German Law Journal*, Vol. 3, No. 9 (2002), p. 22.

17. Compare Brooks, "Drones and the International Rule of Law," pp. 83–88.

18. James Traub, "US Foreign Policy: What Does Obama Believe? United Nations University Conversation Series," Tokyo, March 11, 2015; compare also James Traub, "When Did Obama Give Up?," *Foreign Policy*, February 26, 2015, available at: http://foreignpolicy.com/2015/02/26/when-did-obama-give-up-speeches.

19. Cox and Stokes, *U.S. Foreign Policy*, p. 5.

Bibliography

Acheson, Dean. *Present at the Creation: My Years in the State Department.* New York: W. W. Norton, 1969.

Ackerman, David M. *International Law and the Pre-emptive Use of Force Against Iraq,* CRS Report for Congress RS21314, 2003.

"A Communication from Charles A. Beard," *New Republic,* 1936, 87: 177.

Adams, Charles Francis, ed. *Memoirs of John Quincy Adams, Comprising Portions of His Diary from 1795–1848,* vol. 6. Philadelphia: J. B. Lippincott, 1875.

Adams, John. "Instructions to John Adams, Benjamin Franklin, John Jay, Henry Laurens, and Thomas Jefferson, signed by Saml. Huntington and witnessed by Chas Thompson, Signed 15 June 1781, III. Instructions to the Joint Commission to Negotiate a Peace Treaty," Papers of John Adams Volume II Digital Editions. Available at: http://www.masshist.org/publications/apde2/view?&id=PJA11dg1.

———. *The Works of John Adams, Second President of the United States: With a Life of the Author, Notes and Illustrations, by His Grandson Charles Francis Adams,* 10 vols. Boston: Little, Brown, 1856, vol. 9, chapter "To John Winthrop." Available at: http://oll.libertyfund.org/title/2107/161330/2838396 on 2010–07–01.

Adler, Selig. *The Isolationist Impulse: Its Twentieth Century Reaction.* New York: Abelard-Schulman, 1957.

Akehurst, Michael B. *A Modern Introduction to International Law,* 6th Edition, London: Routledge, 1987.

Allman, T. D. *Unmanifest Destiny,* Michigan: Dial Press, 1984.

Alsop, Joseph, and Stewart Alsop. "Tragedy of Liberalism," *Life,* May 20, 1946, 20: 68–76.

Ammon, Harry. *The Genet Mission.* New York: W. W. Norton, 1973.

Anderson, Fred. *Crucible of War: The Seven Years' War and the Fate of Empire in British North America, 1754–1766.* New York: Alfred A. Knopf, 2000.

Anderson, Stuart. "British Threats and the Settlement of the Oregon Boundary Dispute," *Pacific Northwest Quarterly,* 1975, 66(4): 153–160.

Andradé, Dale. *Trial by Fire: The 1972 Easter Offensive, America's Last Vietnam Battle.* New York: Hippocrene Books, 1995.

Arend, Anthony C. "International Law and the Pre-emptive Use of Force," *The Washington Quarterly,* 2003, 26: 89–103.

Associated Press. "Osama bin Laden Death: Obama Ran Serious Risks with Mission to Kill Terrorist Leader," *Huffington Post,* May 4, 2011.

Bailey, Thomas A. *Woodrow Wilson and the Lost Peace.* New York: Macmillan, 1944.

———. *Woodrow Wilson and the Great Betrayal.* New York: Macmillan, 1945.

Baker, Peter. "Obama Puts His Own Mark on Foreign Policy Issues," *New York Times*, April 13, 2010.

Baker, R. S. *Woodrow Wilson, Life and Letters*, 8 vols. Garden City, NY: Doubleday, 1927–1939.

Baker, R. S. and W. E. Dodd, eds. *The Public Papers of Woodrow Wilson: The New Democracy*, 2 vols. New York: Harper & Row, 1926.

"The Bay of Pigs Invasion and its Aftermath, April 1961–October 1962," U.S. Department of State, Office of the Historian. Available at: https://history.state.gov/milestones/1961-1968/bay-of-pigs.

BBC News. "Osama Bin Laden, al-Qaeda leader, Dead—Barack Obama," BBC U.S. & Canada, May 2, 2011. Available at: http://www.bbc.co.uk/news/world-us-canada-13256676.

———. "Navy Seal Gives Interview on Bin Laden Book No Easy Day," BBC U.S. & Canada, September 10, 2012. Available at: http://www.bbc.co.uk/news/world-us-canada-19540957.

———. "Osama Bin Laden: Legality of Killing Questioned," BBC South Asia, May 12, 2011. Available at: http://www.bbc.co.uk/news/world-south-asia-13318372.

Bemis, Samuel Flagg. *The Diplomacy of the American Revolution*. New York: Appleton-Century-Crofts, 1965.

———. *Jay's Treaty: A Study in Commerce and Diplomacy*. New Haven: Yale University Press, 1962.

———. *Pinckney's Treaty: America's Advantage from Europe's Distress, 1783–1800*. New Haven, Yale University Press, 1960.

———. "Washington's Farewell Address: A Foreign Policy of Independence," *American Historical Review*, 1934, 39: 250–68.

Bergen, Peter L. "President Obama, Warrior in Chief," *New York Times*, April 28, 2012, sec. Opinion/Sunday Review. Available at: http://www.nytimes.com/2012/04/29/opinion/sunday/president-obama-warrior-in-chief.html.

Bergen, Peter and Jennifer Rowland. "Drone Wars," *Washington Quarterly*, 2013, 36(3): 7–26.

Bernstein, Barton J. "The Week We Almost Went to War," *The Bulletin of American Scientists*, February 1976, 62(2):12–21.

Bert, Wayne. *American Military Intervention in Unconventional War*. Palgrave Macmillan, 2011.

Beschloss, Michael. *The Crisis Years: Kennedy and Khrushchev, 1960–63*. New York: Harper-Collins, 1991.

Bialer, Seweryn, and Joan Afferica. "Reagan and Russia," *Foreign Affairs*, Winter, 1982/3, 6: 249–71.

Biden, Joe. "Remarks by Vice President Biden at 45th Munich Conference on Security Policy," The White House, February 7, 2009. Available at: http://www.whitehouse.gov/the-press-office/remarks-vice-president-biden-45th-munich-conference-security-policy.

Black, George. *The Good Neighbor: How the United States Wrote the History of Central America and the Caribbean*. New York: Pantheon Books, 1988.

Blight, James G. and David A Welch. *On the Brink: Americans and Soviets Re-examine the Cuban Missile Crisis*. New York: Noonday, 1989.

Blunt and Bristling Talk Inside the Kremlin: A Private Interview with Aleksei Kosygin, *Life Magazine*, Vol. 64, No. 4, February 2, 1968.

Bolkhovitinov, Nikolai N. "Russia and the Declaration of the Non-colonization Principle: New Archival Evidence," *Oregon Historical Quarterly*, 1972, 72: 10–26.

Borchard E. M. and W. P. Lage. *Neutrality for the United States*, 2nd ed. New Haven, CT: Yale University Press, 1940.

Bourne, Edward G. "The United States and Mexico, 1847–1848," *The American Historical Review*, 1900, 5(3).

Bowcott, Owen. "Osama bin Laden: U.S. Responds to Questions about Killing's Legality," *The Guardian*, May 3, 2011. Available at: http://www.theguardian.com/world/2011/may/03/osama-bin-laden-killing-legality.

Bowett, Derek W. *Self Defence in International Law*. Manchester: Manchester University Press, 1958.

Bowman, Albert Hall. "Pichon, the United States and Louisiana," *Diplomatic History,* 1977, 1(3): 257–270.

———. Bowman, Albert Hall. *The Struggle for Neutrality: Franco-American Diplomacy during the Federalist Era.* Knoxville: University of Tennessee Press, 1974.

Branch, Taylor and George Crile III. "The Kennedy Vendetta: How the CIA Waged a Silent War against Cuba," *Harper's,* August 1975.

Brands, H. W., ed. *The Foreign Policies of Lyndon Johnson: Beyond Vietnam.* College Station: Texas A&M University Press, 1999.

Brennan, John O. "Remarks of John O. Brennan, Assistant to the President for Homeland Security and Counterterrorism, on Ensuring Al-Qa'ida's Demise," The White House, June 29, 2011. Available at: http://www.whitehouse.gov/the-press-office/2011/06/29/remarks-john-o-brennan-assistant-president-homeland-security-and-counter.

Brierly, James L. *The Law of Nations: An Introduction to the International Law of Peace.* 6th ed., edited by Sir Humphrey Waldock, New York: Oxford University Press, 1963.

Britt, Snider, L. *The Agency and the Hill: CIA's Relationship with Congress, 1946–2004.* Center for the Study of Intelligence, Central Intelligence Agency, 2008.

Broad, William J., and David E. Sanger. "U.S. Ramping Up Major Renewal in Nuclear Arms," *New York Times,* 2014.

Brooks, Rosa. "Drones and the International Rule of Law," *Ethics & International Affairs,* 2014, 28 (1): 83–103.

Brown, Adrian. "Osama Bin Laden's Death: How It Happened," BBC, September 10, 2012, sec. South Asia. Available at: http://www.bbc.co.uk/news/world-south-asia-13257330.

Brownlie, Ian. *International Law and the Use of Force by States.* Oxford: Oxford University Press, 1963.

Brune, Lester H. *The Cuba-Caribbean Missile Crisis of October 1962.* Claremont, CA: Regina Books, 1996.

Brzezinski, Zbignew. *Power and Principle: Memoirs of the National Security Adviser.* New York: Farrar, Strauss, Giroux, 1983.

Brzezinski, Zbigniew. "Detente in the 70s," *New Republic,* January 3, 1970.

Buchanan, James J. "Second Annual Message to Congress on the State of the Union," December 6, 1858, The American Presidency Project. Available at: http://www.presidency.ucsb.edu/ws/?pid=29499.

Bundy, McGeorge. *Danger and Survival: Choices about the Bomb in the First Fifty Years.* New York: Random House, 1988.

Bunn, Elaine M. "Pre-emptive Action: When, How, and to What Effect?" *Strategic Forum,* 2003, 200: 1–8.

Burns, Richard Dean. *The Evolution of Arms Control: From Antiquity to the Nuclear Age.* Santa Barbara, CA: Praeger, 2009.

———. *The Missile Defense Systems of George W. Bush: A Critical Assessment.* Santa Barbara, CA: Praeger, 2010.

Burns, Richard Dean, Joseph M. Siracusa, and Jason C. Flanagan. *American Foreign Relations since Independence.* CT: Praeger Security International, 2013.

Bush, George W. "A Period of Consequences," Address at The Citadel, South Carolina, September 23, 1999.

———. "Address to the Nation on Iraq," October 7, 2002.

———. "Graduation Speech at West Point," Washington DC: The White House, December 2002.

———. *National Strategy to Combat Weapons of Mass Destruction (NSCWMD).* Washington DC: The White House, December 2002.

———. *The National Security Strategy of 2006,* Washington DC: The White House, 2006.

———. *The National Security Strategy of the United States of America,* The White House Archives, September 17, 2002. Available at: http://www.state.gov/documents/organization/63562.pdf.

———. "President Discusses Growing Danger Posed by Saddam Hussein's Regime," Radio Address by the President to the Nation, The White House Archives, September 14, 2002.

Available at: http://georgewbush-whitehouse.archives.gov/news/releases/2002/09/20020914.html.

———. "President Outlines Priorities," Presidential Hall, Dwight D. Eisenhower Executive Office Building, November 7, 2002. Available at: http://georgewbush-whitehouse.archives.gov/news/releases/2002/11/20021107-2.html.

———. "Remarks by the President to the Warsaw Conference on Combating Terrorism," November 6, 2001.

———. "State of the Union Address," Washington DC: The White House, January 2002.

Caldwell Lawrence T. and Robert Legvold. "Reagan through Soviet Eyes," *Foreign Policy*, Fall, 1983, 52: 3–21.

Cannon, Lou, *President Reagan: The Role of a Lifetime*. New York: Public Affairs, 1991.

Cannon, Lou. "Dealings with the Soviets Raise Uncomfortable Questions," *Washington Post*, July 2, 1984.

Carter, Jimmy. "Address at Commencement Exercises at the University of Notre Dame," May 22, 1977, The American Presidency Project. Available at: http://www.presidency.ucsb.edu/ws/?pid=7552.

———. "Address to the Nation on the Soviet Invasion of Afghanistan," January 4, 1980, The American Presidency Project. Available at: http://www.presidency.ucsb.edu/ws/?pid=32911.

———. "State of the Union Address Delivered Before a Joint Session of the Congress," January 23, 1980, The American Presidency Project. Available at: http://www.presidency.ucsb.edu/ws/?pid=33079.

Carter, Stephen L. *The Violence of Peace: America's Wars in the Age of Obama*. New York, NY: Beast Books, 2011.

Cassidy, John. "Obama's Well-Earned Victory Lap on the Economy," *New Yorker*, March 19, 2015. Available at: http://www.newyorker.com/news/john-cassidy/obamas-well-earned-victory-lap-on-the-economy.

Castle, Timothy N. *At War in the Shadow of Vietnam: United States Military Aid to the Royal Lao Government, 1955–1975*. New York: Columbia University Press, 1993.

Catanzariti, John, ed. *The Papers of Thomas Jefferson*, vol. 24. Princeton, NJ: Princeton University Press, 1990.

Charles, Joseph. "The Jay Treaty: The Origins of the American Party System," *William and Mary Quarterly*, 1955, 12(4): 581–630.

Cheney, Dick. Interview with *Meet the Press*, NBC, March 16, 2003.

Cheney, Richard B. "Vice President Speaks at VFW 103rd National Convention," The White House Archives, August 26, 2002. Available at: http://georgewbush-whitehouse.archives.gov/news/releases/2002/08/20020826.html.

Churchill, Winston S. *The World Crisis*. Toronto: The MacMillan Company of Canada, 1923.

———. *Triumph and Tragedy*, vol. 6 of *The Second World War*. Boston: Houghton Mifflin, 1953.

———. "Sinews of Peace" Speech, Fulton, MO, 1946, National Churchill Museum. Available at: http://www.nationalchurchillmuseum.org/sinews-of-peace-iron-curtain-speech.html.

Cirincione, Joseph, Jessica T. Mathews, George Perkovich, and Alexis Orton. *WMD in Iraq: Evidence and Implications*. Washington DC: Carnegie Endowment for International Peace, 2004.

Cleland, Robert Glass. "The Early Sentiment for the Annexation of California: An Account of the Growth of American Interest in California from 1835 to 1846," *Southwestern Historical Quarterly*, July 1914, 18(1): 125–147.

Clinton, Bill. *A National Security Strategy of Engagement and Enlargement*, Washington DC: The White House, 1996.

Clinton, Hillary. "Hillary Clinton on Threat in Pakistan," Collection, Fox News, July 20, 2010. Available at: http://video.foxnews.com/v/4287478/hillary-clinton-on-threat-in-pakistan.

"Convention (III) Relative to the Treatment of Prisoners of War. Geneva, 12 August 1949," ICRC Treaties and Documents, 1949. Available at: http://www.icrc.org/ihl/INTRO/375?OpenDocument.

Congressional Joint Resolution, published in *The Washington Post*, October 11, 2002, A12.

The Constitution of the United States of America. Available at: http://www.archives.gov/exhibits/charters/constitution_transcript.html.

Commission on the Intelligence Capabilities of the United States Regarding Weapons of Mass Destruction. "Report to the President," March 31, 2005. Available at: http://govinfo.library.unt.edu/wmd/report/wmd_report.pdf.

Commager, Henry Steele, ed. *Documents of American History*. New York: Appleton-Century-Crofts, 1958.

Cox, Michael, and Doug Stokes. *U.S. Foreign Policy*. Oxford: Oxford University Press, 2008.

Cruikshank, E. A., ed. *The Correspondence of Lieut. Governor John Graves Simcoe, with Allied Documents Relating to His Administration of the Government of Upper Canada*. Toronto: Ontario Historical Society, 1923–1931.

Dangerfield, George. *The Era of Good Feelings*. New York: Harcourt, Brace & World, 1952.

De Tocqueville, Alexis. *Democracy in America*. Vol. 10. Regnery Publishing, 2003.

DeConde, Alexander. *Entangling Alliance: Politics & Diplomacy under George Washington*. Durham, NC: Duke University Press, 1958.

——. *The Quasi-War: The Politics and Diplomacy of the Undeclared War with France 1797–1801*. New York: Charles Scribner's Sons, 1966.

——. *This Affair of Louisiana*. New York: Charles Scribner's Sons, 1976.

Democratic Party Platform of 1844, May 27, 1844, in John T. Woolley and Gerhard Peters, The American Presidency Project, Santa Barbara, CA. Available at: http://www.presidency.ucsb.edu/ws/?pid=29573.

Department of State *Bulletin* 52, April 26, 1965.

DeSantis, Vincent P. "Italy and the Cold War," in Joseph M. Siracusa and Glen Barclay, eds., *The Impact of the Cold War: Reconsiderations*. Port Washington, NY: Kennikat Press, 1977.

Dickey, Christopher. *With the Contras: A Reporter in the Wilds of Nicaragua*. New York: Simon & Schuster, 1987.

Dobbs, Michael. *One Minute to Midnight: Kennedy, Khrushchev, and Castro on the Brink of Nuclear War*. New York: Knopf, 2008.

Dobrynin, Anatoly. *In Confidence*: *Moscow's Ambassador to America's Six Cold War Presidents*. New York; Random House, 1995.

Dostaler, Gilles. *Keynes and His Battles*. Edward Elgar Publishing, 2007.

Draper, Theodore. *A Very Thin Line: The Iran-Contra Affairs*. New York: Hill and Wang, 1991.

Drezner, Daniel W. "Does Obama Have a Grand Strategy? Why We Need Doctrines in Uncertain Times," *Foreign Affairs*, 90, 2011: 57–68.

Dull, Jonathan R. *A Diplomatic History of the American Revolution*. New Haven: Yale University Press, 1985.

——. "Franklin the Diplomat: The French Mission," *Transactions of the American Philosophical Society*, 1982: 1–76.

——. *The French Navy and American Independence: A Study of Arms and Diplomacy, 1774–1787*. Princeton, NJ: Princeton University Press, 1975.

Dulles, John Foster. "Thoughts on Soviet Foreign Policy and What to Do about It," *Life*, June 3, 1946: 113–26.

Dunne, Michael. "Kennedy's Alliance for Progress: Countering Revolution in Latin America. Part I: From the White House to the Charter of Punta del Este," *International Affairs*, 2013, 89(6): 1389–1409.

Eisenhower, Dwight D. *Public Papers of the Presidents of the United States: Dwight D. Eisenhower, 1959*. Best Books, 1960.

——. Speech on the U.S. Role in the Middle East, 1957, Council on Foreign Relations. Available at: http://www.cfr.org/middle-east-and-north-africa/president-eisenhowers-speech-us-role-middle-east-eisenhower-doctrine-1957/p24130.

Elkins, Stanley and Eric McKitrick. *The Age of Federalism*. New York: Oxford University Press, 1993.

Ellis, Jason D. and Geoffrey D. Kiefer. *Combating Proliferation: Strategic Intelligence and National Policy*. Baltimore, MD: Johns Hopkins University Press, 2004.

Emadi, Hafizullah. *State, Revolution, and Superpowers in Afghanistan.* New York: Praeger, 1990.

English, Robert D. *Russia and the Idea of the West: Gorbachev, Intellectuals & the End of the Cold War.* New York: University of Columbia Press, 2000.

Epstein, William. "The Non-Proliferation Treaty and the Review Conferences," in Richard Dean Burns, ed. *Encyclopedia of Arms Control and Disarmament*, 3 vols. New York: Scribners, 1993.

Estes, Todd. *The Jay Treaty Debate, Public Opinion, and the Evolution of Early American Political Culture.* Amherst: University of Massachusetts Press, 2006.

———. "Shaping the Politics of Public Opinion: Federalists and the Jay Treaty Debate," *Journal of the Early Republic*, 2000, 20: 393–422.

Ethridge, Mark. "Memorandum on Bulgaria and Rumania," December 7, 1945, *Foreign Relations of the United States, Diplomatic Papers 1945.* Washington DC: U.S. Government Printing Office, 1967. European Council, "European Security Strategy: A Secure Europe in a Better World." European Union External Action, December 12, 2003. Available at: http://www.consilium.europa.eu/uedocs/cmsUpload/78367.pdf. Fair, C. Christine. "The Bin Laden Aftermath: The U.S. Shouldn't Hold Pakistan's Military against Pakistan's Civilians," *Foreign Policy*, May 5, 2011.

Fallows, James M. *National Defense.* New York: Random House, 1981.

Farrell, John J. ed., *James K. Polk, 1795–1849: Chronology, Documents, Bibliographical Aids.* Dobbs Ferry, NY: Oceana, 1970.

Ferrell, Robert H. *Off the Record: The Private Papers of Harry S. Truman.* New York: Harper and Row, 1980.

Fitzgerald, Frances. *Way Out There in the Blue: Reagan, Star Wars and the End of the Cold War.* New York: Simon & Schuster, 2000.

Fitzsimons, David M. "Tom Paine's New World Order: Idealistic Internationalism in the Ideology of Early American Foreign Relations," *Diplomatic History*, 1995, 19: 569–82.

Fleming, D. F. *The United States and the League of Nations, 1918–1920.* New York: G. P. Putnam's Sons, 1932.

———. *The United States and World Organization, 1920–1933.* New York: Columbia University Press, 1938.

Flowerree, Charles C. "Chemical and Biological Weapons and Arms Control," in Richard Dean Burns, ed., *Encyclopedia of Arms Control and Disarmament*, Vol. 2. Macmillan Reference USA, 1993.

Ford, Worthington Chauncey. "John Quincy Adams and the Monroe Doctrine," *American Historical Review*, 1902, 8(1): 33–38.

Foreign Relations of the United States: The Paris Peace Conference, 13 vols. Washington DC: U.S. Government Printing Office, 1942–1947, vol. 6: 800 ff.

Frankel, Glenn. "New U.S. Doctrine Worries Europeans," *Washington Post*, September 30, 2002, I(A) and 15(A).

Franklin, Benjamin. *The Works of Benjamin Franklin: With Notes and a Life of the Author by J. Sparks.* 1840.

Frazier, Robert. "Did Britain Start the Cold War? Bevin and the Truman Doctrine," *The Historical Journal*, 1984, 27(3): 715–727.

Freedman, Lawrence. *Kennedy's Wars: Berlin, Cuba, Laos, and Vietnam.* New York: Oxford University Press, 2000.

Fursenko, A. A., and Timothy J. Naftali. *One Hell of a Gamble: Khrushchev, Castro, and Kennedy, 1958–1964.* New York: Norton, 1997.

Gaddis, John Lewis. "A Grand Strategy of Transformation," *Foreign Policy*, 2002, 133: 50–57.

———. *We Now Know: Rethinking Cold War History.* New York: Oxford University Press, 1997.

———. *The United States and the Origins of the Cold War, 1941–1947.* New York: Columbia University Press, 1972.

Galloway, Colin G. *The Scratch of a Pen: 1763 and the Transformation of America.* New York: Oxford University Press, 2006.

Gambone, Michael D. *Capturing the Revolution: The United States, Central America, and Nicaragua, 1961–1972*, Greenwood Publishing Group, 2001.

Garthoff, Raymond L. *The Great Transition: American-Soviet Relations and the End of the Cold War*. Washington DC: Brookings Institution, 1994.

Gates, Robert M. *From the Shadows*. New York: Pocket Books, 2007.

Gavin, Francis J. "The Gold Battles Within the Cold War: American Monetary Policy and the Defense of Europe, 1960–1963," *Diplomatic History*, 2002, 26(1): 61–94.

Genscher, Hans-Dietrich. "Toward an Overall Western Strategy for Peace, Freedom, and Progress," *Foreign Affairs*, Fall 1982, 61: 42–66.

"George Washington: Second Term," President Profiles. Available at: http://www.presidentprofiles.com/Washington-Johnson/George-Washington-Second-term.html.

Geyelin, Philip. *Lyndon B. Johnson and the World*. New York: Praeger, 1966.

Gilbert, Felix. *To the Farewell Address: Ideas of Early American Foreign Policy*. Princeton, NJ: Princeton University Press, 1970.

Gilderhaus, Mark T. "The Monroe Doctrine: Meanings and Implications," *Presidential Studies Quarterly*, 2006, 36(1): 5–16.

Goodwin, Doris Kearns. *Team of Rivals: The Political Genius of Abraham Lincoln*. Camberwell, VIC: Penguin, 2009.

Gorbachev, Mikhail. *Reykjavik: Results and Lessons*. Madison, CT: Sphinx Press, 1987.

Graebner, Norman A. *Empire on the Pacific: A Study in American Continental Expansion.* New York: Ronald Press Company, 1955.

———. "The Mexican War: A Study in Causation," *Pacific Historical Review*, 1989, 49: 405–26.

———. "The Soviet-American Conflict: A Strange Phenomenon," *VQR: A National Journal of Literature and Discussion* Autumn, 1984, 60(4).

———. "The Uses and Misuses of Power: The 1980s," *Dialogue: A Magazine of International Affairs*, March 1988, 1(1): 21–35.

Graebner, Norman A. and Edward M. Bennett. *The Versailles Treaty and Its Legacy: The Failure of the Wilsonian Vision.* New York: Cambridge University Press, 2011.

Graebner, Norman A., Richard Dean Burns, and Joseph M. Siracusa. *America and the Cold War, 1941–1991: A Realist Interpretation*, 2 vols. Santa Barbara, CA: Praeger, 2010.

———. *Foreign Affairs and the Founding Fathers: From Confederation to Constitution, 1776–1787*. CT: Praeger Security International, 2011.

———. *Reagan, Bush, Gorbachev: Revisiting the End of the Cold War*. CT: Praeger Security International, 2008.

Graham, Thomas Jr. *Disarmament Sketches: Three Decades of Arms Control and International Law*. Seattle: University of Washington Press, 2002.

Gray, Christine. "President Obama's 2010 United States National Security Strategy and International Law on the Use of Force," *Chinese Journal of International Law*, 2011, 10(1): 35–53.

Grew, Joseph C. *Turbulent Era: A Diplomatic Record of Forty Years, 1904–1945*. Walter Johnson, ed. Boston: Houghton Mifflin, 1952.

Haig, Alexander M. Jr. *Caveat, Realism, Reagan and Foreign Policy*. New York: Macmillan, 1984.

———. "Opening Statement at Confirmation Hearings," January 9, 1981, U.S. Department of State, Bureau of Public Affairs, *Current Policy No. 257*.

"Haig Calls Moscow the Primary Source of Danger to the World," *New York Times*, April 25, 1981.

Hazen, Charles D. *Contemporary American Opinion of the French Revolution*. Baltimore: Johns Hopkins Press, 1897.

Henderson, Christian. "The 2010 United States National Security Strategy and the Obama Doctrine of 'Necessary Force,'" *Journal of Conflict & Security Law*, 2010, 15(3): 403–434.

Hoffmann, Stanley. *Dead Ends: American Foreign Policy in the New Cold War*. Cambridge, MA: Ballinger, 1983.

Hollis, Duncan. "President Elect Obama on International Law," *Opinio Juris*, November 6, 2008. Available at: http://opiniojuris.org/2008/11/06/president-elect-obama-on-international-law.

Hutson, James H. "The American Negotiators: The Diplomacy of Jealousy," in Ronald Hoffman and Peter J. Albert, eds., *Peace and the Peacemakers: The Treaty of 1783*. Charlottesville: University Press of Virginia, 1986.

———. "Intellectual Foundations of Early American Diplomacy," *Diplomatic History*, 1977, Winter 1: 1–19.

Ikenberry, G. John. "America's 'Security Trap,'" in Michael Cox and Doug Stokes, eds., *U.S. Foreign Policy*. Oxford: Oxford University Press, 2008.

Immerman, Richard. "'Trust in the Lord but Keep Your Powder Dry': American Policy Aims at Geneva," in Gunter Bischof and Saki Dockrill, eds., *Cold War Respite: The Geneva Summit of 1955*, Baton Rouge: Louisiana State University, 1955: 35–54.

"Interim Agreement Between the United States of America and the Union of Soviet Socialist Republics on Certain Measures With Respect to the Limitation of Strategic Offensive Arms," Signed at Moscow May 26, 1972, U.S. Department of State. Available at: http://www.state.gov/t/isn/4795.htm.

Jacobs, M. C. *Winning Oregon: A Study of an Expansionist Movement*. Caldwell, ID: Caxton Printers, 1938.

Jay's Treaty, Article 25, Library of Congress. Available at: http://www.loc.gov/rr/program/bib/ourdocs/jay.html.

Jefferson, Thomas. "To the United States Minister in France (Robert E. Livingston)," Washington, April 18, 1802, in Albert Ellery Bergh, ed., *The Writings of Thomas Jefferson*, vol. 10. Washington: Thomas Jefferson Memorial Association, 1907.

———. "To William C. C. Claiborne," Washington, July 13, 1801, *The Papers of Thomas Jefferson*, vol. 34.

Jenkins, Brian M. "A Nuclear 9/11?" This commentary appeared on CNN.com on September 11, 2008 and was republished on the RAND Corporation website. Available at: http://www.rand.org/commentary/2008/09/11/CNN.html.

Jervis, Robert. "Understanding the Bush Doctrine," *Political Science Quarterly*, 2003, 118(3): 365–388.

Jessup, Philip C. *Elihu Root*, 2 vols. New York: Dodd, Mead & Co., 1938.

"John L. O'Sullivan and Manifest Destiny," *New York History*, 1933, 45: 213–34.

Johns, Andrew. *Vietnam's Second Front: Domestic Politics, the Republican Party, and the War*. Kentucky: University Press of Kentucky, 2010.

Johnson, C. O. *Borah of Idaho*. New York: Longmans, Green, 1936.

"Joint Four-Nation Declaration on Austria." The Moscow Conference, October 1943. The Avalon Project. Available at: http://avalon.law.yale.edu/wwii/moscow.asp.

Jones, Howard. *Crucible of Power: A History of U.S. Foreign Relations since 1897*. Rowman & Littlefield, 2001.

Jones, Joseph M. *The Fifteen Weeks*. New York: Viking Press, 1955.

Kalb, Marvin, and Bernard Kalb. *Kissinger*. Boston: Little, Brown, 1974.

Kaplan, Lawrence S. "The Treaties of Paris and Washington, 1778 and 1949: Reflections on Entangling Alliances," in Ronald Hoffman and Peter J. Albert, eds., *Diplomacy and Revolution: The Franco-American Alliance of 1778*. Charlottesville: University Press of Virginia, 1981

Karnow, Stanley. *Vietnam: A History*. Vol. 122. Random House, 1994.

Katzman, Kenneth, "Afghanistan: Post-Taliban Governance, Security, and U.S. Policy," Congressional Research Service report, October 15, 2015. Available at: https://www.fas.org/sgp/crs/row/RL30588.pdf.

Katzman, Kenneth, and Carla E. Humud, "Iraq: Politics and Governance," Congressional Research Service report, November 13, 2015. Available at: https://www.fas.org/sgp/crs/mideast/RS21968.pdf.

Kelsen, Hans. *The Law of the United Nations: A Critical Analysis of Its Fundamental Problems*. New York: Frederick A. Praeger, 1964.

Kennan, George F. *American Diplomacy, 1900–1950*. Chicago: University of Chicago Press, 1951.

———. "Breaking the Spell," *New Yorker*, October 3, 1983: 44–53.

———. *Memoirs: 1925–1950*. Boston: Little, Brown, 1967.

Kennedy, John F. "Address at a White House Reception for Members of Congress and for the Diplomatic Corps of the Latin American Republics," March 13, 1961, in John T. Woolley and Gerhard Peters, The American Presidency Project, Santa Barbara, CA. Available at: http://www.presidency.ucsb.edu/ws/?pid=8531.

———. "Address Before the American Society of Newspaper Editors," April 20, 1961, in John T. Woolley and Gerhard Peters, The American Presidency Project, Santa Barbara, CA. Available at: http://www.presidency.ucsb.edu/ws/?pid=8076.

———. "Radio and Television Report to the American People on the Soviet Arms Buildup in Cuba," October 22, 1962, The American Presidency Project. Available at: http://www.presidency.ucsb.edu/ws/?pid=8986.

———. "The President's News Conference," March 21, 1963, The American Presidency Project. Available at: http://www.presidency.ucsb.edu/ws/?pid=9124.

Kimball, Jeffrey. "The Nixon Doctrine: A Saga of Misunderstanding," *Presidential Studies Quarterly*, 2006, 36 (1): 59–74.

Kissinger, Henry A. *Diplomacy*. New York: Simon & Schuster Paperbacks, 1994.

———. "The Vietnam Negotiations," *Foreign Affairs*, 1969, 47(2): 211–234.

———. *White House Years*. Boston: Little, Brown, 1979.

Klare, Michael T. "The Carter Doctrine Goes Global," *Progressive Magazine*, December, 2004.

———. "Fuelling the Fire: How We Armed the Middle East," *Bulletin of the Atomic Scientists*, January/February, 1991, 47: 19–26.

———. "Oil, Iraq, and American Foreign Policy: The Continuing Salience of the Carter Doctrine," *International Journal*, 2006, 62 (1): 31–42.

Kochavi, Noam. "Limited Accommodation, Perpetuated Conflict: Kennedy, China, and the Laos Crisis, 1961–1963," *Diplomatic History*, 2002, 26(1): 95–135.

Koh, Harold. "The Obama Administration and International Law," U.S. Department of State, March 25, 2010. Available at: http://www.state.gov/s/l/releases/remarks/139119.htm.

Krass, Allan S. *The United States and Arms Control: The Challenge of Leadership*. Westport, CT: Praeger, 1997.

Krock, Arthur. *Memoirs: Sixty Years on the Firing Line*. New York: Funk & Wagnalls, 1968.

Kunz, Josef L. "Individual and Collective Self-Defense in Article 51 of the Charter of the United Nations," *American Journal on International Law*, 1947, 41: 872–878.

LaFeber, Walter. "The Bush Doctrine," *Diplomatic History*, 2002, 26 (4): 543–558.

———. *Inevitable Revolutions: The United States and Central America*. New York, 1983.

Lagon, Mark P. *The Reagan Doctrine: Sources of American Conduct in the Cold War's Last Chapter*. Westport, CT: Praeger, 1994.

Lansing, Robert. "Memorandum by the Counselor for the Department of State (Lansing) on Professor Hugo Münsterberg's Letter to President Wilson of November 19, 1914," *U.S. Department of State Office of the Historian*. Available at: http://history.state.gov/historical-documents/frus1914-20v01/d167.

———. "The Secretary of State to President Wilson," September 6, 1915, Washington DC: U.S. Department of State Office of the Historian. Available at: http://history.state.gov/historicaldocuments/frus1914-20v01/d148.

Lebow, Ned and Janice Gross Stein. *We All Lost the Cold War*. Princeton, NJ: Princeton University Press, 1994.

Lebow, Richard N. "Windows of Opportunity: Do States Jump Through Them?" *International Security*, 1984, 9 (4): 147–186.

Leffler, Melvyn P. *A Preponderance of Power*. Stanford, CA: Stanford University Press, 1992.

"Lessons of Cuba," *New York Times*, September 9, 1962.

"A Letter to Alexander von Humboldt, December 6, 1813," in Helmut de Terra, "Alexander von Humboldt's Correspondence with Jefferson, Madison, and Gallatin," *Proceedings of the American Philosophical Society*, 1959, 103(6): 783–806.

Levinson, Jerome and Juan De Onís. *The Alliance That Lost Its Way*. Chicago: Quadrangle Books, 1970.

Levy, Jack S. "Declining Power and the Preventive Motivation for War," *World Politics*, 1987, 40 (1): 82–107.

Lind, Michael. *Vietnam, the Necessary War: A Reinterpretation of America's Most Disastrous Military Conflict*. New York: Free Press, 1999.

Link, Arthur S., ed. *The Papers of Woodrow Wilson*, vol. 40. Princeton, NJ: Princeton University Press, 1966–1994.

Link, Arthur S. *Wilson: Campaigns for Progressivism and Peace*. Princeton, NJ: Princeton University Press, 1965.

———. *Woodrow Wilson and the Progressive Era, 1910–1917*. New York: Harper & Row, 1954.

Lint, Gregg L. "John Adams on the Drafting of the Treaty Plan of 1776," *Diplomatic History*, 1978, 2: 313–20.

———. "Preparing for Peace: The Objectives of the United States, France, and Spain in the War of the American Revolution," in Ronald Hoffman and Peter J. Albert, eds., *Peace and the Peacemakers: The Treaty of 1783*. Charlottesville: University Press of Virginia, 1986.

Lippmann, Walter. *U.S. Foreign Policy, Shield of the Republic*. Boston: Little, Brown, 1943.

Livingston, Robert R., to Benjamin Franklin, January 2, 1783, National Archives. Available at: http://founders.archives.gov/documents/Franklin/01-38-02-0405#BNFN-01-38-02-0405.

Lodge, H. C. *The Senate and the League of Nations*. New York: Charles Scribner's Sons, 1925.

Loewenberg, Robert J. "Creating a Provisional Government in Oregon: A Revision," *Pacific Northwest Quarterly*, 1977, 68(1): 13–24.

Lord, Kristin M. and Marc Lynch. "America's Extended Hand: Assessing the Obama Administration's Global Engagement Strategy," *Center for a New American Security*, 2010.

Louisiana Purchase Treaty, April 30, 1803. See the Avalon Project of the Lillian Goldman Law Library of Yale Law School. Available at: http://avalon.law.yale.edu/19th_century/louis1.asp.

Lynch, Marc. "Obama and the Middle East: Rightsizing the U.S. Role," *Foreign Affairs*, September/October 2015.

Macris, Jeffrey and Saul Kelly, eds. *Imperial Crossroads: The Great Powers and the Persian Gulf*. Naval Institute Press, 2012.

Manning, William R., ed. *Diplomatic Correspondence of the United States Concerning the Independence of the Latin American Nations*, vol. 3. New York: Oxford University Press, 1925.

Matlock, Jack F. Jr. *Reagan and Gorbachev: How the Cold War Ended*. New York: Random House, 2004.

Matthewson, Tim. "Jefferson and Haiti," *Journal of Southern History*, 1995, 61(2): 209–248.

May, Ernest R. *American Cold War Strategy: Interpreting NSC-68*. New York: Bedford Books, 1993.

McGee, G. W. "The Monroe Doctrine—A Stopgap Measure," *Mississippi Valley Historical Review*, 1951, 38: 233–50.

McNamara, Robert S. et al, *Argument without End: In Search of Answers to the Vietnam Tragedy*. New York: Public Affairs, 1999.

Merk, Frederick. *Albert Gallatin and the Oregon Problem: A Study in Anglo-American Diplomacy*. Cambridge, MA: Harvard University Press, 1950.

———. *Manifest Destiny and Mission in American History: A Reinterpretation*. New York: Alfred A. Knopf, 1963.

———. *The Oregon Question: Essays in Anglo-American Diplomacy and Politics* . Cambridge, MA: Harvard University Press, 1967.

Michaels, Jeffrey H. "Dysfunctional Doctrines? Eisenhower, Carter and U.S. Military Intervention in the Middle East," *Political Science Quarterly*, 2011, 126(3): 465–492.

Middlebrook, Kevin J., and Carlos Rico, eds. *The United States and Latin America in the 1980s*. Pennsylvania: University of Pittsburgh Press, 1986.

Miles, Edwin A. "'Fifty-four Forty or Fight'—An American Political Legend," *Mississippi Valley Historical Review*, 1957, 44: 291–309.

Monroe, James. "Seventh Annual Message to Congress," December 2, 1823. The Avalon Project. Available at: http://avalon.law.yale.edu/19th_century/monroe.asp.

———. "Speech in Congress," May 10, 1820, *Annals of Congress*, 16th Congress, 1st Session.

———. "Speech in the House of Representatives," March 24, 1818, reproduced in *Niles' Weekly Register*, April 18, 1818, 127.

Moore, John Bassett, ed. *The Works of James Buchanan: Comprising His Speeches, State Papers, and Private Correspondence*, vol. 6, 1844–1846. Philadelphia: J. B. Lippincott, 1909.

Moscoso, Teodoro. "Progress Report on the Alliance for Progress," *New York Times Magazine*, August 12, 1962, 11: 59–63.

"Mr. Peña y Peña to Mr. Black," Mexico, October 15, 1845, reproduced in *Niles' National Register*, May 30, 1846.

Murphy, Orville T. "The View from Versailles: Charles Gravier Comte de Vergennes's Perceptions of the American Revolution," in Ronald Hoffman and Peter J. Albert, eds., *Diplomacy and Revolution: The Franco-American Alliance of 1778*. Charlottesville: University Press of Virginia, 1981.

National Intelligence Council, *Iraq's Continuing Program for Weapons of Mass Destruction: Key Judgments*, October 2002.

National Security Council, "Document 68: United States Objectives and Programs for National Security," April 14, 1950, Federation of American Scientists. Available at: http://www.fas.org/irp/offdocs/nsc-hst/nsc-68.htm.

Newhouse, John. "Annals of Diplomacy: The Abolitionist—II," *New Yorker*, January 9, 1989: 51.

———. *Cold Dawn: The Story of SALT*. New York: Holt, Rinehart & Winston, 1973.

New Republic, October 17, 1970.

Newsweek, September 1, 1980.

Newsweek, February 9, 1981.

Newsweek, March 16, 1981.

Newsweek, March 22, 1982.

New Yorker, January 9, 1989.

New York Times, September 9, 1962.

New York Times, September 30, 1967.

New York Times, November 26, 1967.

New York Times, May 9, 1969.

New York Times, September 20, 1969.

New York Times, October 29, 1969.

New York Times, November 4, 1969.

New York Times, December 6, 1969.

New York Times, January 11, 1970.

New York Times, May 1, 1970.

New York Times, September 18, 1970.

New York Times, June 13, 1971.

New York Times, December 23, 1973.

New York Times, August 2, 1975.

New York Times, April 26, 1976.

New York Times, March 23, 1980.

New York Times, May 3, 1981.

New York Times, June 21, 1981.

New York Times, May 9, 1982.

New York Times, June 27, 1982.

New Yorker, October 17, 1982.

New York Times, July 17, 19, 26, 1981.

New York Times, January 3, 1982.

New York Times, February 14, 1982.

New York Times, February 21, 1982.

New York Times, April 11, 1982.

New York Times, September 3, 1983.

New York Times, October 30, 1983.

New York Times, January 1, 1984.

New York Times, November 29, 1984.

New York Times, December 16, 1984.

New York Times, April 6, 1986.

New York Times, May 25, 1986.

New York Times, August 29, 1986.

New York Times, June 7, 1987.

New York Times, July 10, 1988.

Nicoles, Irby C. Jr. "The Russian Ukase and the Monroe Doctrine: A Re-Evaluation," *Pacific Historical Review,* 1967, 36: 13–26.

Nicoles, Irby C. Jr., and Richard A. Ward. "Anglo-American Relations and the Russian Ukase: A Reassessment," *Pacific Historical Review,* 1972, 41: 444–59.

Nitze, Paul H. *From Hiroshima to Glasnost: At the Center of Decision—A Memoir.* New York: Grove Weidenfeld, 1989.

Nixon, Richard M. "Address Accepting the Presidential Nomination at the Republican National Convention in Miami Beach, Florida," August 8, 1968, The American Presidency Project. Available at: http://www.presidency.ucsb.edu/ws/index.php?pid=25968.

———. "Asia after Vietnam," *Foreign Affairs,* October, 1967, 46(1): 121.

———. *No More Vietnams.* London: W. H. Allen, 1986.

———. *RN: The Memoirs of Richard Nixon.* New York: Grosset & Dunlap, 1978.

———. "Third Annual Report to Congress," Washington DC: February 8, 1972.

North Atlantic Treaty, Washington DC, April 4, 1949. Available at: http://www.nato.int/cps/en/natolive/official_texts_17120.htm.

Nye Jr., Joseph S. "The Decline of America's Soft Power," *Foreign Affairs,* 2004, 83(3): 83–95.

NYU Center for Human Rights and Global Justice, "Briefing: Torture by Proxy: International Law Applicable to 'Extraordinary Renditions,'" NYU, December 6, 2005.

O'Hanlon, Michael, Susan E. Rice, and James B. Sterling. "The New National Security Strategy and Pre-emption," Policy Brief #113, The Brookings Institution, December 2002.

O'Sullivan, John L. "The Great Nation of Futurity," *The United States Democratic Review,* 1839, 6(13): 426–430.

Obama, Barack. "Address to Joint Session of Congress," The White House, February 24, 2009.

———. "Executive Order 13491: Ensuring Lawful Interrogations," The White House, January 22, 2009. Available at: http://www.whitehouse.gov/the_press_office/Ensuring_Lawful_Interrogations.

———. "Executive Order 13492: Closure Of Guantanamo Detention Facilities," The White House, January 22, 2009. Available at: http://www.whitehouse.gov/the_press_office/ClosureOfGuantanamoDetentionFacilities.

———. "Obama's Speech at Woodrow Wilson Center," Council on Foreign Relations, August 20, 2007. Available at: http://www.cfr.org/elections/obamas-speech-woodrow-wilson-center/p13974.

———. "The National Security Strategy of the United States of America 2010," The White House, May 2010. Available at: http://www.whitehouse.gov/sites/default/files/rss_viewer/national_security_strategy.pdf.

———. "Remarks by President Barack Obama in Prague," The White House, April 5, 2009. Available at: http://www.whitehouse.gov/the_press_office/Remarks-By-President-Barack-Obama-In-Prague-As-Delivered.

———. "Remarks by President Obama and Prime Minister Reinfeldt of Sweden in Joint Press Conference," The White House, September 4, 2013. Available at: http://www.whitehouse.gov/the-press-office/2013/09/04/remarks-president-obama-and-prime-minister-reinfeldt-sweden-joint-press-.

———. "Remarks by President Obama to the Troops in Afghanistan," The White House, May 1, 2012. Available at: http://www.whitehouse.gov/the-press-office/2012/05/01/remarks-president-obama-troops-afghanistan.

————. "Remarks by the President after the Trilateral Meeting with President Karzai of Afghanistan and President Zardari of Pakistan," The White House, May 6, 2009. Available at: http://www.whitehouse.gov/the-press-office/remarks-president-after-trilateral-meeting-with-president-karzai-afghanistan-and-pr.

————. "Remarks by the President and Governor Romney in the Third Presidential Debate," The White House, October 23, 2012. Available at: http://www.whitehouse.gov/the-press-office/2012/10/23/remarks-president-and-governor-romney-third-presidential-debate.

————. "Remarks by the President at the Acceptance of the Nobel Peace Prize," The White House, December 10, 2009. Available at: http://www.whitehouse.gov/the-press-office/remarks-president-acceptance-nobel-peace-prize.

————. "Remarks by the President at the Democratic National Convention," The White House, September 6, 2012. Available at: http://www.whitehouse.gov/the-press-office/2012/09/07/remarks-president-democratic-national-convention.

————. "Remarks by the President at the National Defense University," The White House, May 23, 2013. Available at: http://www.whitehouse.gov/the-press-office/2013/05/23/remarks-president-national-defense-university.

————. "Remarks by the President in State of Union Address," The White House, January 25, 2011. Available at: http://www.whitehouse.gov/the-press-office/2011/01/25/remarks-president-state-union-address.

————. "Remarks by the President on a New Beginning," The White House, June 4, 2009. Available at: http://www.whitehouse.gov/the_press_office/Remarks-by-the-President-at-Cairo-University-6-04-09.

————. "Remarks by the President on a New Strategy for Afghanistan and Pakistan," The White House, March 27, 2009. Available at: http://www.whitehouse.gov/the-press-office/remarks-president-a-new-strategy-afghanistan-and-pakistan.

————. "Remarks by the President on Request to Congress for Authorization of Force Against ISIS," February 11, 2015.

————. "The State of the Union 2012," The White House, January 24, 2012. Available at: http://www.whitehouse.gov/state-of-the-union-2012.

Oberg, Barbara B., ed. *The Papers of Thomas Jefferson*, vol. 35. Princeton, NJ: Princeton University Press, 2008.

Oregon: The Cost and the Consequences, by "A Disciple of the Washington School," Philadelphia: J. C. Clark's Bookstore, 1846.

Osborne, John. "Why Cambodia?" *New Republic*, June 11, 1970: 7–9.

Overholt, William H., and Marylin Chou. "Foreign Policy Doctrines," *Policy Studies Journal*, 1974, 3(2):185–188.

Pach, Chester. "The Reagan Doctrine: Principle, Pragmatism, and Policy," *Presidential Studies Quarterly*, 2006, 36(1): 75–88.

Paine, Christopher. "A False START," *Bulletin of the Atomic Scientists,* August/September, 1982, 38: 14.

Paine, Thomas. *Common Sense.* London: Penguin Classics, 1982.

Panetta, Leon E. "CIA Chief Panetta: Obama Made 'Gutsy' Decision on Bin Laden Raid," *PBS NewsHour*, May 3, 2011. Available at: http://www.pbs.org/newshour/bb/terrorism/jan-june11/panetta_05-03.html.

Paterson Thomas G., and Dennis Merrill. *Major Problems in American Foreign Relations*, vol. 1, *To 1920*. Lexington, MA: D. C. Heath, 1995.

Peace Treaty Hearings, Senate Document 106, 66 Congress 1 sess., 536.

Pelofsky, Jeremy, and James Vicini. "Bin Laden Killing Was U.S. Self-Defense: U.S.," Reuters, May 4, 2011. Available at: http://www.reuters.com/article/2011/05/04/us-binladen-selfdefense-idUSTRE74353420110504.

Perkins, Bradford. *Castlereagh and Adams: England and America, 1812–1823*. Berkeley: University of California Press, 1964.

————. *The First Rapprochement: England and the United States, 1795–1805*. Philadelphia: University of Philadelphia Press, 1955.

Perkins, Dexter. "Bringing the Monroe Doctrine up to Date," *Foreign Affairs*, 1942, 20(2): 252–262.

————. *A History of the Monroe Doctrine*. Boston: Little, Brown, 1963.

————. *The Monroe Doctrine, 1823–1826*. Cambridge, MA: Harvard University Press, 1927.

————. *The Monroe Doctrine, 1826–1867*. Baltimore: Johns Hopkins Press, 1933.

Phillips, Walter Alison. *The Confederation of Europe: A Study of the European Alliance, 1813–1823, as an Experiment in the International Organization of Peace*. The Lawbook Exchange, Ltd., 2005.

Pincus, Walter H. "CIA learned in '02 That Bin Laden Had No Iraq Ties, Report Says," *Washington Post*, September 15, 2006, A14.

Pitkin, Timothy. *A Political and Civil History of the United States of America from the Year 1763 to the Close of the Administration of President Washington, in March, 1797*. Applewood Books, 2009.

Powell, Colin L. "A Strategy of Partnerships," *Foreign Affairs*, January/February 2004, 83(1): 22–34.

Powers, Francis Gary, and Curt Gentry. *Operation Overflight: The Story of U-2 Sky Pilot Francis Gary Powers*. New York: Holt, Rinehart and Winston, 1970.

Pratt, J. W. "The Origin of 'Manifest Destiny,'" *American Historical Review*, 1927, 32: 795–98.

President of the Russian Federation, "National Security Strategy to 2020," ETH Zuerich Digital Library, May 2009. Available at: http://www.isn.ethz.ch/Digital-Library/Publications/Detail/?id=154915.

"Promoting Democracy and Peace," U.S. Department of State, Bureau of Public Affairs, *Current Policy No. 399*: 3–5.

Quaife, Milo Milton, ed., *The Diary of James K. Polk During His Presidency, 1845 to 1849*, vol. 1. Chicago: A. C. McClurg, 1910.

Rabe, Stephen G. "The Johnson Doctrine," *Presidential Studies Quarterly*, 2006, 36(1): 48–58.

Raskin, M. G., and B. B. Fall, eds. *The Viet-Nam Reader: Articles and Documents of American Foreign Policy and the Viet-Nam Crises*. New York: Vintage Books, 1965.

Ratner, Steven. *New York Times*, August 29, 1982.

Ray, Thomas A. "'Not One Cent for Tribute': The Public Addresses and American Popular Reaction to the XYZ Affair, 1798–1799," *Journal of the Early Republic*, 1983, 3: 389–412.

Reagan, Ronald. "Address Before a Joint Session of Congress on the State of the Union," February 4, 1986, The American Presidency Project. Available at: http://www.presidency.ucsb.edu/ws/index.php?pid=36646%20.

————. "Address to Congress," September 5, 1983, *American Foreign Policy: Current Documents, 1983*. Washington DC: Government Printing Office, 1985: 544–47.

————. "Address on U.S.-Soviet Relations," January 16, 1984, *Public Papers of the Presidents: Ronald Reagan, 1984*, vol. 1. Washington DC: Government Printing Office, 1986.

————. *An American Life: The Autobiography*. New York: Simon & Schuster, 1990.

————. *Public Papers of the Presidents: Ronald Reagan, 1981*. Washington DC: Government Printing Office, 1981.

————. *Ronald Reagan: An American Life*. New York: Pocket Books, 1990.

————. "State of the Union Address," January 25, 1984, *American Foreign Policy: Current Documents, 1984*. Washington DC: Government Printing Office, 1986.

Record, Jeffrey. "The Bush Doctrine and the War with Iraq," *Parameters*, 2003, 33(1): 4–21.

Redick, John R. "Nuclear Weapons-Free Zones," in Richard Dean Burns, ed. *Encyclopedia of Arms Control and Disarmament*, 3 vols. New York: Scribners, 1993.

Reeves, Jesse S. *American Diplomacy under Tyler and Polk*. Baltimore: Johns Hopkins, 1907.

Reiss, Edward. *The Strategic Defense Initiative*. New York: Cambridge University Press, 1992.

"Report from Munich," New York *Daily News*, February 20, 1982.

Republican Party Platform 1952 July 7, 1952, The American Presidency Project. Available at: http://www.presidency.ucsb.edu/ws/?pid=25837.

Republican Party Platform of 1980, July 15, 1980, The American Presidency Project. Available at: http://www.presidency.ucsb.edu/ws/?pid=25844.

Rhodes, Richard. *Arsenals of Folly: The Making of the Nuclear Arms Race*. New York: Knopf, 2007.

Ricard, Serge. "The Roosevelt Corollary," *Presidential Studies Quarterly*, 2006, 36(1): 17–26.

Rice, Condoleezza. "A Balance of Power That Favors Freedom," The Walter Wriston Lecture of the Manhattan Institute, Office of the Press Secretary, New York, Washington DC: The White House, October 1, 2002.

Ricks, Thomas E., and Vernon Loeb. "Bush Developing Military Policy of Striking First," *Washington Post*, June 10, 2002, A01.

Rives, George Lockhart. *The United States and Mexico, 1821–1848: A History of the Relations between the Two Countries from the Independence of Mexico to the Close of the War with the United Sates*, vol. 2. New York: Charles Scribner's Sons, 1918.

Rohrs, Richard C. "The Federalist Party and the Convention of 1800," *Diplomatic History*, 1988, 12(3): 237–60.

Rolle, Andrew. "Exploring an Explorer: Psychohistory and John Charles Frémont," *Pacific Historical Review*, 1982, 51: 145–163.

Rollins, John W., and Heidi M. Peters, "The Islamic State—Frequently Asked Questions: Threats, Global Implications, and U.S. Policy Responses," Congressional Research Service report, November 25, 2015.

Roosevelt, Theodore. *The Winning of the West, Volume Four: Louisiana and the Northwest 1791–1807.* Echo Library, 2007.

Rose, Gideon, "What Obama Gets Right: Keep Calm and Carry the Liberal Order On," *Foreign Affairs*, September/October 2015.

Rosenwasser, Jon, "The Bush Administration's Doctrine of Pre-emption (and Prevention): When, How, Where?" Council on Foreign Relations, February 1, 2004. Available at: http://www.cfr.org/world/bush-administrations-doctrine-preemption-prevention-/p6799.

"Royal Instructions to the Peace Commission of 1778," in S. E. Morison, ed., *Sources and Documents Illustrating the American Revolution, 1764–1788*. Oxford: Clarendon Press, 1923.

Rumsfeld, Donald H. "Secretary Rumsfeld Speaks on '21st Century Transformation' of the U.S. Armed Forces," January 31, 2002.

Sakarov, Andrei. *Moscow and Beyond*. New York: Alfred A. Knopf, 1991.

The Sandinista Military Build-Up, Inter-American Series 119. Washington DC: Department of State, 1985.

Savage, Charlie. "Barack Obama's Q&A," *Boston Globe*, December 20, 2007. Available at: http://www.boston.com/news/politics/2008/specials/CandidateQA/ObamaQA.

Savranskaya, Svetlana, and Thomas Blanton, eds. "The Reykjavik File: Previously Secret Documents from U.S. and Soviet Archives on the 1986 Reagan-Gorbachev Summit," posted October 13, 2006, by the National Security Archive, George Washington University. Available at: http://nsarchive.gwu.edu/NSAEBB/NSAEBB203.

Schellenberg, T. R. "Jeffersonian Origins of the Monroe Doctrine," *The Hispanic American Historical Review*, 1934, 14(1): 1–31.

Schmalenbach, Kirsten. "The Right of Self-Defense and the War on Terrorism," *German Law Journal*, 2002, 3 (9).

Schmitt, Michael N. "Pre-emptive Strategies in International Law," *Michigan Journal of International Law*, 2002, 24: 513–548.

Schoenbaum, Thomas J. *Waging Peace and War: Dean Rusk in the Truman, Kennedy, and Johnson Years*. New York: Simon & Schuster, 1988.

Schouler, James. *History of the United States of America under the Constitution*, rev. ed., 7 vols. New York: Dodd, Mead, 1894–1913.

Scott, Shirley V. *International Law, U.S. Power: The United States' Quest for Legal Security*. Cambridge: Cambridge University Press, 2012.

Sears, L. M. "Nicholas P. Trist, a Diplomat with Ideals," *Mississippi Valley Historical Review*, 1924, 11: 85–98.

Sellers, Charles. *James K. Polk, Jacksonian, 1795–1843*, 2 vols. Norwalk, CT: Easton Press, 1987.

Sexton, Jay. *The Monroe Doctrine: Empire and Nation in Nineteenth Century America*. New York: Hill and Wang, 2011.

Shawcross, William. *Sideshow: Kissinger, Nixon and the Destruction of Cambodia*. New York: Simon & Schuster, 1979.

Sheridan, Eugene R. "The Recall of Edmond Charles Genet: A Study in Transatlantic Politics and Diplomacy," *Diplomatic History*, 1994, 18(4): 463–88.

Shipler, David K. "The Week in Review," *New York Times*, October 26, 1986, E1.

Shotwell, J. T. *At the Paris Peace Conference*. New York: Macmillan, 1937.

Shultz, George P. "Shaping American Foreign Policy: New Realities and New Ways of Thinking," *Foreign Affairs*, 1985, 63(4).

———. *Turmoil and Triumph: My Years as Secretary of State*. New York: Charles Scribner's Sons, 1993.

Simons, Geoffrey Leslie. *Vietnam Syndrome: Impact on U.S. Foreign Policy*. Basingstoke: Macmillan, 1998.

Siracusa, Joseph M. *Diplomacy: A Very Short Introduction*. Oxford: Oxford University Press, 2010.

———. "NSC 68: A Reappraisal," *Naval War College Review*, 1980, 33: 4–14.

———. *Nuclear Weapons: A Very Short Introduction*. Oxford: Oxford University Press, 2008.

———. "Wilson's Image of the Prussian Menace: Ideology and Realpolitik," in John A. Moses and Christopher Pugsley, eds., *The German Empire and Britain's Pacific Dominions, 1871–1919*. Claremont, CA: Regina Books, 2000.

Siracusa, Joseph M., ed. *The Kennedy Years*, New York: Facts on File, 2004.

Smith, Daniel M., and Joseph M. Siracusa. *The Testing of America: 1914–1945*. St. Louis: Forum Press, 1979.

Smith, Gerard C. *Doubletalk: The Story of SALT I*. Garden City, NY: Doubleday, 1980.

The Soviet-Cuban Connection in Central America and the Caribbean. Washington DC: Department of State and Department of Defense, 1985.

Special Task Force on Interrogation and Transfer Policies, "U.S. Task Force Report on Interrogations and Transfers," *The American Journal of International Law*, 2009, 103(4).

Spencer, Samuel R. Jr. *Decision for War, 1917*. Peterborough, NH: Richard R. Smith, 1953.

Sperber, Hans. "'Fifty-Four Forty or Fight': Facts and Fictions," *American Speech*, 1957, 32: 5–11.

Steinbruner, John. "Confusing Ends and Means: The Doctrine of Coercive Pre-emption," *Arms Control Today*, January/February 2003.

Stenberg, Richard R. "Polk and Fremont, 1845–1846," *Pacific Historical Review*, September, 1928, 7: 211–27.

Stepak, Amir and Rachel Whitlark. "The Battle over America's Foreign Policy Doctrine," *Survival*, 2012, 54(5): 45–66.

Stinchcombe, William. *The XYZ Affair*. Westport, CT: Greenwood Press, 1980.

"The Summit Conference at Vienna," June 3–4, 1961, U.S. Department of State Archive. Available at: http://2001-2009.state.gov/r/pa/ho/frus/kennedyjf/xiv/15856.htm.

Szulc, Tad. *Twilight of the Tyrants*. New York: Holt, 1959.

Taffet, Jeffrey. *Foreign Aid as Foreign Policy: The Alliance for Progress in Latin America*. Routledge, 2012.

Taft, William H. IV. "The Legal Basis for Pre-emption," *Council on Foreign Relations Journal*, 2002.

Talbott, Strobe. "Democracy and the National Interest," *Foreign Affairs*, November-December 1996, 74(6).

Talbott, Strobe. *Endgame: The Inside Story of SALT II*. New York: Harper & Row, 1979.

———. *Master of the Game: Paul Nitze and the Nuclear Peace*. New York: Alfred A. Knopf, 1988.

———. *The Russians and Reagan*. New York: Vintage, 1984.

Tansill, C. C. *America Goes to War*. Boston: Little, Brown, 1938.

Tays, George. "Fremont Had No Secret Instructions," *Pacific Historical Review*, September, 1940, 9: 157–72.

Temperley, H. W. V., ed. *A History of the Peace Conference of Paris*, 6 vols. London: Henry Frowde and Hodder & Stoughton, 1920–1924.

Temperley, Harold. *The Foreign Policy of Canning, 1822–1827: England, the Neo-Holy Alliance, and the New World*. London: Frank Cass, 1966.

Tenet, George J. "CIA Letter to Senate on Baghdad's Intentions," Globalsecurity.org, October 7, 2002.

Thielmann, Greg. "Preventive Military Intervention: The Role of Intelligence," Ridgway Center Policy Brief 04-1, October 2004.

Times Herald Record, December 24, 1981.

Tirman, John. "The Politics of Star Wars," in John Tirman, ed., *The Empty Promise: the Growing Case against Star Wars*. Boston: Beacon, 1986.

"Top Bush Officials Push Case Against Saddam," *Inside Politics*, CNN.com, September 8, 2002.

Traub, James. "U.S. Foreign Policy: What Does Obama Believe? United Nations University Conversations Series," Tokyo, March 11, 2015.

———. "When Did Obama Give Up?" *Foreign Policy*, February 26, 2015. Available at: http://foreignpolicy.com/2015/02/26/when-did-obama-give-up-speeches.

Treaty of Alliance Between the United States and France, February 6, 1788, The Avalon Project. Available at: http://avalon.law.yale.edu/18th_century/fr1788-2.asp.

Treaty of Amity and Commerce Between the United States and France, February 6, 1788, The Avalon Project. Available at: http://avalon.law.yale.edu/18th_century/fr1788-1.asp.

Treaty of Paris, September 30, 1783, Library of Congress Digital Reference Section Primary Documents in American History. Available at: http://www.loc.gov/rr/program/bib/ourdocs/paris.html.

Treaty of Versailles, The Avalon Project. Available at: http://avalon.law.yale.edu/subject_menus/versailles_menu.asp.

Treaty on the Non-Proliferation of Nuclear Weapons (NPT), United Nations Office for Disarmament Affairs. Available at: http://www.un.org/disarmament/WMD/Nuclear/NPTtext.shtml.

Truman, Harry S. "Address before a Joint Session of Congress," March 12, 1947, The Avalon Project. Available at: http://avalon.law.yale.edu/20th_century/trudoc.asp.

———. "Special Message to Congress on the Marshall Plan," December 19, 1947, The American Presidency Project. Available at: http://www.presidency.ucsb.edu/ws/?pid=12805.

Tucker, Robert W. "Intervention and the Reagan Doctrine," *Intervention and the Reagan Doctrine*. New York: The Council on Religion and International Affairs, 1985.

Tucker, Robert W., and Hendrickson, David C. *Empire of Liberty: The Statecraft of Thomas Jefferson*. Oxford: Oxford University Press, 1990.

Tudda, Chris. "'A Messiah That Will Never Come': A New Look at Saratoga, Independence, and Revolutionary War Diplomacy," *Diplomatic History*, 2008, 32: 779–810.

Tulchin, Joseph S. "The Promise of Progress: U.S. Relations with Latin America during the Administration of Lyndon B. Johnson," in Warren I. Cohen and Nancy Bernkopf Tucker, eds., *Lyndon Johnson Confronts the World: American Foreign Policy, 1963–1968*. New York: Cambridge University Press, 1994.

The United States Democratic Review, October 1847, 21,112: 291.

U.S. Department of Defense. *Quadrennial Defense Review Report*, September 30, 2001. Available at: http://www.defense.gov/pubs/pdfs/qdr2001.pdf.

U.S. Department of State, Bureau of Public Affairs. *Current Policy No. 275*, 2.

U.S. in World Affairs, 1947–1948. *U.S. in World Affairs*, 1967.

U.S. Senate. Treaty of Peace with Germany, Hearings before the Committee on Foreign Relations, United States Senate. Senate Document No. 106, 66th Cong, 1st sess., 1919.

Ulam, Adam B. *Expansion and Coexistence: The History of Soviet Foreign Policy, 1917–1967*. New York: Praeger, 1968.

UN Charter Article 39, United Nations Charter, June 26, 1945.

UN Charter Article 50, United Nations Charter, June 26, 1945.

"U.N. Chief Ban Hails bin Laden Death as Watershed," Reuters, May 2, 2011. Available at: http://www.reuters.com/article/2011/05/02/us-binladen-un-idUSTRE7414W720110502.

Union of Concerned Scientists, *The Fallacy of Star Wars*. New York: Vintage, 1984.

United Nations News Centre. "UN News: Lessons of Iraq War Underscore Importance of UN Charter; Annan," UN News Service Section, September 16, 2004. Available at: http://www.un.org/apps/news/story.asp?NewsID=11953&#.VESqNEs2n0s.

United Nations News Centre. "UN News: Independent UN Human Rights Experts Seek Facts on Bin Laden Killing," UN News Service Section, May 6, 2011. Available at: http://www.un.org/apps/news/story.asp?NewsID=38293#.UqaLwJEUVSV.

U.S. Department of Justice, "Department of Justice White Paper. Lawfulness of a Lethal Operation Directed Against a U.S. Citizen Who Is a Senior Operational Leader of Al-Qa'ida or An Associated Force," February 4, 2013. Available at: http://msnbcmedia.msn.com/i/msnbc/sections/news/020413_DOJ_White_Paper.pdf.

Vandenberg, A. H. Jr., ed. *The Private Papers of Senator Vandenberg*. Boston: Houghton Mifflin, 1952.

Viereck, George Sylvester. *The Strangest Friendship in History: Woodrow Wilson and Colonel House*. Aware Journalism, 1932.

Von Hoffman, Nicholas. "Terrestrial Wars," *The Spectator*, 1985: 8–9.

Wall Street Journal, March 12, 1981.

Waller, Douglas C. *Congress and the Nuclear Freeze*. Amherst: University of Massachusetts Press, 1987.

Warren, Aiden. *The Obama Administration's Nuclear Weapon Strategy: The Promises of Prague*. New York: Routledge, 2014.

———. *Pre-emption, Prevention and the Nuclear Option: From Bush to Obama*. New York: Routledge, 2011.

Warren, Aiden, and Ingvild Bode. "Altering the Playing Field: The U.S. Redefinition of the Use-of-force," *Contemporary Security Policy*, 36:2.

———. *Governing the Use-of-Force in International Relations. The Post-9/11 US Challenge on International Law*. Basingstoke: Palgrave Macmillan, 2014.

Washington, George. "Proclamation 4: Neutrality of the United States in the War Involving Austria, Prussia, Sardinia, Great Britain, and the United Netherlands Against France," April 22, 1793, The American Presidency Project. Available at: http://www.presidency.ucsb.edu/ws/?pid=65475.

Washington Post, March 8, 1981.

Washington Post, December 12, 1985.

Washington Post, May 30, 1988.

Washington Post, June 1, 1988.

Washington Post, June 7, 1988.

Weatherby, Lauren. "Whatever Happened to the Debate Over Use of Force Against ISIS?" NPR, June 17, 2015. Available at: http://www.npr.org/2015/06/17/415203016/whatever-happened-to-the-debate-over-use-of-force-against-isis.

Webster, Daniel. *The Works of Daniel Webster*, vol. 5. Boston: Little, Brown, 1881.

Weed, Matthew C. "A New Authorization for Use of Military Force Against the Islamic State: Issues and Current Proposals in Brief," Congressional Research Service report, February 20, 2015, pp. 1–2. Available at: http://fas.org/sgp/crs/natsec/R43760.pdf.

Wells, Tom. *The War Within: America's Battle over Vietnam*. New York: Holt, 1994.

The White House, "Press Briefing by Senior Administration Officials on the Killing of Osama Bin Laden," The White House, May 2, 2011. Available at: http://www.whitehouse.gov/the-press-office/2011/05/02/press-briefing-senior-administration-officials-killing-osama-bin-laden.

Willbanks, James H. *Abandoning Vietnam: How America Left and South Vietnam Lost Its War*. Lawrence: University Press of Kansas, 2004.

Wilson, Edwin G. "Edwin G. Wilson to Byrnes," March 18, 1946, FRUS, 1946. Washington DC: U.S. Government Printing Office, 1969.

Wilson, Woodrow. "Address to Congress," April 2, 1917, Library of Congress Internet Archive. Available at: https://ia700504.us.archive.org/22/items/presidentwoodrow00unit/presidentwoodrow00unit.pdf.

————. "Address to a Joint Session of Congress on the Severance of Diplomatic Relations with Germany," February 3, 1917, The American Presidency Project. Available at: http://www.presidency.ucsb.edu/ws/?pid=65397.

————. "Address to the Senate of the United States: A World League for Peace," January 22, 1917, The American Presidency Project. Available at: http://www.presidency.ucsb.edu/ws/?pid=65396.

————. "Message on Neutrality," August, 19, 1914, The American Presidency Project. Available at: http://www.presidency.ucsb.edu/ws/index.php?pid=65382.

————. "President Woodrow Wilson's Fourteen Points," January 8, 1918, The Avalon Project. Available at: http://avalon.law.yale.edu/20th_century/wilson14.asp.

————. *Selected Addresses and Public Papers of Woodrow Wilson*. BiblioBazaar, LLC, 2009.

Wimer, Kurt. "Woodrow Wilson Tries Conciliation: An Effort That Failed," *The Historian*, August, 1963, 25: 419–38.

Winkler, David F. *Cold War at Sea: High-Seas Confrontation between the United States and the Soviet Union*. Annapolis, MD: Naval Institute Press, 2000.

Wirtz, James and James Russell. "U.S. Policy on Preventive War and Pre-emption," *The Nonproliferation Review*, 2003: 113–122.

Woodward, Bob. *Obama's Wars*. New York: Simon & Schuster, 2010.

————. *Plan of Attack*. New York: Simon & Schuster, 2004.

Woodward, Ernest Llewellyn. *War and Peace in Europe 1815–1870*. Oxford: Clarendon Press , 1963.

World Press Review 29, February, 1982.

World Press Review 29, April, 1982.

World Press Review 29, August, 1982.

World Press Review 31, January, 1984.

Worthington Ford, ed. *Writings of John Quincy Adams*, vol. 6. New York: Macmillan, 1916.

Wright, Esmond. "The British Objectives, 1780–1783: 'If Not Dominion Then Trade,'" in Ronald Hoffman and Peter J. Albert, eds., *Peace and the Peacemakers: The Treaty of 1783*. Charlottesville: University Press of Virginia, 1986.

Wright, Tom and Matthew Rosenberg. "Pakistan Warns U.S. Against Raids," *Wall Street Journal*, May 6, 2011. Available at: http://online.wsj.com/news/articles/SB10001424052748704810504576305033789955132.

Wyden, Peter. *Bay of Pigs: The Untold Story*. New York: Simon & Schuster, 1979.

X. "The Sources of Soviet Conduct," *Foreign Affairs*, 1947, 25: 566–82.

Zakaria, Fareed. "Stop Searching for an Obama Doctrine," *Washington Post*, 6, 2011.

Zamani, Nahal. "Rendition Program to Continue Under Obama's Watch," American Civil Liberties Union, August 27, 2009. Available at: https://www.aclu.org/blog/human-rights-national-security/rendition-program-continue-under-obamas-watch.

Zardari, Asif Ali. "Pakistan Did Its Part," *Washington Post*, May 3, 2011, sec. Opinions. Available at: http://www.washingtonpost.com/opinions/pakistan-did-its-part/2011/05/02/AFHxmybF_story.html.

Zubok, Vladislav M. "Soviet Policy Aims at the Geneva Conference, 1955," in Gunter Bischof and Saki Dockrill, eds., *Cold War Respite: The Geneva Summit of 1955*. Baton Rouge: Louisiana State University, 2000.

Zubok, Vladislav M. *A Failed Empire: The Soviet Union in the Cold War from Stalin to Gorbachev*. Chapel Hill: University of North Carolina, 2007.

Index

About the Authors

Joseph M. Siracusa is professor of human security and international diplomacy at the Royal Melbourne Institute of Technology University, in Melbourne, and president of Australia's Council of Humanities, Arts and Social Sciences. American-born, he is the author and co-author of many books, including *Nuclear Weapons: A Very Short Introduction* (2nd ed., 2015); *America and the Cold War, 1941–1991: A Realist Interpretation*, 2 vols. (with Norman A. Graebner and Richard Dean Burns, 2010); and *A Global History of the Nuclear Arms Race: Weapons, Strategy, and Politics*, 2 vols. (with Richard Dean Burns, 2013).

Dr. Aiden Warren is a senior lecturer in the School of Global, Urban and Social Studies at RMIT University in Melbourne, Australia. His teaching and research interests are in the areas of international security, U.S. national security and foreign policy, U.S. politics (ideas and institutions, contemporary and historical), international relations (especially great power politics), and issues associated with the proliferation of weapons of mass destruction, nonproliferation, and arms control. He is the author of *The Obama Administration's Nuclear Weapon Strategy: The Promises of Prague* and *Prevention, Pre-emption and the Nuclear Option: From Bush to Obama* (both released through Routledge) and *Governing the Use of Force in International Relations: The Post-9/11 US Challenge on International Law* (Palgrave-McMillan).

Professor Joseph M. Siracusa and Dr. Aiden Warren are also the editors of the WMD series with Rowman and Littlefield.